Socialism and Commodity Production

Historical Materialism Book Series

The Historical Materialism Book Series is a major publishing initiative of the radical left. The capitalist crisis of the twenty-first century has been met by a resurgence of interest in critical Marxist theory. At the same time, the publishing institutions committed to Marxism have contracted markedly since the high point of the 1970s. The Historical Materialism Book Series is dedicated to addressing this situation by making available important works of Marxist theory. The aim of the series is to publish important theoretical contributions as the basis for vigorous intellectual debate and exchange on the left.

The peer-reviewed series publishes original monographs, translated texts, and reprints of classics across the bounds of academic disciplinary agendas and across the divisions of the left. The series is particularly concerned to encourage the internationalization of Marxist debate and aims to translate significant studies from beyond the English-speaking world.

For a full list of titles in the Historical Materialism Book Series available in paperback from Haymarket Books, visit:
https://www.haymarketbooks.org/series_collections/1-historical-materialism

Socialism and Commodity Production

Essay in Marx Revival

Paresh Chattopadhyay

Haymarket Books
Chicago, IL

First published in 2018 by Brill Academic Publishers, The Netherlands
© 2018 Koninklijke Brill NV, Leiden, The Netherlands

Published in paperback in 2019 by
Haymarket Books
P.O. Box 180165
Chicago, IL 60618
773-583-7884
www.haymarketbooks.org

ISBN: 978-1-64259-050-0

Distributed to the trade in the US through Consortium Book Sales and
Distribution (www.cbsd.com) and internationally through Ingram
Publisher Services International (www.ingramcontent.com).

This book was published with the generous support of Lannan
Foundation and Wallace Action Fund.

Special discounts are available for bulk purchases by organizations and
institutions. Please call 773-583-7884 or email info@haymarketbooks.org
for more information.

Cover design by Jamie Kerry and Ragina Johnson.

Printed in the United States.

10 9 8 7 6 5 4 3 2 1

Library of Congress Cataloging-in-Publication data is available.

Dedicated to the Memory of Maximilien Rubel
Humanist, Savant, Militant, Libertarian
Persona non grata East and West

.
.   .

Contents

Preface   XI

Prologue   1
    Twentieth-Century Socialism   2
    Socialism as Minority Rule   4
    Lenin's Role   4
    The Relevance of Marx   13
    A Caricature of Marx's Socialism   15

1   On Socialism: Association of Free Individuals   27
    (Pre)conditions of Socialism   29
    Associated Mode of Production   47
    Ownership Relation   48
    Exchange Relations   50
    Distribution/Allocation   52
    Labouring Individual under Socialism   56

2   Commodity Production   63
    From Commodity to Capital   64
    Paradoxes and Contradictions   73
    On the Value Form   79
    Commodity Circulation: Possibility of Crisis   95

3   Simple Commodity Production   100
    The Problem   100
    Discussion after Engels   102
    The Critics   104
    Criticisms Discussed   108
    Conclusion   115

4   Commodity Production and Socialism in Marx's Followers   118
    The First Followers: August Bebel and Karl Kautsky   118
    Marxians after Kautsky   121
        Non-Bolsheviks: Korsch, Lukács, Rühle, Hilferding   121
        Bolsheviks on Socialism and Commodity Production   124

5 **On Socialist Accounting**   139
    The Labour Process   140
    Point of Departure   141
    How to Proceed   144
    Labour Time: Neglected Aspects   148
    Labour Time and Non-labour Time   152
    Socialist Accounting Framework   155
    On Planning and the Unit of Calculation   157

6 **Anarchist Communism**   169
    Peter Kropotkin   169
        Kropotkin's Anarchist Communism   170
    Carlo Cafiero   176
    Anarchism and Marx: The Relation   178

7 **Concerning Guild Socialism**   186
    Introduction   186
    Guild Socialism as Democracy   188
    Distribution and Allocation in Guild Socialism   189
    Consumers and Producers   192
    Transformation of the Existing Society   193
    Ambiguities and Contradictions   195

8 **On Market Socialism**   199
    Origin of Market Socialism   200
    The Competitive Solution   209
    Criticisms   212
    Feasible Socialism   217
    Analytical Market Socialism   219
    Market Socialism Proper   221
    Market Socialism – 'Marxian'   223
    Market Socialism is Capitalism   227

9 **The Problematic of a Non-capitalist Road to Socialism**   232
    Capital's Positive Contribution   232
    The Controversy   233
    Controversy Continued   241
    Further Considerations   244

Epilogue. Illusion of the Epoch: Twentieth-Century Socialism   249
    Preliminaries   249
    Nature of Twentieth-Century Socialism   251
    The Party-State   267
    The Fundamental Question   274

References   285
Index   298

Preface

Customarily the word 'socialism' today refers to the social system which came into existence with the seizure of political power by the Bolshevik party in Russia in 1917; it is the Russian system that became the prototype for social-ism *mutatis mutandis* in the different lands which followed. Socialism in this context signifies a society ruled by a single political party, where the means of production are owned mostly by the state and the economy is directed by cent-ral(ised) planning. For its adherents, the abolition of private ownership in the means of production is equivalent to the abolition of capitalism itself, while bringing the means of production under state or 'public' ownership is thought to be tantamount to the abolition of private ownership of the means of pro-duction and thus the establishment of socialism. Finally, the spokespersons of these régimes consider themselves to be Marx's followers and claim the origin of their system in Marx's ideas.

It is notable that most of the discussions on the régimes in question turn on political narratives, dealing with what Marx calls the 'edifice' or 'superstructure' of a society. They leave aside society's very foundation – the material base – the mode of production and the social relations of production derived from it. Of course the absence of these questions in the discourses of 'socialism' does not mean that they are also absent in reality. In fact, following Marx, the character of a society is shown by the type of its social relations of produc-tion. Considered from this angle, it appears that all these régimes, including their prototype, have been commodity societies, marked by what Marx calls the 'commodity mode of production', where all products of human labour, includ-ing labour power, are commodities. Here the producer does not dominate the product, contrariwise, the product alienated from the producer dominates the producer. Here production is meant not for direct satisfaction of needs, but for exchange, and the social necessity of labour involved in production is con-firmed *ex post*. Here individuals exist not in view of solidarity, but as compet-itors for material (monetary) advantage. Here the fundamental form of the system is appropriation by alienation.

In Marx socialism is a profoundly emancipatory concept, that is, socialism is just another name for an 'Association of free and equal individuals' arising from the working people's struggle for self-emancipation through their col-lective self-activity and which excludes all the elements which are oppressive and repressive of the (human) individual, such as contending classes, private ownership of the conditions of production, commodity production including wage/salaried labour and the state.

Now, it is remarkable that the conceptual framework of this socialism, claimed to follow from Marx's ideas, is almost totally limited to the ownership of the means of production as a juridical category, excluding its relational base. In other words, there is hardly any discussion of these régimes' mode of production and the social relation(s) of production following therefrom.

As to the political side of these régimes, these are mostly the products of the seizure of power initiated and led by small groups of radicalised intelligentsia, heading a single party and substituting for a whole class – the working class – who, in fact, far from exercising any initiating or leading role in the process, at best followed the 'leaders'. This is a far cry from the revolutionary process as the outcome of the spontaneous movement of the immense majority in the interest of the immense majority resulting in the working class, and not any party in its name, becoming the ruling class and winning the battle of democracy, as the *Communist Manifesto* envisages.

So, the very inauguration of the new order defined the new rule as minority rule over the majority, by definition undemocratic, completely negating the 1848 *Manifesto*'s predicted outcome of 'winning the battle of democracy'. And these minority régimes *had to be* neverendingly coercive, to be terrorist régimes, in order to survive.

The contrast with socialism as envisaged by Marx could not be sharper. It is equivalent to the contrast between slavery and freedom. Marx's socialism is a society of free individuals based on the Associated mode of production. The present work discusses at length the content of what Marx alternately calls Association, 'communism', 'co-operative society', and 'republic of labour'. Most people, unfamiliar with Marx's own writings, accept Party-State socialism as Marx's own or at least as originating in Marx's ideas, as claimed by the spokespersons of the régimes in question, and they conclude that Marx's socialism is also naturally a coercive régime under state terror. They are hardly aware that Marx was anti-state from the very beginning of his adult life. Marx considered state and slavery indissociable. As regards coercion, in 1853 Marx had written in a New York daily, 'what kind of a pitiable society is that which does not know a better means of defending itself than the hangman!'

Our present work is a very humble contribution towards restoring Marx's immense emancipatory heritage, which has been consigned to oblivion by Marx's epigones, who have made Marx serve the Party-State. This Preface gives the gist of the present work's content.

We are grateful to the following friends who have helped us in different ways: Sebastian Budgen and Peter Thomas for their never-ending encouragement; David Broder and Danny Hayward for their great kindness and patience in view

of my technical backwardness; members of the Calcutta Marx Circle, in particular Rana Bose, Sankar Ray and Sudeb Mitra. And then Andrew Kliman, Alfredo
Saad Filho and Paolo Guissani for having read some parts of the manuscript
and offered helpful suggestions. Also to Manfred Neuhaus and Regina Roth
for arranging a congenial environment for our work as guest researcher at the
Berlin-Brandenburg Academy of Sciences over a period.

Now, a word on the citations in the book. As regards Marx we have cited
him both in his original German and side by side in the corresponding English,
wherever this is available. For *Capital* Volume I, we have also given the texts in
French. The same goes for Lenin's texts (Russian and English). For the rest of
the authors, they are given wherever possible in English.

Prologue

Our present work should be considered as a humble contribution to the ongoing worldwide endeavour to restore Marx's emancipatory vision of socialism, as an Association of free individuals, from the oblivion to which it had been consigned by Marx's historical epigones, who had made Marx serve their 'socialism' conceived as a Party-State régime. This worldwide endeavour is, in a certain sense, comparable to Felix Mendelssohn's famous restoration of J.S. Bach's great choral music, forgotten since about 1750.

In this work socialism, designating the society after capital,[1] is used entirely in the sense of Marx, grounded on Marx's own original writings, finished and unfinished, that have been published so far.[2] This socialism as a portrait of an alternative society arising on the ruins of the society based on a historically determined mode of production, the commodity mode of production (that is, including labour power as a commodity), is the very opposite of the so-called 'real socialism' which has prevailed since the early years of the twentieth century, whose material basis has ever been the 'commodity mode of production',[3] including labour power as a commodity, following from separation of the direct producers from the conditions of production where products, alienated from the producers, dominate the producers, not the inverse. The fundamental characteristic which separates socialism envisaged by Marx from the prevailing socialism is that Marx's socialism is conceived as an Association of free individuals, a completely de-alienated society with no commodity, no money, no waged/salaried labour and no state, all of which are considered as instruments of exploitation and repression that belong to class society and are used to put down the immense majority of humans. The very basis of Marx's socialism, on the contrary, is human emancipation – a de-alienated society whose

---

1   In the present work we employ the term 'capital' in the sense of capitalist society, or what is named in common usage as 'capitalism'. Here we are following Marx's own frequent practice. Another point we would like to stress: we shall in this work try to avoid using two ideologically loaded terms: 'marxist' and 'marxism'.

2   Let us underline that this socialism is a joint theoretical product of Karl Marx and Friedrich Engels. However, Marx's share in this production is overwhelmingly the greater, in Engels's own (rather modest) estimate. Hence, most of the textual references in our work relate to Marx's texts, but Engels's texts will also be recalled wherever relevant.

3   See Marx 1987a, p. 106; 1976a, p. 72; 1954, p. 80.

focus is freedom of the human individual, free from personal as well as material slavery.[4] Here individuals' collective self-authority is the rule.

Twentieth-Century Socialism

In the eyes of a considerable section of the Left, the Bolshevik seizure of power signalled the victory of socialist revolution leading to the establishment of socialism in Russia and setting the stage for a number of such seizures of power by the Communist parties in the different parts of the world – China, Vietnam, Cuba, etc. – excepting those cases in Eastern Europe where power was simply bestowed on the Communist parties, baptised 'working-class' parties, by the victorious Russian army after the defeat of the Nazi régime. In the latter cases, events were considered as not quite amounting to socialist revolutions, but as 'democratic' revolutions preparing the way towards socialism. Nevertheless, the régimes that ultimately resulted in all these lands have also been considered socialist. And the mode of production – in the sense of Marx – of all these régimes has ever been the historically determined commodity mode of production in the Marxian sense as shown above. In this chapter our focus is on socialism in Russia following the Bolshevik victory as the *prototype* of socialisms that followed in other parts of the globe. As regards all these régimes, including the prototype, there is, curiously, a convergence of views between the Left and the Right. In the eyes of both, these régimes have been socialist. This has been possible because for both of them socialism means the same thing – a society ruled by a single party with ownership of at least the principal means of production predominantly by the state – supposed to indicate the absence of private ownership in the means of production – and a system of centralised planning. Of course the Left looks at this 'socialism' positively while the Right views it negatively. Finally – and this is the most remarkable thing – the convergence here is completed in the common position that this 'socialism' originates in Marx. However, as we argue in this book, this socialism has nothing to do with what Marx envisages as socialism, as it appears in Marx's own works, and is, on the contrary, its exact opposite.

Most of the readers of Marx's works occupy themselves uniquely with Marx's critical analysis of the capitalist system. They almost totally leave aside Marx's vision of society after capital. It is undoubtedly true that the bulk of Marx's the-

---

4   We will use – following Marx's practice – the terms 'socialism' and 'Association' interchangeably.

oretical work concerns the critical analysis of the capitalist mode of production in order to 'uncover', as he describes it in the 'Preface' to his *Capital*, 'the economic law of motion of the modern society', that is, capitalist society.[5] True, Marx did not leave any blueprint for a future society. As he stresses in the 'Afterword' to the same book, he is not 'writing receipts for the cook-shops of the future'.[6] However, in a dispersed way in his writings are scattered the building blocks of his vision of the society that he anticipates will succeed capitalism. This pervades even such a work as *Capital*, a work considered by many to be 'esoteric'. In one of his first reviews of this book, Engels, clearly sensing that some eager revolutionaries might be disappointed with the book, after waiting for quite a long time to see here 'finally revealed' the 'secret true socialist doctrine' and 'panacea', warned its readers that there was no 'one-thousand-year communist kingdom' awaiting them here. But 'who has eyes to see, sees here, stated clearly enough, the demand for a social revolution', where 'it is a question of the abolition of capital itself'.[7] Hence it is unfortunate that many readers of Marx neglect this side of his work. In fact, in all the volumes of *Capital*, Marx has something to say on the society after capital, and in what is considered as the first version of Marx's *Capital*, the 1857–1858 manuscripts, very many passages are given to the portrayal of Marx's vision of the future society. It is remarkable that Marx's 1875 brochure *Critique of the Gotha Programme* (hereafter *Gothacritique*) is about the only work which is almost always mentioned as *the* standard reference for any discussion on Marxian socialism. In this orientation a crucial role has been played by Lenin's specific reading of this famous brochure, particularly in his well-known 1917 work *The State and Revolution*. In later chapters we analyse in some detail the contradictions and ambiguities in the Leninist reading of Marxian socialism. We simply note here that while, on the one hand, Lenin, to his great merit, emphasises in his brochure the libertarian side of the struggle for socialism by stressing the transient character of the state, and its disappearance, along with class antagonisms, in the society after capital, he, on the other hand, does just the opposite in the same work and affirms the existence of the state, both as the continuing repository of political power and as the employer of hired wage labour – which, by the way, necessarily implies generalised commodity production – in the first phase of socialism/communism where, again, he conflates Marx's first phase of communism and Marx's transitional phase leading to communism.

---

5   Marx 1987a, p. 67; 1976a, p. 13; 1954, p. 20.

6   Marx 1987a, p. 704; 1976a, p. 19; 1954, p. 26.

7   Engels 1867.

The rest of the twentieth-century 'socialist' régimes have followed Lenin's position almost totally, being, one could say, only the footnotes to Lenin (to paraphrase A.N. Whitehead on Western philosophy in relation to Plato).

Socialism as Minority Rule

In the event, it so happened that in the régimes baptised 'socialist', the state, far from showing any tendency towards disappearance, was increasingly strengthened as a military-bureaucratic machine of repression, even surpassing many of the earlier régimes which they had replaced. The repressive character of these régimes necessarily followed from the specific characteristic that these were the régimes which did not really represent the majority of the country's people, but rather only a small minority. This completely substituted a single party for the class, for all practical purposes.

Lenin's Role

Lenin played a huge role in the conceptualisation of socialism by his epigones worldwide, but he played an even bigger role due to his whole set of ideas concerning the socialist revolution and socialism; ideas which have little in common with Marx's own emancipatory vision of society after capital. And it is this set of ideas – it must be stressed – that became the breeding ground of *minority revolution* and *minority rule* in the different régimes which followed the victorious Russian party, repeating the history of class societies as Engels had so pertinently analysed in his 1895 Introduction to Marx's 1850 *Class struggles in France*, in which he had opined that the era of such minority revolution and minority rule would end with bourgeois rule, since the proletarian revolution is a revolution of the immense majority in the interest of the immense majority. This had far-reaching consequences. Minority rule in its turn necessarily meant that the régimes could not afford to be democratic and *had to be* repressive on a permanent basis in order to survive.

Lenin's starting position is the possibility of a proletarian/socialist revolution breaking out in a backward land, as opposed to Marx's position of such an event taking place in a capitalistically advanced land. Marx believed that it was capitalist development which prepares the necessary conditions for such a revolution. It is remarkable how only a single individual – Lenin – first won over his party (initially with an unenthusiastic leadership) and then practically imposed his own idea on the whole country, defeating all resistance.

His reason for a socialist revolution in Russia he justified not in terms of the materialist conception of history (inappropriately named 'historical materialism', a term nowhere found in Marx), that is, not in terms of a change in the relations of production in society, but in terms of a change in government personnel. He wrote, 'State power in Russia has passed into the hands of a new *class*, namely, the bourgeoisie and landlords who had become bourgeois. *To this extent* the bourgeois-democratic revolution is completed'.[8] About one month later he repeated the same argument, but this time without any qualification: 'the bourgeois revolution is already completed'; this was followed two months later by his assertion that the 'workers' socialist revolution began on October 25'.[9] It should be clear that it is not because of a change in the material base, but purely on the grounds of a perceived change in the superstructure, or the edifice of society, that Lenin sought a socialist revolution, thereby totally reversing Marx's materialist conception of history, which we find condensed in the famous Preface to his 1859 *Contribution to the Critique of Political Economy*.

While for Marx, the active agents of the socialist revolution are the proletarians, Lenin wanted the proletarians as *followers* of his party of 'professional revolutionaries', the Communists, though he called his party a 'working-class party'. In fact for Marx the working class itself plays the role of professional revolutionaries: 'the working class is either revolutionary or it is nothing', wrote Marx in his letter of 1865, 13 February, to his friend Schweitzer.[10] As Marx says (and as we elaborate later in this book), it is the 'historical mission/profession (*Beruf*) of the proletariat to revolutionise the capitalist mode of production and finally to abolish the classes'.[11]

Lenin's position clearly comes out in his 1904 work, *One Step Forward, Two Steps Back*: 'The Party is the vanguard of the working class ... We are the party of a class, and therefore, almost the entire class should/must (*dolzhen*) act under the leadership of our Party, should/must (*dolzhen*) adhere to our Party as closely as possible'.[12] It should be noted that this was the period when Lenin was proclaiming that his party, the Social Democratic Party of Russia, formed not by the independent working-class movement, but by a tiny group of radicalised intelligentsia, had virtually no proletarian adherents. So the so-called

---

8   Lenin 1982b, p. 19; 1975b, p. 37. Emphasis in text.
9   Lenin 1975b, p. 447; Lenin 1982g, p. 51; 1975c, p. 68.
10   Cited in Rubel 1965, p. cxxv.
11   Marx 1987a, p. 703; 1976a, p. 18; 1954, pp. 25–6.
12   Lenin 1970, p. 319.

'working-class party' was a pure fiction. Even later, when the Bolshevik party had a membership of hundreds of thousands on the eve of its seizure of political power, there were practically no proletarians in its supreme leadership. As a well-known historian of communism – Franz Borkenau – very pertinently observes, 'Lenin's revolution is essentially not a proletarian revolution, it is the "revolution" of the intelligentsia, of the professional revolutionaries, but with the proletariat as the chief ally ... the most outstanding personalities of the 1917 revolution were Lenin, Trotsky, Zinoviev, Kamenev, Sverdlov, Smilga, Bukharin, Dzerzhinsky, Stalin: there is not a single worker among them'.[13]

Lenin was bent upon gaining the monopoly of political power for his party, even when his party had only about ten percent of the membership in the first Congress of Soviets. When a minister of Russia's Provisional Government asserted that there was no political party in Russia expressing its readiness to assume full power, Lenin, without consulting anybody in the party, replied 'yes, there is. No party can refuse this, and our Party certainly does not. It is ready to take over full power at any moment'.[14] A few months later, shortly before the seizure of power, Lenin wrote, 'Since the 1905 revolution Russia has been governed by 130,000 landowners ... yet we are told that the 240,000 members of the Bolshevik Party will not be able to govern Russia, govern her in the interests of the poor against the rich'.[15] Lenin's determination to have a party monopoly of power, as well as his deep distrust of, if not disdain for, the soviets, comes out clearly in his private correspondence with his colleagues in the party leadership on the eve of the seizure of power, 'The Crisis has matured'. While loudly proclaiming publicly 'all power to the soviets', Lenin, in this private communication, spoke of this 'vehicle of formal democracy' – and persevered in his attempt to persuade the colleagues with democratic susceptibilities that the party must go it alone (*v svoi ruki*), ignoring the soviets, and capture power; and that 'it would be naïve to wait for a formal majority for the Bolsheviks'. To 'wait' for the Congress of Soviets is complete 'idiocy', or 'total treachery' (*polnaya izmena*) for the Congress will give nothing, and can 'give nothing' (*nichevo ni mozhet dat'*).[16]

In Lenin's view the party completely substituted for the working class. E.H. Carr cites Lenin's fantastic 1919 claim that 'the dictatorship of the working class is carried into effect by the party of the Bolsheviks which since 1905

---

13   Borkenau 1962, pp. 44–5.
14   Lenin 1982f, p. 106; 1975a, p. 119.
15   Lenin 1982b, pp. 367–8; 1975b, p. 369.
16   Lenin 1975d, p. 348; 1982b, pp. 345, 346.

or earlier has been united with the *whole* revolutionary proletariat'.[17] Lenin described the attempt to distinguish between the dictatorship of the class and the dictatorship of the party as 'an unbelievable and inextricable confusion of thought'.[18] The necessity of maintaining the punitive, *coercive* character of the régime is starkly brought out in Lenin's debate with Julius Martov, one of the unduly neglected heroes of the Russian Revolution. The gist of the debate, which touches on the two approaches to the Russian revolution, qualitatively so different – one Lenin's, the other Martov's – is well brought out in Carr's account, according to which,

> Martov attacked the violations of the Soviet constitution: diagnosed 'an apathy of the masses nourished and strengthened by centuries of slavery under Tsars and serf-owners, a paralysis of civic consciousness, readiness to throw all responsibility for one's fate on the shoulders of the government'. Martov then read a declaration demanding the 'restoration of the working of the constitution ... freedom of the press, of association and of assembly, inviolability of the person, abolition of executions without trial, of administrative arrests and of official terror'. Lenin replied that Martov's declaration meant 'back to bourgeois democracy and nothing else. When we hear such declarations from people who announce their sympathy with us, we say to ourselves: No, both terror and the Cheka are absolutely indispensable'.[19]

It may not be out of place to hear something bearing on this issue from the great Austrian-American economist with socialist convictions, Joseph Schumpeter:

> The inevitable conflict that split the party (that is, the social democratic party of Russia) into Bolsheviks and Mensheviks (1903) meant something much more serious than a mere disagreement regarding tactics such as the names of the two groups suggest. At the time no observer, however experienced, could have realised fully the nature of the rift. By now the diagnosis should be obvious. The Marxist phraseology which both groups retained obscured the fact that one of them had irrevocably broken away

---

17 In Carr 1964, p. 230. Emphasis added.
18 In Carr 1964, p. 231. Carr refers to the resolution of the 1923 Twelfth Congress of the party declaring that 'the dictatorship of the working class cannot be assured otherwise than in the form of dictatorship of its leading vanguard, i.e. the Communist Party'. Carr 1964, p. 231.
19 Carr 1964, p. 174.

from the classical Marxism. Lenin had no illusion concerning the Russian situation. He saw that the Tsarist régime could be successfully attacked only when temporarily weakened by military defeat and that in the ensuing disorganisation a resolute and well-disciplined group could by ruthless terror overthrow whatever other régime might attempt to replace it … Such a group could only be recruited from the intellectual stratum, and the best material available was to be found within the party. His attempt to gain control of the latter therefore amounted to an attempt to destroy its very soul. The majority and their leader, Martov, must have felt that. He did not criticise Marx or advocate a new departure. He resisted Lenin in the name of Marx and stood for the Marxist doctrine of proletarian mass party. The novel note was struck by Lenin … Un-Marxian was not merely the idea of socialisation by *pronunciamiento* in an obviously immature situation; much more so was the idea that 'emancipation' was to be not the work of the proletariat itself but of a band of intellectuals officering the rabble.[20]

Lenin was of course 'correct': it would be impossible for the new *minority* régime to survive without continued coercion and terror. Another point worth stressing, which further strengthened the minority character of the régime, was the fact that Lenin was bent on securing the monopoly of power for his party. Thus, about two months before the seizure of power, Lenin wrote to his leadership comrades that when power fell into 'our hands, we shall not give it up'.[21] He again confirmed that when the conditions existed for the Bolsheviks to take power, 'no power on earth can prevent the Bolsheviks from retaining it until the triumph of the world socialist revolution'.[22] This position is manifested in Lenin's dogged opposition, contrary to some of his own party colleagues, like Kamenev and Riazanov, to any coalition and sharing of power with the other socialist parties in the soviets, even though, according to the historians, when workers and soldiers voted for soviet power, they were in fact opting for a multiparty government of the leftist parties.[23] The eminent historian Alexander Rabinowitch, in his blow-by-blow account of the Bolshevik seizure of power, writes, 'the mass mood was not specifically Bolshevik in the sense of a desire for a Bolshevik government. As the flood of post-Kornilov political resolutions revealed, Petrograd soldiers, sailors and workers were attracted more than ever

20   Schumpeter 1950, pp. 329–30.
21   Lenin 1982g, p. 156; 1975a, p. 169.
22   Lenin 1982b, p. 383; 1975b, p. 285.
23   See Suny, in Kaiser 1987, p. 19.

by the goal of creating a soviet government uniting all socialist elements'.[24] Not only did the Leninist leadership refuse to engage in any collaboration with the rest of the socialists in the Soviets, this situation, entirely its own creation, made the Bolsheviks more isolated. This is turn increased their fear of their opponents:

> They had half suppressed them in order to win the civil war; having won the civil war they went on to suppress them for good, and it was necessary to suppress opposition in Bolshevik ranks as well ... The Bolsheviks hardened in the conviction that *any opposition must inevitably become the vehicle of counter-revolution.*[25]

Deutscher refers to Trotsky's argument at the Tenth Congress of the Bolshevik party that 'the Workers' Opposition has come out with dangerous slogans. They have made a *fetish of democratic principles*; they have placed the workers' right to elect representatives above the party, as it were, as if the party was not entitled to assert its dictatorship even if that dictatorship clashes with the passing moods of the workers' democracy'.[26]

Exercise of coercion and violence by the régime is also seen in relation to the country's vast peasantry. It was not only against the kulaks but also against virtually all of the middle peasants who had grain surpluses. No enterprising farmer regarded his own stocks of grain as 'surplus' grown by his own labour on his own land. 'The food detachments took almost all their grain by force and paid almost nothing. The Bolsheviks resorted to mass violence'.[27] Nove observes, 'compulsory delivery of food came to mean a policy in which each peasant household was ordered to deliver its surplus to the state. In some cases this was outright confiscation and in others virtual confiscation since nominal prices were very low and practically nothing could be bought with that money'.[28] Maurice Dobb, a well-known economist and strong sympathiser with the Bolshevik régime, offers a vivid picture of the situation during the period

---

24 Rabinowitch 2004, p. 167.

25 Deutscher 1963, p. 518. Emphasis added.

26 Deutscher 1963, pp. 508–9. Emphasis added. Deutscher adds, 'Trotsky publicly advocated government by coercion. He hoped to persuade people that they needed no government by persuasion. He told them that the workers' state had the right to use forced labour, and he was sincerely disappointed that they did not rush to enrol in the labour camps' (Deutscher 1963, p. 516).

27 Medvedev 1979, p. 168.

28 Nove 1982, pp. 59–60.

of War Communism. We may be allowed to cite here parts of his important observations, which well summarise the whole context of peasant hostility to the new régime:

> It was impossible for the soviet government to obtain resources it needed through normal market process. They could be obtained only by measures of coercion. The surplus product of each peasant farm, above the needs of subsistence and seed-corn, was subject to compulsory requisitioning enforced often by the despatch of armed detachments of workers from towns to the villages ... On May 14, 1918, a decree of the Central Executive Committee (TSIK) declared that the peasants having surplus grains but refusing to deliver them at fixed prices be declared 'enemies of the people' and deprived of rights of citizenship to be brought before a revolutionary tribunal ... Committees of Village Poor established to enforce requisition from the well-to-do peasants precipitated the final break with the Left Social Revolutionaries. Also it antagonised not only the kulaks but also the mass of middle peasantry who constituted the majority in the countryside ... In the degree that the requisitioning policy was extended, peasant resistance grew ... The original requisitioning policy was replaced by arbitrary levies by local allocation departments. Increasingly there were forcible and inquisitorial methods of collection, and this sharpened peasant hostility and resistance ... An epidemic of peasant risings spread over the Volga region and west Siberia and in Tambov gubernia.[29]

An important section of the anti-Stalin Left, mainly the followers of Trotsky, finds the sole cause of the failure of the October Revolution in the civil war and the absence of proletarian revolution (at least) in Europe, not at all in the particular policies pursued by the governing Bolsheviks themselves. However, this argument is only partially true. Having accepted without any question, in fact axiomatically, the Bolshevik claim that the October Revolution was a proletarian revolution, this section of the Left does not at all take into consideration the factor of coercion exercised by the régime against the Left Opposition, and, much more importantly, against the peasantry – as described in Dobb's account given above – which naturally generated peasant resistance against the régime. Roy Medvedev, whose father was liquidated under the régime of Lenin's (nominated) successor, cites Plekhanov's remarkable 'open letter' to the Petrograd workers (29 October 1918):

---

29   Dobb 1966, pp. 102–3, 104, 105, 117, 118.

In the population of your state the proletariat is a minority. It would seem that the peasants, constituting the greater part of the population, is an unreliable ally for the workers in organising the socialist mode of production ... Having seized political power prematurely, the Russian proletariat will not carry out a social(ist) revolution but will only provoke a *civil war* which will ultimately force it to retreat far back from the positions which were won in February and March this year.[30]

After referring to the food detachments and the poor peasants' committees – which had 'nothing socialist about [them]' – to which the working peasant and the middle peasant were opposed, Medvedev added, 'In Russia there were smouldering hotbeds of *civil war* which could potentially burst into flame almost any moment; all that was needed was a pretext, and it was soon found in the form of revolt of the Czech Legion in Russia'.[31]

The policy of monopolising power for the Bolsheviks and thereby exercising a *minority* power over the majority in the country is, again, seen in Lenin's treatment of the question the Constituent Assembly (hereafter CA). This was an institution for which the Russian people had fought and died over a hundred-year period in their struggle for freedom from the monarchical and feudal-ecclesiastical régime. All the different sections of the population were involved in this struggle for a national democratic parliament. Days before the October events, the Bolsheviks had attacked the Provisional Government for its delay in opening the CA. The Bolsheviks claimed that the Provisional Government was not capable of calling the CA, and that only they could call it. But after the seizure of power, when the issue of the CA could no longer be used against their opponents, it became a rallying cry of those who aimed to end the Bolshevik dictatorship. There were disagreements among the Bolsheviks regarding the date when the elections for the Assembly could be held. Some were of the view that the elections should not be postponed since the Bolsheviks had reproached the previous government for that very thing. But Lenin wanted a postponement. On the plea that the situation had changed after October, 'to consider the question of the Constituent Assembly from a formal, legal point of view would be a betrayal of the proletariat's cause, and the adoption of the bourgeois point of view'.[32] In light of the possibility that the opposition

---

30   Medvedev 1979, pp. 71–2.
31   Medvedev 1979, pp. 168–9. Emphasis added.
32   Lenin 1982c, p. 458; 1975d, p. 459. However, there is no evidence that the proletariat had the same view as Lenin.

parties – Kadets, Mensheviks and Socialist-Revolutionaries – might gain a majority, Lenin did not want an early election. In a meeting of the Central Committee of the party two weeks before the *coup de main*, Lenin in fact told his comrades, 'it is senseless to wait for the Constituent Assembly that will not be on our side'.[33] In other words, Lenin was perfectly aware that the *majority* of the country was not on his side.

In any event the Bolsheviks permitted the elections to be held. When, after the CA was finally called on 5 January 1918, it appeared that the Bolsheviks had a little less than a quarter of the total number of the elected representatives, Lenin and the Bolsheviks made up their minds. The assembly was dissolved the next day by a decree of the Soviet of People's Commissars, on spurious grounds. On the day the CA had opened, there was a popular, entirely peaceful, demonstration in honour of the opening of the assembly. As the crowd approached the Tauride palace with the slogan 'All power to the Constituent Assembly', armed soldiers and red guards appeared and demanded that the crowd disperse. When the crowd paid no attention to the order, they were met with volleys of fire. Several were killed and injured. The Bolsheviks and the Left Social Revolutionaries left the assembly, accusing their opponents of setting up the assembly against the Soviets, and thus acting as counter-revolutionaries. Only two Bolsheviks – Lozovsky and the great Marx scholar David Riazanov – to their honour, voted against the withdrawal of the party from the assembly. A few days later Maxim Gorky in his organ *New Life* came out with great emotion, comparing this bloody business of the Bolsheviks with the shooting of unarmed people by Tsarist soldiers on 9 January 1905.[34]

Gorky wrote that when on 22 January 1905, the soldiers, acting in obedience to the Tsar's government, fired on the defenceless and peaceful crowd of workers, members of the intelligentsia and the labourers rushed up to the soldiers shouting

> 'what are you doing? whom are you killing? They are your brothers: they are without arms; they bear no malice; they are not demanding but merely petitioning the Tsar to look into their needs. Think what you are doing, you idiots!' The reply of the soldiers was: 'We have orders. We do not know anything'. On 5 January 1918, the unarmed Petersburg democracy, workers and employees came out to celebrate in honour of the Constituent Assembly. For nearly a century the best of the Russians have dreamed of

---

33   Lenin 1982d, p. 400; 1975c, p. 401.

34   Here we summarise the account as given in Bunyan and Fisher 1934, pp. 387–8.

this day. They visualised the Constituent Assembly as a political organ
capable of giving the Russian democracy an opportunity of freely expressing its will. Thousands of the intelligentsia, tens of thousands of the workers and peasants have died in prison and exile, have been hanged and shot
for the dream. And now that the goal has been reached and the democracy
has come out to rejoice, the 'People's Commissars' have given orders to
shoot. The *Pravda* lies when it says these democrats were the bourgeoisie
and Bankers ... Just as on 9 January 1905, so on 5 January 1918, there are
people who ask those who fired: 'idiots, what are you doing? These are
your own brothers. Can't you see the red banners?' Now, just as then, the
soldiers reply 'we have orders to shoot'.

The same policy of monopolising power without sharing it with other socialists, thus reflecting the *minority rule* under the Bolsheviks, is seen in Lenin's
attempt to create a new International by excluding the socialist parties of other
tendencies, who were not simply the 'patriots' but also the anti-war pacifists,
with self-inflicted negative consequences. As Borkenau remarked, 'if the Russians, instead of seeking friendly relations with the labour movements of other
countries, now set out to split them, they must make the social-democrats their
irreconcilable enemies and thus deprive themselves of the one support abroad
upon which they could have counted, had they renounced their idea of an international split'.[35]

The Relevance of Marx

At this point let us consider some important criticisms aimed at Marx in connection with the claim to Marx's heritage by the partisans of twentieth-century
socialism.

This alleged Marx-connection involves two basic issues. First, since Marx
is supposed to be the progenitor of this socialism, its quasi-disappearance
shows the failure of Marx's ideas in this regard. In particular it involves Marx's
prognostication of the rise of socialism in the advanced capitalist societies
after their disappearance caused by their own internal contradictions. Lenin
affirmed that a socialist revolution could begin in a backward land like Russia, and that 'things have worked differently from what Marx and Engels had

---

expected'.[36] As, demonstrably, capitalism continues to exist in the advanced capitalist countries through all its ups and downs, and as socialism palpably arose, against Marx's prognostication, in societies marked by the dominance of pre-capitalism or backward capitalism, Marx's vision has simply proven to be wrong. Now, we have argued above that the existing socialism has nothing in common with socialism as envisaged by Marx, that is, a society of free and associated individuals. There is a simple answer here based on Marx's materialist conception of history: the absence of the material and the subjective conditions for the advent of a society of free and associated individuals. As regards the relatively backward regions, socially and economically, the causes of this absence should be clear. As to the societies of advanced capitalism, it seems, they have not yet exhausted all the possibilities of their creative potential. Particularly – and this is the most important consideration – the development of the 'greatest productive force' (to use Marx's term for the working class) has not yet reached the point where its great majority can no longer accept the system confronting them and are prepared to revolt, though the necessary process might be on the way. When Lenin declared the possibility and the reality of socialist revolution and the consequent rise of socialism in a backward society, he had to admit that this was not foreseen by Marx and Engels. But, then, Marx and Engels also did not (and could not) imagine that in their name their disciples would create a society marked by the continued existence of state, commodity production and wage labour, with the workers separated and alienated from both political and economic power – the basic enslaving characteristics of the old class society – and call it socialist. To paraphrase Keynes's famous statement about Ricardo, Lenin conquered not only the subsequent revolutionary movement, but also many scholars as completely as the Inquisition had conquered Spain. Uncritically accepting the Leninist claim of the reality of socialist revolution in the backward Russia, some of the most knowledgeable and open-minded Western scholars, such as Carr, Deutscher and Sweezy, came to believe that Lenin rather than Marx was right in holding that proletarian revolution could occur first, not in advanced countries, but in countries which were comparatively backward. Thus, according to Carr, the 'Marxist scheme of revolution was bound to break down when the proletarian revolution occurred in the most backward capitalist country', which showed 'an error of prognostication in the original Marxist scheme'.[37] Carr is here joined by Isaac Deutscher, who opined that 'it was the Russian Marxists, and not Marx

---

36   Lenin 1982b, p. 510; 1975d, pp. 508–9.
37   Carr 1964, pp. 43–4.

and Engels, whom [the events in Russia] proved to be right'.[38] With the proletarian revolution occurring in a country as backward as Russia, the 'Marxist
scheme of revolution broke down'. Later Paul Sweezy expressed the same idea,
enlarging somewhat the context: 'the revolutions that put socialism on history's agenda took place not in economically backward countries, as Marx and
Engels thought they would, but in countries where capitalism was still in early
stages'.[39]

Similarly – from a somewhat different perspective, given the horrible reality
of this socialism in relation to the human individual – it is claimed that Marx's
socialism, which is considered as the progenitor of Party-State socialism, has
proven to be clearly repressive.

A Caricature of Marx's Socialism

We discuss here the arguments of two intellectuals. János Kornai, a deservedly
famous economist from Hungary, and Robin Blackburn, a social scientist from
England. In the context of our theme we first note an important difference
between these two individuals. In his youth inspired and enthused by Marx,
Kornai, living through the reality of Communist rule, has become, in his later
life, very critical of Marx's ideas. Given our theme, here we will leave aside Kornai's critique of Marx's economic ideas, not directly related to Marx's socialism,
which is the topic under consideration, and focus on his critique of Marx's political ideas. *Par contre* Blackburn seems to be a socialist intellectual in the usual
leftist, not necessarily Marxian, sense of the term. However, the difference in
their overall political outlooks does not at all prevent the unity of these two
intellectuals in considering the twentieth-century, post-1917 socialisms as the
inheritors of Marx's socialism.

First we analyse Kornai's position on Marx's socialism (leaving aside his
economic arguments against Marx). He starts with the questions: 'was Marx
responsible for what had occurred in the Soviet Union of Lenin, Stalin, Khrush-
chev, China of Mao or other communist countries? What is the relationship
between Marx's theoretical ideas and the historical reality of the socialist system?'[40] Then he answers: 'The plan of Marx was indeed implemented by the

---

38   Deutscher 1960, p. 184.
39   Sweezy 1993, p. 6.
40   Kornai 2009, p. 973.

socialist system; what arose after 1917 in the communist region and existed until 1989 was in its fundaments a realisation of what Marx saw as the socialist system that would replace capitalism'.[41] In Kornai's view, two salient features of the real system are just 'what Marx expected and prescribed'.[42] First, it came very close to eliminating private ownership in the means of production and public ownership became dominant, mainly in the form of state ownership. Secondly, it came very close to eliminating market conditions, while central planning, bureaucratic coordination and the command economy became dominant.

According to Kornai the kernel of Marx's thinking revolves around the question of property relations, which are private in capitalism, whereas abolishing capitalism would mean placing means of production under public ownership. Following Marx's line of thought (according to Kornai), while private ownership dominates, the exchange of goods and allocation of productive forces are coordinated by the market, which is a bad coordinator, opaque and anarchic. Public ownership will allow the allocation of forces of production and ultimately human labour to become transparent and planned. In support of his argument, Kornai cites Marx's famous sentence from *Capital* Volume I: 'the knell of the private property sounds; the expropriators are expropriated'. He then cites from Marx's 1871 'Civil war in France', where Marx, while discussing the measures the communards were trying to introduce, spoke of 'united cooperative societies regulating national production on a common plan'.[43]

Let us first remark that as regards the first citation from Marx, it is not a question, after the expropriation of capitalist private property, of replacing capitalist private property with so-called 'public' property. Capitalist private property will be replaced by '*socialised* property', as Marx writes.[44] 'Socialised' refers to *society* which replaces state, and the state has no place in Marx's socialism, conceived as an Association of free individuals. Now, neither of these citations correspond to what the Party-State was doing. In fact, what Kornai is ascribing to Marx corresponds in reality to what the Party-State was doing (while claiming Marx's legacy).

Now let us return to Kornai's assertion mentioned earlier concerning the two acts conforming to what 'Marx had expected and prescribed', namely, Party-States' elimination of private ownership in favour of public ownership

---

41   Kornai 2009, 974.

42   Kornai 2009, 975.

43   Kornai 2009, p. 975.

44   Marx 1987a, p. 683; 1976a, p. 558; 1954, p. 715. Emphasis added.

of the means of production, and elimination of the market in favour of central planning. Except for what Kornai considers as Marx's 'prescriptive part', the rest indeed conforms to what Marx anticipated *not* for socialism but for *capitalism* at a certain stage of its development. Let us elaborate. Through the play of immanent laws of capitalist production, the process of accumulation entails concentration of capital as well as centralisation of capital necessitating 'decapitalisation of smaller capitalists by bigger ones'.[45] This ultimate form of expropriation within capitalism finally reaches the point where capital is negated as the property of individuals/households and is transformed into common capital of what Marx calls 'associated capitalists'.[46]

Marx's analysis of the significance of the capitalist collective is of considerable importance. He observes that 'capital which in itself is based on the social mode of production and presupposes social concentration of the means of production and labour, directly assumes here the form of social capital in opposition to private capital'. 'This is the abolition (*Aufhebung*) of capital as private property within the limits of capitalist production itself'.[47] Marx also envisages the 'state as capitalist' so far as governments 'employ wage labour' in productive activities.[48] The state could very well take over the totality of society's capital, in which case, as Marx underlines in the French version of *Capital*, the 'centralisation of capital would reach its last limit where the total national capital would constitute only a single capital in the hands of a single capitalist'.[49]

The Party-State's claim to having realised socialism was fundamentally based on the argument that the régime had eliminated private property in the means of production. And its advocates, exactly like Kornai, never mention what Marx had thought to be the principal criterion for characterising a society in a particular period: the mode of production, involving the relations of production as shown, principally, in the relations between the means of production and the immediate producers. Both the régimes in question and Kornai himself remarkably abstract from this fundamental idea of Marx's materialist conception of history. As a matter of fact, property relations as a juridical category arise from production relations. To consider property relations as a 'category apart' is a 'metaphysical or juridical illusion'.[50]

---

45   Marx 1987a, p. 682; 1976a, p. 557; 1954, p. 714.
46   Marx 1987a, p. 572; 1954, p. 587. This expression seems to be absent in the French version.
47   Marx 1992, p. 502; 1984, p. 436.
48   Marx 2008, p. 636; 1956, p. 100. Actually the expression used is *Staatskapital*.
49   Marx 1976a, p. 448. This whole sentence, absent in the German original, appears only here.
50   Marx 1965, p. 118.

As regards the very concept of 'private property', it is very different in Marx when compared with the concept that we find in the work of the Party-State partisans. According to the latter it means the private property (in the means of production) of an individual/household or a business enterprise, the same as in bourgeois jurisprudence (as well as with Kornai). But Marx gives to the concept a more profound meaning. As we treat this subject in some detail in our chapter on 'Socialism' in the present volume, we will be brief here. In all class societies the ownership of means of production belongs to a minority, excluding the majority from this ownership. While in pre-capitalist societies the labouring persons (slaves, serfs, lower caste persons) were considered as an integral part of the means of production, in capitalism the workers as individuals are completely separated from the means of production. Marx calls such property in an early 1860s manuscript 'private property of a part of society', 'the property of a class'.[51] The *Communist Manifesto* asserts that the Communists could sum up their theory in a single expression, 'abolition of private property', since the existence of private property for the few means its 'non-existence for the immense majority'. The 'abolition of private property' is explicitly used in the sense of 'disappearance of *class* property'.[52] The same expression occurs again in Marx's *Civil War in France*, 'the Commune intended to abolish that class property which makes the labour of the many the wealth of the few'.[53] Contrary to the affirmation of the spokespersons of the régimes in question, as well as to the assertion of Kornai, private property in the means of production in the Party-State régimes was not abolished, and remained class private property, because the great majority in these régimes continued to be separated from the means of production, as seen in the continued existence of this majority as wage and salary earners.

Similarly, as regards Kornai's 'second salient feature' of the régimes in question, showing their alleged Marx connection, commodity production – the 'market' – far from being eliminated, continued to prevail in these régimes after the seizure of political power, the initial illusion of the spokespersons (during 'war communism') notwithstanding. As a well-known Polish authority on the 'soviet' economy underlined, 'Soviet planning did not do away with the market. It had introduced new rules of the game'.[54]

---

51   Marx 1956b, pp. 20,21; 1963, pp. 54, 56.

52   Marx and Engels, 1970b, pp. 47, 49. Emphasis added.

53   Marx 1971b, p. 75.

54   Zaleski, 1962, p. 297. We are placing the term soviet within inverted commas just to stress that after the Bolsheviks, with their monopoly of power, liquidated the soviets arising in February 1917 as independent self-governing organs of the working people, the term lost its *raison d'être*.

In turn, in his widely discussed book, Rudolf Bahro pointed out that 'eventually the entire "socialist" economy had necessarily to be recognised as one of commodity production and the law of value had again to give sway'.[55] Kornai himself, in an earlier work (published in the 1980s) had underlined, with reference to what he called 'soviet type societies', what he called a 'general definition of [the] market', that is, 'a system in which isolated producers and consumers are functioning as actors, [and] products are exchanged between them for money', including 'the firm manufacturing the means of production and the firm using the means as *seller and buyer*'.[56]

Kornai writes that he has found in no scholar sympathetic to Marx 'a quotation from Marx where Marx speaks comprehensively of political government, the state or the relation between oppression and freedom'.[57] But instead of depending on secondary sources, why not go directly to Marx's own work, beginning with that from the early 1840s, which is so rich in emancipatory messages![58] Kornai considers Marx to be anti-democratic, and as someone according to whom 'democracy is nothing other than the dictatorship of the bourgeoisie, to be replaced by the revolutionary dictatorship'. This type of criticism could only come from somebody who is totally unaware of Marx's own trajectory, starting from his critique of Hegel's political philosophy, where he had fought Hegel's apotheosis of monarchy in the name of democracy. We read there, 'In democracy the human does not exist for the sake of the law, but the law exists for the sake of the human, it is *human existence*, whereas in other political systems the human is a *legal existence*'.[59] Again, 'Democracy is the solution to the *riddle* of every constitution'.[60] In a chapter in this work we discuss Marx's idea of democracy at some length, focusing on his critique of Hegel. As regards the much-misunderstood term 'dictatorship of the proletariat', it simply signifies the rule of the class which constitutes, according to the 1848 *Manifesto*, the immense *majority* of society, totally in opposition to the rule of a *minority*, which has been the case so far in human annals. And it has nothing to do with the absolute rule of a single party which has exercised its power through a formidable military-bureaucratic state machinery in twentieth-century 'social-

55   Bahro, 1978, p. 135.
56   Kornai 1983, p. 153. Emphasis added.
57   Kornai 2009, p. 978.
58   One could almost say, paraphrasing Goethe, 'why wander far away, when the thing is so near' (from his *Erinnerung*).
59   Marx 1975, p. 88. Emphasis in text.
60   Marx 1975, p. 87. Emphasis in text.

ism', in the name of the working class after 1917. This topic, again, is discussed at some length in a chapter in the present book. We can only mention here that both Marx and Engels considered this proletarian rule as a 'democratic republic'.

'What Marx saw as the socialist system that will replace capitalism' according to Kornai,[61] is nowhere given in his present work. Instead we are given to understand that what arose after 1917 in the Communist region and existed until 1989 was basically a realisation of Marx's socialism. And wonder of wonders, he nowhere mentions Marx's own works on what Marx envisioned to be the society succeeding capital. The reader is supposed to accept Kornai's assurance that Marx's socialism is *grosso modo* the socialism of the régime(s) arising in his name. However, what Kornai and the post-1917 'socialist' régimes offer us as Marx's socialism is a caricatural representation of Marx's socialism.

We have, in the present work, devoted a whole chapter to this subject. Still a broad outline in brief can be offered here.

Marx's socialism is a thoroughly emancipatory project, starting with the self-emancipation of the most oppressed part of the capitalist society – the proletariat – which Marx supposes to constitute the great majority in capitalist society (under the supposition of advanced capitalism). The emancipation of the most oppressed in society, its lowest stratum, immediately implies the emancipation of the rest of society. The new mode of production Marx calls the Associated Mode of Production (AMP) as opposed to the Capitalist Mode of Production (CMP). As opposed to CMP's defining characteristic of separation of the immediate producers from the means of production, which, owned and dominated by the capitalists, confront the immediate producers as an independent, alien power, the relation of production under AMP is the (re)union of the immediate producers with the means of production, where the producers dominate the means of production, their own creation. In conformity with the new production relation there is a new ownership relation. In place of the earlier private ownership – individual or collective – of the means of production, from which the great majority of society – the labouring individuals – were excluded, there is now collective appropriation by society as a whole, where all are simple producers, not wage slaves. And with the disappearance of production by private labours, executed in reciprocal independence, that is, commodity production, there appears the form of directly social, collective production. As Marx stresses, in the 'cooperative society' producers do not

---

61   Kornai 2009, p. 974.

exchange their products (*Critique of the Gotha Programme*).[62] There is now only allocation/distribution of the products on the one hand among the different branches of production and on the other among the members of the new society. This allocation/distribution does not require any mediation through individual exchange – contrary to capitalism, it is directly operated. One part of the total social product goes for the enlarged reproduction of society's productive apparatus and society's insurance and reserve funds against uncertainty. The rest goes for individual and collective consumption of the society's members.

Finally, we turn to Robin Blackburn's critique of Marx – as he terms this critique, 'responsibility of Marx(ism) for October Revolution and the State issuing therefrom'. Now, this is apparently not the theme of his whole, long discourse. In a larger sense the theme is economic calculation in a socialist society, such as what was attempted, according to him, in the period 1917–89. But his critique of Marx is a convenient starting point, inasmuch as the whole project, according to Blackburn, arose from Marx's ideas. In this critical affirmation he is at one with Kornai, who also thinks, as we just saw, that the post-1917 power-holders of Russia were implementing Marx's project.

Now, if 'Marxism' means the ensemble of Marx's own ideas, then ascribing any responsibility for 'October' to Marx is simply preposterous. Though we take up this question in more detail in another chapter of this book, we can briefly say the following. The October Revolution started with the *coup de main* guided and organised by a tiny group of radicalised intelligentsia belonging to a single political party, far removed from the locus of material production and exploitation and without any popular mandate, at the back and over the heads of the soviets, thereby putting a brake on the immense revolutionary process spontaneously generated by millions of working people in Russia in February 1917. Thus there is an unbridgeable gap between this near-Bakuninist process of seizing power and the Marxian process, entirely based on self-emancipation of the whole proletariat and leading to the emancipation of the rest of society, and representing the 'immense majority in the interest of the immense majority', to use the oft-cited expression of the *Communist Manifesto*, enabling the proletariat as a class to become the ruling class.

Now Blackburn. According to Blackburn, to disclaim any responsibility for the disaster that befell the 1917–89 Russian régime is wrong, because 'leaders from Lenin to Gorbachev have appealed to Marx, sought to organise support for this state on the basis that they were Marxists, and at a subjective level believed

62   Marx in Marx and Engels 1970b, p. 319.

that they were furthering socialist causes as they understood it'. It is also wrong because the 'soviet system has appeared to implement key aspects of the classical Marxist and socialist programme, implicating, in some degree, any politics that chooses public ownership as a means and popular welfare as the goal. The economic order of the Soviet Union was certainly based on state ownership and planning'.[63]

There are several parts to this argument. The first is the appeal made by these leaders to Marx and their belief that they were furthering their socialist cause 'as they understood it'. Is not this case analogous, for example, to the case of the Japanese soldiers – all devout Buddhists – during the Second World War, who, before journeying to their killing spree, prayed to Buddha, who for this reason cannot disclaim any responsibility for the crime? Secondly, just because these leaders at a *subjective level* believed that they were furthering the socialist cause, that is, that of Marx, does not demonstrate at an objective level that they were really doing so. And, by critically examining what they were doing in practice, we can see clearly that they were doing just the opposite. In the text of this book we have extensively dealt with this subject in light of the Bolshevik practice. So we highlight here a couple of points.

As mentioned above, Blackburn speaks of classical Marxist and socialist programmes as being those that implement any politics that chooses public ownership as a means and popular welfare as goal. First of all, it is not clear what he means by a 'classical Marxist and socialist' programme. One does not know what is meant by 'classical', and how does he distinguish 'Marxist' from 'socialist'? There are of course socialisms different from the Marxian, like, for example, anarchist socialism, guild socialism and market socialism (all treated in this book), none of which is Marxian, by which we mean socialism/communism as found in Marx's own ideas as they were elaborated in his own original writings. If Blackburn thinks adequate the illustrations that he provides in support of his argument that the leaders of the socialist régime were following Marx, namely, public ownership of means of production with a view to popular welfare, and centrally based state-ownership and planning – we beg to differ.

The starting point for us is the notion of socialism in the sense of Marx. Given the appropriate objective conditions produced by capital itself, socialism is the outcome of the struggle for self-emancipation of the proletariat, the lowest and the most oppressed stratum of society constituting its immense majority. It is an Association of free individuals based on the Associated Mode of Production, as opposed to capitalism based on the Capitalist Mode of Production. In

---

63   Blackburn 1991, p. 9.

the second, working people are wage slaves, while in the first they are free in a double sense: free from personal dependence and free from material dependence. Here production as well as appropriation of products are collective. This is also a classless society where, consequently, besides not having generalised commodity production, there is also no state, hence no state ownership of the means of production. Instead, there is social ownership. It is remarkable that Blackburn nowhere mentions the specificity of the mode of production in what he considers to be Marxian socialism. And unsurprisingly he avoids any mention of the continuing existence of commodity production and wage labour in the régimes under those whom he considers to be Marx's followers. Contrariwise, in Marx's own work we read

> The collective character of production would from the start make the product collective and general. The original exchange taking place in production would not be an exchange of values, but of activities which would be determined by communal needs and communal goals and would from the outset include the share of the individual in the world of collective production.[64]

Of course the economy is planned here. But it is quite a different kind of planning. It is not centralised, bureaucratised 'soviet' type planning, basically the work of 'experts', pure technicians, outside any discussion and active control by the citizens. Contrariwise, we have altogether a different kind of planning in Marx's own socialism. We read, 'the form of social life process, that is, the material process of production, and the relations which it implies, will strip off its veil only when, as the product of socialised individuals, it is brought under their *planned* control'.[65] Let us remark, *en passant*, that Blackburn's placing of Trotsky by the side of Martov on the question of democracy is, to say the least, rather strange. Martov was a thoroughgoing democrat, one of the noblest characters of the Russian Revolution, while the Bolshevik Trotsky – in sharp contrast with the pre-Bolshevik Trotsky – had the same negative attitude to democracy as Lenin and Bukharin. Deutscher cites from Trotsky's aggressively anti-democratic speech at the tenth Party Congress, which we cited above. Indeed, Trotsky had the 'honour' of establishing on 4 June 1918, years before the Nazis, concentration camps for the Czechoslovaks who refused to surrender

---

64   Marx 1953, p. 88; 1993, p. 171.

65   Marx 1987a, p. 110; 1976a, p. 74; 1954, p. 84. The expression 'the relations which it implies' appears only in the French version. Our emphasis.

their arms, the order being extended to include the officers of the old army who refused to enrol in the Red Army, and, increasingly, to many others of different categories.[66] Trotsky had another feat to his 'credit': the first 'show trial', years before it was generalised by Lenin's nominated successor. Trotsky single-handedly had organised, in early summer 1918, the trial of the Baltic fleet commander Aleksei Shchastny, accusing him of acts he had not committed. As a well-known academic historian has written, 'Trotsky single-handedly organised an investigation, sham trial, and death sentence on the spurious charge of attempting to overthrow the Petrograd Commune with the long-term goal of fighting the Soviet Republic'.[67] The historian commented, 'Trotsky was the sole witness allowed to testify at the trial, possibly the first *show trial*. In 1995 Shchastny was cleared posthumously of all charges against him and rehabilitated'.[68] Speaking of Trotsky again, the eminent historian of Kronstadt Israel Getzler writes that unlike the Right Mensheviks as well as Kerensky, who could not bring themselves to take serious repressive action against the Kronstadters in 1917, 'Trotsky and the communists did not falter when making good their threat to "shoot them down like pheasants" in March 1921'.[69] Then he adds

> Trotsky took recourse to facile sociology. He pointed to the alleged replacement of 'vast numbers of revolutionary sailors' by such 'accidental elements' as 'Latvians, Lithuanians and Finnish sailors', thus robbing the Kronstadters of their glorious past and revolutionary potentials. While he never managed to live down his own gruesome role in the Kronstadt tragedy, he certainly did succeed in saddling its historiography with tendentious sociology.[70]

It should be clear that there is nothing in common between what Blackburn considers to be Marxian socialism and what we find in Marx's own work.[71] Blackburn's paper is an apologia for a commodity society, 'market socialism', which is the subject of a whole chapter in our present book. So, instead of introducing an excursion on market socialism as such, we would like to examine a couple of his positions. When he speaks of Marx's 'rhetoric', he does not explain

66   See Heller and Nekrich 1982, p. 54.
67   Rabinowitch 2007, p. 243.
68   Rabinowitch 2007, p. 435. Emphasis ours.
69   Getzler 1983, p. 656.
70   Getzler 1983, p. 257.
71   As the mathematicians would say, the intersection of these two ensembles is a nulle ensemble.

in what this 'rhetoric' consists. Nevertheless, Blackburn should be commended for reminding his readers of Marx's 'aphorism' that the 'free development of each is the condition for the free development of all', though he seems not to be aware that this is unrealisable in a commodity society, what he calls market socialism (a *contradictio in adjecto*) where the product, alienated from the producer, dominates the producer, not the inverse. The commodity society, the material abode of Party-State socialism, is a false society where the individual is not a personal, but a contingent individual. Within this false society, society confronts the individual as an independent power. It is only in the Association that there will exist the 'totally developed individual', to use Marx's phrase.[72]

Marx had written, 'the real basis of a higher form of society, [is] a society in which the full and free development of every individual forms the fundamental principle'.[73] While Marx had conceived human emancipation to be centred on the emancipation of the human individual from both subjective and objective constraints, in the 'socialist' régimes of the twentieth century, it was precisely the human individuals as persons who were totally subjugated by the Party-State. Being a one-party minority rule, the régime had to be a *terror régime* from the start, as we saw earlier with Lenin's reply to Martov. Any opposition to the régime was considered 'counter-revolutionary', resembling the last years of the Jacobin régime of the great French Revolution, whose portrait is vividly drawn in Alfred de Vigny's *Stello*, in the character of André Chénier, initially an enthusiastic devotee of the Revolution, who later turns dissident in the face of the increasing terror of the régime and is, ultimately, guillotined. (Later it was made into an opera by Umberto Giordano).[74]

How very different was the standpoint of Rosa Luxemburg, who wrote about one year after the Bolshevik victory: 'the proletarian revolution has no need for *terror*. It is not the desperate attempt of *a minority* to shape the world according to its own principles but an act of the people, of *millions* who are on a historical mission to turn what is historically necessary into reality!'[75] One can presume that the writer had the Bolsheviks in mind.

A case very different from if not the exact opposite of what we find in Kornai-Blackburn, we encounter in the character of Harold Isaacs, the author of the important book *The Tragedy of the Chinese Revolution* (1938), highly praised by

---

72 Marx 1987a, p. 466; 1976a, p. 347; 1954, p. 458.

73 Marx 1987a, p. 543; 1954, 555. This phrase is absent in the French version.

74 We find a fascinating portrait of the Robespierre terror in Anatole France's *Les Dieux ont soif* (Gods are thirsty).

75 Luxemburg in Kuhn 2012, pp. 101–2. Emphasis added. In another chapter of this book we have further elaborated on Luxemburg's position.

Leon Trotsky, whose follower he was. Isaacs started out as a Trotskyist when he
wrote the book. But, as his son Arnold Isaacs explains in a new preface to the
2010 edition of the book, Harold wrote in a preface to the 1951 edition that he 'no
longer agreed with the fundamental Leninist principles that Trotsky held until
his death in 1940, in particular, the principle that a proletarian dictatorship
led by a single revolutionary party must exercise sole power in a revolutionary state'.[76] Arnold cites his father, 'the one-party monopoly of political life,
developing into a bureaucratic oligarchy, an outcome that clearly rose out of
some of the basic premises of Bolshevism, cannot serve socialist ends; the contradiction between authoritarianism and democratic socialism is complete'.[77]
Speaking of Harold Isaacs, the son Arnold concludes, 'in later years he rejected
all labels and was suspicious of all isms – most of all, perhaps, revolutionism
(to borrow Trotsky's word) which preached a better world but made the twentieth century an era of unprecedented butchery and drowned its believers' hopes
in vast seas of blood'.[78] We must underline that unlike Kornai and Blackburn,
Isaacs does not anywhere mention Marx as the original sinner responsible for
the Bolshevik (mis)deeds.

---

76   Isaacs 2010, p. vii.
77   Isaacs 2010, p. viii.
78   Isaacs 2010, p. vii.

CHAPTER 1

On Socialism: Association of Free Individuals

First, a word on terminology. To start with, there is a widespread idea that, after capitalism, socialism and communism are two different, successive, societies, that socialism is the transition to communism, and precedes communism. However, for Marx (and Engels) socialism is neither the lower phase of nor the transition to communism. Socialism *is* communism. In fact Marx calls capitalism itself the 'simple transitional point' or 'transitional phase' (to the higher form of society).[1] For Marx socialism and communism are simply equivalent and alternative terms for the same society that he envisages for the post-capitalist epoch, which he calls, in different texts, equivalently: communism, socialism, the Republic of Labour, society of free and associated producers or simply Association, Cooperative Society, or (re)union of free individuals. Hence what Marx says in one of his famous texts – *Critique of the Gotha Programme* (hereafter *Gothacritique*) – about the two stages of communism could equally be applied to socialism, which would then undergo the same two stages. To drive home our point that socialism and communism in Marx mean the same social formation, and thereby to refute the uncritically accepted idea – a sequel to the Bolshevik tradition – of socialism being only the transition to communism, we can mention at least four of Marx's texts where, referring to the future society after capital, Marx speaks exclusively of 'socialism' and does not mention 'communism'. First,

> Generally a revolution – overthrow of the existing power and the dissolution of the old relations – is a political act. Without revolution socialism cannot be viable. It needs this political act to the extent that it needs destruction and dissolution. However, where its organizing activity begins, where its aim and soul stand out, socialism throws away its political cover.[2]

The second and the third texts are almost identical, appearing respectively in one of his 1861–3 notebooks (second notebook of the 23 notebooks) and in the

---

1 Marx 1953, p. 438; 1993, p. 540; 1962a; pp. 425–6; 1971a, p. 428.
2 Marx 1975, p. 420.

so-called 'main manuscript' for *Capital* Volume III. Here is the 1861–3 text, in Marx's own English:

> Capitalist production ... is a greater spendthrift than any other mode of production of man, of living labour, spendthrift not only of flesh and blood and muscles, but of brains and nerves. It is, in fact, at [the cost of] the greatest waste of individual development that the development of general men [general development of human beings] is secured in those epochs of history which prelude to [which presage] a socialist constitution of mankind [our bracketed insertions].[3]

This text is repeated almost word for word in the 'main manuscript' of Volume III of *Capital*.[4] Finally, in the course of correcting and improving the text of a book by a worker (Johann Most), meant to popularise *Capital*, Marx inserted: 'The capitalist mode of production is really a transitional form which by its own organism must lead to a higher, to a co-operative mode of production, to socialism'.[5]

One could also mention that Engels, speaking of the society after capital in both *Anti-Dühring* (1878) and *Socialism Utopian and Scientific* (1880), always calls it 'socialism/socialist', and not 'communism/communist'. Remarkably, in an article (published in Italian) in 1894, he simply substitutes the term 'socialists' for the term 'communists' in a sentence of the original 1848 *Manifesto*, jointly written by both Marx and himself: '... In the various stages of development which the struggle of the working class against the bourgeoisie has to pass through they (that is "communists") always represent the interests of the movement as a whole' (section II). In the 1894 article, Engels now puts 'socialists', replacing the term 'communists'. In what follows in the present chapter, wherever the term 'communism' is used in the text of Marx it should be clear that the term is used in the same sense as socialism, even if the latter term is not there.

---

3 Marx 1976b, pp. 324–5.
4 See Marx 1992, pp. 124–5; 1964b, p. 99; 1984, p. 88. Engels, in his edition of the book, which was translated into English, before the new original MEGA edition was published, had translated the passage into German, but not literally.
5 Most 1989, p. 783. Even in the text of his *Gothacritique* (1875) where 'communism' is in question, Marx, in one place, attacks the Lassallian 'servile belief in the state' as 'remote from socialism', where obviously the latter is just an alternative term for communism (Marx, in Marx and Engels 1970b, p. 329).

'Communism' (Socialism) appears in two different senses in the works of Marx and Engels. First, as a theoretical expression. As Engels succinctly underlines: 'to the extent that it (communism) is theoretical, it is the theoretical expression of the place of the proletariat in the class struggle between the proletariat and the bourgeoisie, the résumé of the conditions of the emancipation of the proletariat'.[6] Shortly thereafter the *Communist Manifesto* echoes this: 'the theoretical principles of the communists ... are only the general expressions of the real relations of the existing class struggle, of a historical movement that is going on before our eyes'.[7] In the second sense, communism refers to the society which is envisaged as arising after the demise of capital. The real movement which abolishes the present state of things inaugurates a communist society which is also designated – by Marx – alternatively, and with the same meaning in each case, as 'Socialism', the '(Re)union of Free Individuals', 'Republic of Labour', 'Cooperative Society', 'Society of Free and Associated Producers' or simply (*more frequently*) 'Association', based on the 'Associated Mode of Production' (AMP) as opposed to the 'Capitalist Mode of Production' (CMP). What follows is a portrait of this society after capital. The chapter is divided into six sections. The first section touches on the conditions for the rise of the new society, the four succeeding sections deal respectively with the new mode of production, its ownership relation, exchange relations and allocation/distribution. It concludes with a discussion of the place of the individual in the new society.

(Pre)conditions of Socialism

The starting point in a discussion of the society after capital is to stress the historical, transient character of capitalism. 'The present day society is no solid crystal, it is an organism that is capable of changing and is constantly changing', wrote Marx in his Preface to Volume I of his masterwork.[8] Again, in the third volume of the same work, the 'capitalist mode of production is not an absolute, but only a historical mode of production corresponding to a definite limited epoch in the development of the material requirements of production'.[9] Similarly, in one of Marx's early 1860s notebooks, we read of the 'historically

---

6 Engels 1847.
7 Marx and Engels 1970b, pp. 46–7.
8 Marx 1987a, p. 68; 1976a, p. 14; 1954, p. 21.
9 Marx 1992, p. 333; 1984, p. 259.

transitory character of (capitalist) relations of production which themselves create the means of their own abolition'.[10]

The conditions for the rise of socialism are not given by nature. Socialism is a product of history. Hence it is very important to emphasise the singularity of these conditions, which is very often neglected. In an early article Marx wrote that 'individuals build a new world from the historical acquisitions of their foundering world. They must themselves in course of their development first produce the *material conditions* of a new society, and no effort of spirit or will can free them from this destiny'.[11] Even with the strongest will and the greatest subjective effort, if the material conditions of production and the corresponding relations of circulation for a classless society do not exist in a latent form, 'all attempts to explode the society would be quixotism'.[12] As we read in an early text, 'If the material elements of a total revolution, the existing forces of production and the formation of a revolutionary mass which revolts not only against certain conditions of the past society but against the "old production of life itself" and its foundation, the "total activity", if these elements are absent, it does not matter at all for the practical development that the *idea* of this revolution has already been formulated one hundred times'.[13] About one year earlier, Marx and Engels had stressed that 'ideas can never lead beyond an ancient order of the world, they can only lead beyond the ideas of the ancient world order. Ideas can realize absolutely nothing; for realizing the ideas the humans have to employ themselves into practice'.[14]

The future society arises from the contradictions of the present society itself. This process is best understood by recalling the two methodological principles, derived respectively from Spinoza and Hegel, which inform Marx's whole 'Critique of Political Economy'. In his first manuscript for *Capital* Volume II, Marx completed Spinoza's famous saying 'all determination is negation' by adding 'and all negation is determination'.[15] Years earlier, in his 1844 Parisian manuscripts, while critically commenting on Hegel's *Phenomenology of Spirit*, Marx had observed that the latter's 'greatness' lay in the 'dialectic of negativity as the moving and creating principle'.[16]

---

10   Marx 1962a, p. 263; 1971a, p. 265.

11   Marx 1847.

12   Marx 1953, p. 77; 1993, p. 159.

13   Marx and Engels 1845–6. Emphasis in text.

14   Marx and Engels 1845.

15   Marx 1988a, p. 216.

16   Marx 1975, pp. 385–6. Translation modified.

Marx shows how capital creates the material and subjective conditions of its own negation and, simultaneously, the elements of the new society destined to supersede it. The material conditions are a great increase of the productive forces and a high degree of their development. This is also a 'necessary practical presupposition, because without this high level of development, only the shortage will be generalised and there will be a return of struggle around necessities, and, with it, a return to the old misery'.[17] It is precisely capital's negative side which contributes to this positive outcome. 'The material and the spiritual conditions of the negation of wage labor and capital – themselves the negation of the earlier forms of unfree social production – are in turn the result of its (capital's) (own) process of production'.[18] It is only capital that by separating the producers from the conditions of production – their own creation – and pursuing the path of production for production's sake – the logic of accumulation – creates, independently of the will of the individual capitalists, an abundance of material wealth and the socialisation of labour and production – the fundamental conditions for building the new society.

The original unity between the worker and the conditions of production (abstracting from the relations of slavery where the worker herself/himself is a part of the conditions of production) has two principal forms: the Asiatic community (natural communism) and small family agriculture (connected with domestic industry).

These two forms are infantile forms and little suited for transforming labour into social labour. Hence the necessity of separation, of violent rupture, of opposition between labour and ownership (in the conditions of production, that is). The most extreme form of this tearing apart (*Zerreissung*), within which at the same time the productive forces are most powerfully developed, is capital. Only on the material basis which it creates, and through the revolutions which the working class and the whole society undergo, can the original unity be re-established.[19]

In his 1847 discourse to the workers, Marx talked of the big industries, free competition and world market as the 'positive side of capital' and added that 'without these relations of production neither the means of production, the material means for the liberation of the proletariat and for founding a new society, could be created, nor could the proletariat take the road to union or undertake the (necessary) development enabling it to revolutionize soci-

17 Marx and Engels 1845–6.
18 Marx 1953, p. 635; 1993, p. 749.
19 Marx 1962a, p. 419; 1971a, p. 423.

ety and itself'.[20] A few years later Marx puts the question in a sharper form while referring to Ricardo's contribution to capitalist development. Considering Ricardo's advocacy of production for production's sake, he takes Ricardo's 'sentimental' critics to task for attacking the mercilessness of the Ricardian approach on the ground that this approach is destructive of the human individual. Marx holds that such arguments would mean that no war should be waged in which individuals perish. 'What these critics fail to understand is that the development of the faculties of the human species (*Fähigkeiten der Gattung Mensch*) though taking place at the cost of the majority of individuals and even whole classes of humans, ends by surmounting this antagonism and by coinciding with the higher development of the singular individual, therefore, the higher development of the individuality is bought at the cost of a historical process in which individuals are sacrificed'.[21]

Marx argues that at a certain stage of capitalism's development its social relations of production turn into fetters for the further development of the forces of production – including the 'greatest productive force, the revolutionary class'[22] – forces which have been engendered by capital itself and have progressed under it hitherto. This indicates that the old (capitalist) society has reached the limits of its development and that it is time for it to yield its place to a new, higher social order – which thus signals the beginning of the 'epoch of social revolution'.[23] 'The increasing unsuitability of the hitherto existing production relations of society for its productive development', writes Marx, 'is expressed in sharp contradictions, crises, convulsions. The violent destruction of capital, not through the relations external to it, but as the condition of its self-preservation, is the most striking form in which the advice is given to it to be gone and give room to a higher state of social production'.[24] In a famous, often misunderstood, text, Marx underlined, 'No social formation ever

---

20   Marx 1973c, p. 556.

21   Marx 1959, p. 107; 1968a, p. 118. Readers will notice the similarity between this statement from the notebook number 11 and the statement cited earlier from the second notebook of the same 1861–3 manuscripts. A few years later, in a letter to his friend Kugelmann (7 March 1868), Marx wrote, 'I have presented big industry not only as the mother of antagonisms, but also as the producer of the material and intellectual conditions for the solution of these antagonisms, which, indeed, cannot take place in a comfortable way'. In Padover 1978, p. 245.

22   Marx 1965ba, p. 135.

23   Marx 1980a, pp. 100–1; 1970a, p. 21.

24   Marx 1953, p. 635; 1993, p. 749. Part of the passage beginning with 'advice ... social production' is in English in the manuscript.

perishes before all the productive forces, which it is large enough to contain, have developed, and new, higher relations of production, never appear before the material conditions have been hatched within the womb of the old society itself. That is why humanity always sets itself only the task which it can solve, and the task itself only appears where the material conditions of its solution already exist or at least are in the process of formation'.[25]

More concretely, two and a half decades later, in his polemic with Bakunin, Marx wrote: 'A radical social revolution is bound up with certain historical conditions of economic development. The latter are its preconditions. It is therefore only possible where, with capitalist development, the industrial proletariat occupies at least a significant position'.[26] Besides the material conditions, as regards the subjective – 'spiritual' – condition, it is, again, provided by capital itself by begetting its own 'grave diggers' – the proletariat.

We would like to refer here to a remarkable piece by Marx, his speech (in English) at a Chartist banquet (14 April 1856). Here it is in his own English:

> In our days everything seems pregnant with its contrary ... At the same pace that mankind masters nature, man seems to become enslaved to other men or to his own infamy ... All our invention and progress seem to result in endowing material forces with intellectual life, and stultifying human life into a material force ... Steam, electricity and the self-acting mule were (are) revolutionists of a rather more dangerous kind than even citizens Barbès, Raspail, Blanqui (great revolutionaries of the period). This antagonism between the productive powers and the social relations of our epoch is a fact. Some parties may wail over it, we on our part do not mistake the shape of the shrewd spirit. We know that to work well the new-fangled forces of society, they only want to be mastered by new-fangled men – and such are the working men. They are as much the product of modern time as machinery itself ... We do recognize our brave friend Robin Goodfellow, the old mole that can work in the earth so fast, that worthy pioneer – the Revolution.[27]

Marx stresses the importance of the economy of time in creating disposable time. In a communitarian society the less time the society requires to produce its necessities, the 'more time it has for other activities, material or spiritual'.

---

25   Marx 1980a, pp. 100–1; 1970a, p. 21. Translation modified.
26   Marx 1874–5.
27   Marx 1980b, pp. 655–6.

'Economy of time is that to which all the economy is reduced; similarly, society
has to allocate its time appropriately (*zweckmässig*) with a view to realising a
production conforming to its needs ... Economy of time as well as the appropriate distribution of the labour time in the different branches of production
remain the first economic law in the collective system of production'.[28] Closely
connected with economy of time is the question of free time, as opposed to
what Marx calls 'time of labour', which always remains the creative substance of
wealth and the measure of production costs. But 'free time, disposable time, is
wealth itself partly for enjoyment of products and partly for free activity which,
unlike labour, is not determined by the constraint of an extraneous purpose,
the fulfilment of which is considered as a natural necessity or a social duty as
one likes'.[29]

It must be stressed that capitalist relations are not revolutionised within capitalism automatically even with all the requisite material conditions prepared
by capital itself. It is the proletariat's *categorical imperative to overthrow all the
relations* in which the individual is a degraded, enslaved, abandoned, despised
being'.[30] It is the working class – the 'greatest productive force' – which is the
active agent for eliminating capital and building the socialist society. As a justification of this special role of the proletariat, Marx and Engels had already
written, more than four decades earlier, that

> The conditions of existence of the proletariat resume all the conditions of
> the present society which have reached the paroxysm of inhumanity. In
> the proletariat the human individual has lost her/him self, but has, at the
> same time, gained the theoretical consciousness of this loss. The prolet-
> ariat feels itself constrained to revolt directly against this inhumanity. It
> is for these reasons that the proletariat can and must liberate itself. But it
> cannot liberate itself without abolishing its own conditions of existence.
> It cannot abolish its own conditions of existence without abolishing all
> the inhuman conditions of the present society which are resumed in its
> own situation.[31]

---

28   Marx 1953, p. 89; 1993, pp. 172–3.
29   Marx 1962a, p. 255; 1971, p. 257.
30   Marx 1975, p. 251. Emphasis in text.
31   Marx and Engels 1844–5. Shortly thereafter the two authors wrote, 'the proletariat, the
     lowest stratum of the present society cannot stir, cannot raise itself up without the whole
     superincumbent strata of official society being sprung into the air'. See Marx and Engels
     1970b, p. 45.

'The proletariat is the "bad side" of the present society', and 'history moves by the bad side', as Marx reminded Proudhon.[32]

Now, a proletarian (socialist) revolution is impossible without the proletariat being fully aware of what this revolution is about. But how does this consciousness arise? On this question there has been an important tendency among Marx's followers, beginning at least with Karl Kautsky, to argue that the workers on their own are not capable of developing spontaneously this (socialist) revolutionary consciousness, and that this has to be carried to them by the (revolutionary) intelligentsia from outside. He was, however, careful to add that this task of the intellectuals in no way entitled them to be in the leadership of the revolutionary movement.[33] Closely following Kautsky, his then-disciple V.I. Lenin extended the master's argument further. He distinguished between workers' organisation and the organisation of 'professional revolutionaries', that is, those who make 'revolutionary activity their profession'.[34] Now Marx and Engels had already stressed that the consciousness of the necessity of a profound revolution arises from this class (that is, the working class) itself.[35] More than a decade later, in the notebook 4 of his massive 1857–8 manuscripts, Marx wrote, 'the recognition of the product as his/her and the judgment of its separation from the conditions of realisation as something improper, imposed by force, is an enormous consciousness, itself the product of the mode of production based on capital, and as much the knell to its doom, as with the consciousness of the slave that s/he cannot be the property of another, with his/her awareness as a person, the existence of slavery becomes merely an artificial, vegetative existence, and ceases to be able to continue as a foundation of production'.[36] In his turn Engels, in his 1890 Preface to the *Communist Manifesto*, stressed that 'for the ultimate triumph of the ideas set forth in the *Manifesto* Marx relied solely and exclusively on the intellectual development of the working class as it necessarily had to come from united action and discussion'.[37]

As regards the need for an organisation of 'professional revolutionaries' to 'bring about the (political) revolution' apart from the workers' own organisa-

---

32   Marx 1965b, p. 89.

33   For this account of Kautsky we draw on the outstanding article of Massimo Salvadori, in Grisoni 1976, pp. 81–205.

34   Lenin 1982a, pp. 170–1; 1970, p. 207.

35   Marx and Engels 1845–6.

36   Marx 1953, p. 366; 1993, p. 463.

37   Engels, in Marx and Engels 1970b, p. 33. Note that Engels nowhere mentions the intellectuals importing (exporting) revolutionary consciousness to the workers from outside.

tion, as emphasised by Lenin,[38] Marx had, as mentioned above, already called the working class itself the 'revolutionary class' in his 1847 Proudhon critique. In close succession, the 1848 *Manifesto* emphasised that of all the classes standing in opposition to the bourgeoisie today, only the 'proletariat is really a revolutionary class'.[39] Indeed, 'the proletariat is either revolutionary or it is nothing', as Marx wrote to a friend many years later (13 February 1865).[40] And, more clearly, in the 'Afterword' to the first volume of *Capital*, Marx stressed that the 'historical profession (*Beruf*) of the proletariat is to revolutionise the capitalist mode of production and the final abolition of classes'.[41] In other words, the proletariat as a class is itself a class of 'professional revolutionaries', to use Lenin's terminology. It is also of contextual relevance to refer here to the positions of two of the best-known followers of Marx (and Engels) on this question: Rosa Luxemburg and Antonio Gramsci.

In her brochure *Mass Strike, Party and Revolution* (1906), speaking of the need for the destruction of Russia's absolutism, Luxemburg observed that to achieve this, 'the proletariat needs a high degree of political education, class consciousness, and organisation – the conditions which can be satisfied not through brochures and pamphlets, but simply by the living political school, from the struggle, from the progressive course of the revolution'.[42] Luxemburg here clearly follows basically the thought of Marx and Engels on the question as given above. Gramsci, in his turn, discussed the analogous problem in his prison notebooks (c. early 1930s) in the context of the problematic of the concept of unity of theory and practice, where he brought in the role of the intellectuals. He observed, 'Critical self-consciousness signifies historically and politically the creation of an intellectual elite; a human mass does not "distinguish" itself and does not become independent on its own without organisation in large sense (*in senso lato*) and there is no organisation without intellectuals, that is, without organisers and without leaders ... without there being a stratum (*strato*) of persons specialised in the conceptual and philosophical elaboration'.[43] A broad affinity with Kautsky-Lenin thought is clear here.

Let us conclude this discussion with what Marx and Engels wrote in their famous October 1879 'Circular Letter' to some of their followers:

---

38   Lenin 1982a, pp. 170–1; 1970, p. 207.
39   Marx and Engels 1970b, p. 44.
40   Rubel citing Marx, in Marx 1965a, p. cxxv.
41   Marx 1987a, p. 703; 1976a, p. 18; 1954, pp. 25–6.
42   Luxembourg, in Hudis and Anderson 2004. Translation modified.
43   Gramsci 1996, p. 18.

It is an inevitable manifestation, and one rooted in the process of development, that people from what had hitherto been the ruling class also join
the militant proletariat and supply it with educative elements. We have
already said so in the *Manifesto*. But in this context there are two observations to be made. First, if these people are to be of use to the proletarian
movement they must introduce genuine educative elements. Secondly,
when people of this kind join the proletarian movement, the first requirement is that they should not bring with them the remnants of bourgeois,
petty bourgeois etc. prejudices, but should unreservedly adopt the proletarian outlook. Within a workers' party they are an adulterating element.
Should there be any reason to tolerate their presence for a while, it should
be our duty only to tolerate them, to allow them no say in the Party leadership. As for ourselves, there is only one course open to us. For almost 40
years we have emphasised that the class struggle is the immediate motive
force of history, that class struggle is the lever of modern social revolution.
At the founding of the International we expressly formulated the battle
cry: the emancipation of the working class must be achieved by the working class itself. Hence we cannot co-operate with those who say that the
workers are too uneducated to emancipate themselves and must first be
emancipated from above by the philanthropic members of the upper and
lower middle classes.[44]

The emancipation of the proletariat is the task of the proletariat itself. At the
same time, the proletariat being the lowest class of the capitalist society, as we
just saw, Marx and Engels stress that the emancipation of the proletariat signifies at the same time the emancipation of the humanity itself.[45]

It is important to note the specificity of the proletarian revolution. From the
fact that socialism in Marx and Engels arises from the reality of the capitalist
society, which is revolutionised into a new society, it follows that their starting
assumption is historically severely limited to the capitalist epoch which itself
is considered as historically transitory. In particular, it is only advanced capitalism in which the society has already freed itself from the millennial fetters of
the individual's personal unfreedom under slavery and serfdom. At the same
time, here the capitalist mode of production and correspondingly capitalist
relations of production have sufficiently advanced to a degree such that the

---

44   Marx and Engels 1879.
45   Marx, in his last programmatic pronouncement to the French workers, repeated the same
       idea: 'the emancipation of the producing class is that of all humanity without distinction
       of sex or race'; see Marx 1965c, p. 1538.

immense majority of the population are neither themselves part of the means of production (as were the slaves and serfs) nor in possession of any material means of production as their own. They, on the contrary, have only their own labour power – manual and mental – to sell 'freely' to the possessors of the means of production in exchange for wages/salary (high or low), in order to live and reproduce the labour power.

Secondly, unlike the bourgeoisie, who started to undermine the pre-capitalist relations of production long *before* attaining (political) domination, the proletariat must first have its own political power in order to *start* the transformation process.[46] As Engels noted, 'the bourgeoisie came more and more to combine social wealth and social power in its hands while it still for a long period remained excluded from political power'.[47] Again, the proletarian movement, unlike all previous social movements, is an independent movement of the immense majority in the interests of the immense majority, as the *Communist Manifesto* stresses.[48] It follows that 'all revolutions till now have resulted in the displacement of one definite class rule by another. And all ruling classes up to now have only been small minorities in relation to the ruled mass of the people'.[49] The proletarian revolution will be the first real majoritarian revolution in the annals of humanity.

As noted above, while the bourgeois revolution finds its crowning point and comes to power after undermining the pre-capitalist social order, thereby at the end of the revolutionary process, the working class must first gain its political power in order to launch the whole revolutionary process of transforming the existing capitalist social order. It should be stressed that the dissolution of the old society – for that is what a social revolution boils down to – is not a momentary event, not a moment but a *process*. It is secular, *epochal*, in the sense Marx speaks of when he writes about the 'beginning of the epoch of social revolution'.[50]

At this point we would like to refer to a common mistake concerning the significance of the socialist (proletarian) revolution. Even when we ignore the crude mistake of equating the whole working class with a party calling itself 'Communist' or 'Socialist', and consequently the party power with the class power (which has been the practice of twentieth-century 'socialism'), even then there remains a serious mistake in the supposition that the seizure of

---

46   See Marx and Engels 1970b, p. 45.
47   Engels, in Marx and Engels 1970b, p. 371.
48   See Marx and Engels 1970b, p. 45.
49   Engels, in Marx and Engels 1970b, p. 645.
50   Marx 1980a, p. 101; 1970a, p. 21.

political power is tantamount to the 'victory' of the revolution, like the supposed 'victory' of the Russian or Chinese or Cuban revolution. We saw above
that this kind of social revolution is only true for the bourgeois revolution,
where the victory of revolution coincides with the gaining of political power.
Let us very briefly mention here two cases involving two celebrated authors.
First Hal Draper. He interprets Marx as holding that following the 'conquest of
political power', *equated to* 'socialist revolution', there follows the 'dictatorship
of the proletariat'. Draper also calls the period after the seizure of power the
'post-revolutionary period'.[51] The same position was taken by the well-known
radical economist Paul M. Sweezy, who wrote a whole book under this title,
Post-Revolutionary Society.[52] Then there is Istvan Mészáros, who, speaking of
the 1917 Russian Revolution, says that it was the 'first successful revolution
which projected the socialist transformation of society breaking out in Tsarist Russia'.[53] So in Russia the revolution for socialism did not only break out
but was also 'successful'. As we can see in the cases under consideration, for all
three authors the (socialist) revolution is a momentary event and not 'epochal'
as Marx would have it in his 1859 'Preface' cited earlier. This is clearly the case
in the 1848 *Manifesto* where we read that the raising of the working class to the
position of the ruling class constitutes only the 'first step in the revolution by
the working class'.[54]

From this point onwards begins the process of revolutionising the bourgeois
mode of production, and it continues till the whole existing mode of production is transformed. Marx called it the 'revolutionary transformation period' to
which corresponds a 'political transition period' ruled by the working class constituting the immense majority of society.[55] It is during this prolonged 'transition period' that the whole capitalist mode of production and therewith the
whole bourgeois social order are superseded. Until capital totally disappears,
the workers do not cease to be proletarians, and hence the absolute rule by
the proletariat, 'the *revolutionary dictatorship of the proletariat*', as Marx calls
it,[56] continues throughout the transition period, the period of preparation for

---

51   Draper 1986, pp. 1–2.
52   Sweezy 1980.
53   Mészáros 2008, p. 295.
54   Marx and Engels 1970b, p. 52.
55   Marx, in Marx and Engels 1970b, p. 327.
56   Marx, in Marx and Engels 1970b, p. 327. Emphasis in original. Years earlier, in his 'Class
     Struggles in France', referring to what he calls 'revolutionary socialism', Marx wrote, 'This
     socialism is the declaration of the permanence of the revolution, the class dictatorship of
     the proletariat as the transit point to the abolition of all class distinctions generally, to the

the advent of the Association. Marx characterises this period as the 'prolonged birth pangs' within the womb of the capitalist society.[57]

On the question of the revolutionary transformation period between capitalism and socialism (communism) and, particularly, the revolutionary dictatorship of the proletariat corresponding to it, there has been a lot of misreading and misunderstanding of the texts of Marx and Engels. First of all, the overwhelming stress has mostly been on the political part, the proletarian dictatorship, which is only supposed by Marx to correspond to the *primary aspect* of the transition period, the transformation of the capitalist social order into the socialist social order. As noted earlier, it is this transformation period which is inaugurated by the proletariat as the ruling class by gaining the political supremacy as only the 'first step' in the revolution. The transformation in question cannot be effected by any legislation, by any quick juridical measure by the victorious proletariat; an existing social order cannot be just legislated away.[58] Marx indicates this in more than one text. Thus in the third notebook of his 1844 Paris Manuscripts, referring to the human emancipation through communist practice, Marx observed that 'history will bring this about, and the movement will pass through a rude and prolonged process'.[59] A few years later, in an 1850 (September) discourse of the central committee of the Communist League, Marx told the workers, 'you will have to go through 15, 20, 50 years of civil war and national struggles not only to change the social conditions but also to change yourselves in order to render you capable of exercising political power'.[60] And, in *Capital*, while discussing 'commodity fetishism', he observed that 'the social life process, that is, the material process of production, will strip off its mystical veil only when it is treated as the product of the freely associated individuals and brought under their conscious planned control. But this demands a set of material conditions of existence, which themselves are the natural products of a long and painful development'.[61] Later, with a real situation of a workers' rule being exercised in the Paris Commune (1871) before his eyes, Marx affirmed that the 'superseding of economical conditions of the

---

abolition of all relations of production on which they rest, to the abolition of all the social relations that result from all these relations'. See Marx 1850.

57   Marx, in Marx and Engels 1970b, p. 320.
58   Precisely the 'socialisms' of the last century were inaugurated by the juridical 'abolition' of private property in the means of production, beginning with the 1936 constitution of the USSR. More on this later.
59   Marx 1975, p. 365.
60   Marx, in Marx 1994, p. 587.
61   Marx 1987a, p. 110; 1976a, p. 74; 1954, p. 84.

slavery of labour by the conditions of free and associated labour can only be the progressive work of time … in a long process of development of new conditions, through long struggles … through a series of historic processes, *changing circumstances and men*.[62] The transformation affects the totality of the existing social order.

All the above citations taken from Marx's writings between 1844 and 1871 – refuting in fact the notion of momentary, instantaneous victory of socialism – relate to what was referred to above as the 'revolutionary transformation period' between capitalism and communism.[63]

The question of transition from capitalism to socialism as Marx (and Engels) envisaged it was considerably obscured by Lenin's distinction in his 1917 unfinished work *State and Revolution* between socialism and communism (absent in Marx's texts as shown earlier), equating them respectably with Marx's first and second phase, as well as Lenin's acceptance of two transitions, one from capitalism to socialism and another from socialism to communism. Also, in Marx the passage from capitalism to the first phase of communism is qualitatively different from the passage from the first to the second phase of communism, inasmuch as the former involves a revolution in the social relations of production whereas the latter does not. There is no new mode of production in the second phase because the mode of production has already been revolutionised to form the basis of the first phase. It is not without reason that Marx reserves the phrase 'revolutionary transformation period' only for the first passage, that is, the passage from capitalism to the new society, and not for the passage between the first and the second phase of the Association.[64]

Let us turn to the problematic of the proletarian dictatorship. We encounter a paradox here. The transition period ending in the inauguration of a Union of Free Individuals has been conceived mainly as a *coercive* régime in Bolshevik theory, as we clearly see in the writings of Lenin in the first place. Here we

---

62   Marx, in Marx and Engels 1971b, pp. 76, 156–7. Emphasis added.

63   Marx, in Marx and Engels 1970b, p. 327. The question of a period of transformation necessary as a preparatory stage for building the new society is quasi-absent in contemporary discourses on socialism.

64   Now it so happens that in one of the original drafts for his book in question, while treating the problem of state, Lenin does not mention 'socialism' but only 'communism' as the society succeeding capitalism. And the analysis strictly follows Marx. Thus, according to Lenin, first, under capitalism there is the state in its proper sense; second, there is the state of the transition – dictatorship of the proletariat – no longer a state in its proper sense. Thirdly, the end of the process, communist society, disappearance of the state. See Lenin 1962a, p. 179.

refer to three of his texts. First, in *State and Revolution*, while speaking of the first stage of communism, also considered by Lenin as the transition to communism, Lenin underlines that all citizens will be 'transformed into the hired employees of the state ... The whole society will become a single office and a single factory with equal labour and equal pay'.[65] This clearly means that the citizens will be transformed into wage labourers in the first phase of communism. Lenin's second text in question was composed a few months after the seizure of power: 'The Immediate Tasks of the Soviet Government' (1918). This discourse is an apology for coercion. He held that 'in the interests of socialism' people must 'unquestionably obey the single will of the leaders of labour' who constitute the 'proletarian vanguard'.[66] He added that in the history of the revolution, 'dictatorship of individuals was often the expression of the dictatorship of the revolutionary classes'.[67] At the Ninth Congress of the Party (1920), again, Lenin stressed the necessity of 'fighting against the survivals of the notorious democratism (*preslovootogo demokratisma*)', and denounced 'all this outcry against appointees, all this old harmful rubbish (*vredniy khlam*) which have found their way into various resolutions and conversations'.[68] Henceforward proletarian dictatorship was conceived mostly as an instrument of coercion in the Bolshevik tradition. To the same extent the secular transforming tasks of the period – 'changing circumstances and men' in Marx's words (cited earlier) – got lost and were shelved until the arrival of a far-distant 'full communism', in Lenin's repeated expression in *State and Revolution*. However, this position found its full blossoming in Bukharin's discussion of the transition period between capitalism and communism.

Bukharin starts by affirming that in the transition period, when one structure of production yields place to another structure of production, revolutionary violence serves as the midwife whose task it is to blow up the fetters which obstruct the development of society. This means, on the one hand, the old forms of 'concentrated violence' which have become a counter-revolutionary factor, that is, the old state and the old type of production relations. The revolutionary class, on the other hand, must promote the building of new production relations and thereby the new society. Its state power is the proletarian dictatorship which constitutes a factor of destruction of the old economic relations and of the construction of the new. The political power of the proletariat as the

---

65   Lenin 1982g, pp. 307–8; 1975a, p. 312.
66   Lenin 1982b, p. 617; 1975d, p. 611.
67   Lenin 1982b, p. 617; 1975d, p. 610.
68   Lenin 1971a, p. 339; 1982c, p. 279.

concentrated power (*kontsentrirovannoe nasilie*) constitutes a 'factor of self-organisation and coerced self-discipline of the workers'. So there are 'two sides of coercion, in relation to the non-proletarian strata as well as in relation to the proletariat itself and the groups close to it'.[69] To the extent the proletariat gains victory in its struggles with the non-proletarian strata, classes and groups, there is an 'accelerated decomposition (*razlozheniya*) of the old mindset' of the persons who are useful to the new system, in the first place the technical intelligentsia. However, without the pressure of coercion they cannot be usefully put to work for a well-directed plan for the society. External state coercion is here absolutely necessary. Then Bukharin particularly emphasises that 'this coercion does not limit itself only to the former ruling class and groups close to it; in the transformation period it is carried over – in different forms – also to the working people themselves, also to the ruling class (proletariat) itself. Even the vanguard of the proletariat which is integrated in the communist party, the party of the revolution, is not immune to this coerced self-discipline (*prinudite'niu samoditsiplinu*) in its own ranks'.[70]

This characterisation of proletarian rule as mostly coercive and repressive was attributed to Marx both by his self-anointed 'followers' and his detractors. The main features of proletarian rule are discussed by Marx mostly in his 1871 *Civil War in France*, and Engels brilliantly outlines those features in his introduction to this work. Both believed the 1871 Commune to involve working-class rule, the first working-class government. This was a thoroughly democratic rule. The 1848 *Manifesto* had already stressed that the beginning of the proletarian revolution arising from the independent movement of the immense majority in the interests of the immense majority, and raising the proletariat to the rank of the ruling class, was the *conquest of democracy*.[71] That is, the proletariat, representing the 'immense majority' of society as the ruling class, is equated to the conquest of democracy. To Marx and Engels the 1871 Commune represen-

---

69   Bukharin 1989, pp. 162–63.

70   Bukharin 1989, p. 166. Let us note that the identification of the 'vanguard of the oppressed as the ruling class' with the 'proletarian dictatorship' that Lenin made in his *State and Revolution* is totally contrary to the position of the *Communist Manifesto*, where it is a question of the whole working class, not its 'vanguard' (implicitly the Communist Party), as the ruling class, in the same sense as the 1871 Paris Commune. It is remarkable how in Lenin's supposedly libertarian work Marx's emancipatory position has been seriously compromised. Let us remark, *en passant*, that Bukharin's stress on the exercise of coercion against the Communist Party itself would be tragically illustrated in his own case only a few years later.

71   See Marx and Engels 1970b, pp. 45, 52.

ted such a rule within its space. 'The majority of its members were working men, or acknowledged representatives of the working class ... The Commune was the true representative of all the healthy elements of the French society'.[72] The Commune, the living dictatorship of the proletariat, was not, contrary to Bukharin's idea of such a dictatorship discussed earlier, primarily a machine for coercing and suppressing the non-proletarian classes. It suppressed the bureaucracy and the standing army and filled all its posts by election on the basis of universal suffrage of all concerned, subject to the right of recall at any time by the same electors. Years later, Engels, in his 1891 critique of the Social Democratic Party's Erfurt Programme, wrote, 'The working class can only come to power under the form of a democratic republic. This is the specific form of the dictatorship of the proletariat'.[73] In his 1975 *Gothacritique*, Marx observed that 'Vulgar democracy, which sees the millennium in the democratic republic ... has no suspicion that it is precisely in this last form of state of bourgeois society that the class struggle has to be fought out to a conclusion'.[74] One wonders how this idea of the proletarian dictatorship being a 'democratic republic' could be compatible with the Leninist idea of the dictatorship of a single individual representing the class dictatorship. Indeed, little of this democratic aspect of the proletarian dictatorship – the principal aspect – finds its place in the usual discussion of the proletarian dictatorship. It is interesting to recall that Lenin, while citing Marx and Engels on the Paris Commune, adds that one of the reasons for the defeat of the Commune was that it did not suppress the bourgeoisie with 'sufficient determination' (*nedostatochno reshitel'no eto delala*).[75] In the context of the Bolsheviks' declared adhesion to the principles of the Paris Commune, even as they interpreted the proletarian dictatorship as a uniquely coercive instrument, it may not be out of place to refer to what Karl Kautsky – whom the Bolsheviks had savagely attacked as a 'renegade' for his denunciation of the way they had come to power – wrote. The 'renegade' returned the compliment in his 1921 polemic with Trotsky:

> The Commune and Marx prescribed the abolition of the old army and its replacement with a militia. The Soviet Government has started by dissolving the old army. But it has created the red army, a permanent army, one of the strongest in Europe. The Commune and Marx prescribed the dissolution of the State police. The Soviet Republic has dissolved the old

72   Marx in Marx and Engels 1971b, pp. 71,79.
73   Engels 1891.
74   Marx in Marx and Engels 1970b, p. 328.
75   See Lenin 1975a, p. 268; 1982c, p. 260.

police in order to build the police apparat of Tcheka, a political police provided with power, more extensive, more unlimited and more discretionary than what the French Bonapartism and the Tsarist bureaucracy had at their disposal. The Paris Commune and Marx had prescribed the substitution of the State bureaucracy by the functionaries elected by the people through universal suffrage. The Soviet Republic has destroyed the old Tsarist bureaucracy, but at its place, has installed a new bureaucracy as centralised as the old and having at its disposal powers much more extensive than the precedent, since it serves to control not only the liberty but also people's subsistence.[76]

In the context of the present discussion, let us examine the criticism of Marx by a famous scholar and intellectual, Hannah Arendt, on what she considers to be a contradiction in Marx on the question of his perception of the Paris Commune of 1871. She referred to Marx's statement in the *Civil War in France* to the effect that the Communal constitution showed the political form which might well be the form for the liberation of labour. Then she added,

> But he soon became aware to what extent this political form contradicted all notions of 'dictatorship of the proletariat' by means of a socialist or communist party whose monopoly of power and violence was modeled upon the highly centralised governments of nation states.[77]

This is an astounding statement from such an eminent scholar. This only shows how little she was aware of Marx's own relevant texts. We already stressed earlier that for Marx (and Engels) a proletarian dictatorship, by the very fact of its constitution by society's overwhelming majority in the interest of the overwhelming majority, is by definition a democracy. It is a democratic republic. As opposed to all the earlier revolutions, for the first time in human annals this is a majority revolution. So the entire process could only be democratic. And, contrary to Arendt's assertion, in no text does Marx mention a 'socialist' or 'communist' *party* as the holder of proletarian power. Following *real* proletarian practice as exemplified in the Commune, the state of the proletariat is not a state – possessing special repressive machinery – in the proper sense of the term. Marx's famous statement in the *Gothacritique* that during the transition period between capitalism and communism 'the state can *only* be the revolu-

---

76   Kautsky 1921.
77   Arendt 1963, pp. 260–1.

tionary dictatorship of the proletariat',[78] can only mean that during the period of workers' self-rule the power of the proletariat can only have this minimally repressive character (repressive just enough to put down the revolt of the 'slave holders').

On the other hand, far from modelling his idea of proletarian dictatorship on the highly centralised government of a nation state, Marx was agreeably surprised to see the realisation in the Commune of what he had already thought would be the case in a workers' revolution in Europe in his text of 1851–2, *The Eighteenth Brumaire of Louis Bonaparte*: the destruction of the centralised state power. In a letter to his friend Kugelmann written during the 1871 events in Paris, Marx recalled his earlier expectations.[79] In fact this had been Marx's passion at least since the mid-1840s. So it seems Arendt had been seeing Marx through Bolshevik lenses.

Now, with the end of the revolutionary transformation period, classes and class rule also end. The proletariat together with its political rule ceases to exist, leaving individuals as simple producers. Once we have arrived at this point, all political power will cease to exist, since political power is the official résumé of the antagonism in civil society.[80] We read in the programmatic part of the *Communist Manifesto* that while all the instruments of production are 'centralised in the hands of the state ... in the beginning', it is only 'in the course of development [that] class distinctions disappear, all production is concentrated in the hands of the associated individuals, [and] public power loses its political character ... The proletariat abolishes the old relations of production and thereby its own rule as a class'.[81] As Engels succinctly put it later, 'In place of the rule over persons, there will be administration of things and the direction of the processes of production. The state will not be "abolished", it will pass away'.[82] In fact the state starts to lose its power as the process of socialisation advances, till society completely replaces the state, totally reversing the earlier history. And then the first phase of the Association begins.

---

78   Marx in Marx and Engels 1970b, p. 327. Emphasis added.

79   Marx wrote to Kugelmann, 'If you look at the last chapter of my *Eighteenth Brumaire*, you will find that I declare that the next attempt of the French Revolution will no longer be, as before, to transfer the bureaucratic-military machine from one hand to another, but to *smash* it ... and this is what our heroic Party comrades in Paris are attempting' (in Marx and Engels 1971b, p. 284. Emphasis in original).

80   Marx 1965b, p. 136.

81   Marx and Engels 1970b, p. 53.

82   Engels 1962, p. 262.

Associated Mode of Production

The outcome of the workers' self-emancipatory revolution is the communist society based on the AMP and the corresponding relations of production. This is 'a (re)union' or an 'association' of 'free individuals'. The expression 'free individuals' here signifies that individuals are neither under personal dependence as in slavery or serfdom nor subject to material dependence as in commodity-capitalist production.[83] The term '(re)union' or 'association' has a profound meaning here. It has a double sense; as opposed to capitalism's reciprocal separation of the producers themselves, as well as the producers' separation from the conditions of production – their own creation – it is now a voluntary, unmediated union or association of individuals as producers (after having ceased to be proletarians) as well as a union or association of the producers and their conditions of production. This union or association thus constitutes a double negation of the individual's alienation: from the other individuals in society as well as from oneself (through the alienation from one's own product).

This 'union', the exact opposite of capitalism's *separation*, is, however, not the restitution of the earlier union in either of its versions – either constrained as in slavery/serfdom or voluntary as in 'natural communism' or in small family enterprise, inasmuch as under neither of these could there be a universal development of the productive powers of labour, engendering an abundance of material wealth – nor could labour and production be socialised at a universal level – the two basic conditions for building the new society, as mentioned earlier. Thus the new union is built 'on the basis of the acquisitions of the capitalist era'.[84] After the labourers cease to be proletarians, labour loses its earlier meaning. It is no longer commanded and enforced by an alien power on the labourer. Labour now is transformed into free and conscious *self-activity* exercised by the individual producer – as a part of the free Association – with a view to developing the individual's human essence. Thus in the new society we have the complete *de-alienation* – as opposed to capitalism's *alienation* – of individuals, both in regard to their own kind and to their own material creations. As opposed to the hitherto existing 'false community', which as an autonomous power confronted and subjected the singular individual, there is now a 'true community' whose members are universally developed social individuals subjecting their social relations to their own control.[85]

---

83   Marx 1953, p. 75; 1993, p. 157.
84   Marx 1987a, p. 683; 1976a, p. 557; 1954, p. 715.
85   Marx 1975, pp. 265–6; 1953, pp. 593–4; 1993, p. 706; 1987a, 109; 1976a, p. 74; 1954, p. 83.

Ownership Relation

Ownership relations are 'simply the juridical expression of the production relations'.[86] With the change in the relations of production, the ownership relations also change. Ownership here refers to the ownership of the means of
production/means of labour. In all class societies, including capitalist society, this ownership has belonged to a small minority, the great majority has
been deprived of this ownership. While in pre-capitalist societies the labouring people (mostly slaves and serfs and their likes) were themselves considered
an integral part of the means of production, under capital the wage and salary
earners are separated from these means altogether. In his sixth notebook (1861–
3) Marx calls this class monopoly of ownership – never recognised by jurisprudence – 'ownership of a definite class' or 'private ownership of a part of society'.[87] This is independent of the question of ownership by *individual* capitalists
in their private capacity. Within this broad class ownership there could be different forms of private ownership. In modern jurisprudence private ownership
refers to the ownership (of means of production) by an individual/household
or by a business enterprise. Quite understandably the substitution of *this* capitalist private ownership by 'public' (state) ownership is considered by many
people as abolition of private ownership in the means of production. However,
this view is mistaken. Here is a confusion between ownership *form* and ownership *relation* itself, which is simply the juridical representation of the production relation of a society. The capitalist (class) ownership relation is given
as soon as the capitalist production relation is given. This specific ownership
relation is defined by the producers' *separation* from the means of production.
This ownership relation could have different *forms*, such as ownership of the
individual capitalist or of 'associated capitalists' (joint stock company) or even
of the state.[88]

---

86   Marx 1980a, p. 100; 1970a, p. 21.
87   Marx 1956b, pp. 9, 21; 1963, pp. 43, 56. When the *Communist Manifesto* declares that the
      communists can sum up their theory in a single expression 'abolition of private owner-
      ship', the latter is expressly used in the sense of 'disappearance of class property' (Marx and
      Engels 1970b, pp. 47, 49). In his 'Address' on the Commune (1871) Marx said, 'the Commune
      intends to abolish that class-property, which makes the labour of the many the wealth of
      the few' (1971b, p. 75).
88   Marx 1987a, p. 572; 1976a, p. 448; 1954, p. 588; 2008, p. 636; 1956, p. 100. As the last limit of
      centralisation of capital, Marx even envisages in *Capital*'s French version, the existence,
      over the whole economy, of a single capital under a single ownership (1976a, p. 448). (This
      expression does not appear in *Capital*'s first or second editions, written before the French

Thus the state ownership of the means of production does not at all mean the end of 'private ownership of a part of society' – class ownership – of the means of production, as long as the great majority, separated from the means of production, remains wage/salary earners. It simply signifies the end of the juridically recognised *individual* (including corporate) private ownership of the means of production. Indeed, the *Communist Manifesto* underlines the need for the juridical elimination of *individual* private ownership of the means of production and of bringing it under the ownership of the proletarian political power only as an *initial* measure of the revolution.[89] And since the installation of the workers' political power does not signify the immediate disappearance of capital (as a relation of production), proletarian state ownership does not at all mean the end of capitalist 'class private ownership' in the means of production. Hence, whereas the juridical elimination of individual capitalist private ownership is perfectly possible within capitalism, the 'invisible' class private ownership cannot be abolished juridically, as that would be tantamount to abolishing the bourgeois production-relation itself – whose juridical expression is this ownership – by mere legal enactment. As Marx stresses, a society cannot simply 'jump over' or 'enact away' its natural phases of development.[90] This class private ownership disappears only with the disappearance of the capitalist relation itself (along with the proletarian state). Capitalist private ownership of the means of production – both in its individual and class sense – yields place to their ownership by society as a whole-social appropriation. As Marx and Engels stress, 'with the appropriation by the associated individuals of the totality of the productive forces, private ownership disappears'.[91] This appropriation, contrary to its earlier forms, which had a limited character, has now a total, universal character. This is because non-ownership of the means of production by the great majority, that is, the latter's deprivation within the last antagonistic social formation, is total, and, secondly, given the universal character of the development of the productive forces attained under capital, the appropriation of the productive forces has also to be universal, appropriation by the collective body of the emancipated producers. Thereby the social

---

version, but later was added by Engels for the third and the fourth editions.) It is important to stress that Marx conceives the individual capitalist not necessarily as a private owner of capital, but as a 'functionary of capital', 'the real agent of capitalist production' earning 'wages of management' for exploiting labourer (1962a, p. 475; 1971a, p. 477; 1992, pp. 452, 460); 1984, pp. 380, 389.

89   Marx and Engels 1970b, p. 52.
90   Marx 1987a, p. 67; 1976a, 13; 1954, p. 20.
91   Marx and Engels 1845–6.

individual becomes a total, integral individual. In this sense the former private ownership is transformed into 'individual ownership'.[92] Almost paraphrasing the language of *Capital*, Marx observes in his discourse on the Paris Commune that 'it aimed at the expropriation of the expropriators. It wanted to make individual property a truth by transforming the means of production ... into mere instruments of free and associated labour ... This is communism'.[93]

Exchange Relations

Like the ownership relation, exchange relations also change following the transformation of the social relations of production. As in earlier societies, the two types of exchange carried on by humans, namely, material exchange with nature and social exchange among themselves, continue to operate in communism. As to the material exchanges of individuals with nature, while the CMP – compared with earlier modes of production – renders humans less dependent on the powers of nature by progressively subjecting these powers to human intelligence through an unprecedented increase in the material forces of production, its technology, at the same time, it seriously damages the natural environment by undermining the natural powers of the earth along with those of the human producer, 'the twin fountains of all wealth'.[94] Under the AMP the social individuals not only free themselves from their subjugation by nature's blind force through a rational regulation of their material exchanges with nature, but also carry on these exchanges in conditions 'most worthy of and in fullest conformity with their human nature'.[95] We should add here an important point. After the demise of capital, and after its absurd goal of production for production's sake is displaced by production uniquely for the sake of human needs, there is no reason why the associated producers who are supposed to be at a higher level of enlightenment with a changed mindset will not take care of their own ecological concerns which, even at present, preoccupy so many. Need for a healthy life of the members of society will surely prevent bad ecology and promote good ecology without capitalist constraints.[96]

---

92   Marx 1987a, p. 683; 1976a, p. 557; 1954, p. 715.

93   Marx, in Marx and Engels 1971b, p. 75.

94   See Marx 1953, p. 597; 1993, p. 709; 1987a, p. 477; 1976a, p. 361; 1954, p. 475; 1992, p. 753; 1984, p. 813.

95   Marx 1992, p. 838; 1984, p. 820.

96   This entire process is a part of the revolutionary transformation process, 'transforming cir-

Coming to the exchange relations among individuals, it should be noted that in any society the labour of the individual producers creating useful objects for one another has, by this very fact, a social character. However, in a society with generalised commodity production, where products from private labours are executed in reciprocal independence, the social character of this process is not established directly. Their social character has to be mediated by exchanging products as *commodities*. The social relations of individuals take the form of social relations of their products. Products dominate the producers, confronting them as an independent power. Marx considers the whole process as a process of mystification and famously names it 'commodity fetishism' in *Capital*.

In the Association, with the collective (social) appropriation of the conditions of production, individual labour is directly social from the beginning. In place of exchange of products taking value form, there is now 'free exchange of activities' among social individuals 'determined by collective social needs and aims'.[97] Under capital the social character of production is posited only *post festum*, only after the products are promoted to the rank of exchange value. Under communism, on the contrary, the labour of the individual is posited as social labour from the start, the social character of production is presupposed, precluding the need for any transaction based on exchange value.[98] Not that, strictly speaking, no mediation is necessary for production and distribution in the new situation. As Marx stresses in his 1857–8 manuscripts, whereas in the commodity (including capitalist) society the social character of production is posited *post festum*, in the new society the social character of production is posited right at the beginning of the production process, even before production starts. 'Here community is posited before production' and 'the individual's participation in the world of collective products is not mediated by independent labours or products of labour. It is mediated by the social conditions of production within which the individual's activity is inserted'.[99] About two decades later Marx writes, 'In the co-operative society based on common ownership of the means of production producers do not exchange their products, just as little the labour employed in products appear here *as value* of these products'.[100] A

---

cumstances and humans', in Marx's words already quoted earlier in this chapter, preparing the associated individuals to create the new society.

97   Marx 1953, p. 88; 1993, p. 172.
98   See Marx 1980a, p. 113; 1970a, pp. 34–5.
99   Marx 1953, p. 89; 1993, pp. 172–3.
100 Marx, in Marx and Engels 1970, p. 319. About two decades earlier Marx had written, 'Noth-

few years earlier Engels in his turn had observed that 'as soon as society takes possession of the means of production and employs them towards directly socialised production, the labour of everybody – however different its useful character – is from the beginning directly social labour. How much quantity of social labour is contained in a product could be known directly without going through a detour (of exchange value)'.[101]

Distribution/Allocation

Distribution in any society can be viewed both as the distribution of the conditions of production and of products where the first determines the second. The distribution of the conditions of production, again, includes the distribution of the material means of production and of the labouring individuals of society among different branches of production. The distribution of the conditions of production is in fact the distribution of the total social labour time – dead as well as living – across the economy. Thus viewed, the distribution of the conditions of production is a 'moment of production' itself or an aspect of the mode of production itself.[102] First we discuss the distribution of the conditions of production, and then take up that of products.

Social labour time refers to society's time available for production. The regulation of production by a proper distribution of society's available labour time among different productive spheres is common to all societies. Another issue, equally general, concerns the absolute magnitude of society's labour time itself. There is an absolute need for economising society's global time for production, not only indicating greater productive efficiency but also in order to release more time to allow society's individuals personal enjoyment and development. Thus 'all economy is finally reduced to the economy of time'. However, though the economy of time and its distribution in society are effected in different ways in different societies, in a society based on conscious, collective production they assume such a different character that they constitute the 'first economic law' in such a society.[103]

The interbranch allocation of society's labour time is a question of the latter's alternative uses in suitable proportions. More time is bestowed on certain

---

ing is more false or more absurd than to suppose the control of the associated individuals over their production on the basis of exchange value'. Marx 1953, p. 76; 1993, p. 158.

101   Engels 1962, p. 288.

102   Marx 1953, p. 20; 1993, p. 99, in Marx and Engels 1970b, p. 321; 1992, p. 900; 1984, p. 883.

103   Marx 1953, p. 89; 1993, pp. 172–3.

branches of production, less time remains for the rest. This allocation problem, common to all societies, is solved differently in different societies. Economy of time and its distribution take different forms in different societies. In the collective economy this distribution is essentially different from measuring exchange value by labour time. Thus whereas under capital the distribution of society's labour time is mediated by the *value form* of the products of labour, the new society solves the problem in a conscious, controlled way without the need for social relations to appear as relations between things.

Within the broad context of society's allocation of its available labour time, there are, again, two particular situations that all economies face. The first concerns the replacement of the means of production that perish or wear out over a period. Given the fluctuations in the volume of durable parts of the means of production as a function of changing consumption needs – both personal and productive – and the need for maintaining a corresponding level of the volume of raw materials and semi-finished products, the problem is how to effect the reproduction of the means of production in their totality. Whereas capitalism 'solves' this problem anarchically, the real solution lies in 'continuous relative overproduction' of the means of production, possible only when society consciously controls and plans the process of its own reproduction, 'as in communism'.[104]

The second problem relates to the temporal lag between employment of resources and obtaining use values therefrom. The lag is of course long in some lines of production and relatively short in others. This again is a situation independent of any specific mode of production. The problem of allocating resources to production lines with a longer time lag, compared with others with a shorter time lag, is 'solved' in CMP *post festum* and at the cost of abiding disturbances, while in AMP society will consciously calculate and plan in advance the necessary scale of operation and allocate the resources, that is, the total labour time, accordingly. Marx observes that from a purely objective point of view the necessity of such calculation increases with the growing social character of production, for example, in capitalism compared with simple commodity production. Given that communism (socialism) is at a still higher scale of socialisation and that it is a consciously planned economy, the necessity of such calculation – social bookkeeping – is naturally even greater in AMP compared to any earlier mode of production.[105] Not only is the allocation of labour time as between different lines of production effected in a different way under AMP

---

104   Marx 2008, p. 770; 1956a, p. 473.
105   Marx 2008, p. 304; 1956a, p. 318.

compared with CMP, the saving of society's global labour time itself, devoted to material production, takes on an altogether different character in the new society. The creation of disposable time by minimising the global labour time signifies, for all class societies, non-labour time for the non-producing few. However, unlike the pre-capitalist modes of production, the CMP continuously strives to increase, beyond the necessary labour time of the producers, their *surplus labour time*, the appropriation of which as surplus value is considered society's wealth, given exchange value and not use value as its objective. Surplus labour is the labour of the worker beyond her/his own needs. This in fact is labour for society which under the CMP the capitalist appropriates in the name of society. The surplus labour is the basis of society's free time, and, simultaneously, the material basis of society's many-sided development.

However, since capitalism on the one hand creates disposable time, while on the other it converts this disposable time into surplus time leading ultimately to the crisis of overproduction and non-valorisation of surplus labour, the process is contradictory. The contradiction is overcome in AMP. First of all, in the conditions of social appropriation of the conditions of production, the earlier distinction between necessary and surplus labour time loses its meaning. From now on necessary labour time will be measured in terms of needs of the 'social individual', not in terms of the needs of valorisation. Similarly, the increase in disposable time will no longer signify non-labour time for the few. It is disposable or free time for all 'social individuals'. It is now society's free time and no longer labour time that becomes the measure of society's wealth. And this in a double sense. First, its increase indicates that labour time produces more and more wealth due to the immense increase in the productive forces, unconstrained by earlier contradictions – the wealth for the enrichment of all individuals. Secondly, free time itself signifies wealth in an unusual sense because it means the enjoyment of different kinds of creation and because it means free activity, which unlike labour time is not determined by any external finality that has to be satisfied either as a natural necessity or as a social obligation. On the other hand, labour time itself, the basis of free time, has now a new significance. Labour in the new society is directly social, unmediated hierarchically or by the value form of the products of labour and bereft of its earlier antagonistic form.

There is another important aspect of distribution under communism which concerns the division of the total social product between society's production and consumption needs as well as the distribution of the means of consumption among the 'social individuals'. As to the first problem, one part of the social product serves as common funds that includes replacement and extension of society's productive apparatus as well as society's insurance and reserve funds against uncertainty. The rest serves as means of collective consumption – mainly society's health and educational needs and provision for those who are unable to work – and personal consumption.[106]

As regards the mode of distribution of the means of consumption among individual producers, this follows from the way in which the conditions of production are distributed. As producers are (re)united with the conditions of production under communism, they are, to start with, no longer sellers of their labour power, and the wage form of return to their labour ceases right from the beginning of the new society. Here the producers receive from their own Association not wages but some kind of token indicating the labour time that each individual has contributed to the total social labour time, after necessary deductions for the common funds. These tokens allow the producers to draw from the social stock of means of consumption the amount costing the same amount of labour. Naturally, in the absence of commodity production these tokens are not money, they do not circulate.[107]

At the initial phase of the communist society, which has just come out of the bourgeois society after a 'prolonged birth pang', afflicted with the birth marks of the old society, the latter's principle of equal exchange, that is, equivalent exchange of labour against labour of the same amount, cannot be avoided. Hence this equal right is still 'bourgeois right'. But there is a big difference between the two situations. In the old society there is a contradiction between principle and practice; the principle of exchange of equivalents exists and can exist *only as an average*, it cannot exist for each individual case, which is unascertainable. The opposite is the case with collective, social appropriation. Here, with directly social labour in production, the share of each producer in total social labour time is palpable. Hence there is no contradiction between principle and practice. The unavoidable persistence of this 'bourgeois right' at the initial stage of the Association is wholly overcome only at a higher stage of the Association when all-round development of the 'social individual', along with the development of the productive forces, takes place, and when all the springs of 'co-operative wealth' flow more fully. Only then will prevail the principle, 'from each according to one's ability to each according to one's needs'.[108]

---

106   Marx 1987a, p. 109; 1976a, p. 73; 1954, pp. 82–3; in Marx and Engels 1970b 318–19.

107   Marx 1987a, p. 122; 1956a, p. 577; 1954, p. 98; 2008, p. 347; 1956a, p. 362; in Marx and Engels 1970b, p. 319.

108   Marx 1953, p. 88; 1993, p. 172; in Marx and Engels 1970b, p. 321. We think that today, given the immense increase in the material forces of production and taking account of ecological considerations, in the Association, distribution according to needs is conceivable,

Labouring Individual under Socialism

We end our chapter by touching on a theme which forms the very core of the human emancipatory project of the future society in the works of Marx and Engels, namely, the situation of the human individual in socialism. Not much attention has been paid to this theme by the readers of their works.[109]

Quite early Marx set the tone: '*all* emancipation is the *reduction* of the human world, of the relations, to the *human individual her/himself*'.[110] Later, in a justly famous statement, Marx and Engels affirmed that in the Association the 'free development of each' would be the 'condition for the free development of all'.[111] Engels later held: 'it is self-evident that society cannot liberate itself without liberating each individual'.[112] Marx particularly focuses on the situation of the producing individual in the Association. In this perspective there is a remarkable passage in one of Marx's manuscripts which sums up the whole human social evolution focused uniquely on the (labouring) individual:

> The relations of personal dependence ... are the first social forms in the midst of which the human productivity develops (but) only in reduced proportions and in isolated places. Personal independence based on material dependence is the second great form only within which is constituted a system of general social metabolism made of universal relations, faculties and needs. Free individuality based on the universal development of the individuals and their domination of their common, social productivity as their (own) social power is the third stage.[113]

Three stages here of course refer respectively to pre-capitalism, capitalism and socialism.

The starting point here is a very important distinction that Marx makes between the individual's labour as such and an individual's labour as *self-*

---

assuming that humanity has gotten rid of the huge waste involved in military and other means of coercion.

109   Marx announced his (and Engels's) 'new materialism' (1845) thus: 'The standpoint of the old materialism is civil society, the standpoint of the new materialism is the *human society* or *social humanity*' (Marx, in Marx and Engels 1970b, p. 30; emphasis added).

110   Marx 1975, p. 234. Emphasis in original.

111   Marx and Engels 1970b, p. 53. Later Marx added this sentence in *Capital* in a somewhat enlarged form. See Marx 1987a, p. 543; 1954, p. 555. It is absent in the French version.

112   Engels 1962, p. 273.

113   Marx 1953, p. 75; 1993, p. 157.

activity, a distinction which most of Marx's readers generally leave aside. The neglect of this point by readers leads them to a wrong understanding of Marx's explicit emphasis in some texts on the *abolition* of division of labour and of labour itself in the coming society. This position of Marx (and Engels) appears most explicitly in the *German Ideology*. At first sight this position looks strange. Even many Marxists by and large are embarrassed in the face of this seemingly 'utopian' idea. Let us see the matter more closely. Basically Marx stresses that labour, as it has been practised by human individuals in society across the ages, has so far been principally *involuntary*, at the service of others, commanded by others. This was palpably the case with individuals under 'personal dependence', as seen in slavery and serfdom (in their different forms). Under 'material dependence', with wage labour, this is less palpable but here also an individual's labour is imposed on the labourer by forces external to the labourer. Labour under capital, as we saw earlier, remains alienated from the labourer. In one of the 1844 notebooks Marx wrote, 'My labour would be the free expression, the enjoyment of life. In the framework of private property it is the alienation of life, my individuality has been alienated to the point where I loathe this activity, it is torture for me ... it is only a forced labour imposed on me'.[114] One year later, in his critique of Friedrich List, Marx remarks that the labourer's activity is not a 'free manifestation of his human life, it is rather an alienation of his powers to capital'. Marx calls such activity 'labour' and writes that 'labour by nature is unfree, inhuman activity' and calls for the 'abolition of *labour*'.[115] Indeed Marx cites Adam Smith's view that labour in history so far, including labour under capital, has been repulsive, appearing as sacrifice, as externally enforced labour, and that non-labour is freedom and luck.[116] As regards the existing division of labour, Marx underlines that the activity of the individual here is not voluntary. His own act stands in opposition to him as an alien power which instead of being mastered by him enslaves him. 'As soon as the labour begins to be divided, each labouring individual has a definite, exclusive circle of activity imposed on him and from which s/he cannot come out'.[117] In his manuscripts of the late 1850s and early 1860s, Marx wrote – echoing his earlier Parisian manuscripts –

---

114   Marx 1975, p. 278.
115   Marx 1972, p. 436. Emphasis in original.
116   See Marx 1953, p. 505; 1993, p. 611. The great Marx scholar Maximilien Rubel very pertin-
      ently discusses the origin of the term 'labour' (*Arbeit*) and connects this term to 'orbbo',
      which signifies in the Indo-Germanic languages 'small', poor, low, in Latin 'labor', becom-
      ing in English 'labour'. See his remarks in Marx 1982b, p. 1823.
117   Marx and Engels 1845–6.

that (under capital) the product of living labour, the 'objectified labour with its own soul stands opposed to it as an alien power'. The 'realisation process of labour is at the same time the de-realisation process of labour'.[118] Referring to the process of simple reproduction of capital, Marx underlines in his masterwork that 'inasmuch as before entering the labour process the labour of the labourer is already appropriated by the capitalist and incorporated by capital, this labour is objectified during the process constantly into alien product'.[119] Referring to the division of labour in capitalism, Marx says that this process seizes not only the economic sphere but also other special spheres, introducing everywhere the process of 'parcellisation of the (labouring) individual'. Marx also calls such individuals 'detail', that is, 'fragmented individuals'. Very pertinently, Marx cited what he called the 'outcry' of Adam Smith's teacher Adam Ferguson: 'We make a nation of helots [serfs in ancient Sparta], we have no free citizens'.[120] In other words, going back to an earlier text, we have here what Marx calls 'abstract individuals'.[121] Hence it is a question of abolishing *this* 'labour' and *this* 'division of labour' as the task of the 'communist revolution'.[122] It is in this spirit that Marx wrote in one of his 1861–3 manuscripts: 'As if division of labour was not just as well possible if its conditions appertained to the associated labourers, and the labourers related themselves to these conditions as their own products and the objective elements of their own activity which by their nature they are'.[123] This is the sense we get in Marx's *Critique of the Gotha Programme*. Discussing the lower and the higher phases of the communist society, Marx observes that the lower phase of the new society, which has just come out of the capitalist society with all its birth marks, cannot completely get rid of the legacy of the mode of labour of the old society, including the division of labour, particularly that between mental and physical labour. Only the higher phase of the new society will completely transcend the narrow bourgeois horizon, such that labour will not simply be a means of life but will become life's first need, and not all division of labour will be abolished but only the division of labour which 'puts the individual under its enslaving subordination', along with the opposition between mental and physical labour.[124]

---

118   Marx 1953, p. 358; 1993, p. 454; 1982b, p. 2239; 1994, p. 202.

119   Marx 1987a, p. 527; 1976a, p. 406; 1954, p. 535.

120   Marx 1987a, pp. 349, 463, 466; 1976a, pp. 257, 344, 347; 1954, pp. 334, 454, 457.

121   Marx and Engels 1845–6.

122   Marx and Engels 1845–6.

123   Marx 1962a, p. 271; 1971a, p. 273.

124   Marx, in Marx and Engels 1970b, pp. 320–1.

Earlier we discussed in a general way the relation between necessary and surplus labour time in the perspective of AMP as opposed to CMP. Now we focus on this distinction specifically from the perspective of the labouring individual. In all modes of production, necessary labour is what is required for preserving and reproducing the labour power, while surplus labour is labour beyond necessary labour whose product takes the form of surplus value in capitalism. Once the capitalist form of production disappears, a part of total human activity still remains necessary in the earlier sense of preserving and reproducing the labour power of the individual labourer through the provisions for collective and individual consumption – including food, housing, health and education. However, in contrast with capitalism, the domain of necessary labour is much further extended in conformity with the requirements of the total development of the individual, subject only to the limit set by society's productive powers. The labour beyond this necessary labour – the surplus labour – which under capitalism used to serve mainly capital accumulation, disappears.

On the other hand, a part of what is considered under capitalism as surplus labour, the part which today serves as reserve and accumulation funds, would, in the absence of capital, be counted as necessary labour for insurance and reserve funds and continuing enlarged reproduction of means of production, keeping pace, not with the requirements of (non-existing) *capital accumulation* but with the requirements of growing social needs of the associated individuals, including provisions for those who are not in a position to work. All this falls in the domain of material production. So the whole labour devoted to material production is counted as necessary labour under communism. The time beyond this necessary labour time required for material production is really the free time, or disposable time, which is wealth itself, on the one hand for enjoying existing products and, on the other hand, for free activity, activity which is not determined by the constraint of an external finality which has to be satisfied, a satisfaction which is a natural necessity or a social duty. In a justly famous passage Marx observes:

> The kingdom of freedom begins where the labour determined by necessity and external expediency ceases. It lies therefore by nature of things beyond the sphere of material production really speaking. Just as the savage has to wrestle with nature in order to satisfy his needs, to preserve his life and to reproduce, the civilised person also must do the same in all social forms and under all possible modes of production. With his development increases this kingdom of natural necessity because his needs increase, but at the same time the productive powers increase to satisfy

them ... [Only] beyond this begins the development of human powers as
an end in itself, the true freedom, which, however, can bloom only on the
basis of the other kingdom, that of necessity.[125]

It is important to note that Engels, treating the relation between freedom and
necessity with regard to communism as opposed to the earlier class societies,
comes to a conclusion somewhat different from Marx's. For him communism
constitutes 'humanity's leap from the kingdom of necessity to the kingdom of
freedom'.[126]

Even the non-disposable or necessary labour time in communism has a qualitatively different character compared to the necessary labour time in a class
society, inasmuch as this time is not imposed by an alien power but is willingly
undertaken by the associated producers as self-activity, as self-affirmation. 'The
time of labour of an individual who is at the same time an individual of disposable time must possess a quality much superior to that of a beast of labour'.[127]
It seems that when Marx was speaking of labour not only as means of life, but
as life's first need in the *Gothacritique* (as referred to above), and, earlier, in his
inaugural address to the First International (1864), of the distinction between
the previous kind of labour and 'associated labour plying its toil with a willing
hand, a ready mind and a joyous heart', he was precisely referring to the 'necessary labour' in communism in the sphere of material production. As regards
the necessary labour time bestowed on material production itself in communism, the continuous development of productive forces at a high rate, helped by
advancing science and technology, would allow continuous decrease of necessary labour time and corresponding increase of disposable, that is, free time for
every individual. 'The true wealth is the developed productive power of all individuals. It is then no more the labour time but the disposable time which is the
measure of wealth. The labour time as the measure of wealth posits wealth as

---

125   Marx 1992, p. 838; 1984, p. 820. In his Parisian manuscripts Marx observed that 'com-
       munism' as 'perfect humanism' is the 'true solution of the struggle between existence
       and essence, objectification and self-affirmation, freedom and necessity, it is the solved
       enigma of history' (Marx 1975, p. 348).

126   Engels 1962, p. 264.

127   Marx 1962a, pp. 255–6; 1971a, p. 257. In his 1865 discourse (in English) to the workers of the
       International Marx observed, 'Time is the room of human development. A man who has
       to dispose of no free time, whose whole lifetime apart from the mere physical interrup-
       tions by sleep, meals and so forth, is absorbed by his labour for the capitalist, is less than a
       beast of burden. He is a mere machine for producing Foreign Wealth, broken in body and
       brutalized in mind' (in Marx and Engels 1970b, p. 219).

founded on poverty ... This is to posit the whole time of an individual as labour time and thus to degrade the individual to the position of simple labourer, subsumed under labour'.[128] Marx refers to the idea of the ancients that the aim of production is the human individual, and considers this as 'sublime' compared to the modern world, where the aim of the human is production and the aim of production is wealth (and not the human individual). Then Marx adds,

> Once the limited bourgeois form disappears, wealth appears as nothing but the universality of needs, of capacities, of enjoyments, productive powers of the individuals, the absolute elaboration of the individual's creative aptitudes with no other presupposition but the previous historical development which makes an end in itself the totality of development of all human powers as such, not measured by a standard, previously set, where the individual is not reproduced according to a particular determinacy, but creates her (his) totality. In the bourgeois economy, and the corresponding epoch of production, this complete elaboration of the human interiority appears as complete emptiness.[129]

In consonance with the three-stage analysis of the situation of the individual given above, Marx discusses (in English) the changing relation through time of what he calls the 'Man of Labour' and the 'Means of Labour' in his 1865 discourse to the workers of the International: the 'original union', then its 'decomposition', and finally the restoration of the original union in a 'new historical form'.[130] Here the last form refers to socialism, where through the appropriation of the 'means of labour' by the collective body of the freely

---

128   Marx 1953, p. 596; 1993, pp. 708–9.
129   Marx 1953, p. 387; 1993, pp. 487–8.
130   Marx in Marx and Engels 1970b, p. 208. 'The original unity between the labourer and the conditions of production', writes Marx, 'has two main forms (leaving aside slavery where the labourer himself is a part of the objective conditions of production): the Asiatic community (natural communism) and the small family agriculture (bound with household industry) in one or the other forms. Both are infantile forms and equally little suited to develop labour as social labour and productive power of *social labour*, whence the necessity of separation, of rupture, of the opposition between labour and ownership (in the conditions of production). The extreme form of this rupture within which at the same time the productive forces of social labour are most powerfully developed is the form of capital. On the material basis which it creates and by the means of the revolutions which the working class and the whole society undergoes in the process of creating it can the original unity be restored' (1962a, p. 419; 1971a, p. 423. Emphasis in manuscript).

associated individuals, the 'reunion' takes place. Once this re-union is established, the human individual ceases to be personally or materially dependent,
and no more exists as an alienated, parcellised, fragmented individual; he or
she becomes a 'totally developed', 'integral' individual. This 'free individuality'
signifies the 'real appropriation of the human essence by the human for the
human, a conscious return to the human essence conserving all the wealth
of previous development'.[131] With this begins humanity's real history, leaving,
in Marx's celebrated phrase, 'the pre-history of the human society' behind.[132]
Socialism (communism) is indeed the beginning, and not the end, of human
history.

---

131   Marx 1975, p. 348.
132   Marx 1980a, p. 101; 1970a, p. 22.

CHAPTER 2

Commodity Production

Why is the question of commodity production relevant for Marx's socialism (it is, to recall, socialism in Marx's sense that is the subject of our study)? To answer this question, one has to understand first of all that socialism arises by directly negating capital, which itself is generated through the development of exchange value. As Marx observes, 'the value form of the commodity is the economic cell-form of the bourgeois society'.[1] Therefore the negation of capital automatically signifies negating exchange value or the product taking the form of the commodity. In his 1847 lecture to the workers, Marx poses the question as follows: 'how does an amount of exchange value become capital?' He answers, 'by maintaining and multiplying itself as an independent social power of a part of society, by means of its exchange for direct, living labour power'.[2] However, there is no direct relation between capital and labour. The labourer in capitalism is not personally dependent on the owner of the means of production to gain her/his livelihood. S/he is a juridically independent individual, freely disposing of her/his labour power as a commodity for sale. Hence the relation between capitalist and labourer has to be mediated by exchange in the circulation process. 'In order to develop the concept of capital', Marx reminds his readers, 'it is necessary to start not from labour but from value, and particularly from exchange value already developed in circulation. It is impossible to directly pass from labour to capital as it is to pass from different human races to the banker or from nature to the steam engine'.[3] In fact, 'for capital, [the] labourer is not the condition of production, only labour is. If it [capital] could make machines do it, or through water, air, *tant mieux* [so much the better]. And it does not appropriate the labourer, but only labour – not directly but through the mediation of exchange'.[4]

One month before the publication of *Capital* Volume I, Marx, in a letter to Engels, wrote that till now the bourgeois economists had overlooked the simplest thing – that the 'simplest form of value in which value is not yet

---

1   Marx 1987a, p. 66; 1976a, p. 11; 1954, p. 19.
2   Marx, in Marx and Engels 1973b, pp. 408–9; Marx and Engels 1970b, p. 81.
3   Marx 1953, p. 170; 1993, p. 259; 1976b, p. 28; 1988b, p. 20. The same passage appears in both the manuscripts.
4   Marx 1953, p. 397; 1993, p. 498.

expressed as a relation with other commodities but only as something different from its own natural form, contains the whole secret of the money form
and thereby in germ all the bourgeois forms of the product of labour' (22 June
1867).[5] In a different text Marx expresses the same idea in a more condensed
form: 'for bourgeois society the commodity form of the product of labour –
or the value form of the commodity – is the economic cell form'.[6] So Marx's
starting point for his investigation into the economic law of motion of capitalist society is the commodity, the form which wealth assumes in capitalist
society. 'The first category in which bourgeois wealth appears is the category
of commodity', writes Marx in his 1857–8 manuscripts.[7] He elaborates this in
his *Contribution* (1859), characterising 'bourgeois wealth' as 'an immense collection of commodities [with the] singular commodity as its elementary form
(*Dasein*)',[8] and later in his masterwork (1867), in almost identical terms: 'the
wealth of societies in which reigns the bourgeois mode of production appears
as an immense accumulation of commodities, the singular commodity being
its elementary form'.[9]

From Commodity to Capital

In general, useful objects become commodities when produced by private
labours operating independently of one another, not for the direct use of the
producers themselves but for the use of others. Each commodity presents itself
under a double aspect: use value and exchange value. It is use value destined to
satisfy human needs, and its material side is common to the most varied kinds
of social formation. Indeed, whatever be the social form of wealth, use value
always forms its content. And use value is the necessary presupposition of the
commodity. A use value is transformed into a commodity by being the bearer of
exchange value. Exchange value appears as the quantitative relation in which
use values are reciprocally exchangeable, each having the same magnitude of
exchange value.

---

5 Marx 1987c, p. 383.
6 Marx 1987a, p. 66; 1976a, p. 11; 1954, p. 19.
7 Marx 1953, p. 763; 1993, p. 881.
8 Marx 1980a, p. 107; 1970a, p. 27.
9 Marx 1987a, p. 69; 1976a, p. 41; 1954, p. 43. The formulation undergoes slight change in the
   French version. See also 1988a, p. 24; 1994, p. 355. Later in this chapter we deal briefly with
   Marx's idea of the genesis of money as the general equivalent as a development starting with
   the simplest form of value and the associated contradictions of the equivalent form of value.

Though immediately united in the commodity, use value and exchange value are also immediately separated. Not only does the exchange value appear not to be determined by use value, but, furthermore, the commodity becomes commodity, is realised in exchange value, insofar as its possessor is not related to it as use value. It is only by its externalisation, its exchange with other commodities, that the possessor appropriates the use value. 'Appropriation by alienation (*Entäusserung*) is the basic form of the social system of production whose exchange value is the simplest and the most abstract form. What is pre-supposed is the use value of the commodity, not for its owner, but for society in general'.[10] Use values are immediately the means of life. However, these means of life are themselves the products of social life, result of the expenditure of the vital force expended by the human being, objectified labour. Indifferent as to the specific material of use value, labour positing exchange value is therefore indifferent as regards the specific form of labour itself. The different use values, further, are products of the activities of different individuals, thus results of different individual labours. 'As exchange values they present themselves, however, as equal, indistinguishable labour, that is, labour in which the individuality of the labourer is dissolved. Therefore labour positing exchange value is abstract general labour'.[11] This abstract general labour is common to all exchange values – a mere coagulation of indistinct human labour, of labour power expended without regard to the mode of its expenditure, differing only in a bigger or a smaller magnitude. 'As crystals of this social substance, common to all of them, they are values ... The common something presenting itself in the exchange relation or exchange value of commodities is their value. Exchange value is the necessary form of expression or phenomenal form of value'.[12] Thus, following Marx, a product has value only because abstract human labour is objectified or materialised in it. Each unit of human labour power is equal to any other unit insofar as it possesses the character of the social average. That is, in the production of a commodity it employs only the 'socially necessary labour time', where socially necessary labour time signifies that 'labour time which is executed with the average degree of skill and intensity in the existing socially normal conditions of production'.[13] In his 1857–8 manuscripts, while stress-

---

10   Marx 1953, p. 763; 1993, pp. 881–2. The term 'sale' for the term '*Entäusserung*' in the English
      translation does not quite correspond to the spirit of this important passage correspond-
      ing to Marx's revolutionary 1844 Parisian manuscripts. We propose to analyse the revolu-
      tionary significance of this important work later in the text.

11   Marx 1980a, p. 109; 1970a, p. 29.

12   Marx 1987a, p. 72; 1976a, p. 43; 1954, p. 46.

13   See Marx 1987a, p. 73; 1976a, p. 44; 1954, p. 46. However, it should be pointed out that this

ing the distinction between commodity and value,[14] Marx designates value as 'exchangeability (*Austauschbarkeit* / *Austauschfähigkeit*) of the commodity'.[15] Later, in the first edition of *Capital*, Volume I, Marx equates 'value form' with the 'form of exchangeability' (*Austauschbarkeit*).[16] In the book's French version, again, the 'value form' is equated to the 'form of (general) exchangeability'.[17] in fact while value is a social relation, commodity is the material medium of this relation.[18] This fundamental distinction is Marx's own contribution. Let us recall *en passant* that Marx reproaches classical political economy – the 'bourgeois science' – for having neglected the distinction between 'value' and 'exchange value' or 'value form'. 'It is one of the fundamental defects of the classical political economy that it never succeeded to find, from the analysis of the commodity, specially of the value of the commodity, the form of value under which value becomes exchange value'.[19]

Corresponding to the two-fold character of commodity as use value and as exchange value, there is a two-fold character of labour that produces the commodity – abstract labour creating exchange value and concrete labour creating use value. Marx calls this the 'pivot around which the understanding of political

---

is only a preliminary definition of socially necessary labour time. This preliminary definition considers socially necessary labour time only from the side of production and leaves aside the side of social needs, which must also be satisfied by the product. Under commodity production, 'there exists no necessary connection between the *total quantity of social labour* which is employed in a particular article, and therefore between the *volume* which this particular article occupies in the total production, and the *volume* whereby society demands the satisfaction of needs by this article'. Marx 1992, pp. 261–2; 1984, p. 187 (emphasis in text). In other words, 'in order that a commodity be sold at market value, that is, in proportion to the *socially necessary labour* contained in it, the total quantity of social labour employed in the production of the total mass of the commodity must have to correspond to the quantity of social needs, that is, payable quantity of needs'. Marx 1992, p. 267; 1984, p. 192. Emphasis in text.

14   'Value of the commodity is distinct from the commodity itself. Value is commodity only in exchange'. Marx 1953, p. 59; 1993, p. 140.

15   Marx 1953, p. 59; 1993, p. 140. On the same page Marx elaborates, 'Value is not only the exchangeability of the commodity in general, but also its specific exchangeability'.

16   Marx 1983a, p. 38; 1976c, p. 30.

17   Marx 1976a, p. 89. This equation does not appear in the English translation.

18   'Value is, at the same time, the exponent of the relation in which commodity is exchanged with other commodities, and the exponent of the relation in which it has already been exchanged with other commodities – materialized labour time – in production'. Marx 1953, p. 59; 1993, p. 140.

19   Marx 1987a, p. 111; 1976a, pp. 74–5; 1954, p. 85. The text is somewhat altered in the French version.

economy turns' and claims that he is the 'first to have demonstrated (*nachgew-iesen*) critically this dual character' of the commodity-producing labour.[20]

Commodities like wheat and iron are very different as regards their different characteristics and are measured with different units of measurement. They are incommensurable. As exchange values the commodities are quantitatively different but qualitatively equal. They are reciprocally convertible, serving reciprocally as measure, and are exchanged against one another. Value is their social relation. As exchange value one commodity at the same time serves as equivalent for all other commodities in a definite relation. As equivalent, all its natural properties are blotted out (*ausgelöscht*); it ceases to be in any specific qualitative relation with other commodities. 'All the properties which are counted as properties of money, are the properties of commodity as exchange value. The exchange value of the commodity as particular existence by the side of the commodity itself is money, the form in which every commodity is equalised, compared, measured, into which all commodities are dissolved, the form which is dissolved in all commodities: the general equivalent'.[21] In a later manuscript Marx wrote, 'Every commodity is *itself* money'.[22] Product as value, as already noted, is embodiment of social labour, and as such directly transformable from one use value into every other use value.

Private labour has to be represented as its direct opposite, social labour. This transformed labour is abstract, general labour, which is therefore represented in a general equivalent. Only by its alienation does individual labour manifest itself really as its opposite. This necessity to express individual labour as general labour is the same as the necessity of expressing a commodity as money. 'To the

20   Marx 1987a, p. 75; 1976a, p. 45; 1954, p. 49. In a letter to Engels at about the same time (24 August 1867) Marx wrote, referring to his master work, that 'the best part of my book – on which depends all understanding of facts – is that right in the first chapter is stressed the double character of labour, according as it is expressed in use vale or in exchange value' (then he went on to mention another aspect of his book – his analysis of surplus value independently of profit – as also belonging to this 'best part'). See Marx, in Marx and Engels 1987c, p. 407. In this connection it is interesting to recall an important point made by Marx several years earlier in his 1859 *Contribution*, which is very much related to what Marx is saying here. In this book, Marx, speaking very highly of the British economist James Steuart, mentioned that 'contrary to his predecessors and successors Steuart sharply distinguished between the specific social labour which is represented in exchange value and the real labour which creates use value'. See Marx 1980a, p. 135; 1970, p. 58. Here clearly the first term corresponds to what Marx calls abstract labour while the second stands for Marx's concrete labour.
21   Marx, 1953, p. 60; 1993, p. 142.
22   Marx 1956b, p. 137; 1963, p. 174. Emphasis in manuscript.

extent money serves as measure and as expression of value of the commodity in *price*, the commodity gets this expression. It is only through real transformation in money, sale, that the commodity wins this adequate representation as exchange value'.[23]

For each possessor of a commodity, every commodity excepting one's own is a particular equivalent of her/his commodity. Hence her/his commodity is the general equivalent of all the other commodities. But as all the exchangers are in the same situation, no commodity can serve as general equivalent. This general equivalent could only be the result of social action. A specific commodity is thus set aside by a common act of all commodities in which they all express their values. And this specific commodity thus assumes the form of the general equivalent. Thus it becomes money.

Money is a crystal which is a necessary product of the exchange process, in which various kinds of products of labour are in fact equalised and thereby in fact transformed into commodities. The historical development and deepening of exchange develop the opposition between use value and value, latent (*schlummerend*) in the nature of value. The need of expressing this opposition for the purpose of commerce is the driving force towards the establishment of an independent form of commodity value and finds no peace or rest till this form is achieved by the doubling (*Verdopplung*) of the commodity in commodity and money. To the same extent that products of labour are transformed into commodities, the commodity is also transformed into money.[24]

The exchange process of the commodity finds its completion in two opposite and reciprocally complementary metamorphoses, namely, the transformation of commodity in money and its retransformation from money into commodity. These two metamorphoses of the commodity present, from the point of view of its possessor, two acts: exchange of the commodity for money, and exchange of money for the commodity. In a word, sale and purchase, and, considered together, selling for buying. This can be seen as two phases: commodity changing into money and money changing into commodity (C – M – C), where C represents commodity and M represents money. 'The first metamorphosis of a commodity, its transformation from commodity form into money, is always, at the same time, the second, opposite transformation into another commodity, its retransformation from money form into commodity form ... The two opposite phases of the movement of the metamorphosis of a commodity constitute a circle: commodity form, stripping of the commodity form, returning to the

---

23   Marx 1962a, p. 134; 1971a, p. 136. Emphasis in original.
24   Marx 1987a, p. 116; 1976a, pp. 78–9; 1954, p. 90.

commodity form'.[25] 'The circle which the series of metamorphosis of each commodity describes is swallowed up (*verschlingt sich*) with the circles of other commodities. The totality of the process presents itself as *circulation of commodities*'.[26]

There are two forms of circulation: C – M – C, and M – C – M. The first form signifies the exchange of the commodity for money as the first act, and the exchange of money for the commodity is the second act. It is the opposite operation with the second form, where the first act is the exchange of money for the commodity and the second act is the exchange of the commodity for money. The commodity which exchanges for another commodity mediated by money comes out of circulation in order to be consumed as use value. Its determination as exchange value and thereby as commodity disappears. However, if it is rendered autonomous in circulation as money, it represents only the general form of wealth without substance and becomes a useless use value like gold or silver, so long as it does not re-enter the circulation as a means of purchase or a means of payment. 'In fact it is contradictory that the autonomous exchange value should be the absolute existence of exchange value by withdrawing from exchange'.[27]

From the point of view of form, that which is generated in circulation, is developed there, is money itself, nothing more. Commodities are exchanged there but they are not produced there. Circulation, considered in itself, is a process of mediation between the two pre-posited extremes (poles), but it does not posit them. The repetition of the two factors, money and commodity, does not have its genesis in the conditions of circulation itself. 'Circulation does not contain itself the principle of self-renewal. Commodities must be incessantly thrown into circulation from outside like combustible material into fire. Otherwise the process will cease, dissolved into money as an indifferent result without any connection with the commodity'.[28] Simple circulation is, on the one hand, the exchange of the pre-existing commodities, while on the other hand it is a simple mediation between the two poles which are anterior and external to it. Its entire activity is limited to exchanging and positing formal determinations which the commodity traverses as the unity of exchange value and use value. 'In reality this unity as commodity does not exist when the commodity is at rest (*als ein ruhndes Sein*), but exists only in the social movement of circulation where the two determinations of commodity – use value and

---

25   Marx 1987a, pp. 134, 136; 1976a, p. 93, 94; 1954, pp. 111, 113.

26   Marx 1987a, p. 136; 1976a, p. 95; 1954, p. 113. Emphasis in original.

27   Marx 1980a, p. 63; 1987b, p. 478.

28   Marx 1980a, p. 64; 1987b, p. 477.

exchange value – are at the two opposite poles of exchange. It is the exchange value for the seller, and use value for the buyer'.[29]

For the ulterior development of the determinate form generated by the circulation process we have to consider how the form – exchange value – pursues its development and acquires deeper determinations by virtue of the process of circulation itself. In other words, we have to study the trajectory of money. We have to investigate the form M – C – M. In money exchange value becomes circulation's content and end – in itself, the autonomy of exchange value as such. Selling in order to buy is aimed at acquiring use value, buying in order to sell is aimed at exchange value itself.

It is now seen that exchange value has a double mode of existence, as commodity and money, the latter as its adequate form. Further, in order that money is conserved as money it must not be dissolved in the simple means of circulation which disappears in the form of the commodity in order to become simply use value. In other words, 'money's conversion into commodity has to be only a simple change of form which permits it to reappear in its adequate form, as the *adequate exchange value*, but at the same time as *multiplied, increased exchange value, valorised exchange value*'.[30] Money that undergoes this movement is *capital*. The point of departure of this type of circulation, therefore, is itself the product of the circulation of commodities, since it is only in circulation and by circulation that the commodity takes the form of money, is transformed into money. Further, the value arising from circulation in this way and becoming autonomous in the form of money re-enters circulation, becomes commodity but returns from the commodity form to the money form while at the same time the magnitude of its value is increased. 'In the form (C – M – C), selling for buying, where the use value and therefore the satisfaction of needs are the final objective, we do not find directly in the form the conditions of its renewal after the end of the process; thereby the movement ends. Contrariwise in the form (M – C – M) it is already clear from the simple form of its movement that there is no end of the movement and that the end already contains the principle and the urge for its renewal'.[31] Concerning this never-ending movement, Marx writes later in *Capital*, 'The perpetual increase of exchange value which the hoarder strives after by saving the money from circulation, is gained by the cleverer capitalist by always throwing it afresh into circulation'.[32]

---

29   Marx 1980a, p. 69; 1987b, p. 484.

30   Marx 1980a, p. 77; 1987b, p. 492. Emphasis in original.

31   Marx 1976b, p. 15; 1988b, p. 19.

32   Marx 1987a, p. 171; 1976a, p. 154; 1954, p. 151. The French version is somewhat different from the German original.

M – C – C – M: here money appears not only as measure, not only as medium, but as its own end in itself, and therefore outside of circulation. This is the third determination of money, besides the other two, namely, medium of exchange and measure of value. To the extent that money in its autonomous existence comes out of circulation, it appears in circulation itself as a result of circulation. It closes itself together with its circulation. 'In this determination its determination as *capital* is already latent'.[33]

It should be stressed that money's autonomous existence is not the abolition of its relation with circulation, it is only a negative relation with circulation. This lies in this autonomy as a result of M – C – C – M.

In money as capital the following is already posited: (1) it is the presupposition as well as the result of circulation; (2) its autonomy, therefore, is itself a negative relation, but always a relation with circulation; (3) it is itself posited as an instrument of production, inasmuch as circulation no longer appears in its first simplicity, as quantitative exchange, but as process of production, as real material metamorphosis (*Stoffwechsel*). Thus money itself is determined as a particular moment of this process of production ... In production it is no longer a question of simple determination of price, that is, translation of exchange values of commodities into a common unity, but it is a question of the creation of exchange value, therefore creation of the determinacy (*Bestimmtheit*) of price. Not only a simple positing of the form, but also of the content.[34]

The exchange value of the commodity is only the average social labour objectified in its use value. Money and commodity are distinguished only by the form in which this objectified labour is expressed. In money the objectified labour is expressed as general social labour, which thereby is directly exchangeable with all other commodities to the extent that these latter contain as much labour. When money is transformed into the commodity or the commodity is transformed into money, value only changes its form, not its substance – substance being its objectified labour – or its magnitude – magnitude signifying a definite quantity of objectified labour. 'The unique opposition to the objectified labour is constituted by the non-objectified labour, the living labour. The one is the labour existing in space, the other is the labour existing in time, the one is past, the other is present, the one is embodied in use value, the other is in the human activity engaged in the process of its objectification, the one is value, the other is the creator of value'.[35] The distinction between C – M – C

33   Marx 1953, p. 130; 1993, p. 217. Emphasis added.
34   Marx 1953, pp. 130–1; 1993, p. 217.
35   Marx 1976b, p. 30; 1988b, p. 32.

and M – C – M was made earlier in this chapter. Whereas the first circuit starts
with one commodity and ends with another and falls out of circulation, the
second circuit starts and ends with money. Both the poles in the second circuit
are identical, hence such exchange seems meaningless. A sensible exchange
could only have meaning when they are quantitatively different. More money
should come out at the end than the money that existed at the start. This is
true not only in the case of merchant capital but also in the case of productive
capital – money is changed into a commodity and through the sale of the commodity is reconverted into additional money. Properly speaking, the second
kind of circuit should be M – C – M', where M' > M, an excess over the original M.
However, a quantity of labour by its simple existence in the form of commodity or money cannot modify, far less increase, the magnitude of its value. An
increase of value can only mean an increase of objectified labour, and it is only
by the living labour that the objectified labour can be conserved or increased.
The increase of value by which money could be transformed into capital cannot be generated by money itself. If it serves as the means of purchase or means
of payment it only realises the price of the commodity purchased or paid for.
The change of value expressed by the form M – C – M' has to come from the
commodity itself. But this cannot be effected by the second act C – M', resale,
where the commodity simply passes on from its natural form to the money
form. When we consider the first act M – C, the purchase, we find that there is
exchange between equivalents, that is, the commodity does not contain more
value than the money converted into it. The change, then, could only origin-
ate from the use value of this commodity itself, that is, from its consumption.
The value – objectified labour existing in the form of money – could increase
only by exchanging against a commodity whose consumption would be syn-
onymous with the creation of value or the objectification of labour. Now, only
the power of the living labour possesses such a use value. In short, value, that
is, money, can only be transformed into capital through its exchange against
living labour power. This means that in the commodity market – within circulation – there already exist free labourers to exchange their labour power against
money. In this context the term 'free labourers' signifies that these labourers are
not in a relation of personal dependence in regard to the ones on the opposite
side of the exchange. The relation between the two sides is only that of sellers
and buyers. 'The labourer is free in so far as on the one hand s/he freely disposes
of her/his labour power as a commodity and on the other hand s/he cannot dispose of any other commodity, that is, freed – detached and emptied (*los und
ledig*) – from all the objective conditions of realisation of her/his labour power,
and, consequently, s/he is a simple subject, simple personification of her/his
own labour power, a *labourer* in the same sense as the possessor of money as

subject and bearer of objectified labour, self-conserving value, is *capitalist*.[36] Marx defines 'labour power' as the 'totality of physical and mental capacities which exists in the body, in the living personality, of an individual and which s/he puts in motion whenever s/he produces any use value'.[37]

Paradoxes and Contradictions

The contradictions in commodity production start with the antagonism arising from the two-fold character of the commodity itself, as use value and as exchange value. The commodity, considered from a double point of view, is the direct unity of opposites: use value and exchange value. The commodity is both use value and at the same time a non-use value. If it were a use value for the possessor of the commodity, a direct means of satisfying her/his own needs, it would not be a commodity. For her/him it is use value only so far as it is exchange value. Now, the commodity must express itself not only as different from its use value but also must represent itself as autonomised in relation to its use value, which is to say that commodity production must end up in the formation of money. This contradiction results in an antagonistic relation in the movements of use value and exchange value. Now, in all societies wealth always consists of use values. Marx approvingly cites the great French classical economist Boisguillebert, 'The real wealth [is] the total enjoyment, not only of the needs of life, but also of the superfluities, and of all that gives pleasure to the senses'.[38] An increase in the quantity of use values means increase in material wealth, which, at the same time, corresponds also to a decrease in its value. This contradictory movement originates from the double character of labour. The efficiency of useful labour at a given period depends on its productive power. Useful, concrete labour becomes, therefore, a source of more or less abundant products, directly due to the increase or diminution of its productive power. Contrariwise, a change in its productive power does not directly affect the labour represented in *value*. As the productive power belongs to useful, concrete labour, it can no longer have any bearing on that labour as soon as abstraction is made from its useful form. Independently of variations in the productive force of labour, the same labour of identical duration will produce the same value. But it furnishes in a definite period more use val-

---

36 Marx 1976b, p. 33; 1988b, p. 37. Emphasis in manuscript.
37 Marx 1987a, p. 183; 1976a, p. 129; 1954, p. 164.
38 Marx 1980a, p. 133; 1970a, p. 55.

ues if its productive power increases, less if its productive power decreases. All changes in the productive power which increase the fruitfulness of labour and, consequently, the mass of use values delivered by it, decreases the value of this increased mass, if it shortens the total time necessary for this production, and inversely. 'The magnitude of value of a commodity, therefore, varies directly as the *quantity* and inversely as the productive power of labour realised in it'.[39] In his early 1860s analysis of the communist/socialist literature opposed to Ricardo (on the basis of Ricardo's own work) Marx mentions an anonymous 1821 brochure – considered as 'an important advance on Ricardo' – which holds that *'wealth is disposable time and nothing more'*. Then Marx elaborates – on the basis of Ricardo's own statement that wealth consists of the maximum quantity of use values produced by the shortest possible labour time – that 'this means that the greatest quantity of wealth is created by the shortest possible labour time', in other words, 'having the disposable time and enjoying what others have created during their time of labour as the real wealth, but as everything in capitalist production, and, correspondingly, in its interpreters, this appears in a contradictory form'.[40] About a decade earlier, in his 1851 'London Notebooks', referring to Ricardo's statement that wealth depends on abundance while value depends on the facility or difficulty of production, Marx wrote:

> Bourgeois wealth and the aim of all bourgeois production is exchange value not use value or enjoyment (*Genus*). To increase this exchange value there are no other means than the multiplication of products, more to produce. But in the same proportion as the productive force of a given quantity of labour increases the exchange value of the products falls. To produce more commodities is never the aim of bourgeois production, the aim is to produce more value. In spite of this the real increase of the productive force and of commodities take place, and the contradiction between this increase of value which itself is transformed (*sich selbst aufhebt*) through its own movement into increase of products lies at the root of all crises.[41]

Let us return to the simple circulation. The first thing to note in the simple circulation (c – m – c) is that all particularities in the relation between the two concerned individuals disappear (it is now only a question of exchange value as

39	Marx 1987a, p. 74; 1954, p. 48; 1976a, p. 45. Emphasis in the French text.
40	Marx 1962a, pp. 254, 255; 1971a, p. 256, 257.
41	Marx 1986, p. 364.

such) just as all (hitherto existing) political, patriarchal and other kinds of relations arising from the specificity of the relation between individuals are lost. Each relates to the other as an abstract social person, representing uniquely the exchange value, with money as such as the sole link. 'Thus disappears the geniality (*gemüthliche Schein*) which had enveloped (*umhüllte*) the earlier form of transaction'.[42] The basic idea of this statement already appears strikingly in a text that Marx had written about fifteen years earlier in what could be called his first '*Critique of Political Economy*' (1844). In this posthumous work Marx had expressed the central idea of the nature of exchange in a commodity world as a relation between individuals, not as that of human being to human being as such, but as a relation between human beings as owners of property. 'The mediating movement of the exchanging individual is not a social, not a *human movement*, not a *human relation*, it is the *abstract relation* of private property to private property, and this *abstract* relation is value'.[43]

As mentioned earlier, in simple circulation the two poles of circulation already exist as use values produced by human labour (aided originally by nature's gifts) before circulation begins. Labour and the appropriation of the fruits of one's own labour constitute the basic conditions without which there could be no secondary appropriation of the product created by alien labour, which is effected only through circulation. In the 1858 'primitive version' of Marx's 1859 text *Contribution to the Critique of Political Economy*, we read: 'If the appropriation of commodities by personal labour constitutes the first necessity, the second is the social process that first makes the product an exchange value and then reconverts the exchange value into use value. After the law of appropriation by labour or the materialisation of labour, the second is the *alienation or the conversion of this labour into a social form*'.[44]

42 Marx 1980a, p. 19; 1987b, p. 430.
43 Marx 1932, p. 532; 1975, p. 261. Emphasis in text.
44 Marx 1980a, p. 50; 1987b, p. 464. Emphasis in manuscript. This position was elaborated slightly earlier, in another of Marx's posthumously published texts, as follows: 'In the simple circulation as the exchange value in its movement the action of individuals in relation to other individuals is, as regards content, only the reciprocal (self) interested satisfaction of needs, and as regards form, only the exchanges and the positing of equality (equivalence), so that here property is still posited only as the appropriation of the product of labour by labour and of the product of alien labour by one's own labour in so far as the product of one's own labour is bought by alien labour. The ownership of alien labour is mediated by the equivalence with one's own labour. This form of ownership – wholly as freedom and equality – is posited in this simple relation. In the further development of the exchange value this will be transformed and it will finally appear that private ownership of the product of one's own labour is identical with the separation of labour

Now, the exchange of human activity in production as well as of human products among individuals is a species-activity and species-enjoyment; thus a social activity and social enjoyment. However, the true community of human beings is their inter-relations among themselves (and with nature). Therein lies the affirmation of the human essence. This is the 'social being which is not an abstract ... general power against isolated individuals but the essence of each individual, her/his own activity, her/his own life, own spirit, own wealth'.[45] The relation between human beings not as human beings but as private property owners – for that is what commodity exchange amounts to, as we saw above – is an inversion of this natural relation. Human society considered as a 'commercial society' – following Adam Smith, cited by Marx in his 1844 commentary on James Mill – is a society where individuals' own creation appears as an alien power, their own wealth as poverty, the individual's separation from other individuals as the individual's real existence. 'The individual's own power over the object appears as the power of the object over the individual. Master of her/his production, the individual appears as the slave of this production'.[46]

The buyers and sellers of commodities in the exchange process – these *determinate social types* – it should be stressed, in no way have their origin in human individualities. On the contrary, their origin is to be found in the relations of exchange among the producers whose products are exchanged. The great *paradox* is precisely the fact that 'these relations represented in the relation of buyer and seller are so little purely individual relations that each one enters this relation only to the extent that her/his individual labour is negated, that is to say, becomes money, because it is the labour of no particular individual'.[47] In a somewhat different though sharper version, which Marx had written one year earlier, 'It is in money, that is, in the form which is the most

---

from ownership, so that labour will create alien ownership and ownership will command the alien labour' (Marx 1953, p. 148; 1993, p. 238). In this connection it is interesting to note that the last sentence in this text finds direct echo in the 1858 (primitive) version of the 'Critique' where, after citing Cherbuliez's words that the 'labourer has the exclusive right to the value resulting from his/her own labour', Marx went on to assert that 'labour is the original mode of appropriation' and added: 'the circulation process as it appears on the *surface* of society does not know any other mode of appropriation than the one based on labour, and if in the progress of investigation contradictions appear they must be deduced from the *development of exchange value itself as was done for the law of original appropriation based on labour*'. See Marx 1980a, p. 49; 1987b, p. 463. Emphasis in text.

45   Marx 1932, p. 535; 1975, p. 265.
46   Marx 1932, p. 536; 1975, p. 266.
47   Marx 1980a, p. 164; 1970a, p. 95.

abstract, therefore, emptiest of any sense, and the most difficult to grasp – a form in which all mediation has disappeared – in which the reciprocal social relations appear as fixed, overpowering and subjugating the individuals. And this phenomenon is all the more brutal that it finds its genesis (precisely) in the premises of free, atomistic private persons, voluntarily related to one another only by their mutual needs in production'.[48]

In his 1857–8 manuscripts, Marx underlines several contradictions arising from the simple circulation c – m – c. First, the simple fact that the commodity has a double existence, first as a particular product, then as exchange value, money, which in its turn has cast off the natural form of existence of the product. This double existence must necessarily progress towards difference, and from difference to opposition and contradiction. 'The same contradiction between the particular nature of the commodity as product and its general nature as exchange value which creates the necessity of positing them doubly – one time as this definite commodity, and another time as money, the contradiction between its specific natural properties (*Eigenschaften*) and its general social properties contains from the start the possibility that these two separated forms of existence of commodity are not reciprocally convertible'.[49]

Secondly, just as the exchange value of the commodity exists doubly, as a determined commodity and as money, in the same way the act of exchange stands separated between two independent acts: exchange of commodity against money and exchange of money against commodity, purchase and sale. As these two latter acts have acquired forms of existence which are separated spatially and temporally, and reciprocally indifferent, their immediate identity is broken. Marx writes,

> There could be correspondence or non-correspondence between them. They could coincide or not coincide (*decken*). There could be disproportion between them. In place of the earlier equality there is now the perpetual movement towards equalisation which precisely presupposes continuing inequality.[50]

Thirdly, just as the exchange itself is divided in two independent acts, in the same way the whole movement is separated from the exchangers, the commodity producers. Exchange for exchange is separated from exchange of com-

---

48 Marx 1980a, p. 74; 1987b, p. 489.
49 Marx 1953, p. 65; 1993, p. 147.
50 Marx 1953, p. 66; 1993, p. 148.

modities. There arises a whole community of merchants who stand between the producers, a community which purchases only to sell, and sells only to purchase. Their aim is not to possess commodities as products but simply to hold exchange values as such, hold money. To the autonomisation of exchange value in money, detached from the producers, corresponds the autonomisation of exchange as a function detached from the exchangers. The objective of commerce is not direct consumption, but the acquisition of money, of exchange value. This doubling of exchange – exchange for consumption and exchange for exchange – begets a new disproportion. What determines the trader in her/his exchange is simply the difference between the purchase and sale of commodities, but the consumer buying a commodity has definitely to replace the exchange value of the commodity. 'The circulation, the exchange within the community of traders, and the end of circulation – exchange between the traders' community and the consumers – are determined by totally different laws and motives and can enter into the sharpest contradiction with one another. In this separation there already lies the possibility of commercial crisis'.

Finally, as Marx observes, 'just as exchange value appears in money as the universal commodity by the side of all particular commodities, in the same way exchange value appears in money as particular commodity (because it possesses a particular existence) by the side of other commodities. There is incongruence here from the fact that money, because it exists only in exchange, stands, as universal exchangeability, opposed to the particular exchangeability which it immediately blots out (*auslöscht*), even though both have to remain mutually convertible all the time; thus money enters into contradiction with itself and its determination, inasmuch as it is itself a particular commodity, and consequently, in its exchange with other commodities, is subject to particular conditions of exchange which contradict its unlimited and universal exchangeability'.[51] As observed here, money becomes a commodity like other commodities, but at the same time money is not a commodity like other commodities. It is not only a universal exchange value, but it is at the same time a particular exchange value by the side of other particular exchange values. We thus see that it is immanent in money to 'accomplish its finalities by simultaneously negating them; to autonomise itself in relation to commodities; from a means to become an end; to realise the exchange value of commodities by separating itself from them; to facilitate exchange by dividing it; to overcome the difficulties of immediate exchange of commodities by generalising them;

---

51   Marx 1953, pp. 68–9; 1993, p. 150.

to autonomise exchange in relation to the producers to the same extent as the producers are made dependent on exchange'.[52]

On the Value Form

Let us have a look at this point at Marx's analysis of what he considered as the most difficult part of his analysis of value: the 'value form'. It is remarkable that very few writers in the Anglo-American tradition of Marx studies have paid attention to Marx's crucial analysis of value form.[53] However, in contrast with

---

52   Marx 1953, p. 69; 1993, p. 150.

53   Thus neither Maurice Dobb 1940, 1973, nor Paul Sweezy 1942 – to name the two best known economists in this tradition – mention this problem. Dobb's case is all the more remarkable in that his second book specifically on 'theories of value' (and distribution) does not mention at all this vital part of Marx's value theory, preoccupied as he is to show that Marx after all was a great disciple of Ricardo. (We recall *en passant* that a part of Marx's criticism of the classical economists including Ricardo was precisely that they had neglected value form, as they were preoccupied only with the quantitative aspect of value. See, for example, Chapter One, Section Four of *Capital* vol. I). Also little is said on this question by Meek (1956). In his turn D.K. Foley, in his widely studied popular book on *Capital*, while saying that Marx, taking the 'labour theory of value from Ricardo, makes important critical corrections to his formulation', does not mention at all Marx's critique of value in Ricardo precisely on the point of the value-form of the commodity. See Foley 1986, p. 15. Apart from most of the Marxist and Marx-sympathetic economists, this neglect of Max's value form and forms of value also characterises – needless to say – the rest of the economists writing on Marx. One important example of the latter we find in a widely used text on the history of economic thought by Mark Blaug, who writes, while suggesting how to read Marx's *Capital*, 'the reader will miss little by skipping the pedantic third section of Chapter I' (of *Capital* Volume I). See Blaug 1997, p. 256. Joseph Schumpeter, sympathetic to Marx, in his great book on the history of economic analysis, considers Marx the 'only great follower of Ricardo' and adds that 'Marx adopted Ricardo's conceptual lay-out', but nowhere mentions the basic differences – including, most importantly, the value theory – between the two. (See Schumpeter 1994, pp. 390, 596). Naturally, he nowhere mentions Marx's value form. To our knowledge, the honourable exception in the Anglo-American tradition of Marx studies in this regard is the important Cleaver 2000, which offers a fine analysis of this question in Marx, but does not refer to any debate on the question. We should add here that there has been in the Anglo-American circle also another, almost parallel, discussion on what the concerned scholars also call the 'value form approach'. That narrative, however, has little to do with the 'value form' we are discussing here, based on the opening chapters of *Capital* Volume I. (For this parallel narrative see Saad-Filho 2002, pp. 26–9, and Samuel Knafo 2012, pp. 367–72).

the Anglo-American world of Marx scholarship, there have been in recent decades some lively debates among the Marx scholars in Germany on the problem of Marx's value categories, including the value form.[54] There have also been important discussions on value form in other countries, of which two contributions – one from Russia and another from Japan – dealing particularly with the discussion on Marx's money form, have been available to us.[55] To our knowledge, however, the German discussion has been more extensive. So while we will just mention *en passant* the works of the Russian and the Japanese scholars, we will be concerned here with the German discussion, and we will try to give an account of the principal points under discussion at some length, given its relative non-availability to the English-reading public.

The initiative of the recent controversy came from the adherents of the Frankfurt School, with their 'new Marx reading' (*neue Marx-Lektüre*), particularly from Helmut Reichelt and H.G. Backhaus, whose contributions have attracted the most attention. The impetus for a 'new reading' of Marx was generated in the aftermath of the student movement(s) of the 60s of the last century and was fed by the reaction to the ossified 'Party State' Marxism (Leninism) of Russia and the German Democratic Republic. In the realm of ideas, Reichelt and Backhaus were additionally stimulated by Adorno and Horkheimer, who saw an increasing tendency to water down the dialectical method in Marx's critique of political economy in Marx's own attempt to popularise his *Capital*.[56] In a joint paper Backhaus and Reichelt laid down a severe indictment of the increasing tendency by Marx to 'hide' his dialectical method from the readers of *Capital*, which they call 'reduction of the dialectic by Marx himself'.[57] They underline that 'if Marx practiced this "reduced" method of development, then it is admittedly problematic if this method could still be generally characterised

---

54 For an outline account see Heinrich 2003, Chapter 6. He has himself been a participant in the debate.

55 The concerned Marx scholars have been I.I. Rubin in Russia (see his recently published – in German translation – manuscript on Marx's theory of money (Heinrich 2012) and Samezō Kuruma on the genesis of money in Marx (Kuruma 2009). We should mention that this great Japanese scholar had edited the justly famous 15-volume *Marx-Lexikon zur Politischen Ökonomie*).

56 Among the different critics of the Backhaus-Reichelt approach in Germany, two are particularly noticeable – Schwarz 1987 and D. Wolf, in Wolf and Paragenings 2004.

57 Backhaus and Reichelt 1994, p. 106. They of course borrowed the term 'hidden' from Marx himself. In a letter to Engels (9 December 1861, see Marx 1985, p. 332), Marx wrote 'my writing is becoming more popular and the method more hidden'. He was referring to his earlier 1859 *Contribution* for comparison.

as dialectical'.[58] What they call Marx's 'emphatic dialectic', that is, where Marx did not 'hide' his method, where his dialectic is in its pure state, is found, they claim, only in his 1857–8 *Grundrisse* and the succeeding so-called 1858 'primit-ive text' (*Urtext*) of the 1859 *Contribution*.

It appears that by 'dialectic' these authors mean Hegel's dialectic, what Back-haus calls 'the kernel of Hegel's dialectical philosophy'.[59] For lack of space we will not enter into a long philosophical discussion. We will discuss here rather its repercussion on Marx's value form analysis, offered mostly by Backhaus.

Having maintained (along with Reichelt) that 'before beginning the work on the 1859 *Contribution*, Marx had broken off the experiment started in the *Grundrisse* and abandoned his systematic elaboration of value-theoretical and methodological fundamental thought',[60] Backhaus tries to show how in the process of the writing of *Capital*, Marx's developmental method in relation to value analysis – the analysis of the value form in particular – became more and more impoverished. Leaving aside the *Grundrisse*, where there supposedly appears in its purest form Marx's dialectical method of development, there have been, as regards the value analysis, basically, four variants. These are (1) the 1859 *Contribution*, (2) the first edition of *Capital* Volume I (1867), (3) the 'Sup-plement' to the first edition of *Capital* Volume I (1867), (4) the second edition of *Capital* Volume I (1872).[61] This trajectory of Marx's work on *Capital* Volume I, according to Backhaus, had involved the steady deterioration of the dialect-ical method in *Capital* through Marx's own work of increasing popularisation, as well as the accompanying historicisation of the work. Comparing the first and the second editions of Marx's book, Backhaus holds that the logically con-ceived form of development, as seen in the statements of the first edition, fully 'concur with the *esoteric* parts of the second edition, as is seen in the third (value) form' (form C, the general equivalent).[62] To give the gist of Backhaus's critique of Marx's presentation of the value form in the two respective edi-tions, it suffices to say that this crucially concerns the fourth value form in the two editions. More specifically, in the first edition the fourth form (Form IV) is the 'general equivalent form', the 'money form' does not yet appear, and in fact appears only in the second chapter on the 'exchange process'. In the second

---

58   Backhaus and Reichelt 1994, p. 112.

59   Backhaus 1997, p. 15.

60   Backhaus and Reichelt 1994, p. 106.

61   There was no further change in this regard in the later third and fourth German editions
      or the French edition of the book.

62   Backhaus 1997, p. 290. Emphasis in text.

edition the fourth form (Form D) is the 'money form'.[63] Backhaus cites from the second edition that the third form 'really relates the commodities in their reciprocal relations as values'.[64] However, Backhaus holds that the commodity here is 'commodity in itself (*an sich*)', not the *real* commodity. Hence, 'if commodity-in-itself is not at all a real commodity then the "exchange process" built with such a "commodity in itself" is just as little a real process and should in no case have been mixed up with the real exchange process'.[65] And Backhaus precisely reproaches Marx for conceiving the exchange process as 'supra-historical', inasmuch as Marx's exchange process is a 'generic notion' which includes 'barter, the spontaneous process of exchange'. In other words, the exchange process includes 'pre-monetary commodities'. This is a descent into the world of 'imaginary contradictions of the pre-historic development of the barter of primitive fisher and hunter'.[66] 'It is easy to see how Marx's own work of popularizing his value theory – by the replacement of the section "Form IV" of the first edition by the section "Form D" in the second edition – brought about its regression to the Ricardian value theory'.[67]

The formulations and constructions in the second edition of Marx's book under consideration, opines Backhaus, mark its characteristic difference with the first edition of 1867. 'This revision in the second edition towards historicizing is a step backward in the logical method of development compared to the conceptual development of money in the first edition, and still more (to that) in the "Contribution" of 1859'.[68] Backhaus refers to Engels's letter to Marx of 1867 (16 June) where Engels counselled Marx to make the presentation of the value form analysis of the first chapter more accessible to a larger number of readers.[69] Backhaus says that this impetus by Engels to popularise the value form analysis – leading to the 'Supplement' to the first edition – set the stage for the revised version of the first chapter in the second edition. More importantly this marks the 'beginning of a development leading ultimately, through the popularised and historicised text, to the abandonment of the concept of a dialectical theory of value and money'.[70] Then he concludes, 'if one takes seriously

---

63   See in this respect the development in Schwarz 1987, especially pp. 201–4.
64   Marx 1987a, p. 97; 1976a, p. 64; 1954, p. 70. The French version omits altogether the term 'real' (*wirklich*) while the English edition translates this term as 'effectively'.
65   Backhaus 1997, p. 291.
66   Backhaus 1997, pp. 291, 296.
67   Backhaus 1997, p. 293.
68   Backhaus 1997, p. 230.
69   Marx 1987c, p. 381.
70   Backhaus 1997, p. 258.

the historical development of money, then the proper logic of its conceptual development vanishes; but if one undertakes seriously to get the definition of the essence of money, then the theoretical relevance of the historical development vanishes, and the latter can only serve as illustration'.[71]

Backhaus distinguishes between Marx's value theory and Marx's theory of money and, correspondingly, between 'pre-monetary' value theory and 'monetary' theory of value, stressing that the former has nothing to do with the price-determined commodities, hence nothing to do with money, while in the latter everything is determined by money which already exists. For Backhaus, 'Marx's road of development from commodity to money is non-passable. One has to accept the category of money as the logical first of the economic theory, its irreducible basic category'.[72]

Backhaus refers to Marx's 1858 letter (2 April) to Engels – where Marx gives 'an outline' of his planned project.[73] Backhaus holds that this letter offers the 'singular authentic form of Marx's value theory'.[74] Now, coming to *Capital* Volume I, Backhaus opines that the connection between value theory and the theory of money, which was 'transparent' in the first edition of Marx's book, became unrecognisable due to a 'fatal revision' of the first edition's value form analysis. However, it seems that even the first edition is not free from 'contamination'; 'the pseudo-dialectic of logical and historical has in the first edition also led to some fatal contaminations, particularly drastic being the case with the mixing up of the heterogeneous elements in the example of the concept of exchange process. In the second edition, in the chapter on exchange process, this concept was further loaded in a particularly crass fashion with the historical context'.[75]

Now let us have a closer look at some of the important points in the argument advanced by Backhaus and Reichelt in their Marx critique. In what follows, the majority of references to Marx's works relates to those which are considered by our authors to be 'uncontaminated' or far less 'contaminated' (in their sense as given above) than the second edition of *Capital*, in order to serve as counter-examples to their argument. But for the sake of logical relevance we will also refer to the rest when necessary. The first point to note is that these

---

71   Backhaus 1997, p. 260. Dieter Wolf in his critical remark on Backhaus very pertinently underlines that 'Marx's road from commodity to money fails to conform to Hegel's logic of essence'. See Wolf 2004, p. 128.

72   Backhaus 1997, p. 181.

73   See Marx 1983b, p. 296.

74   Backhaus 1997, p. 13. He seems to mean the authentic dialectical form of value theory.

75   Backhaus 1997, p. 293.

authors' obsession with the Hegelian dialectic as the *unique dialectic* has led
them to completely ignore Marx's *own dialectic*, which Marx himself famously
explains in his 'Afterword' to the second edition of *Capital* Volume I, the very
edition, let it be underlined, that these authors consider as the least dialectical of all the texts of his critique of political economy. In this 1873 text, Marx
emphasises that in relation to Hegel's dialectic, his (own) 'dialectical method,
as to its foundation, is not only different but is its direct opposite'.[76] Hegel
'transforms the thought process even under the name Idea into an autonomous subject, the demiurgos of the Real'.[77] This Hegelian 'dialectic of the concept'
Marx had criticised much earlier in the 'German Ideology' (1845). While opposing his and Engels's 'materialist conception of history' (widely though inexactly
called 'historical materialism') to Hegel's idealist conception of history, Marx
wrote, in this 1845 text: 'at the end of his *Philosophy of History* Hegel confessed
that he had "considered uniquely the progress of the *Concept*, and that he had
presented in history the true Theodicy"'.[78] This same materialist position was
expressed by Marx many years later in his last theoretical text, the one directed against Adolph Wagner. 'Use value and exchange value', wrote Marx, 'have
to be derived by Mr. Wagner from the *concept of value* and not as I do from a
concrete form, the commodity'.[79] Then he continues, 'I do not proceed from
"concepts", therefore not from the "value concept", my point of departure is ...

---

76   Marx added at the same place that 'the mystifying side of Hegel's dialectic I have already
      criticized about thirty years ago when it was still fashionable'. It should be pointed out
      that in that same text, on the same page, Marx, in his reaction to the superficial, vulgar
      critics of Hegel, stressed that while mystifying the dialectic Hegel was, nevertheless, the
      first to present the movement in its totality in a conscious manner and that he himself was
      a 'pupil of that great thinker'. A few years earlier, in his second manuscript of the second
      volume of his masterwork, Marx had declared that Hegel was 'my master', whose dialectic
      nevertheless he felt free to 'demystify and had thereby essentially changed' (Marx 2008,
      p. 32). The relevant passage does not appear in the current English version, which has been
      translated from Engels's edition.

77   Marx 1987a, p. 709; 1976a, p. 21; 1954, p. 29. The Moore-Aveling translation leaves out the
      important term 'foundation'. Let us note that a couple of pages earlier in the same text
      Marx speaks of the 'materialist foundation' of his method. See Marx 1987a, p. 707; 1976,
      p. 19; 1954, p. 27.

78   Marx and Engels 1962, p. 49; 1968, p. 17. Emphasis in text. We should note that in the *Holy
      Family* Engels had posed the following question to his opponents: 'Who has annihilated
      the dialectic of the concept'? He replied: 'Feuerbach'. See Marx and Engels 1972, p. 198;
      1975, p. 92. The later criticism of Feuerbach by the two authors did not affect *this* aspect of
      Feuerbach.

79   Marx 1962b, pp. 361–2; 1989, p. 46. Emphasis in text.

the commodity'.[80] Also interesting is that in an earlier text, in the *Grundrisse*, which is supposed by Backhaus (and Reichelt) to represent the acme of the dialectical method – as mentioned above – the same position is affirmed by Marx. In the context of his discussion of the commodity, value and exchange value, Marx insists on the 'necessity of correcting the *idealist manner* of presentation, which gives the impression as if (all) this is a matter only of the determination of *concepts* and of the dialectic of these concepts'.[81] So, when Marx wrote in his letter to Engels (7 November 1867) that his was the 'first attempt at applying the dialectical method to Political Economy',[82] he could only be speaking of his own (materialist) dialectical method, which very soon thereafter he would squarely differentiate from Hegel's idealist dialectic, as we saw above. It is interesting to bring in here a view on the value analysis of the first chapter of just that much denigrated second edition of *Capital* Volume I, a view which is very different from, if not the exact opposite of, the view presented by our two authors under consideration. Karl Korsch, in his 'Introduction' to his own edition of this work by Marx, affirms that in the development from the 'value form' to 'the money form' in that chapter, 'we move through an absolute masterpiece of dialectical development unsurpassed even by Hegel'.[83]

Now we come to the alleged negative role of historical considerations in Marx's dialectical method. To start with, if real historical considerations are excluded from Marx's method of development in order to maintain its virginal purity, then in what way could this method still be considered to follow from Marx's 'materialist conception of history', which he and Engels so mightily opposed to the 'idealist conception of history' which abstracts from all real history? Would it not be then reduced precisely to the mere (Hegelian) 'progression of the Concept', that is, away from all real history? Indeed, Marx reproached the bourgeois economists for taking capitalism along with its economic categories as eternal and not historical. Already in his polemic with Proudhon, Marx criticises Ricardo for applying the bourgeois concept of rent to landed property of all epochs and all countries. He wrote in the same text, 'this is the error of all the economists who represent the relations of bourgeois production as eternal categories'.[84] Let us see what we find in this regard, precisely in those texts of Marx which our two authors believe to provide the very model of Marx's 'uncontaminated' dialectical method of development. Let us take

---

80   Marx 1962b, p. 368; 1989, p. 67.

81   Marx 1953, p. 69; 1993, p. 151. Emphasis added.

82   Marx 1987c, p. 463.

83   Korsch 1971, p. 55.

84   Marx 1965b, p. 123.

his 1857–8 economic manuscripts. Referring to the 'bourgeois economists who consider capital as an eternal and natural (*naturgemässe*), and not historical (*geschichtsgemässe*) form of production', Marx affirms, 'our *method* shows the points where historical considerations must come in, where the bourgeois economy as a mere historical form of production process refers beyond itself to the earlier modes of production'.[85] Again in the same work, Marx writes, regarding the development of value which appears as an abstraction, 'such determinations as value, which appear purely as abstraction, show the historical basis from which they are abstracted, and on which basis only they can appear ... The economic concept of value is not found among the ancients'.[86] Again, in his 1858 letter to Engels (2 April), regarded by Backhaus as the 'singular authentic form' of Marx's value theory,[87] Marx writes, 'Value (is) the most abstract form of bourgeois wealth. This is a *historical abstraction* which could be effected only on the basis of a definite economic development of society'.[88]

Not entirely unrelated to Marx's 'historicising' is the reproach about Marx's 'popularising' of his work on *Capital*, particularly its first volume, associated with the alleged progressive enfeeblement of his dialectical method. Our two authors have even stressed 'the necessity of de-popularising (*Ent-Popularisierung*) all the infected fundamental concepts'.[89] The crucial question one has to answer in this connection is: for whom mainly did Marx think he was writing? The answer is clear from his own words. In the 1873 'Afterword' (referred to earlier) to the second edition of *Capital* Volume I, this comes out clearly. After stating that, due to the peculiar historical development of Germany, there could be no original development of bourgeois (political) economy in that country, he added, 'However, that could not prevent the rise of its critique. In so far as such a critique represents a class, it can represent only that class whose historical vocation (*Beruf*) is to revolutionise the capitalist mode of production and the final abolition of classes – the proletariat'.[90] Marx certainly did not write mainly for cloistered scholars. In the same text, Marx wrote that 'the understanding which *Capital* quickly gained in the wide circles of the German working class is the best reward of my labour'.[91] In his 1872 letter (18 March) to

---

85   Marx 1953, p. 364; 1993, p. 460. Emphasis on the term 'method' added.
86   Marx 1953, p. 662; 1993, p. 776.
87   Backhaus 1997, p. 13.
88   Marx 1983b, p. 296. Emphasis added.
89   Backhaus and Reichelt 1994, p. 106.
90   Marx 1987a, p. 703; 1976a, p. 18; 1954, pp. 25–6.
91   Marx 1987a, p. 701; 1976a, p. 15; 1954, p. 23. In the same text Marx specifically mentioned Kugelmann for having convinced him, in the interest of 'most readers', to make a double

Maurice La Châtre, speaking of the coming French edition of *Capital* Volume I, Marx characteristically asserts (in French) that the 'consideration of accessibility of the work to the working class prevails over all other considerations for me'.[92] We see the same consideration in Marx's 1867 (30 Nov) letter to Kugelmann in Germany, where he asks his friend to try to direct the workers' attention – in their meetings – to the newly published *Capital*.[93] No mention there of the German world of scholarship. In the same vein, years later, Marx praised Carlo Cafiero in his 1879 letter (29 July) for the latter's Italian résumé of *Capital* Volume I, which he considered much superior to two other attempts – one Serbian and another American – at popularising the same book, criticising them for being 'too pedantic' as regards the 'scientific form of development'.[94]

Finally, let us turn to Backhaus's position (given above) that there is no passage from exchange value (commodity) to money, and that one has to start from money as the 'logical first'. We have found no text by Marx – including the absolutely 'uncontaminated' ones – where this is asserted. In fact Marx's position in all his relevant texts is just the opposite. Thus, in the *Grundrisse*, 'Product becomes commodity, commodity becomes exchange value; the exchange value of the commodity is its immanent monetary property (*Geldeigenschaft*) which is severed from exchange value as money, gaining a universal (general) social existence separated from particular commodities ... Just as the real exchange of products generates its exchange value, in the same way exchange value generates money'.[95] A careful reader will see that this position of Marx remains invariant in all the editions of his masterwork. In another writing of the same 'uncontaminated' genre – Marx's famous 1858 (2 April) letter, already referred to above – Marx wrote, 'The category of money is the result of the contradiction which opposes the general character of value to its material existence in a definite commodity'.[96] At the same period, in the first draft of what he called 'Index to the 7 Notebooks' (of which consists the *Grundrisse*), Marx speaks of the 'transition/passage (*Übergang*) from value to money, the product of exchange

---

exposition of the value form of the first edition, leading to a 'Supplement' that provided a more 'didactic exposition' of the value form. See Marx 1987a, p. 701; 1976a, p. 15; 1954, p. 23.

92   Marx 1976a, p. 35.

93   Marx 1987c, p. 489.

94   Marx 1991, p. 365. In his 1862 (28 December) letter to Kugelmann, Marx wrote that the 'scientific attempt at revolutionizing a science can never be really popular. But once scientific foundations are laid, popularisation is easy' (Marx 1985, p. 435).

95   Marx 1953, p. 65; 1993, p. 147.

96   Marx 1983b, p. 296.

itself'.[97] In the 1859 *Contribution*, the least 'infected' text according to Backhaus and Reichelt,[98] we read, 'the main difficulty in the analysis of money disappears as soon as its origin from the commodity is grasped'.[99]

It so happens that as regards the relation between value and money, Backhaus's position – that is, that there is no passage (*nicht gangbar*) from value to money – is *grosso modo* the same position as that of Samuel Bailey, which Marx precisely combatted in one of his early 1860s manuscripts. There Marx observes that, according to Bailey, with his 'queer manner of thinking which sticks only to the surface phenomena', the 'concept of value is formed only because besides commodities money exists, and we are so habituated to consider values of commodities not as their relations to one another but only in relation to a third, a third relation distinct from the immediate relation. For Bailey it is not the determination of product as value which is the driving force to the formation of money and is expressed as money, but contrariwise it is the existence of money which is the driving force to the fiction of the concept of value'.[100]

Let us remember that Marx himself, in the 'Preface' to the first edition of *Capital* Volume I, indicated that the section on value form in the first chapter, third section of the book was the most difficult part.[101] On the question of the difficulty of understanding Marx's category of value form, the great Marx scholar and economist from Russia, I.I. Rubin – who was liquidated in 1937 – one of the few economists who thoroughly studied the question of the genesis of money in Marx – in an incomplete manuscript composed shortly before his death, but published only recently (in German translation), had this to say:

> By the side of his historical remarks on the genesis of money we find, particularly in his theory of money, a special entanglement (Verflechtung) of historical and theoretical aspects. Not infrequently Marx presents the earlier phases of historical development as singular 'moments' (in the sense of Hegel) of the later, more developed form of the same phenomenon, or, conversely, presents the stages of logical analysis of a complex phenomenon in the form of successive phases of historical development. Such entanglement of historical and theoretical investigations of the value-form makes its understanding exceedingly difficult.[102]

97   Marx 1980a, p. 3.
98   Backhaus and Reichelt 1994, p. 106.
99   Marx 1980a, p. 139; 1970a, p. 64.
100   Marx 1962a, pp. 143–4; 1971a, p. 145. The English term 'queer' is Marx's own.
101   Marx 1987a, p. 66; 1976a, p. 11; 1954, p. 19.
102   Rubin 2012, pp. 43–4.

To start with, it is very relevant to recall here a crucial passage from the first volume of *Capital* (Chapter I, Section 3 of the second edition):

> Everybody knows, if s/he knows nothing else, that the commodities possess a particular form of value which contrasts in the most striking manner with their colourful (*bunte*) natural forms – the money form. Here it is a question of performing (*leisten*) something which the bourgeois economy never sought to do, namely, to demonstrate the genesis of this money form, [and] thus to develop the expression of value contained in the value relation of commodities from its simplest, least perceptible form to the dazzling money form. Thereby will disappear at the same time the enigma of money.[103]

So to understand the origin of money, the 'general equivalent', one has to examine how this form of value developed from its simplest to the highest form, the general equivalent, money. As value, a commodity is at the same time equivalent to all other commodities in a definite relation. While, as value, the commodity is in an equivalent relation, as equivalent, all its natural properties are obliterated. It is no longer in a specific qualitative relation with other commodities. Contrariwise, it is as much the general measure as it is the general representative, the general medium of exchange with other commodities. As value it is money. 'As value the commodity is at the same time different from itself as product. Since commodities as values differ from one another only quantitatively, each commodity must differ from its own value qualitatively. Its value

---

103   Marx 1987a, pp. 80–1; 1976a, p. 50; 1954, p. 54. The term 'particular' was added in the French version. This specific paragraph, absent in the first edition, was added in the second and subsequent editions. On the question of the money riddle, the great Japanese Marx scholar Samezō Kuruma has very pertinently remarked that 'The riddle of the money form is ultimately rooted in the peculiar fact that the value of a commodity is expressed in the oppositional element to *value*: a commodity's *use-value*. In order to solve the riddle of the money-form, therefore, we must first answer the fundamental question of how it is possible, exactly, for a commodity's value to be expressed in the use-value of another commodity. The problem does not present itself in that manner when we directly consider the money-form'. See Kuruma 2009, p. 98. It is interesting to note that Reichelt, in his earlier 1973 work (Reichelt 1973, p. 143) approvingly cited this passage from Marx, which clearly contradicts Backhaus's 1997 contention on the commodity-money relation, which we discussed above. Let us recall that Marx wrote to Weydemeyer (1 February 1859), while giving him a sketch of his *Contribution* to be soon published, that 'the analysis of the simple forms of money is the most abstract and hence the most difficult part of political economy' (1983b, p. 374).

must, therefore, have an existence which is qualitatively differentiable from it, and in real exchange this separability must become real separation, because the natural difference of commodities must necessarily enter into contradiction with their economic equivalence, and the two can exist, one by the side of the other, because the commodity has acquired (*gewinnt*) a double existence; by the side of its natural existence there is a purely economic existence'.[104]

As regards money, the general equivalent, what is particularly difficult to grasp in it is that here a social relation, a definite relation between individuals, appears as a metal, a stone, a pure bodily thing. But gold or silver does not produce any money, any more than it produces bankers or a rate of exchange. 'It does not appear at all that it is the simple result of the social process; this is all the more striking in that its immediate use value for the living individual has no relation to this role at all and that the memory of use value, different from exchange value, has totally disappeared in this incarnation of pure exchange. Thus here appears in all its purity the basic contradiction which lies in exchange value and in the mode of production corresponding to it'.[105]

The function of money to equalise the unequal, and, to the extent it serves as the general equivalent, implies several contradictions.[106] First, use value becomes the phenomenal form of exchange value. In general, the commodity in which the exchange value of another commodity is expressed is never expressed as exchange value, never as relation, but as a definite quantity in its natural constitution. If a bushel of wheat equals three bushels of rye in value, it is only the bushel of wheat that is expressed as value and not the bushel of rye. When one commodity is expressed in another commodity, it is as relation, while the other is posited as a simple quantity of itself (in its natural state). 'In the determination of money as the unit of exchange value, as its measure, as the general point of comparison, money (itself) appears as essentially a natural material, gold, silver, since it is the price of the commodity, not an exchange value, not a relation, but a definite weight of gold or silver'.[107] In other words, the exchange value of a commodity is necessarily expressed in the use value of another commodity, that is, a particular commodity which necessarily functions as a general equivalent.

---

104   Marx 1953, p. 60; 1993, p. 141.

105   Marx 1953, p. 151; 1993, pp. 239–40.

106   Marx calls them 'particularities' (*Eigentümlichkeiten*). We would like to call them 'contradictions', which they really are, as the reading of Marx's text clearly shows.

107   Marx 1953, p. 121; 1993, p. 207.

Hence the enigmatic character of the equivalent form which only strikes the crude bourgeois notice of the political economist as soon as this form appears in front of her/him in its finished shape. Then s/he seeks to explain away the mystical character of gold and silver by substituting them with less puzzling commodities, and with renewed pleasure goes over and over again the catalogue of articles which have in their times played the role of equivalent. S/he has no presentiment that already the simplest expression of value such as 20 yards of linen equals one coat offers the solution of the riddle.[108]

We now consider the second contradiction. The body of the commodity serving as the equivalent form counts always as the bodily form of abstract human labour and is always the product of definite, useful, concrete labour. This concrete labour thus only serves to express abstract human labour. In terms of Marx's example, if the coat counts as a simple materialisation of human labour, then the activity of tailoring which is materialised in it is a simple form of materialisation of abstract labour. In the expression of value of the linen, the utility of tailoring consists not in the fact that it makes clothes but in the fact that it makes a material which is regarded as value, thus a coagulation of labour which is in no way different from the labour materialised in the value of linen.

In the form of tailoring, as in the form of weaving, human labour power is expended. Both possess, therefore, the general characteristic of human labour, and in definite cases, for instance, in the production of value, and could be regarded from this point of view. There is nothing mysterious in this. However, 'in the case of the expression of value of the commodity, there takes place an inversion. To express weaving, not as the concrete labour of weaving, but in its quality of human labour in general which forms the value of linen, one has to posit in opposition another labour, the concrete labour of tailoring, which produces the equivalent of linen as the palpable form of materialisation of abstract human labour'.[109] Hence the second contradiction of the equivalent form: concrete labour becomes the phenomenal form of its opposite, abstract human labour.

Thirdly, products of labour are commodities precisely because they are products of private labour, executed independently one from the other. The social interconnection of these private labours exists materially so far as they

108   Marx 1987a, p. 90; 1976a, p. 58; 1954, p. 63. The term 'bourgeois' is displaced and appears directly to qualify the expression 'political economist' in the French version and in the English edition.
109   Marx 1987a, p. 90; 1976a, p. 58; 1954, p. 64.

are the members of social division of labour and satisfy a system of social needs. However, this interconnection is a *mediated* interconnection and is realised only through *exchange* of the products of these labours. The product of private labour possesses a social form only to the extent that its own bodily form is simultaneously the form of exchangeability against the other commodity, that is, counts as the value form of the other commodity. This happens only when the latter commodity plays the role of equivalent to the other commodity. This implies equality of the labour contained in one commodity with the labour contained in the other commodity. This equality, however, is possible only to the extent that both are human labour in general, abstract human labour, that is, expenditure of human labour power. 'Hence we have the third contradiction of the equivalent form, private labour becomes the form of its opposite, labour appearing in directly social form'.[110]

In the first edition of *Capital* Volume I, Marx wrote a 'supplement' on 'value form', in which he added a fourth contradiction: '("particularity") of the equivalent form: the fourth particularity of the equivalent form is that fetishism of the value form is more striking (*frappenter*) in the equivalent form than in the relative form'.[111]

The fact that the products of labour, the useful things like wheat, iron, etc., are values, definite magnitudes of value, and in general, commodities, this characteristic occurs only in commerce, and does not come from nature, like being light/heavy, or being cold/hot. Inside commerce these things behave as between themselves as commodities. In this world the producers of these things like tailors or weavers enter into a definite social relation of production where they equalise their different kinds of useful labour. It is equally a definite social relation of production of the producers in which quantities of labour are measured by the labour time of the expenditure of human labour power. But, within this commerce these social characters of their own labours appear as the natural characteristics, as objective determinations, of products of labour of themselves. However, writes Marx, 'the commodity form and the value relation of the products of labour have nothing to do with their physical nature and the real relations springing from them. It is only the definite social relations of individuals themselves which take the phantasmagoric form of relations between

---

110 Marx 1987a, p. 91; 1976a, pp. 58–9; 1954, p. 64. In this text we have substituted 'contradiction' for Marx's 'particularity' for the reason mentioned earlier. In the French version the whole cited part is absent. In its turn the English edition substitutes Marx's 'private labour' for 'labour of private individuals', which are of course not exactly identical.

111 Marx 1983a, p. 637; 1978, p. 142.

things. This is what I call *fetishism* which adheres (*anklebt*) to the products of labour as soon as they are produced as commodities'.[112] The fetish character comes out more strikingly in the equivalent form than in the relative form. The relative value form is mediated precisely by the relation of this commodity to another commodity. Through this value form the value of the commodity is expressed as something totally different from its own sensual existence. This implies that the value relation of this commodity to another can only be the phenomenal form of a social relation hidden behind it. Quite the opposite is the case with the equivalent form. This consists precisely in the fact that the *bodily or natural form* of a commodity counts *directly* as social form: as the value form for the other commodity. Since inside the expression of value A, the equivalent form comes naturally to the commodity B, it appears that the latter comes from outside of this relation. 'Hence the enigma (*Räthselhafte*) of gold which, besides its other natural properties like light colour, non-oxydability, etc. also appears to possess the equivalent form from nature (itself), that is, a social quality of being *directly exchangeable* with the other commodity'.[113]

There is one important aspect of the meaning of Marx's term 'equivalent' which one should notice.[114] There is a shift in the meaning of the term 'equivalent' between Marx's two fundamental works: 1859's *Contribution to the Critique*

---

112   Marx 1983a, p. 638; 1978, p. 142. Emphasis in text.
113   Marx 1983a, p. 638; 1978, p. 143. Emphasis in text. In the same first edition of his master work Marx elaborates the central aspect of the *fetish* character of commodity production, the inversion process: 'Within the value relation and the expression of value contained in it the abstract general does not count as the property of the concrete, the sensuous-real, but, contrariwise the sensuous-concrete as the simple phenomenal or definite form of realisation of the abstract-general. Tailor's labour which is embodied in the equivalent coat, possesses, within the value expression of the linen, not general property of also being labour, It is the opposite (*Umgekehrt*). To be human labour is its essence, to be tailor's labour is only the phenomenal form or the form of realisation of this essence. This *quid pro quo* is unavoidable because the labour represented in the product of labour creates value only to the extent that it is undifferentiated human labour so that the labour objectified in the value of a product is not at all differentiated from the labour objectified in a product of different kind. This *inversion* through which the sensuous-concrete is only the phenomenal form of the abstract-general, not contrariwise, the abstract-general is the property of the concrete, characterises the expression of value. At the same time this makes its understanding difficult'. Marx 1983a, p. 634; 1978, pp. 139–40. Emphasis in original.
114   We here draw on a remarkable text of the outstanding French Marx scholar P.D. Dognin – not much known outside France and almost unknown to the English reading public – who as far as we know, was one of the first, if not the first to underline this aspect. See Dognin 1977, p. 59.

of Political Economy and 1867's *Capital*. In the first book, Marx, while discussing the value relation of commodities, uses 'equivalent' in the general sense of *equality*. He writes,

> So far as the two products represent the same quantity of general labour time, and, therefore, equivalents for each use value containing the same quantity of labour time, they are *equivalents for each other*. It is only because the labour time of the spinner and the labour time of the weaver present themselves as the general labour time, and therefore their products *present themselves as general equivalents*, that the labour of the spinner for the weaver and the labour of the weaver for the spinner become the general labour time that the labour of the one for the labour of the other, that is, their respective labours acquire a social existence.[115]

It is clear that Marx attributes the concept of 'equivalence', even 'general equivalence', to *both the terms* of the value expression. In *Capital* Volume I, Chapter 1, the meaning of the concept is not the same. In the latter book we read that the value of a commodity (linen) expresses itself in the *body* of another commodity (coat), the value of the first by the use value of the second. In the value relation between commodity A and commodity B, the natural form of B becomes the value form of the commodity A. The first commodity, linen, manifests its quality of having a value by the fact that the coat, *without assuming a value form different from its bodily form*, is equated to linen. 'Linen has its own existence of value by the fact that the coat is directly (unmediated, *unmittelbar*) exchangeable with it. Therefore the equivalent form of a commodity is the form of its direct exchangeability with other commodities'.[116] Here, very differently from Marx's earlier book, the term 'equivalent' is uniquely attributed to only *one term*, not to both, in the value relation. Dognin explains that

> Marx wants to show how the 'equivalent' develops till it becomes in money the 'general equivalent'. Now money constitutes only one of the terms of the exchange relation. Therefore the qualification 'equivalent' has to be attributed from the beginning only to one term of the same relation. Marx also wants to show that this development is the work of the commodities themselves.[117]

---

115   Marx 1980a, p. 112; 1970a, p. 33. Emphasis ours.
116   Marx 1987a, p. 88; 1976a, p. 55; 1954, p. 61. The last sentence does not appear in the French version.
117   Dognin 1977, p. 57.

It is important to be clear about the distinction between unmediated exchangeability and mediated exchangeability in the value relation. The 'general equivalent' or money is the unique commodity which is immediately or directly exchangeable, whereas all other commodities have to be mediated by money before acquiring any commodity.

Commodity Circulation: Possibility of Crisis

We will be dealing in this section only with the 'simple circulation' of commodities, c – m – c, from which the possibility of crisis arises. The cycle c – m – c is decomposed into the movement c – m, exchange of commodity against money or sale, the movement m – c, exchange of money against commodity or purchase, and, finally, the unity of the two movements, exchange of commodity against money and exchange of money against commodity. However, in the result in which the process itself disappears we obtain c – c, exchange of commodity against commodity, a real metabolism.

c – m or sale: a particular article enters the circulation process as a use value with a definite price. This price, which is an indicator of the labour time contained in the article as a commodity, expresses at the same time the effort of its possessor to give the labour time that it contains the form of general social labour time. If this transformation fails to occur, the article ceases not only to be a commodity but also to be a product, since it is a commodity only if it is a non-use value for its possessor, or its labour is only real labour as useful labour for others. And it is only useful for the possessor as abstract general labour. Taking Marx's example that the particular article is iron, one could say that 'the task of the iron or its possessor is to find the point in the world of commodities where iron attracts gold. This difficulty, the mortal leap (*salto mortale*) of the commodity, is overcome if the sale – as it is supposed here in the analysis of simple circulation – really goes through'.[118]

The opposition between use vale and exchange value is polarised in two extremes. As we have seen above, c – m signifies sale, the transformation of the commodity into money. But from the other extreme, the same process appears as m – c, purchase, the transformation of money into commodity. In the first case the initiative comes from the commodity while in the second case the initiative comes from money. Representing the first transformation of commodity into money as the result of the passage of the first stage of circulation, we sup-

---

118   Marx 1980a, p. 159; 1970a, p. 88.

pose at the same time that another commodity has already been transformed
into money and thus already exists in the second stage of the circulation. We
thus enter into 'a vicious (*fehlerhaften*) circle of presuppositions. The circulation itself is this vicious circle'.[119] Indeed, the commodity is exchanged for
money, money is exchanged for the commodity, and the operation continues
and is repeated to infinity, 'a series without beginning and end'.[120] Hence 'at first
sight circulation appears as a process of bad infinity'.[121] However, a closer look
at the process reveals that there are still other phenomena involved, the phenomena of being linked together or the return to the point of departure. The
buyer becomes again seller, the seller becomes again buyer. Therefore each is
posited in a double and opposite determination and thus in the living unity of
both determinations. Nevertheless, it is wrong to consider only the end results
without the process which mediates them, only the unity and not the difference, only the affirmation and not the negation. In other words, the acts of
buying and selling appear as reciprocally indifferent, disjoint in space and time.
'So far as buying and selling are two essential moments of circulation, indifferent to each other, separated with respect to each other in space and time,
there is no need for them to come together; but so far as they are the essential moments of a totality, there must come a moment when the autonomous
form is violently broken from outside. This is how the germ of crisis lies already
in the determination of money as the mediator in the disjunction (*Ausein-
anderfallen*) of exchange in two acts, at least the possibility of crisis'.[122] The
separation between purchase and sale in the exchange process, which 'destroys
the local-spontaneous, antic, pious, genial, absurd (*alberne*) barriers to social
metabolism, is, at the same time, the general form of dismemberment of its
moments that were bound together and which become fixed in a relation of
opposition to one another. In a word this creates the possibility of commercial
crisis if only because the contradiction between commodity and money is the
abstract, general form of contradiction contained in bourgeois labour'.[123]

The inherent contradictions in commodity circulation are further deepened
in Marx's early 1860s critique of Ricardo's (and Say's) position in regard to the
commodity-money relation: that 'a (hu)man never sells, but with an intention
to purchase some other commodity'. Now, as was noted earlier, the possibility of

119   Marx 1980a, p. 160; 1970a, p. 90.
120   Marx 1980a, p. 163; 1970a, p. 93.
121   Marx 1953, p. 112; 1993, p. 197. The expression 'bad infinity' Marx borrowed from Hegel's
       Science of Logic.
122   Marx 1953, p. 113; 1993, p. 198.
123   Marx 1980a, p. 165; 1970a, p. 96.

crisis appears in the metamorphosis of the commodity. The possibility of crisis, so far as it shows itself in the simple form of metamorphosis, arises only from the fact that the differences in form – the phases – which the commodity goes through are, first, the forms and phases which are necessarily complementary, and secondly, in spite of this necessary internal coherence, exist indifferently to each other in time and space, and are separated and reciprocally independent. Thus the possibility of crisis exists uniquely in the separation of sale from purchase. 'It is only in the form of commodity that the commodity has to go through the difficulty'.[124]

In commodity production the transformation of the product into money, the sale, is an indispensable condition. Production for direct satisfaction of one's own needs disappears. If the sale fails to take place, there is crisis. The difficulty that the commodity, the particular product of individual labour, has to be transformed into money – its opposite – in abstract, general, social labour, lies in the fact that money does not appear as the particular product of individual labour, that one who has sold the commodity and possesses the commodity in the form of money, is not obliged to buy, to transform money again into a particular product of individual labour. The difficulty of the seller – under the supposition that the product has use value – arises simply from the ease with which the buyer can defer the reconversion of money into commodity. In other words, 'the difficulty of converting the commodity into money, of selling it, arises from the fact that though the commodity must be transformed into money, money need not necessarily immediately be transformed into the commodity, and that sale and purchase can be disjoined. This form includes the possibility of crisis, that is to say, the possibility that the moments which belong together, which are inseparable, are separated, and therefore, have to be violently united, their coherence realised by violence to the reciprocal autonomy'.[125] Here is the dense presentation of this process as we read it later in *Capital*:

> Since the first metamorphosis of the commodity is at the same time sale and purchase, this partial process is simultaneously an autonomous process. The buyer has the commodity, the seller has the money. Nobody can sell unless another person buys. But nobody needs to buy immediately simply because s\he her(him)self has sold. Circulation bursts (*springt*) through the temporal, spatial and individual barriers of barter (exchange) such that it destroys the immediate identity between sale and purchase,

---

124   Marx 1959, p. 504; 1968, p. 508.
125   Marx 1959, pp. 505–6; 1968, p. 509.

and generates opposition between them. The fact that the autonomous, mutually opposing process builds an inner unity, means precisely that their inner unity moves into external opposition. True, purchase and sale are necessary complements, but it is no less true that their unity is the unity of opposites. If the separation between two complementary processes of the metamorphosis of the commodity is prolonged, if the separation between sale and purchase is accentuated, their internal unity is affirmed by a crisis. The contradictions which are immanent in the commodity between use value and exchange value, private labour appearing as social labour, concrete labour validating only as abstract general labour, personification of things and reification (*Versachlichung*) of persons – these contradictions immanent in the commodity obtain their forms of movement in circulation. These forms contain, therefore, the possibility – and only the possibility – of crisis.[126]

Besides the temporal and spatial separation between selling and purchasing, there is a second factor contributing to the possibility of crisis in simple circulation. This factor is the role of money as means of payment. 'Crisis in the first form is the metamorphosis of the commodity itself, the disjunction of purchase and sale. Under its second form crisis is the function of money as the means of payment, where money figures in the two moments separated in time, in two different functions'.[127]

Having discussed the first factor in the possibility of crisis, let us have a look at the second factor – money as means of payment. Again, there are two different functions which money performs as means of payment: as measure of value and as realisation of value. These two moments do not coincide. If the value changes within the interval, if the value which the commodity had at the moment when money had functioned as measure of value, and therefore, of the mutual obligations, the amount of sale of the commodity, does not allow the fulfilment of the obligation, then a whole series of earlier transactions which depend on this one transaction cannot be balanced. Moreover, even if the value of the commodity has not changed, it is sufficient that it cannot be sold within a stipulated period such that money cannot function, since it has to accomplish this function within a definite, already-defined period. Now as the same sum of money functions in this case for a series of transactions and reciprocal obligations, the inability to pay does not occur only at one point,

126   Marx 1987a, p. 138; 1976a, p. 96; 1954, p. 115.

127   Marx 1959, p. 506; 1968, p. 510.

but at several points. Hence the crisis. If the crisis occurs because of the non-coincidence of purchase and sale, it develops as monetary crisis as soon as money has developed as means of payment, and this second form of crisis is self-explanatory as soon as the first form has appeared.

The function of money as means of payment includes an unmediated contradiction. To the extent that the payments are equalised, money functions only ideally as money of account or measure of value. So far as the real payment is concerned, money does not appear as a medium of circulation, as only a vanishing and mediating form of change of products, but intervenes as the individual incarnation of social labour, the independent form of exchange value, as the absolute commodity. The contradiction bursts forth in the times of industrial and commercial crisis which go by the name of monetary crisis. This is produced only where the chain of payments and an artificial system destined to serve the purposes of compensation are fully developed. With the general disturbance of this mechanism, originating from anywhere, money goes through a sudden reversal without transition, does not function any more in the purely ideal form of money of account. It turns into hard cash and can no longer be replaced by profane commodities. The use value of the commodity becomes worthless, and vanishes in front of its own value form. 'Even only the day before, the bourgeois, with the presumptuous self-sufficiency, with intoxicating prosperity, declared that money was a vain illusion, only the commodity is money; but now the cry, resounding throughout the world market, is that money alone is commodity. As the hart cries for fresh water, so cries the bourgeois soul after money, the only wealth'.[128] Marx adds, 'the opposition between the commodity and its value form, money, rises to an absolute contradiction'.[129]

---

128   Marx 1987a, p. 159; 1976a, p. 111; 1954, pp. 137–8.
129   Marx 1987a, p. 159; 1976a, p. 111; 1954, p. 138.

CHAPTER 3

Simple Commodity Production

The concept of 'simple commodity production', and its place in Marx's work as analysed by Engels in his editorial remarks on *Capital* Volume III (in the book's 'Preface' and 'Supplement') on the occasion of its publication (1894), became a subject of controversy. In recent years the controversy got a new lease of life, particularly in Germany, after the publication of the book's so-called 'main manuscript' in the new version of the 'Complete Works of Marx and Engels' (MEGA²). There are several issues at stake in the controversy: the textual validity of Engels's use of the concept – claimed to be absent in Marx – his 'historicisation' of the concept, his affirmation that simple commodity production is the starting point of *Capital* Volume I, and his interpretation of the method of Marx's critique of political economy as 'logical-historical'. One issue, not directly related to the controversy on simple commodity production, but which arose as a consequence of Engels's use of the concept, was the conclusion drawn by some followers of Marx (not always explicitly referring to Engels) – the Marxist adherents of 'market socialism' and the partisans of the twentieth-century régimes called 'socialist' – that if commodity production could exist historically, independently of capitalism, it could also exist after capitalism without necessarily giving rise to capitalism. However, we will not pursue this last issue here. Here we simply note that this latter point of view concerning the relation of commodity production to socialism was completely alien to the points of view of both Marx and Engels. Later a separate chapter will be devoted to 'market socialism'.

The Problem

The point of departure of Engels on simple commodity production is encapsulated in two statements. The first is that the starting point of *Capital* Volume I is 'simple commodity production'. He writes in the Preface to his edition of *Capital* Volume III:

> It is self-evident that where things and their interrelationships are conceived, not as fixed but as changing, their mental images, the ideas, are not encapsulated in rigid definitions, but are developed in their historical or logical process of formation. This makes clear why in the beginning

of his first book Marx proceeds from simple commodity production as the historical premise ultimately to arrive from this basis to capital. He proceeds from simple commodity instead of a logically and historically secondary form – from an already capitalistically modified commodity.[1]

Engels's second statement appears in his 'Supplement' to the same book. There, in connection with the law of value, he says that what was involved was not merely 'a logical process but also a historical process and its explanatory reflection in thought', the logical pursuance of its inner connections.[2] He then cites Marx:

> The exchange of commodities at their values ... necessitates a much lower stage than the exchange of commodities at their prices of production, which requires a definite level of capitalist development. It is therefore totally consistent (*durchaus sachgemäss*) with the reality to consider values not only theoretically but also historically prior to the prices of production. This is valid for the situations where the means of production belong to the worker, and this situation is found in the old and the new world for the artisan and the self-cultivating peasant proprietor.[3]

Engels historicises Marx's theoretical statement as given here. He writes:

> The Marxian law of value holds generally ... for the whole period of simple commodity production. Thus the Marxian law of value has general economic validity for a period lasting from the beginning of exchange which transforms the product into commodity, down to the fifteenth century of the present era ... Thus the law of value has prevailed during a period from five to seven thousand years.[4]

Engels's methodological statement on the historical-logical is earlier seen in his review of Marx's *Contribution to the Critique of Political Economy* (1859), which appeared in *Das Volk* (1859):

> The critique of political economy could be laid out in two ways: historical and logical. Since in history as in its literary reflection the development on

---

1 Marx 1964, p. 20; 1984, pp. 13–14.
2 Marx 1964, p. 905; 1984, p. 895.
3 Marx 1992, p. 252; 1964; p. 186; 1984, p. 177.
4 Marx 1964, p. 909; 1984, pp. 899–900.

the whole progresses from the simplest to the more complex relations, in the same way the historical development of the literature of political economy furnished a natural leading thread to which the critique could be attached, and on the whole the economic categories would appear in the same order as in the logical development ... The logical method is nothing else than the historical method, divested of its historical form and disturbing hazards. The march of ideas must begin at the point where the history begins, and its further development will be only the reflection of the historical course in abstract and theoretically consistent form, a corrected reflection, but corrected according to the laws furnished by the real course of history itself.[5]

Discussion after Engels

The category of simple commodity production as a historical category preceding the capitalist mode of production was later taken up by some eminent followers of Marx and Engels. Thus Hilferding, in his well-known book on finance capital, speaks of the 'progress from simple commodity production to the capitalist commodity production', illustrated by the evolution from 'independent artisans to capitalist entrepreneurs'.[6] In turn, Rosa Luxemburg, in her posthumously published lectures on political economy, explicitly discusses the historical process from the dissolution of primitive communism to a 'simple commodity economy' based on independent artisans and then to modern capitalism.[7] Neither of these writers mentioned Engels in this connection. Furthermore, neither posited 'simple commodity production' as the starting point of *Capital*. Oskar Lange was the first academic economist with pronounced Marxian sympathies to underline, in a journal article in 1935, that 'simple commodity production' was the point of departure of what he called 'Marx's theory of value', 'undergoing later (only) slight modification when applied to a capitalist economy'.[8] A few years later he wrote that according to Marx the 'law of value applies not only under capitalism but also under commodity production of any kind'. In particular it applies also under 'what Marx called *simple commodity production*', an exchange economy of small independent producers not

---

5   In Marx 1980a, pp. 252–3; 1970a, p. 225.
6   Hilferding 1968, p. 26.
7   Luxemburg 1972, p. 187.
8   Lange, in Kowalik 1993, p. 12.

employing wage labour.[9] In neither of the papers does he mention Engels. Paul Sweezy, in his widely read book on capitalist development, stated:

> The first chapter of *Capital* is entitled 'commodities' … [where] Marx begins by analysing 'simple commodity production' … in starting with simple commodity production Marx was following a well-established tradition of economic theory.[10]

He did not mention Engels. Later Maurice Dobb in his book dealing with theories of value and distribution, explicitly accepted Lange's position about the point of departure of *Capital*, but did not mention Engels either.[11] Ronald Meek was the most thoroughgoing Engelsian in this respect. He totally accepted both the positions of Engels. In other words, he accepted 'simple commodity production' both as a historical category preceding the capitalist mode of production and as the starting point of *Capital*. According to Meek, Marx 'postulated' a society in which although 'commodity production and free competition were assumed to reign more or less supreme', the labourers still owned the whole produce of their labour. Marx, according to the author, then 'imagined capitalism suddenly impinging upon this society'. Meek underlined that Marx 'postulated an abstract pre-capitalist society based on what he called simple commodity production'.[12] Further, Meek wrote that 'Marx begins [*Capital*] with an analysis of simple commodity production' and that Marx goes on to consider its 'logically and historically secondary form, a capitalistically modified commodity'.[13] Not only this, but Meek accepted as well Engels's methodological position on the logical-historical method ascribed to Marx. Meek cited Engels's text on the method of the critique of political economy, written in his review of Marx's 1859 book – the text which we quoted earlier – saying that Engels's 'description' of the method 'had not been bettered'.[14] He even presented the Sraffa system as appearing in three stages: first as 'simple commodity production', the second as early capitalism and the third as developed capitalism. This he did, as he said, in order to make the Sraffa system more accessible to ordinary readers.[15]

---

9   Lange 1945, p. 29. Emphasis added.
10   Sweezy 1942, p. 23.
11   Dobb 1973, p. 147.
12   Meek 1967, p. 98.
13   Meek 1956, p. 180.
14   Meek 1956, p. 148.
15   Meek 1967.

The Critics

Let us return to the criticisms levelled against Engels on the issues in question. We first give a general account of the issues raised by the critics against
Engels's position on simple commodity production; then we critically examine the particular objections of the critics. We will deal here only with those
contributions which appear to us to be significant. We start with the critical remarks of the well-known Marx scholar from Germany, Rolf Hecker. As
regards the concept 'simple commodity production', Hecker underlines that it
was Engels who 'introduced' the concept in his 'Preface' to *Capital* Volume III,
whereas in the 'Appendix' (*Anhang*) to the first edition of *Capital* Volume I,
and in the revised second edition of the same book, the distinction between
'simple commodity production' and 'commodity production by capital' is 'non-
existent'. Secondly, according to Hecker, for Marx, as opposed to Engels, the
point of departure is the commodity produced by capital and not the pre-
capitalist commodity. Further, Marx sees the historical development of commodity production in the process of transformation of exchange of products
into exchange of commodities.[16] Here Hecker cites from the second edition of
Capital Volume I:

> Just as commodity production at a certain stage of development neces-
> sarily becomes capitalist commodity production – and in fact only on
> the basis of the capitalist mode of production do commodities become
> the general, predominant form of production – in the same way the laws
> of ownership of commodity production turn into the laws of capitalist
> appropriation.[17]

To strengthen his argument, Hecker adds that Engels had struck out these
lines from the fourth edition of *Capital*. As regards the beginning of *Capital*
Volume I, Hecker observes that though commodity and money are historically older than capital, methodologically it was decisive for Marx to present
the commodity, value and capital not in their pre-capitalist form but in the
sphere of simple circulation. Engels had simply confused 'simple circulation of
commodities' with 'simple commodity production'. Engels, continues Hecker,
understands by 'simple commodity production' a type of production which is

---

16   Hecker 2001, p. 85.
17   Hecker 2001, p. 85. The citation comes from Marx 1987a, p. 538. It does not appear in the
      English translation, as the translation is from the fourth edition, not from the second.

based on artisanal or peasant production and private ownership in the means of production, but essentially not yet on wage labour.[18] Finally, Hecker holds that Engels's statement in his 'Preface' to *Capital* Volume II, showing how the average rate of profit is formed on the basis of the law of value, offered an opportunity to Marx's later critics – such as Böhm-Bawerk and Bortkiewicz – to argue for Marx's logical inconsistency as between his two positions, namely, the exchange of commodities at their values and exchange at prices of production. In other words, according to them, there is a contradiction in Marx's theory of value between *Capital* Volume I and *Capital* Volume III. 'Obviously this turn of events was unanticipated by Engels'.[19] Going further and outbidding Hecker, Chris Arthur from England emphasised that Marx 'never' called anything 'simple commodity production, the term cannot be found in Marx's writings', and that it was 'invented by Engels'.[20] Hans-Georg Backhaus from Germany asserts that the concept 'simple commodity production' was 'coined (*geprägte*) by Engels and is not detectable in Marx's work'. Engels, with his concept of 'simple commodity production', had 'in an absurd way' misunderstood Marx's basic concept of 'simple circulation'. Further, with his interpretation of *Capital*'s first chapter as the value theory of a 'pre-monetary theory of a natural economy', and of the book's third chapter as the 'monetary theory of simple commodity production', Engels had totally ignored the 'monetary-theoretical intention of Marx's value theory'.[21] Later, Backhaus and Helmut Reichelt of the Frankfurt school, appearing as co-authors of a work that was destined otherwise to serve as a critique of the new MEGA edition, affirmed, among other things, that for Engels the concept of simple commodity production was 'historical, referring to a definite mode of production, the pre-capitalist mode of production'. In their view Engels had difficulty with dialectical reasoning. These authors have gone further. They hold that Marx himself had not a little contributed to Engels's shortcoming in this regard, particularly due to his own work of 'popularising' the fundamental concept of his method – the concept of substance of value – and 'hiding his dialectical method'. Based on their reading of a letter Marx had written to Engels in 1861, Backhaus and Reichelt have detected the beginning of this process of 'deterioration' after the *Grundrisse* (1857–8) and the original version (*Urtext*) of Marx's 1859 *Contribu-*

---

18   Hecker 2001, p. 87.
19   Hecker 2001, p. 87.
20   Arthur 1999, p. 5. It should be pointed out that the original version of Hecker's paper was published in 1997. The reference will appear in the bibliography.
21   Backhaus 1997, pp. 86, 113, 131.

tion to the Critique of Political Economy.[22] The dialectical method, 'not hidden'
in the *Grundrisse*, became 'partly hidden' in Marx's 1859 *Critique*, and 'much
more hidden' in *Capital.*[23] We elaborate this Backhaus-Reichelt position further in our chapter on the 'commodity' in this book.

The outstanding Russian dissident 'soviet' Marx scholar and economist Vladimir Shkredov – virtually unknown to 'Western' Marx readers – has focused
on Engels's method, rather than his treatment of 'simple commodity production' as such. In view of the general lack of knowledge of his work among Marx
readers in the 'West', we propose to undertake here a somewhat extended treatment of his contribution to the Engels debate. According to Shkredov, Engels's
theoretical work in the field of political economy possesses 'its own scientific
value; he was never Marx's *Alter Ego*, simply reproducing Marx's work'.[24] Shkredov stresses that the 'explanation-clarification of the materialist character of
Marx's method was one of the essential merits of Engels'.[25] Engels saw political economy not as a theoretical but as an empirical science. He laid great
value on reasoning through historical and contemporary facts. This tendency
had influenced him in his preparation of the second and the third volumes
of *Capital*. Engels's 'historicising' of Marx's value theory 'promoted the development and spread of a materialist conception of value and other categories
of political economy'. However, at the same time, it influenced the succeeding (*nachfolgenden*) interpretations of *Capital* and finally led to 'vulgarising
the dialectical method which Marx had applied in his work'.[26] Engels's interpretation of dialectical method contradicted Marx's, which in his economic
manuscripts and his *Capital* was laid bare. However, the real significance of
Engels's review of Marx's 1859 book – where he had described his method of
political economy – lay not in the explanation of the essence of the dialectical method, but in 'breaking the wall of silence' on Marx's book.[27] Shkredov
compares Engels's method as described in his *Das Volk* 'Review' (1859) with
Marx's method as given in his 1857 manuscript 'Introduction', which remained
unknown to Engels. While, according to Engels, the thought process has to
begin at the point precisely where history begins, in Marx's view the opposite
is the case. Here Shkredov cites[28] Marx's famous statement that 'the anatomy

22   Backhaus and Reichelt 1994, p. 106.
23   Backhaus and Reichelt 1994, p. 106.
24   Shkredov 1997, p. 114.
25   Shkredov 1997, p. 113.
26   Shkredov 1997, p. 118.
27   Shkredov 1997, p. 118.
28   Shkredov 1997, p. 119.

of the human is the key to the anatomy of the ape'.[29] Referring to Engels's treatment of the relation of value to price of production – mentioned above – Shkredov observes that the transformation of value into production price reflects
the inner dialectic of the production and reproduction of capital. 'The production price is the form in which value is reflected on the surface of the capitalist
society'.[30] The theoretical system of Marx's *Capital*, in its pure form, affirms
Shkredov, exclusively reflects the inner dialectic of capital's production and
reproduction process under the conditions of mature bourgeois society. In the
consideration of the object as the 'subject' of the objective economic process,
in whose result the formation and transformation of all of capitalism's forms
are realised, is also included the dialectical logic of *Capital*. 'For its realisation it
is not necessary to trace the genesis of the capitalist mode of production'.[31] For
the scientific analysis of the modern bourgeois society, the works of Engels,
in which he described the situation of the working class in the nineteenth
century, 'retain their actuality'.[32] Shkredov stresses that the 'dogmatics have
made Engels into a founder of "political economy of socialism"'.[33] Referring to
Anti-Dühring, Shkredov underlines that Engels could not know that, one hundred years later, this work would be 'mechanically tied with the real socialism,
thereby limiting its significance in the history of political economy'.[34]

The critics of Engels do not feel very comfortable when faced with one particular text of Marx, contained in the manuscript of *Capital* Volume III, which –
as we have seen above – Engels, in the 'Supplement' to his edition, had cited in
defence of his position on the historical character of 'simple commodity production'. Michael Heinrich from Germany dismisses this text as an 'incidental
remark', which Engels had cited 'to prove that this was also Marx's opinion'.
The first part of the first volume of *Capital*, opines Heinrich, was considered
by Engels as presenting the laws of pre-capitalist production, and thus 'Engels
fostered a historical reading' of Marx's book.[35] Morishima and Catephores, in
their turn, do not contest the concept of 'simple commodity production', or that
it exists in Marx's work. What they dispute is the view – shared, in their opinion, by Engels and a number of later Marxian economists following Engels's
lead – that this form of production constituted a whole economic system before

---

29 Marx 1953, p. 26; 1993, p. 105.
30 Shkredov 1997, p. 122.
31 Shkredov 1997, pp. 124–5.
32 Shkredov 1997, p. 126.
33 Shkredov 1997, p. 127.
34 Shkredov 1997, p. 128.
35 Heinrich 1996–7, p. 463.

capitalism, that there existed a whole 'epoch of simple commodity production'.[36] They particularly question the so-called 'historical transformation problem', that values are transformed into prices of production through a historical
process.[37] They also find in Marx a certain inconsistency in his presentation
of simple commodity production. While generally Marx refused to consider
ancient economies as based on simple commodity production or simple commodity production as an independent socio-economic formation like feudalism or capitalism, and while considering particular historical epochs of socio-
economic formations in his 1959 *Critique*, Marx did not mention simple commodity production as an independent socio-economic formation along with
the others, he also in some texts treated simple commodity production as a
'distinct socio-economic formation on a par with feudalism and capitalism'.[38]
Referring to the particular passage in *Capital* Volume III (cited above) which
constituted the rationale of Engels's argument to 'historicise' simple commodity production, including the 'historical transformation of values into prices of
production', they call it a 'striking passage taking the opposite tack to all we
have been arguing'.[39] Then, seizing on a remark by Engels about the unfinished
character of the particular passage, they concluded: 'In view of the evidence
on the total approach of Marx to the question of value', it is perhaps possible
to speculate that 'he could equally well have deleted it completely'.[40] In other
words, these critics think that this statement by Marx contradicts his general
position.

Criticisms Discussed

As already mentioned, the issues involved are several: the textual validity of
'simple commodity production', 'simple commodity' as the starting point of
Capital, 'historicisation' of the concept of 'simple commodity', the method
of political economy. First, does Marx ever use 'simple commodity (production)' in his work, or is the concept Engels's pure invention, as several critics
allege? There are a number of places in Marx's work – too many to mention
here – where the concept *does* appear explicitly.[41] Marx clearly distinguishes

36   Morishima and Catephores 1975, p. 311.
37   Morishima and Catephores 1975, p. 312.
38   Morishima and Catephores 1975, p. 314.
39   Morishima and Catephores 1975, p. 319.
40   Morishima and Catephores 1975, p. 319.
41   We hold that Chris Arthur's remark, cited above, about the alleged total absence of the

between the simple commodity or commodity as such and the commodity as the product of capital. In other words, the commodity which is not the product of capital is a simple commodity. Let us now turn to some of Marx's own texts in order to verify the arguments of the critics of Engels. The very first question is: did Marx ever use the concept 'simple commodity'? It appears that the answer is 'yes he did'. In this connection Marx employed two German terms (*einfach* and *bloss*) equivalently – either of them meaning 'simple' in English. Sometimes the specific *term/expression* does not appear but the *concept* is clear enough to seize from the (con)text. The concept 'simple commodity' itself signifies for Marx the commodity which is not the product of capital. In the very first notebook (among 23) of 1861–3, Marx distinguishes between 'commodity as such' – which only requires that the particular product (use value) is destined for direct personal consumption through sale, and the product as 'commodity as the universal and necessary form of all products' (of human labour), possible 'only on the basis of a specifically determined mode of production'. In the first case 'we would not have gone beyond simple commodity production' (*einfache Ware*), whereas in the second case the value of the commodity produced generates a greater value compared to the initial value, that is, it is a case of the 'commodity produced by capital'.[42] Elsewhere, in a text from the unpublished so-called 'sixth chapter' of *Capital* Volume I, we read: 'Capital, like the *einfache Ware*, has the double form as use value and as exchange value'. But in both these forms (under capital) there enter other, more developed determinations, which are different from those of the 'simple commodity considered independently'.

The product of the capitalist process of production is neither 'simple product (*blosses Product*)', use value, nor 'simple commodity (*blosse Ware*)', that is, '[it is] a product that has an exchange value, but its specific product is surplus value'.[43] Similarly, in a manuscript of the early 1860s criticising Ricardo's position that the product exchanges for product or service, and that money is only the simple mediation in this exchange, Marx observes that

> in the first place, the commodity in which the opposition between use value and exchange value exists is reduced to simple product (*blosses Product*) and thus exchange of commodities is transformed into simple

---

term 'simple commodity production' in Marx's texts only shows his astonishing innocence of Marx's relevant texts. The same goes for Backhaus referred to above.

42   Marx 1976b, pp. 34, 60; 1988b, pp. 39,68.

43   Marx 1988a, pp. 55, 56, 76; 1994, pp. 388, 389, 409.

barter, simple use value. It is a relapse not only behind capitalist production but even behind simple commodity production (*blosse Waren-
produktion*).[44]

In the same way, in his recently published so-called 'main manuscript' of the
third volume of *Capital*, the very volume whose alleged miseditorship by Engels
was denounced by his critics on this score, Marx clearly distinguishes between
'commodity capital' and '*einfache Ware*' (in fact this distinction appears identic-
ally in Engels's edition too). Thus, after saying that in the (capitalist) circulation
process, capital functions as '*commodity capital*', Marx adds that

> in the act of circulation commodity capital functions as *commodity*, not
> as *capital*. It is commodity capital as distinguished from 'simple commod-
> ity' (*einfachen Waare*) because it is already 'pregnant (*geschwängert*) with
> surplus value, [and] the realisation of its value is at the same time the real-
> isation of its surplus value'

and because its function as commodity is a moment of its reproduction process
as capital.[45] We turn now to some particular critics. We have mentioned above
that Rolf Hecker has a specific criticism of Engels in regard to the latter's alleged
'introduction' of 'simple commodity production'. According to Hecker – as
mentioned above – contrary to Engels's presentation, neither in the 'Appendix'
to the first edition nor in the revised second edition of *Capital* Volume I does
the distinction between 'simple commodity production' and commodity production by capital appear. Now if 'simple commodity' means commodity not
produced by capital, as Marx holds – as we saw above – then the distinction
referred to by Hecker does exist *bel et bien* in the second edition of the book.
Here is a passage:

> The unity of the labour process and the process of formation of value is
> the *production process of commodities*, the unity of the labour process and
> the process of producing surplus value is the capitalist production pro-
> cess, the *capitalist form of commodity production*.[46]

---

44   Marx 1959, p. 497; 1968a, p. 501.
45   Marx 1992, p. 415; 1984, p. 342.
46   Marx 1987a, p. 209; 1954, p. 191. Emphasis added.

Next, let us note another important criticism of Engels by Hecker mentioned above. Hecker stresses that, following Marx, the historical development of commodity production passes through the transformation of the exchange of products into the exchange of commodities. In this connection we have seen Hecker citing a paragraph from the second edition of *Capital* (citation given above), and holding that this passage was eliminated by Engels in the fourth edition of the book. We submit that this is only partially true. True, it does not appear in the fourth edition of the book. However, what has escaped Hecker's notice is that in the *third edition* of the book, equally edited by Engels, exactly the same passage appears in the same chapter on 'conversion of surplus value into capital', in the same place as in the second edition. What is also of great importance to note, and equally absent in Hecker, is that in the French version of the book, the work of Marx himself (aided by the translator), the passage in question completely disappears, along with some other changes. Next, as regards the paragraph from *Capital* Volume III which was cited earlier, and which is an embarrassment for Engels's critics, that is, where value determination is posited before the determination of prices of production as logical and historical, well, that is not an incidental or unique statement by Marx on the question. Earlier in his 1860s manuscripts he had said substantially the same thing, albeit in a very condensed way. Thus while discussing Ricardo's theory of ground rent he states:

> The transformation of values into cost prices is the consequence and result of the development of capitalist production (*Entwicklung der kapitalistischen Produktion*). Originally commodities are (on the average) sold at their values.[47]

Similarly he refers to Ricardo's mistake at the beginning of his *Principles* of identifying 'cost price and value', which again comes from the fact that, at a point where as yet he had to develop only value, therefore 'only commodity' (*nur noch Ware*), Ricardo plunged into the general rate of profit and all the 'presuppositions springing from the developed capitalist relations of production (*entwickeltern kapitalistischen Produktionsverhältnissen*)'.[48] Again, Marx put the matter succinctly when he wrote in a critical remark on Cherbuliez that

---

47 Marx 1959, p. 325; 1968a, p. 333. 'Cost price' here means advances (c+v) plus average profit, that is, 'prices of production'. Cost price in this sense is frequently used in Marx's 1861–3 manuscripts.

48 Marx 1959, p. 200; 1968a, p. 208.

'value is the primary factor, antecedent to the rate of profit and to the establishment of production prices'.[49]

As regards the critics' charge against Engels of 'historicising' commodity production, Marx, in the same place from where the embarrassing paragraph from
Capital Volume III was cited, refers to the situation – in the old and the new
world – where the 'working peasant and artisan' possessing their respective
means of production 'exchange mutually their commodities'.[50] Again this is
not the only place where Marx himself 'historicises' – so to speak – simple commodity production. In various places, Marx, indeed, refers to the existence of
the simple commodity – in the sense of the commodity not produced by capital – in pre-bourgeois society.[51] We will not go into the question whether this
was indeed the case in real history. For the purposes of the present chapter
the relevant point is to see to what extent Marx's own texts allow for the existence of pre-bourgeois commodity production independently of what actually
happened in history. Even if Marx's texts confirm this existence, a very important point, missed by most of the adversaries of Engels as well as by some of his
partisans, is that Marx underlines that such commodity production concerned
a pre-bourgeois society only within a limited sphere, at first only between
different communities and then gradually inside particular communities. It
mostly involved exchange of surplus over immediate consumption, the basic
aim of production was use values and not exchange values (including their
self-expansion). Commodity production was not the dominant mode of production, it was not the production in general before capital arrived. It is only
under capital that commodity production becomes generalised. On the other
hand, when the whole or at least the major part of the economy is commodified, where 'purchase and sale seize not merely the surplus of production but
its substance itself' (in a different text 'subsistence itself'),[52] this would only
indicate that use values have ceased to be the main aim of production, and that
the main aim of production has become exchange values necessarily leading
to self-expansion of exchange values, which is just another mode of expression for capital. At this point let us say that there is a misreading of some of
Marx's texts by Morishima and Catephores when they interpret them as showing some inconsistency in Marx's position on the historical character of simple

---

49   Marx 1962a, p. 371; 1971a, p. 377.

50   Marx 1992, p. 252; 1984, p. 177.

51   See Marx 2008, p. 650; 1956a, p. 113, where Marx refers to commodity production in differ-
      ent 'social modes of production', such as production based on slavery, on peasants, or on
      the communal form etc.

52   Marx 1976b, p. 286; 1988b, p. 316.

commodity production: on the one hand, Marx generally does not consider this form of production as the prevailing form for a whole society at any time in the pre-capitalist period, while in some texts, on the other hand, Marx, they allege, holds 'simple commodity production on a par with feudalism and capitalism'.[53] In defence of their position they quote a couple of passages from *Capital* which allegedly contradict Marx's general position. We will refer here to the shorter passage they cite from the first volume of the book:

> In the colonies ... the capitalist régime everywhere comes into collision with the resistance of the producer, who as owner of his own conditions of labour, employs that labour to enrich himself, instead of the capitalist.[54]

Let us add to this statement what Marx says in this connection only a few lines after this passage. Marx says that this is the social environment in which 'modes of production and appropriation, based on independent labour of the producer' prevail.[55] From these two citations from Marx, referring to a precapitalist society, we see that there is absolutely no indication here of this *whole society* being based on (simple) commodity production.

Now, in his posthumous publication *Conspectus on 'Capital'*, what Engels wrote is not very different from this central idea of Marx: to become commodity, the product is not to be produced as immediate means of subsistence. The mass of commodities can take commodity form

> only *within a definite mode of production, the capitalist mode of production* though commodity production and commodity circulation can already be found where the mass of products never become commodities.[56]

However, Engels's position that Marx's point of departure in the first volume of *Capital* is the 'simple commodity' as the 'historical presupposition' is palpably contradicted by Marx's different texts.[57] At the same time we should note that in his reviews as well as *Conspectus of 'Capital'*, Engels strictly accepted

---

53   Morishima and Catephores 1975, p. 314.

54   They cite the passage from the English edition of the book. See Marx 1954, p. 716.

55   Marx 1954, p. 716.

56   Engels 1973, p. 75; emphasis in text.

57   See Marx 1953, p. 763; 1993, p. 881; Marx 1962a, p. 109; 1971a, p. 112; Marx 1976b, p. 286; 1988b, p. 316; Marx 1987a, p. 69; 1976a, p. 42. 1954, p. 43; Marx 1988a, p. 24; 1994, p. 355.

Marx's position that the commodity which is posited there is already a product of capital. Similarly, in *Anti-Dühring*, Engels underlined Dühring's inability to see, as regards Marx's analysis of 'commodity value' in *Capital*, that Marx's 'sole preoccupation is the investigation of commodity value' as it appears 'in to-day's capitalist society (*in der heutigen kapitalistischen Gesellschaft*)'.[58] Again, independently of the question of the historical validity or otherwise of Engels's affirmation of the prevalence of the law of value over thousands of years, his position in *Anti-Dühring* is that commodity production is 'not at all the exclusive form of social production'. Such was for example the case of old Indian (village) communities and that of south Slavic family communities, where products were 'not transformed into commodities (at least within the community)'.[59] We should note that Engels's position on commodity production as given here – which basically conforms to Marx's – appears to contradict his own position, as stated later in his 1894 'Supplement' to *Capital* Volume III, in the passage we discussed above. Let us recall that in this 'Supplement' he held that over centuries before capitalism the 'law of value had prevailed'. Later we find similar ideas in several Marx readers, either followers or sympathisers of Marx. Thus Rosa Luxemburg speaks of 'simple commodity economy' preceding modern capitalism.[60] Similarly, even more precisely, Paul Sweezy refers to 'a society of simple commodity producers' or 'a simple commodity producing society like Adam Smith's hunters'.[61] Ronald Meek elaborates this idea. Totally misreading Marx, Meek says, without giving any supporting textual evidence, that 'Marx adopted this kind of approach', and then proceeds

> Postulating a society in which although commodity production and free competition were assumed to reign more or less supreme ... Marx was following and developing further a long and respectable tradition established by Smith and Ricardo. Marx's postulation of an abstract, pre-capitalist society based on simple commodity production was not essentially different from Adam Smith's postulation of an 'early and rude society inhabited by deer and fish hunters'.[62]

---

58   Engels 1962, p. 184.

59   Engels 1962, pp. 287–8.

60   Luxemburg 1972, p. 187.

61   Sweezy 1970, pp. 46, 47. In a different text Sweezy distinguishes between what he calls 'two forms of society' where 'Marxian value theory applies', the one under capitalism, the other where 'simple commodity production' prevails. See Sweezy 1949, p. 157.

62   Meek 1967, p. 98.

Finally, Oskar Lange – as already mentioned – holds, like Engels in his 'Supplement' much earlier, that the law of value applies not only under capitalism but also under 'commodity production of any kind'.[63]

Conclusion

To put the record straight, let us now go back to Marx and consider in light of his texts the two important propositions – just enunciated – which we have found in some of his eminent followers as seen above: the late Engels, Rosa Luxemburg, Paul Sweezy, Ronald Meek, and, in a pronounced way, Oskar Lange (though not all of these authors use exactly identical terms). The two propositions are, first, that the commodity not produced by capital existed and *prevailed* in society over a long period, and that, equivalently, the law of value applied under 'simple commodity production' over the same period. We have already argued with reference to Marx's text(s) that before capitalism a society could have commodity production, but that the latter's prevalence in such a society would be only limited, partial, and that it is only under capitalism that commodity production becomes the general form of production. In other words, a commodity society *is* a capitalist society. The second proposition concerning the 'law of value' requires some elucidation. Marx speaks of the 'law of value' for the first time in his 1847 'Anti-Proudhon'. There he affirms that the 'determination of value by labour time is for Ricardo the law of exchange value'.[64] The formulation is elaborated and made more precise by him twelve years later. In his later text Marx observes that, although Adam Smith determines commodity value by labour time, he shifts its reality back to 'pre-Adamite times'. As opposed to this

> Ricardo analyses clearly the determination of the value of the commodity by labour time. Ricardo's research is exclusively limited to the *magnitude of value* by labour time, in respect to which he has at least the presentiment that its operation depends on definite historical conditions. He says in effect that the determination of the magnitude of value by labour time is valid only for commodities which 'industry can multiply at will and whose production is governed by unlimited competition'. This means in

---

63   Lange 1945, p. 129.
64   Marx 1965b, p. 25.

effect that the law of value in its full development presupposes the society
of big industrial production and free competition, in other words, modern
bourgeois society.[65]

The important criticism of mixing up 'simple commodity production' and
'simple commodity society', specifically in Meek's work, has been very clearly
made by the Italian Marxist Gianfranco La Grassa, who underlines that in
Marx's 'theoretical system', while 'simple commodity production exists, there
is no place for simple commodity society'.[66]

The critics of Engels under consideration (with the exception of Shkredov),
particularly Backhaus and Reichelt, obsessed with Marx's alleged undermining of dialectic by his 'watering down' of *Capital* – where Engels also allegedly
played a role – by 'popularising' the book, have surprisingly neglected to mention the specific character of Marx's own dialectical method which, as Marx
stresses, is 'not only different from but also directly opposite to Hegel's'.[67] We
have elaborated this aspect at some length in the chapter on the 'commodity'.

Again, these critics of Engels's 'historicisation' – again with about the sole
exception of Shkredov – seem in particular not to have paid much attention
to the absolutely basic standpoint of Marx's critique of political economy,
namely, that all its categories are *historical* and not eternal. As Marx and Engels
wrote in their very first elaboration of their materialist conception of history:[68]
'We know only one science, the science of history'.[69] It would indeed seem
strange to conceive of a 'materialist conception of history' without history.
This would reduce materialist dialectic to the idealist 'dialectic of concepts', or
to the 'progress of the concept'.[70] Marx's 'uncovering of the *specifically histor-*

65   Marx 1980a, p. 136; 1970a, p. 60. Marx has slightly altered the wordings of Ricardo's text,
      which literally speaks of 'such commodities only as can be increased in quantity by
      the exertion of human industry, and on the production of which competition operates
      without restraint'. See Ricardo 1962, p. 13. Substantially, of course, Marx's slightly altered
      text conforms to Ricardo's original text as cited here. An important point needs to be
      stressed here. In light of Marx's statement as cited above, it is clear that Meek's statement
      (referred to earlier) attributing to Marx the 'postulation of a society in which although
      commodity production and free competition were assumed to reign more or less supreme
      the labourers still owned the whole produce of their labour', is a blatant misreading of
      Marx.

66   La Grassa 1975, p. 70. See also pp. 67–8.
67   Marx 1987a, p. 709; 1976a, p. 21; 1954, p. 29.
68   Frequently, and inexactly, called 'historical materialism'.
69   Marx and Engels 1845.
70   Marx and Engels 1845.

ical nature of all economic categories as they characterize capitalism' is of the 'greatest scientific significance', as Shkredov holds.[71] Indeed, in his 1847 polemic against Proudhon, Marx already reproaches Ricardo for applying the bourgeois concept of rent to the landed property of 'all epochs and of all countries'. This is the 'error of all economists who represent bourgeois production relations as eternal'.[72]

---

71   Shkredov 1987, p. 232; emphasis in original. For a masterly analysis of Marx's method in *Capital*, see Shkredov 1973.
72   Marx 1965b, p. 123.

CHAPTER 4

Commodity Production and Socialism in Marx's Followers

In this chapter we discuss how the followers of Marx (and Engels) did envisage the existence of money-commodity production in the society after capital. The time frame within which we deal with this problem begins with the immediate followers like Bebel and Kautsky and ends with the latter-day followers, particularly in Russia, until the lively discussion on the question of the validity of the law of value in 'soviet' socialism in the twenties and thirties reached a consensus in the late forties of the last century. Given the length of the period, we here somewhat arbitrarily select the followers on the basis of, in our view, the importance of their contributions.

The First Followers: August Bebel and Karl Kautsky

Bebel in his work does not devote a lot of space to economic questions concerning socialism. His remarks on them are short. In his famous work *Woman and Socialism* (1879) he held that the capitalist mode of production enabled the capitalist class to exploit and oppress the masses. 'Accordingly', he wrote, 'the most rapid and direct way to remove the insecurity of existence and degradation of the exploited classes would be to transform capitalist property into common or social property by general appropriation. The *production of commodities will be socialised*, it will become a production for and by society'.[1] Here is scope for some ambiguity. If commodities are 'socialised' it may mean society-wide commodity production, in which case we are dealing with a capitalist society, though the author seems to have meant a society without commodity production. However, in the same work, in a later chapter, Bebel states without any ambiguity that 'since in the new society there is no commodity to buy and sell, it produces uniquely life's needs which are used up. There is no money either', therewith the 'totality of trade also disappears'.[2] Very interestingly for such a non-commodity society, Bebel attaches great importance to statistics

---

1 Bebel 1879. Our emphasis.
2 Bebel 1879.

to take account of the number and the kind of means of labour, means of transportation and their efficiency. The same justification goes for the statistics concerning needs for different articles and objects for the subsistence of the society within a specific period. 'For all these things statistics play a primordial role'.[3]

Kautsky's views on commodity-money relations in the society after capital changed over the years.[4] In his discussion on the Erfurt Programme (1892) Kautsky holds that the 'abolition of the present system of production means substituting production for use for production for sale, and secondly, social or co-operative production for the satisfaction of the commonwealth'.[5] Kautsky holds that commodity production and private ownership of the means of production go together, and emphasises abolition of commodity production. This obviously means absence of commodity-money relations in socialism. However, coming to the question of personal distribution of consumer products in socialism, separated from the question of exchange of products, Kautsky does not affirm abolition of the wage system for the workers. He writes, 'All forms of today's wage payment – time wage, piece wage – are compatible with the nature of socialist society, naturally with corresponding changes'.[6]

Only a few years later (1902), in the second volume of his book *The Social Revolution* (in the chapter 'On the day after the revolution'), Kautsky poses the question: 'will there be wages in the new society? Shall we not have abolished wages and money?', and answers, 'the objection will be valid if social revolution proposed the abolition of money immediately'.[7] He adds that this would be impossible and that money is the simplest means that makes it possible in as complicated a mechanism as that of the modern production process, with its far-reaching division of labour, to secure circulation of products and distribution to the individual members of society. 'So long as money and prices of products are there, labour will also be paid in money'.[8] However, Kautsky asserts, 'As a matter of fact wages under a proletarian régime would be totally different from that under capitalism. The labourer will no longer be compelled to sell his labour power. In a society ruled by the proletariat, labour power will

---

3 Bebel 1879. Years later Otto Neurath underlined the necessity of such statistics for his non-monetary natural (in kind) economy. In the chapter on 'socialist accounting' in the present book, this theme is discussed in greater detail.

4 Over a period of about three decades (1892–1924).

5 Kautsky 1892.

6 Kautsky 1892.

7 Kautsky 1902.

8 Kautsky 1902.

cease to be a commodity whose price is determined by its cost of re-production, and its price would be independent of the supply-demand relation'.[9]

Years later, in his book *Labour Revolution* (1924), speaking of money, he poses the following question: 'will not money be abolished in a socialist society? Is this not implied by the idea of production for use?'[10] Then he responds by arguing that if the money is to be abolished, the only way to do so is to render superfluous the functions which money has hitherto performed, of which the most important is the facilitation of exchange and circulation of commodities.[11] He ridicules Otto Neurath for advancing the idea of a moneyless society after capital. He stresses, 'A socialist society would not be able to exist without a system of exchange of products'.[12]

Kautsky opines that without money, two kinds of economy are possible. First, the primitive economy, which would mean that the whole of the productive activity in the state would form a single factory under single central control. 'The ideal of such a condition is the prison or the barrack'.[13] Another form of socialism without money, Kautsky continues, is 'the Leninite interpretation of what Marx described as the second phase of communism: each to produce on one's own accord as much as one can, the productivity of labour being so high

---

9   Kautsky 1902. Let us stress that this argument concerning the existence of a wage system without capital(ism), advanced by Kautsky, will be taken over and perpetuated by later 'Marxians' in their notion of 'socialism', which becomes a régime of money-commodity relations together with wage labour. Kautsky's expression 'a society ruled by the proletariat' is not without ambiguities. It cannot be socialism/communism in the sense of Marx, since socialism/communism in the latter sense has no proletariat in the absence of capitalists. It is a classless society. Kautsky's phrase on proletarian rule could at best mean the period of revolutionary transformation between capitalism and socialism. Indeed, Carl Landauer, in his important work on *European Socialism*, observes that 'as the name of his [Kautsky's] pamphlet indicates, Kautsky was not concerned with the final form of socialist society, but with the transitional regime that would be established in the first years after the decisive victory of the Social Democratic party'. See Landauer 1959, p. 1609.

10   Kautsky 1924.

11   In the same 1924 book, Kautsky fortifies his argument for maintaining money by his reference to the catastrophic economic situation created by the experience of 'war communism' under the Bolsheviks. He wants a stable currency and not depreciation by inflation as under the Bolsheviks.

12   Kautsky 1924. We should remind readers that in Marx's vision of socialism, conceived as a 'co-operative society based on common ownership of the means of production ... the producers do not exchange their products'. See the *Gothacritique*, in Marx and Engels 1970, p. 310.

13   Kautsky 1924.

that everyone may be trusted to take what one needs'.[14] Kautsky concludes that such a society would not require money, but that 'the socialism with which we are concerned to-day will unfortunately not have this enviable freedom and abundance at its disposal and will therefore not be able to do without money'.[15]

Speaking of 'socialist money', Kautsky writes that money in socialism must be distinguished from money in capitalism, inasmuch as 'means of production in socialism are all social property, so that all conditions will be lacking for transforming the money into capital'.[16] However, as the measure of value and the means of circulation of products, money will continue to exist in social-ism 'until the dawn of that blessed second phase of communism which we do not know yet whether that will ever be more than pious wish, similar to the Millennial Kingdom'.[17]

Marxians after Kautsky

In the following we discuss, selectively, the essential ideas of followers of Marx and Engels, post-Kautsky, on their position on the question of the rela-tion between socialism and the commodity-money relation (which implies the question of wage labour). Among these followers, we treat separately the Bolsheviks and those who were not Bolsheviks. Again, in the present context, by Bolsheviks we mean those who upheld the Bolshevik régime as its stake-holders.

Non-Bolsheviks: Korsch, Lukács, Rühle, Hilferding

Karl Korsch, a council communist and a critic of Lenin, nevertheless seems in his discussion of the society after capital to be strongly influenced by what we consider to be Lenin's questionable reading of Marx's *Gothacritique* in his *State and Revolution*,[18] and appears not to accept any qualitative difference between what Marx considers to be the 'revolutionary transformation period' between capitalism and socialism (communism) and the early phase of social-ism/communism regarding *social relations of production*. Thus, in his view, in the first phase of the communist society that has just come out of the prolet-arian revolution and where a more or less large part of the 'economic structure

---

14   Kautsky 1924.
15   Kautsky 1924.
16   Kautsky 1924.
17   Kautsky 1924.
18   This important question is analysed in another chapter of the present book.

is still based on to-day's *commodity production*', the antagonism of classes and class struggle continue, 'and takes its sharpest political form under the dictatorship of the proletariat'.[19] Contrariwise, in the developed communist society, commodity, value, and money as well as the state will cease to exist, along with all the class oppositions and class struggles.[20]

In his turn Lukács, calling 'socialism' the 'first transitional phase', affirms that Marx establishes here that the 'structure of *commodity* exchange, despite all other fundamental changes, will function in this phase in the same way as in capitalism'.[21] He adds that it is only at a higher phase that the structure of commodity exchange, the effectiveness of the law of value for the individuals as consumers, ceases. 'It is evident of course that in production itself, socially necessary labour time and hence the law of value as regulator of production must remain unchanged in their validity with the growth of the productive forces'.[22] Here again, this author's position, essentially like Korsch's, is a variation on Lenin's theme – Lenin's questionable interpretation of Marx's *Gotha-critique*.

Otto Rühle advanced his arguments on commodity production and socialism against the points of view of Max Weber and, particularly, Ludwig von Mises, that there could be no rational economic calculation in a society such as socialism where there was no market due to the absence of individual private ownership in the means of production.[23] 'In the first period of the socialist economy', opines Rühle, 'the money-form will probably remain. In Russia the wage is paid in money'.[24] The author then tries to refute Weber and Mises:

---

19   Korsch 1967, p. 142. Emphasis added.
20   See Korsch 1967, pp. 142–3. Any close reader of Marx's discussion of society after capital will find that Korsch is mixing up the early phase of socialism with the revolutionary transformation period under the proletarian rule.
21   Lukács 1978, p. 165. Emphasis added.
22   Lukács 1978, p. 166.
23   We discuss extensively the question of the market in relation to socialism, including Mises' position on the question, in the chapter on 'market socialism' in the present book.
24   Rühle 1971, p. 206. It should be noted that the author considers the Russia of the period (circa late 1920s) to be socialist. However, this was not the abiding position of the author. One of the most expressive and dominant positions of the author on the post-1917 'soviet' Russian régime we find in his work of 1924, 'From the bourgeois to the proletarian revolution', where he affirms that though the Russian revolution appeared with the ambition of a social and proletarian revolution it was basically a retarded and miscarried bourgeois revolution (*verspätete und verunglückte bürgerliche Revolution*) (p. 1).

> The market is not abolished nor destroyed (in socialist economy). Only the free market, the market in the capitalist sense, disappears. The market's function has changed. The market is socialistically modernised and is built as the economy of need. This Weber and Mises have not recognised. The supposition that in the socialist economy there is no market any more is an error ... Price, wage, money, market, all the economic categories and functions change and receive a new meaning.[25]

The features of a post-capitalist (socialist) society as we see in this paragraph from Rühle seem, very interestingly, not to be basically different from those which we found above in Kautsky's idea of a socialist society, which Rühle, however, qualifies as 'primitive, crude, bureaucratic State socialism', and continues, 'the old features remain: commodity, market, labour power as a commodity, price formation, wage system, money, and State socialism appears as a reformed and modernised capitalism, promoted upwards (*emporgehoben*) at a higher level of history, a State of the future of lesser evil'.[26]

Now Hilferding. In his famous work *Finance capital* (1910), the relation between commodity production and socialism is a secondary issue, but he briefly touches on this issue just to show that in contrast to the capitalist society where commodity production requiring money prevails, there could be an alternative society of a very different kind which requires neither commodity nor money. (And, let us add *en passant*, without the commodity-money relation, there can be no wage labour either). Most readers of this book neglect Hilferding's very important remarks on this question. Thus, right in the opening chapter, while analysing the necessity of money, he starts with the question of the type of society which requires money for its transactions, that is, a commodity society, as opposed to the type which does not, that is, a socialist society, creating organs which, as the representatives of social consciousness, fix the extent and the method of production, and, without any commodity exchange, distribute the products of society among its members.

> Given the material and human-made conditions of production, all decisions on method, place, quantity and available tools involved in the production of new goods are made by the national commissars of socialist society who can have the knowledge of requirements of their society by means of comprehensive statistics of production and consumption.

---

25   Rühle 1971, pp. 206–7.
26   Rühle 1971, pp. 80–1.

> They can thus design, with conscious foresight, the whole economic life
> of the community in accordance with the requirements of the members
> of society.[27]

Hilferding then adds, 'their relations of production are directly shown as social
relations, and economic relations between individuals can be seen as determined by the social order rather than by private wishes; relations of production
are accepted as those which are established as desired by the whole community'.[28] The readers of Marx will see here that what Hilferding, unlike the
authors we have treated so far, says about society after capital fairly closely follows Marx's idea of the 'Union of free individuals', sometimes even paraphrasing Marx's text. He does not mix up – unlike some of the authors considered
above – socialism with the transitional phase between capitalism and socialism.

   Hilferding of course raises the question of the status of exchange relations in
socialism, and answers that 'exchange may take place also in socialism', but 'that
would be a type of exchange occurring *only after the products have already been
distributed according to society's desired norm*. It would have no more importance than does the exchange of dolls among children in a nursery'.[29] According
to Hilferding exchange becomes a distinct social force when it supplies the
integrating factor in a society in which private ownership and division of labour
have dissociated individuals and, at the same time, made them interdepend-
ent. 'The outcome of achieving all possible acts of exchange in such a society
is what would have been accomplished in a *communist*, consciously planned,
society by the planning authorities – namely, what is produced, how much and
by whom, in short, exchange must allocate among the producers of commodities what would be allocated to the members of a *socialist society* by authorities
who consciously regulate production, plan the labour process etc'.[30]

Bolsheviks on Socialism and Commodity Production
One common assumption underlying the discussion in this section, particularly among the Bolsheviks, was that there had been a *socialist* revolution in
their country – equated to the seizure of political power by the Bolsheviks (in

---

27   Hilferding 1968, p. 24.
28   Hilferding 1968, p. 24.
29   Hilferding 1968, p. 25. Emphasis added.
30   Hilferding 1968, p. 26. Emphasis added. It should be noted here that Hilferding makes
      no distinction between communism and socialism. Here, again, he follows Marx (and
      Engels).

the name of the proletariat) – and that, *in this sense*, the related discussion concerned the economic problems of a so-called 'post-revolutionary' Russia, basically the Russia of the (transition) period between capitalism and communism.

Lenin sets the tone and prepares the ground for the discussion on the character of the economy of the new régime. In his 1919 article 'Economics and Politics in the Era of the Dictatorship of the Proletariat', Lenin qualifies the period as the 'transition period between capitalism and communism', partaking of the features of both, and observes that the basic forms of social economy are capitalism, petty commodity production, and communism; the basic forces are 'the bourgeoisie, petty bourgeoisie (peasantry in particular) and the proletariat'.[31] Making his formulation sharper, Lenin adds, 'The economic system of Russia in the epoch of the dictatorship of the proletariat, represents the struggle of labour united on communist principles and making its first steps the struggle against petty commodity production and against capitalism which still persists'.[32] Lenin's final formulation of the transitional features of the Russian economy we find in his 1921 work 'The Tax in Kind'. There he enumerates five elements: natural peasant farming, small commodity production, private capitalism, state capitalism, socialism.[33]

Apart from his preoccupation with the economy of the transition period, Lenin's discussion of the economic questions of socialism as a *mode of production* does not amount to much. Within this short range, however, Lenin makes clear that as regards exchange relations in socialism, commodity production including money is excluded. The end of capitalism, according to him, would signify the suppression of commodity production, and the new society would be characterised by organised, state-wide distribution of 'products' replacing commerce.[34] Henceforth all the discussions on the Russian economy would take place broadly within this Leninist economic framework. In what follows we, rather arbitrarily, analyse what we consider to be the most significant contributions on the question. The most important followers of Lenin in this regard are, we believe, Nikolai Bukharin and Yevgeni Preobrazhensky. In the 1920 work *ABC of Communism*, drawn up jointly by these two authors with a view to explaining the recently adopted Party Programme, the central categories are directly derived from Lenin, or, rather, from the way Lenin had read Marx's *Gothacritique*. From this perspective they mean by socialism

---

31   Lenin 1971a, p. 290; 1982c, p. 221.
32   Lenin 1971a, p. 290; 1982, p. 221.
33   See Lenin 1971b, p. 590; 1982f, p. 531.
34   See Lenin 1962b, p. 151.

not what Marx had conceived it to be, that is, a new society (alternatively and equivalently called 'communism' by Marx) emerging after the disappearance of capital, but rather the transitional régime between capitalism and communism whose first phase is called socialism.[35]

With the existence of such a distinction between communism and socialism in their mind(s), the two authors hold that while there would be no money in communism, 'a very different state of affairs prevails in socialist society which is an intermediate stage between capitalism and communism where money is needed, for it has a part to play in the commodity economy. In socialist society a commodity economy will to some extent persist'.[36]

At about the same time (1920), Bukharin published his *Economics of the Transformation Period*. Written during the period of the civil war and under the influence of the Party Programme, the book deals with the organisation of production in an economy transitional between capitalism and communism.[37] His point of departure is 'state capitalism' reached by capitalism in its latter-day period or 'organised' phase, which is supposed to have eliminated the market with its free competition along with anarchy of production. He opines that modern capitalism is characterised by state capitalist trusts and finance capital. 'Finance capital has abolished the anarchy of production in the big capitalist countries and created a new type of production relation in which the unorganised commodity-capitalist has been transformed into a finance capitalist organisation'.[38]

Dealing with the transition period which prepares the society for communism, Bukharin underlines the changes in the economic categories of capitalism. Under the state power of the proletariat and with nationalisation of production, the process of producing surplus value as the specific category of

---

35   We go into this whole question of conceptual clarification in the chapter on Socialism.
36   Bukharin and Preobrazhensky 1967, pp. 333–4.
37   In what follows we use two versions of the same book, the Russian of 1920, and the German of 1921. Of the eleven chapters of the book, eight chapters of the Russian version are accessible to us (published in 1989), whereas we have all eleven chapters of the German version available to us (published in 1970). So the references relating to the first three chapters indicate the German version of 1970, the rest all relate to the Russian of 1989.
38   Bukharin 1970, pp. 9, 12. Bukharin's inversion of the materialist method is clearly seen in his characterisation of state capitalism as a new type of production relation. He does not show in what way this new phenomenon changes the relation between the immediate producers and the conditions of production – which *is* the production relation in a society. The question is, do the immediate producers continue to remain wage/salaried labourers under the new dispensation? If they do then there is no change in the (social) relations of production.

bourgeois society disappears with the dialectical transformation of bourgeois dictatorship into proletarian dictatorship. In the same way, the production of surplus value is changed into the production of surplus product, which serves as the reproduction fund for enlarged reproduction. 'There occurs the trans- formation of the process of producing surplus value into a process of planned satisfaction of social needs'.[39]

Calling the proletarian dictatorship a 'system of socialist dictatorship' and, alternatively, 'state socialism', Bukharin affirms that it is the 'dialectical nega- tion of state capitalism', where production relations change radically, since the foundation of all capitalist order, the ownership-relations, 'become different'.[40] The question which Bukharin raises is whether the method and the theoretical categories which Marx made use of to investigate capital's laws of motion are relevant now, at the time of capital's breakdown and the construction of the foundation of the new society. Now some of the basic categories of capitalism are commodity, value, price and wage. Bukharin underlines that in the trans- ition period between capitalism and communism these categories 'exist and do not exist in reality. They exist as if they do not exist'.[41]

Bukharin affirms that value emerges when there is regular commodity pro- duction. Here there is no accidental, but regular anarchic connections com- pelled by exchange. It follows that value as the capitalist commodity system in its equilibrium is least usable in the transformation period, where commodity production to a large extent disappears and where equilibrium is wanting.

> Wage becomes (simply) a phenomenal magnitude without any content. In so far as the working class is the ruling class, wage labour disappears; in socialised production there is no wage labour. In so far as there is no wage labour, there is no wage as the price of labour power for the capitalist to pay for. What remains of the wage is simply the outer cover – the money form.[42]

Within a few years – after the adoption by the régime of the New Economic Policy – Bukharin acknowledges in a 1925 report, 'On the New Economic Policy and our tasks', his 'mistake' in believing earlier in the abolition of the market, the installation of a planned economy, and the elimination of the capitalist

---

39   Bukharin 1989, p. 106.
40   Bukharin 1989, p. 138. Here again Bukharin stands the materialist method on its head. Soci- ety's production relation is made to follow from its political and juridical edifice.
41   Bukharin 1989, p. 151.
42   Bukharin 1989, p. 159.

mode of production immediately after the establishment of proletarian rule. On the contrary, Bukharin now opines that 'market relations, money, the stock exchange, banks play a very big role' in the transitional economy.[43] He also speaks of the transitional economy's relative lack of plan and asserts the possibility of a planned economy only for a 'developed socialist society'.[44] Three years later, in his 1928 'Notes of an economist', Bukharin, contrary to his earlier negative position on the relevance of the Marxian economic categories for the transitional period, holds that the reproduction schemes of *Capital* Volume II are relevant for the dynamic equilibrium of the transitional economy.[45]

In his last work on socialism, dated 1933, the fiftieth anniversary of Marx's demise – 'Marx's Teaching and its Historical Significance' – a text apparently free from any immediate relation with actual reality – the author clearly distinguishes between socialism and the transition period but does not add much that is new to the basic Leninist framework (as opposed to Marx's) concerning the nature of society after capital.[46]

We now turn to Preobrazhensky's principal theoretical work, *The New Economics* (1926). The period in which this treatise was written was very different from the one in which Bukharin's work on the transition was undertaken. Whereas Bukharin's book was written during the period of so-called 'War Communism', which had clearly marked it, Preobrazhensky's was penned during the period of the 'New Economic Policy'. Unlike Bukharin's book discussed above, this book does not have as its subject the 'transition period' or socialism as such. According to its author the book was about the 'economic theory of the USSR'.[47] According to the author, the economy of the USSR is a combination of the 'law of value and the principle of planning whose basic tendencies take the form of primitive socialist accumulation'.[48] Preobrazhensky seems to have in mind Marx's famous discussion of 'primitive accumulation' of capital mainly through expropriation of the peasantry and through colonial exploitation, providing means for industrial development in the metropolitan lands. In the case of the USSR Preobrazhensky distinguishes between socialist accumulation and primitive socialist accumulation. The first is defined by 'addition

43   Bukharin 1988, p. 128.
44   Bukharin 1988, p. 396.
45   Bukharin 1988, pp. 395–6.
46   In a different chapter of this book we deal with the basic difference between these two approaches to the post-capitalist society, where the emancipatory character of the new society, a society of free, associated individuals as Marx envisaged it, is emphasised.
47   Preobrazhensky 1926, p. 20.
48   Preobrazhensky 1926, pp. 62–3.

to the means of production in use by the surplus product created within the developed socialist economy, the process serving enlarged reproduction, while the second signifies accumulation of material wealth in the hands of the state from the sources external to the state sector'.[49] In the country's 'relations of production two principles intermix, the commodity principle and the socialist principle, resulting in the struggle between two contending forces'.[50] Seen as a whole, the economic system of the USSR is a system of socialist-commodity economy. 'The fact that the USSR economy constitutes an example without precedent, in economic history, of the co-existence of two distinct and antagonist systems by nature, with two different types of regulation, makes this economy an arena not only of struggle, but also of a certain equilibrium'.[51]

Following Preobrazhensky the law of value operates spontaneously as a regulator of production and distribution in an unorganised economy. In a backward transitional economy of the USSR type, with a low level of productive forces and the majority of the population engaged in backward agriculture, the simple commodity sector remains extensive, within which the law of value operates as the dominant regulator. On the other hand, within the organised state sector of the economy, where the state is both monopoly producer and the unique purchaser of its own products, there is an atrophy in the operation of the law of value.

Preobrazhensky considers the law of primitive socialist accumulation to have 'universal significance'. In its struggle against the law of value this law tries progressively to evict the commodity sector in favour of the state or socialist sector over the whole economy. 'This accumulation must play a role of colossal importance in a backward agricultural economy (such as the USSR) in accelerating, to an immense degree, the arrival of the moment where the state economy will start the process of reedification and where this economy will finally receive the greatest economic supremacy'.[52] According to the author the 'period of primitive socialist accumulation is not only a period of amassing the material resources of the new economy in view of its final victory over the capitalist form, but also a period of direct struggle of the state economy with the private economy; one of the most interesting questions of soviet economic

---

49   Preobrazhensky 1926, pp. 93–4. Preobrazhensky reminds readers here that the expression 'primitive socialist accumulation' belongs to his 'comrade Smirnov'. This expression was already used by Bukharin in the same sense in his work on the transformation period, where also Smirnov is mentioned as its author. See Bukharin 1989, pp. 133–4.

50   Preobrazhensky 1926, p. 71.

51   Preobrazhensky 1926, p. 154.

52   Preobrazhensky 1926, p. 94.

theory is to know under what concrete forms will be produced the eviction of all the pre-socialist forms by the historically superior socialist economy'.[53] The sources of the primitive socialist accumulation lie in the pre-socialist part of the economy, such as the alienation of the surplus product of the independent artisans and peasants as well as the surplus value of the remaining capitalist sector of the economy. 'During the primitive socialist accumulation the state economy cannot avoid the alienation of a part of the surplus product of the rural area and of the artisans as well as deductions from the capitalist accumulation for the gain of the socialist accumulation'.[54] A concrete policy of effecting this unequal exchange would involve charging high prices for industrial products in exchange for low prices for agricultural products. In other words, the principal mechanism of the exploitation of the pre-socialist forms by the state is the transfer of surplus product from agriculture to the nationalised industry through non-equivalent exchange, that is, exchange in value form of a greater quantity of labour from agriculture against a lesser quantity of labour from industry. As a distinguished historian of the USSR economy, discussing Preobrazhensky's position on unequal exchange, has succinctly put it, 'the state should use its position as the supplier of industrial products to pump resources out of the private sector and so finance the industrial investment of the state sector; this is the gist of the conflict between the law of value and the principle of primitive socialist accumulation'.[55]

Like Bukharin before him, Preobrazhensky too denies the relevance of Marx's economic categories for the socialist-commodity economy of the USSR, since, according to him, those categories are valid only for the capitalist-commodity economy. 'The market relations within the state sector do not arise from the laws inherent to the structure of the state economy. The market relations are purely formal here, arising from its connections with the private sector'.[56] Again, 'the category of price plays in the state sector only a purely formal role'.[57]

Among those economists who opposed Preobrazhensky's theory, two eminent economists, I.A. Lapidus and K. Ostrovitianov, stand out. They expressed their ideas towards the end of the 1920s in a text on political economy in

53   Preobrazhensky 1926, p. 138. Let us note that, following the Bolshevik tradition, Preobrazhensky, like Bukharin, equates the state sector with the socialist sector. In other words they are not following Marx's libertarian position on socialism – a classless society which has no state.
54   Preobrazhensky 1926, p. 99.
55   Nove 1982, p. 126.
56   Preobrazhensky 1926, p. 160.
57   Preobrazhensky 1926, p. 182.

relation to the soviet economy. One of their principal concerns was, as with Preobrazhensky, the question of the regulator of the soviet economy during the transition from capitalism to socialism. 'With the soviet economy uniting two principles, plan and spontaneity, there are two regulators, the rational regulator for the socialist sector of the economy and the spontaneous regulator – the law of value – for the rural sector, and in a general way, the sector of private property. These two mutually opposing principles are in combat, and one will eliminate the other'.[58] Here we see not much difference with the position of Preobrazhensky. However, Lapidus and Ostrovitianov now stress the importance for every society of having a certain equilibrium between production and consumption and underline the necessity for every society of keeping a certain proportion in the matter of allocation of labour in the different branches of production. They call it the law of proportionality of labour expenditure, which exercises its regulatory action by the law of value and plan. The rational direction of the economy uses the law of value as an instrument to serve the economy's interest. Speaking of the Marxian categories of capitalism the two authors hold, broadly in common with Bukharin and Preobrazhensky, that the 'production relations of the two sectors – state socialist sector and the peasant sector – are not, really, capitalist relations, and that the categories of the capitalist economy do not apply here, even though their outward forms are maintained'.[59] In the same way, the peasants must contribute to the accumulation fund of the socialist sector, and the 'appropriation of a part of the cultivator's income by the state cannot be considered as an act of exploitation. Hence the relations established between the socialist and the peasant sectors of the soviet economy cannot be assimilated to capitalist relations'.[60] The thought of the two authors so far considered does not show any real difference with the thought of Preobrazhensky discussed earlier. However, on the specific question of how to extract surplus from the non-state/socialist sector for the latter sector, in other words, on the operation of Preobrazhensky's 'primitive socialist accumulation', Lapidus and Ostrovitianov have important differences with the latter, inasmuch as in their view Preobrazhensky's ideas go against Lenin's idea of co-operation with the peasantry. 'Preobrazhensky, proceeding from the theory of primitive socialist accumulation, refuses to consider co-operation as the road to development of agriculture towards socialism'.[61] They conclude, 'If one considers the union between socialist industry and small agriculture, between

58   Lapidus and Ostrovitianov 1929, p. 409.
59   Lapidus and Ostrovitianov 1929, p. 410.
60   Lapidus and Ostrovitianov 1929, p. 412.
61   Lapidus and Ostrovitianov 1929, p. 448.

the proletariat and the peasantry which it leads, if one recognises the possibility and necessity of transforming small agriculture into large-scale socialist
agriculture, the analogy of primitive accumulation must be categorically and
resolutely abandoned, and this theory has to be recognised as mistaken'.[62]

In sum, at the close of NEP there seems to be a general consensus among the
soviet economists that, during the transition period, commodity categories like
value, price and market continue to subsist in the socialist sector, but that their
content is different from that in capitalism. However, what specific kind of production relations characterise the new régime does not come out clearly from
the discussion. It took some time before things began to move, with the publication of an unsigned article in the party journal *Under the Banner of Marxism*
in 1943, dealing with the 'Teaching of Economics in the Soviet Union'.[63]

Beginning in 1936, the régime was considered to have completed the phase
of 'transition to socialism' and was proclaimed as 'socialist' on the basis of the
predominance of state and cooperative ownership of the means of production
following the fulfilment of the Second Five Year Plan (1933–7).

The 1943 text – the work of a group of economists – analyses different
aspects of the appropriate 'political economy of soviet socialism'. We here try
to summarise the basic ideas of this longish text. Moreover, given our pre-
occupations, our discussion will be confined basically to what it says on the
value-commodity relation. The text's analysis offers a series of criticisms of the
earlier ways of teaching the subject and offers corresponding rectifications.

Regarding value-commodity relation, 'one must keep in mind that commodity production, exchange and money precede the appearance of capitalism by
thousands of years'.[64] In support of this argument the text refers to Engels's
well-known observation on the pre-capitalist existence of the law of value.[65]
When teaching political economy, it is necessary to consider such categories as
the commodity and money, not only in the section devoted to capitalism but
also in the preceding parts of the course.

The text recalls that following the 1936 Constitution of the USSR, the 'economic basis of the USSR is the socialist economic system and the socialist
property in the tools and means of production, established through the liquida-

---

62   Lapidus and Ostrovitianov 1929, p. 448. At about the same time (1928), Bukharin had
       defended the peasant-worker alliance and the acceleration of exchange between urban
       and rural areas. See Bukharin 1988, pp. 391–418.
63   The article was translated by Raya Dunayevskaya in the *American Economic Review* 1944,
       September issue, pp. 501–29.
64   Teaching 1943, p. 509.
65   Teaching 1943, p. 519.

tion of the capitalist economic system, the abolition of exploitation of (hu)man by (hu)man'.[66] The text considers that it is necessary first of all to 'elucidate the *character of the economic laws of socialism*, the key to this elucidation being the rich experience in the practice of socialist construction'.[67] The fundamental mistake in the past has been the thought that if under capitalism certain laws or categories existed, then in the soviet system these were necessarily absent; in fact, the opposite was true. Such a faulty approach made it 'essentially impossible to understand the real relations of the soviet economic system ... to deny the existence of economic laws under socialism is to slip into the most vulgar voluntarism'.[68]

These economic laws of socialism, in their character, content and method of action, are fundamentally different from the economic laws of capitalism. Whereas 'socialist society cannot develop outside of the planned administration of the national economy, that socialism and planning are indissoluble, under capitalism planned administration of the national economy is unrealizable, since the system is based on private property in the means of production'.[69]

Under socialism, distribution according to labour prevails. The guiding principle of social life under socialism is: from each according to his ability, to each according to his labour. As regards the laws and categories of capitalism, the incorrect idea had taken root that these laws and categories had no place under socialism. Particularly this concerns the *law of value*. Now the fact of the matter is that 'after the abolition of capitalism socialist society subordinates the law of value, and consciously makes use of its mechanisms – money, trade, price – in the interests of socialism'.[70] It would of course be an absurd approach to presume that Marx and Engels could foresee the concrete way to employ the law of value in the interests of socialism. On the basis of the practice of soviet socialism 'these ways were generalised by the genius of comrade Stalin, who showed how the soviet state puts at the service of socialism such instruments as money, banks, trade etc ... the political economy of socialism (was) created by comrade Stalin'.[71]

The labour of citizens of a socialist society is not qualitatively uniform. There exist differences between skilled and unskilled labour and between labour of

---

66   Teaching 1943, p. 512.
67   Teaching 1943, p. 512. Emphasis in text.
68   Teaching 1943, p. 514.
69   Teaching 1943, p. 518.
70   Teaching 1943, p. 519.
71   Teaching 1943, p. 521.

various degrees of skill. As a result of this, the measure of labour and measure of consumption in socialism can be calculated only on the basis of the law
of value. The labour of members of a socialist society produces commodities,
and they reach the consumer through trade helped by money.[72] The errors of
the former teaching, in denying the operation of the law of value in socialist
society, created 'insurmountable difficulties in explaining the existence under
socialism of such categories as money, banks, credit'.[73]

However, the commodity which is the product of socialist production no
longer contains the contradictions of the commodity production of the earlier
régime, the contradictions which, in their further development, lead to the
rise of capitalist exploitation. On the contrary, 'the law of value functions in
a transformed manner ... The law of value will be overcome only in the highly
developed stage of communism'.[74] The law of value in a socialist society, briefly
stated in this text, would be elaborated only about a decade later, in 1952, in
Stalin's work *Economic Problems of Socialism in the USSR*, and also in the 1954
collective work *Politicheskaya Ekonomia, Uchebnik* (*Textbook of political economy*).[75]

On the question of the operation of the law of value in socialism – our
main concern – there is (naturally) no difference between the two works. In
fact Stalin begins his discourse as a kind of response to the ongoing questions
arising from the draft of the *Uchebnik*.

The general affirmation of the operation of the law of value in socialism is
something that the 'Textbook' shares entirely with the 1943 work we discussed
above. But the reasons thereof are elaborated in the 1954 text.

Right at the beginning of his discourse Stalin stresses the objective character of the laws of economic development under socialism, created independently of the human will. Unlike the laws of natural sciences, these laws are
not eternal, existing during a certain historical period and yielding place to
other laws.[76] As the 'Textbook' puts it – in harmony with Stalin's presentation – 'the necessity of commodity production under socialism arises from
the presence of two basic forms of ownership of socialist production – the
state form and the kolkhoz form. In the state enterprises the means of production and the products are the property of the whole people, whereas in the
kolkhoz the means of production and their products belong to a group, they

---

72   Teaching 1943, p. 522.
73   Teaching 1943, p. 523.
74   Teaching 1943, pp. 525–7.
75   We will cite indifferently this work and Stalin's discourse of 1952.
76   Stalin 1952.

are the kolkhoz-cooperative property'.[77] 'Thanks to the means of production being state property and collective-cooperative property, the wage system and exploitation of human by human have been liquidated, and commodity production here cannot be transformed into capitalist production'.[78]

'All that is produced and realised as commodity under socialism has use value created by concrete labour and value created by abstract labour'.[79] In other words, under socialism the commodity has a double character determined by the double character of labour. Since under socialism there is no private property in the means of production, labour also is not private but is directly social. Society plans the production process and distributes labour among the different branches of production and different units of production. That is why 'commodity fetishism is surmounted, and social relations between humans do not take the deceptive appearance of relations between things'.[80]

Since under socialism commodity production and commodity circulation exist, the law of value continues to play a role. The 'Textbook' emphasises the role of money under socialism. 'Since in the socialist society commodity production and commodity circulation exist, money necessarily exists'.[81] It also serves as means of payment and means of accumulation.

Beginning with the second edition (1955) of the *Uchebnik*, its successive editions adopted positions which increased the field of action of the law of value by including within it transactions between the units of production of the means of production themselves, excluded by Stalin in his 1952 presentation.[82] In a collective work on the political economy of socialism published about a decade before the total evaporation of 'soviet socialism', the authors mention the fact that the existence of commodity production in socialism was explained earlier by the existence of two forms of socialist property. Then they add that the 'existence of commodity relations under socialism is not fully explained by the existence of two forms of socialist property; the actual conditions of building socialism call for broad utilisation of commodity relations not only in the sphere of the interrelations of two broad production sectors of socialist society but also within the leading public sector. In recent years commodity relations

---

77   *Uchebnik* 1954, p. 440.
78   *Uchebnik* 1954, p. 441.
79   *Uchebnik* 1954, p. 442.
80   *Uchebnik* 1954, p. 443.
81   *Uchebnik* 1954, p. 449.
82   Henri Chambre very interestingly traces the evolution of this tendency in the successive editions of the 'Textbook'. See Chambre 1974.

have also become common in the co-operative-collective farm sector'.[83] Out-side the USSR, Charles Bettelheim, to his credit, was one of the first – if not the first – to show the falsity of Stalin's oversimplified juridical argument of the existence of commodity production wholly on the basis of ownership of the means of production. After raising the issue of the real existence of commodity relations *within* the state sector of the economy, he asked why 'within the state sector products were *bought* and *sold*, and not simply distributed between the state-owned enterprises, and why did the state provide its own enterprises with the monetary and financial means to enable them to purchase the means of production which they required'.[84]

The publication of the text 'Teaching of Economics in the Soviet Union' in English translation in the American journal mentioned above gave rise to a lively debate in the pages of the *New York Times* and particularly in the *American Economic Review* (1944–5), with a number of participants besides Dunayevskaya, the translator: Oskar Lange, Leo Rogin and Paul Baran, to name the most eminent among them. In the debate virtually Dunayevskaya alone, basing herself on Marx's own writings, attacked the text as 'a new revision of Marxian Economics',[85] inasmuch as the text asserted the existence of the law of value in socialism, which in her view was quite foreign to Marx's idea of social-ism. Of the rest, arguing against Dunayevskaya, the most vocal was Lange, who was out to show, against Dunayevskaya's attempt to denigrate the 'Teaching' in the name of Marx, the textual fidelity to Marx of the authors of the 'Teaching'. On the basis of an astonishingly superficial reading of Marx's writings, Lange argued that the text of 'Teaching' was correctly following Marx on the question of the law of value in socialism. He wrote, 'A careful study of Marx's writings establishes clearly that he held the view that the theory of value applied to a socialist economy'.[86] He then referred to the final section of the first chapter of *Capital* Volume I, where in one of the subsections Marx speaks of the 'Union of Free Individuals' as an alternative to the existing society. There Marx discusses the role of labour time both in maintaining the proportion between different kinds of work and as a measure of the share of common labour borne by each individual and the share of the total product destined for individual consump-tion. For Lange this example of the role of labour time as a quantity seemed to belong to the Marxian labour theory of value.

---

83   Kozlov (ed.) 1977, p. 120.

84   Bettelheim 1970, p. 49. Emphasis in text.

85   Dunayevskaya 1944, p. 531.

86   Lange 1945, p. 128.

First of all: The irony here is that this Union of Free Individuals Marx posits first of all under the subsection of 'fetishism of commodities', signifying the domination of product (as commodity) over the producer, which negates the existence of free individuals.[87] Secondly, the explicit context of this discussion is that commodity production is presented here as a particular social form of production by the side of other social forms of production: 'The moment we envisage other (social) forms of production we see the immediate disappearance of all this mysticism which obscures the products of labour in the modern period'.[88] Then Marx proceeds to discuss a few of the 'other forms of production', one of which is precisely the form of 'the union of free individuals' mentioned above. Lange seems not to be able to grasp that labour as magnitude alone does not constitute value, which, Marx affirms, has three dimensions: magnitude, substance, and form. One important critique of classical political economy by Marx is precisely that 'it is value as magnitude which absorbs its attention'.[89]

In our view, on a purely *theoretical* plane, Dunayevskaya was completely right as far as the fidelity with Marx's own texts was concerned. The soviet discussants on the socialist economy had indeed stood Marx completely on his head. However, the fact of the matter is that like most of the observers of the soviet scene, internal and external, she too started with the unstated assumption that the Bolsheviks were building a socialist society in Russia after having liquidated *grosso modo* the capitalist mode of production in the land. This is seen openly affirmed later in her other texts. There she affirmed her support for the 'practice of the 1917 Revolution', giving rise to the 'first workers' state'.[90] In another text she spoke of the 'Russian Revolution of 1917' as the 'greatest of all proletarian revolutions'.[91] This was the *illusion* of the epoch. The *ground reality* was of course very different. In a much neglected insightful paper, a little known East European economist, A.M. Vacić, analysing the reality of the European (including soviet) socialism in light of Marx's theoretical position on socialism and commodity production, observed that 'In spite of the organised economic, political, and sometimes even physical pressure, commodity production maintained itself, it spread, renewed itself, and extended to many fields. It may be said of several socialist countries, that their economies are more of a commod-

---

87   We here refer to the French version of the masterwork, which is clearer than its German
      or the standard English version on this issue.

88   Marx 1976a, p. 72.

89   Marx 1976a, p. 572.

90   Dunayevskaya 2002, pp. 109, 216.

91   Dunayevskaya 1981, p. 108.

ity producing nature than before the revolution when their main economic branch, agriculture, had been largely organised on the basis of "natural" production'.[92]

The experience of 'war communism' (1918–21), when the units of production practically ceased to be economic units and their relations were determined in physical terms (compulsory delivery of surplus products) and distribution of personal income was determined in kind and paid in kind without the use of money, confirmed for many the veracity of Marx's original position of socialism as a system without commodity production. Alec Nove cites R.W. Davies: 'News spread that the civil war system of complete state ownership and abolition of market was the full socialism of Marx and Engels, and that money was therefore an anachronism'.[93]

Hence, once one accepted that the USSR was building socialism, the economic reality of the country increasingly contradicted the received opinion that socialism negated commodity production, that is, the law of value. Later an eminent Russian economist wrote that according to the 'declaration of the "classics of Marxism-Leninism", commodity production ceased to exist with the building of socialism: this idea was prevalent in the 1920s. The exploration of the practice of socialist construction in the USSR, however, showed that towards the end of 1920s there was gradual recognition of the connection of socialism with the law of value'.[94] He added that the negative attitude towards value relations 'had caused the economy great harm, and between 1930 and 1933 the Party undertook various measures to regulate and consolidate bookkeeping, trade, monetary circulation. All these measures were based on the recognition that commodity-money-forms would continue to stay and must be used'.[95] That was the reality of the situation. Now having proclaimed the establishment of socialism in their land, where the law of value was enduring, the self-anointed 'Marxist' spokespersons of the régime had to underline that their law of value and the wage system were not capitalist but were very different from what prevailed under capitalism. Content-wise, the law of value and the wage system in the régime, independently of their phenomenal forms, were really the socialist law of value and the socialist wage system.

---

92   Vacić 1977, p. 233.

93   Nove 1982, p. 65.

94   Manevitch 1972, p. 66.

95   Manevitch 1972, p. 67.

CHAPTER 5

On Socialist Accounting

Accounting here refers to the economic calculation regarding allocation/distribution of resources for production and of final goods for consumption. The problematic of economic accounting in any society Marx sums up in his two letters written in 1868 to his two friends Engels and Kugelmann. He wrote to Engels (8 January) that no social form could prevent the regulation of production by the available labour time, adding that so long, however, as this regulation could not be achieved by society through directly conscious control, but only through the movement of commodity prices, the situation remained exactly the same as the one that Engels himself had so pertinently described in his own 1844 work *Outline of a Critique of Political Economy*.[1] Similarly, in his letter to Kugelmann a few months later (11 July) Marx wrote:

> Every child knows that the masses of products corresponding to the diverse social needs require diverse and quantitatively determined masses of total social labour. It is self-evident that this *necessity of distribution* of social labour of definite proportions cannot at all be eliminated by the *definite form* of social production, that it is only the *way it manifests* that can change. The natural laws cannot generally be eliminated. What can in historically different circumstances be changed is only the *form* in which this law can be imposed. And the form in which this proportional distribution of labour is realised in a social situation as *private exchange* of the individual products of labour is precisely the *exchange value* of products.[2]

---

1 Marx had earlier (1859) called this brochure a 'genial sketch'. See Marx 1980a, p. 101; 1970a, p. 22. The standard English translation uses, not quite appropriately, the term 'brilliant'.
2 Marx 1988c, p. 67. Emphasis in original.

The Labour Process

Human labour[3] occupies the centre stage in Marx as the creating and transforming agent in society.[4] The starting point here is the 'labour process'. In this
process are involved, first, the personal activity of the individual, labour, really
speaking, secondly, the object on which the labour operates, thirdly, the means
with which the labour operates. Though in the labour process both the human
individual and nature participate, it is the human individual who regulates
and controls the 'material exchange' (*Stoffwechsel*) between the individual and
nature.[5] 'By thus acting on the external world and changing it, the individual
at the same time changes his/her own nature. S/he develops its slumbering
powers and subjugates them, bringing them under his/her domination'.[6] In the
labour process human activity, with the help of instruments of labour, effects
a change in the material on which work was being carried on and there comes
out a product which is a use value. The labour process creates use values in the
form of products. Though the outcome of the labour process is a use value, yet
other use values, products of previous labour, enter into it as means of production. The same use value is both the product of a previous labour process and a
means of production in a later labour process. The machines and other means
of labour that do not serve the labour process are useless. They are as good
as dead. The living labour must seize these things and awaken them from their
dead state. 'Lapped by the flame of labour, appropriated as its organs, enthused
to fulfil their functions, they are also consumed, but for a definite purpose, as
elements of formation of new use values, products capable of satisfying either
individual consumption or as means of production entering the new labour
process'.[7] The labour process in its simple and abstract moments as the activ-

---

3   Let us add that by 'labour power' Marx means the 'totality of the physical and mental capacit-
    ies which exist in the body, in the living personality of a human being, and are put in motion
    whenever s/he produces any kind of use value'. Marx 1987a, p. 183; 1976a, p. 129; 1954, p. 164.
4   Marx wrote in 1875: 'Society will find its equilibrium only when it revolves around its sun –
    labour.' See Marx 1960, p. 470.
5   Marx wrote in his 1844 Parisian manuscripts: 'The universality of the human appears precisely
    in the fact that the whole Nature constitutes her/his non-organic prolongation. Nature is the
    non-organic body of the human. The human is a part of Nature. By producing in practice a
    world of objects, by fashioning the non-organic nature, the human affirms her/himself as a
    conscious generic being'. Marx, in Marx and Engels 1973, p. 516; Marx 1975, p. 328.
6   Marx 1987a, p. 192; 1976a, p. 136; 1954, pp. 173–4.
7   Marx 1987a, p. 197; 1976a, p. 140; 1954, p. 178. In the same place Marx distinguishes between
    'productive consumption' and 'individual consumption'. The first refers to labour's consump-
    tion of its objects and instruments in the production process while the second refers to the

ity with a view to producing use values is the general condition of material exchange between the human and Nature, a physical necessity of human life, independent of all social forms, or, rather, common to all social forms. 'One does not guess from the taste of wheat who has cultivated it any more than one can see under what conditions this process has taken place – whether under the slave supervisor's brutal lash or under the anxious eye of the capitalist'.[8] The use value as the product of the labour process is productive labour, though not considered as such in capitalist production.[9]

Point of Departure

It should now be clear that for Marx the central problem of allocation/distribution in a society boils down to the allocation/distribution of total social labour – living as well as past or 'materialised labour' – and the way this operation is carried on is determined by the particular form of society in which it takes place, as his two 1868 letters, cited earlier, stress. The point of departure of socialist accounting is the consideration that whereas in capitalism production is directed towards realising maximum profit towards the accumulation of capital, in the new society it is the satisfaction of needs – individual and collective – of the humans that is the aim of production. As Marx already observed in his 1847 polemic with Proudhon, 'In a future society, where class antagonism would have ceased, where there would no longer be classes, the usefulness (*usage*) would no longer be determined by the *minimum* production time, but the production time bestowed on different objects would be determined by their social utility'.[10] So, for socialist accounting, the starting point is to find out the existing conditions in which people live, and inquire into what their needs are. This would be a kind of household survey of the labouring people. A pioneering

---

consumption of products as means of individual enjoyment. The term *Lebensmittel* in the German edition, literally translated into English as 'means of subsistence', was given a wider meaning by Marx as 'means of enjoyment' (*moyens de jouissance*) in the French version.

8   Marx 1987a, p. 198; 1976a, p. 141; 1954, p. 179.

9   'This determination of productive labour resulting from the simple labour process is not at all sufficient for the case of the capitalist process of production' Marx 1987a, p. 195; 1976a, p. 138; 1954, p. 176. Earlier Marx had very positively referred to James Steuart's distinction between the labour that produces use value – calling it 'real labour' – and the labour that produces exchange value, calling it 'industry'. See Marx 1980a, p. 135; 1970a, p. 58.

10   Marx 1965b, p. 37. The term 'minimum' is emphasised in original.

example in this regard we find in Marx's own 1880 questionnaire *Enquête Ouvrière*.[11] In the Preamble to the text, Marx affirmed that 'only the workers in the urban and rural areas, and not the "providential savers", could apply energetically the remedies for the social miseries affecting them'. Stressing that it was the 'working class to whom the future belongs', Marx pointed out that these 'Labour Notebooks' were the first work which imposes on the socialist democracy the task of *'preparing the social renewal'*.[12]

Long after Marx, the Austrian socialist Otto Neurath, to his credit, has been one of the few socialists/communists who have treated at any length the question of inquiring into the conditions of life of society's labouring people as a preliminary step for a meaningful socialist accounting. By condition of life is meant food, housing, clothing, health, education, entertainment, work etc. In his work on this question Neurath's starting reference point, as well as object of admiration, is Friedrich Engels's well known 1845 booklet *Condition of the Working Class in England*, from which Neurath cites: 'The condition of the working class is the real basis and the point of departure of all social movements at present'. Neurath then remarks: 'We have in this work a perfectly consistent description of the conditions of life such as can be *incorporated in the framework of scientific presentation'*.[13] In this spirit, Neurath, in a 1917 essay, speaks of the need of compiling an inventory of people's 'conditions of life', arranging them according to the pleasurableness of the qualities of life, for example what food the individuals consume per year, what their housing conditions are, what and how much they read, how much they work, how often they fall ill, how much time they spend enjoying works of art etc. The basis for these surveys is provided by household descriptions and related data, he underlines.[14] Neurath very pertinently observes that this kind of household survey is very different from the 'household budgets' discussed in (bourgeois) economics text-

---

11   This questionnaire was originally written for the most part in English, except for a few paragraphs written in French. It appeared, with the author remaining anonymous, in *La Revue socialiste* on 20 April 1880. The full text was published with the author's name in the *Vie ouvrière* (20 June 1911). See Marx 1965c, p. 1527.

12   Marx 1965c, p. 1518. Emphasis added.

13   Neurath 2004, p. 411. Emphasis added. In a work with a number of references to Marx's texts, it is rather surprising to see the complete absence of any reference to Marx's 1880 *Enquête*, which could only be due to Neurath's lack of knowledge of this work, though it was already published in 1911, as mentioned earlier. Neurath's work in question here appeared in 1925.

14   Neurath 2004, p. 326. As can be clearly seen, Neurath's idea of the need for household surveys strongly recalls Marx's 1880 *Enquête*.

books, where only the things that could be bought with money are taken into consideration. We should also mention here the important work, with a pronounced libertarian accent, of the eminent Dutch socialist Anton Pannekoek, who emphasised the need for comprehensive statistical surveys towards socialist accounting.[15] Social organisation of production has as its basis good management helped by statistics and countable data. Statistics on consumption – both productive and personal – of different goods, statistics on the productive capacity of different enterprises, on the machines, land, mines, means of transport, on the population and resources of towns, the regions, the country – all these, when the data are presented in a well-ordered way, constitute the basis of the economic process and the point of departure of the organisation of production. To produce adequate quantities of goods one must know the quantities that are used or necessary. Social accounting which encompasses the administrations of different enterprises brings them together in a table of the economic process of society. In uniting globally the results of enterprises of the same type (which cooperate with one another), it compares their efficiency, establishes the average necessary labour and orients the attention to the possibilities of progress. At different levels it registers the total process of transformation of the material, and accompanies it, beginning with the extraction of raw materials, across all the factories and manipulations until we reach the finished products ready to be consumed. Once production has been organised, management becomes a simple task of a network of accounting offices related to one another. Each enterprise, each group of connected enterprises, each branch of production, each region will have its office of administration for gathering and discussing the figures of production and consumption, and for presenting them in a form which is clear and easy to examine. The process of production is exposed to every one through a simple numerical table which is accessible, and easy to understand. Only then do the 'individuals control their own lives'. 'What the workers with their organised collective collaboration decide and plan is translated by the accounting figures; since these results are always before the eyes of every producer, the direction of the production process by the producers themselves could finally be realised'.[16] This organisation of economic life is totally different from the forms of organisation under the rule of capital, where the complications and difficulties are due to the mutual

---

15   See his text on workers' councils (Pannekoek 2003). In the following discussion on the
      need for social statistics with a view to socialist accounting, we draw on both these
      authors.
16   Pannekoek 2003, pp. 26–7.

struggles and the war of all against all, 'demanding domination over or annihil-ation of the competitors. All this disappears in the new society'. The 'simplicity of fixing the aim – of providing humans with their necessities – lends simplicity to the whole structure'.[17] So socialist accounting starts with a comprehensive survey, on the one hand, of collective and individual needs, and, on the other hand, of the natural resources and means of production fabricated by the past or 'dead' labour and the present or living labour working with them; and it aims to fulfil those needs with a view to enhancing what Neurath calls the 'quality of life'[18] of the social individuals.

Referring to this 'universal statistics', Neurath anticipates Leontief's famous input-output analysis (in physical terms). Following Neurath, the transfer of goods according to amounts and destination, combined with production stat-istics, 'will show quantitatively, via input charts, which raw materials things are made from, how certain quantities of mines, fields, forests, etc., machines, etc., yield certain quantities of coal, and via output charts, what raw materials are good for what things'.[19] The statistical tables will show what enters as 'raw material and auxiliary inputs (like energy) into individual processes of produc-tion, what is produced out of them, how fertilizer, seeds, etc., enter agricultural production, how milk, butter, meat are produced from it. Whatever enters as "increase" in one table will figure as "decrease" in another table till a closed statistic system is reached'.[20]

How to Proceed

Given the availability of this 'universal statistics', how would the socialist calcu-lation proceed? In other words, how would the operation of allocation/distri-bution of the use values – resources as well as the final products ready to be con-sumed (productively and personally) – and living labour take place? The prob-lem boils down to the *mode* of allocating/distributing the total social labour, including past and present labour – materialised and living labour – and the use values produced for final consumption. Under commodity production, includ-ing its ultimate form, capital, the operation is carried on by means of exchange value, money, as the universal equivalent. But for the 'Association of free and equal producers' – to use Marx's alternative term for socialism – this mediation

17   Pannekoek 2003, p. 26.
18   Neurath 2004, pp. 346–7.
19   Neurath 2004, p. 357.
20   Neurath 2004, p. 357.

is by definition excluded. What was in pre-capitalist society the 'domination of person over person', is replaced by, in (generalised) commodity production, the 'universal domination of things over persons', of the product over the producer, and, just as the 'determination of alienation of private property lies in equivalent, in value, similarly money is now the sensuous objective existence of this alienation'.[21] That a social relation of production appears as an 'object outside of the individuals' and that the determinate relations of these individuals in the process of production appear as 'the specific properties of an object', this 'inversion, this mystification, characterises all the social forms of labour that posit exchange value. In money this is manifested only in a more striking way than in the commodity'.[22] Some people on the Left seeking a libertarian alternative to capitalism stress the need for the price system – 'market' – to be a necessary part of it.[23] This is, for example, the case with a distinguished proponent of what he calls 'participatory economics' (PARECON), Michael Albert, who writes, 'If one means by market system a system in which there are prices and in which supply and demand come into accord during allocation, then, yes, participatory planning will be a market system'.[24] The writer, like a number of others, does not seem to appreciate what Marx calls the 'material dependence' of individuals under the commodity (capitalist) system – with the product dominating the producer. The sole concern of these authors is with what Marx calls 'personal dependence' – a trait of the pre-capitalist society – which they want to abolish. That is why the wage system which, at least in principle, is based on personal independence, continues in their system. That a post-capitalist society, if it is to be a society superior to capitalist society in terms of the human individual, has necessarily to be a society with neither personal nor material dependence, in which would prevail what Marx calls 'free individuality',[25] does not seem to cross their minds. Similar ideas are also expressed by the humanist libertarians who, while justly stressing the value of individual liberty, never question the existence of material dependence of the individual. This is the

---

21   Marx 1932, p. 540; 1975, p. 270.

22   Marx 1980a, p. 128; 1970a, p. 49.

23   In the present book there is a whole chapter devoted to 'market socialism', where we also take up the position of the left market socialists and subject them to critique.

24   Albert 2003, p. 266. The same non-recognition of the existence of material dependence of the individual under commodity-capitalist production we find in a proponent of 'economic democracy', Pat Devine, whose proposed regime will involve the 'continued existence of the labour markets' and of the 'consumer markets'. See Devine 1988, particularly p. 23.

25   See Marx 1953, p. 75; 1993, p. 157.

case, for example, with the well-known moral philosopher John Rawls. While stressing the 'consistency of market arrangements with socialist institutions', he underlines that 'it is necessary to recognize that market institutions are common to both private property and socialist régimes', and then adds that, although the 'market is not indeed the ideal arrangement', given the requisite background institutions, 'the worst aspects of the so-called wage slavery are removed', and concludes, 'it seems improbable that the control of economic activity by the bureaucracy that would be bound to develop in a socially regulated system would be more just on balance than control exercised by means of prices'.[26]

Now, if along with private, reciprocally autonomous production, exchange value, money, disappears as the medium of social accounting, there remain only two ways in which social accounting can operate – in labour time and in kind, that is, in use values as such. As regards labour time employed in production, labour as the human activity in the process of production creating socially useful products signifies both the present and the past labour materialised in the means of production, in other words, both the living and the past labour time. In a work of the late 1840s, Marx observed that 'The determination of the price of a commodity by cost of production is equivalent to the determination of price by labour time necessary for the fabrication of a commodity. These costs of production consist of (1) raw materials and depreciation of the instruments of production, that is, industrial products whose production has cost a certain number of labour days and which represent a definite amount of labour time, and (2) direct labour whose measure is likewise the time'.[27] In this sense, Marx wrote in one of his later manuscripts, 'Labour time, even if exchange value is abolished, remains the creative substance of wealth and the measure of the cost of production'.[28]

Now the productive human labour under consideration here has a social dimension. An individual producing an article for his or her own immediate use creates a product which has no social dimension. But whenever the individual creates articles for the use of others, for satisfying some need of the society at large, and, in the process, participates in the social division of labour, the production in question assumes a social character. This is also the case with commodities produced by human labour.[29] However, this is a special kind of

---

26   Rawls 1971, pp. 273, 274, 280, 281. It should be clear that the argument involves simple
      (unproven) assumptions about socialism, the meaning of which also remains unclear.

27   Marx in Marx and Engels 1970b, p. 78.

28   Marx 1962a, p. 255; 1971a, p. 257.

29   See Marx, in Marx and Engels 1970b, pp. 201–2.

sociality. Even though, as purposeful activity appropriating natural materials in one or another form, labour is the natural condition of human existence, independent of all social forms, and thus the condition of material exchange between humanity and nature, 'it is labour positing exchange value which is a specific social form of labour'.[30] Under commodity production, the specific social character of each producer's labour does not show itself except in the case of exchange. Here the labour of the individual asserts itself as a part of the labour of society only by means of relations which exchange establishes directly between products and indirectly, through them, between producers. The relations between the labouring individuals do not appear as directly social relations. As Marx puts it in the first volume of his *Capital*, 'the specific social character of private labours appears only within these exchanges',[31] or, in a slightly different way in the book's French version, 'it is only within the limits of this exchange that the specific social character of [the producers'] labours is affirmed'.[32] Needless to say, in the free Association the opposite is the case. In the first Notebook of his manuscript of the late 1850s, Marx wrote:

> The necessity itself of transforming at first the product or the activity of the individuals into exchange value, money, so that this product and this activity can, under this material form, receive and demonstrate their social power, proves two things: (1) that the individuals produce only in the society and for the society; (2) that their production is not directly social, that it is not the offspring of association which distributes the labour among its members; the individuals remain subsumed under the social production which stays outside of them as a fatality (*Verhängnis*). But the social production is not subsumed under the individuals who handle it as their common power.[33]

In the Association the collective and general character of labour follows naturally from the collective character of production. Here the original exchange in production, which would not be an exchange of commodities, but an exchange of activities determined by common needs and common ends, would comprise from the start the share of individuals in the world of collective products. In the case of commodity production, the 'social character of production is posited

---

30   Marx 1980a, p. 115; Marx 1970a, p. 36.
31   Marx 1987a, p. 104; 1976a, p. 70; 1954, p. 78.
32   Marx 1976a, p. 69.
33   Marx 1953, p. 76; 1993, p. 158. The expression 'offspring of association' is in English in the text.

only *post festum* by the promotion of products to the rank of exchange values and are exchanged as exchange values, whereas in the opposite case the social character of production is pre-supposed, and the participation in production, in consumption, is not mediated by the reciprocal exchange of independent labours or products of labour. It is mediated by the very social conditions of production within which individuals carry on their activities'.[34] Let us stress that both these two kinds of labour are 'socially necessary labour', but in one case the 'social necessity' is established through the market, backed by adequate purchasing power as an index of social recognition of the particular products, that is, indirectly, while in the other case this social necessity corresponding to the satisfaction of society's needs – independently of any mediation by exchange value – is predetermined, that is, determined directly, following from the collective character of production determined by social needs. In a later manuscript, Marx puts the matter succinctly: 'it is only where production is under the real, predetermining control of society that society creates a relation between the magnitude of social labour time employed in producing definite articles and the quantity of social needs to be satisfied by these articles'.[35]

Labour Time: Neglected Aspects

In the discussion on the question of labour time, its three vital aspects are not always treated with sufficient consideration, leading to: neglect of labour time as a totality, that is, only living or present labour time is considered, neglecting the materialised or past labour time; consideration only of the indirectly social labour connected with commodity production (exchange value), neglecting the directly social labour; and, the most neglected of all, the importance of non-labour time as the free time for the all-round development of the

---

34   Marx 1953, p. 89; 1993, pp. 172–3. In a text which was composed somewhat later, Marx put the matter more succinctly. Speaking of common labour in its primitive form, Marx wrote, 'Here the social character of labour is obviously not mediated by the labour of the individual taking the form of abstract generality or her/his product taking the form of a general equivalent. Here the community is posited before production, which prevents the labour of the individual from being private labour and her/his product from being private product, and allows the individual labour to appear directly as the function of a member of the social organism. The labour which is represented in exchange value is pre-supposed as the labour of the isolated individual. It becomes social by the form of its opposite, the form of abstract generality'. Marx 1980a, p. 113; 1970a, p. 33.

35   Marx 1992, p. 262; 1984, p. 187.

social individual. All this becomes apparent when one considers (for or against) labour time as the measure of calculation for social(ist) accounting. Thus the well-known Polish economist Oskar Lange, citing Marx's 1868 letter to Kugelmann on the allocation of society's labour time – quoted above – opined that in Marx's thought 'labour seems to have been the only kind of scarce resource to be distributed between different uses and he wanted to solve the problem by the labour theory of value'.[36] Here Lange clearly took into consideration only the living labour as the resource, inasmuch as outside of the virgin, untreated natural resources, all the resources available for use by humans would be either living or materialised labour. Secondly, as regards Marx's alleged application of the labour theory of value, this is a theory implying the determination of the value of commodities by labour time that, as Marx stresses, presupposes only the 'modern bourgeois society'.[37] It is rather for Proudhon, as Marx underlines, that the determination of value by labour time is *la formule régénératrice de l'avenir*.[38] In other words, here it is a question of the necessary labour which is only indirectly social, creating products which appear as (exchange) value. In socialism, on the contrary, it is the necessary labour which is directly social, creating use value requiring no mediation of (exchange) value. In her turn, Joan Robinson refers to a passage in *Capital* Volume III where Marx says that 'after the disappearance of the capitalist mode of production, but with *social* production still maintained, the determination of value will remain predominant in the sense that the regulation of labour time and the distribution of social labour among different branches of production, finally the bookkeeping, become more essential than ever'.[39] On the basis of these lines, she concludes that the law of value will come into its own in society after capitalism has disappeared.[40] On the basis of the same passage, the eminent economist from Hungary, András Bródy, opines that though Marx believes that in the absence of commodity production there will be no exchange value, nevertheless 'the

---

36 Lange 1964, pp. 132–3.
37 Marx 1980a, p. 137; 1970a, p. 60. Marx says here, in effect, paraphrasing and interpreting Ricardo: 'the law of value for its full development presupposes a society of big industrial production and free competition, that is, the modern bourgeois society'. Years later, in his 1880 polemic with Adolph Wagner, referring to Schaffle's attribution of 'social state' to him, along with the value theory that was a part of it, Marx wrote that in his investigation on value it was 'a question of bourgeois relations', not even once a relation with the 'social state' constructed by Schaffle. See Marx 1962b, pp. 360–1.
38 Marx 1965b, p. 42.
39 Marx 1992, p. 871; 1984, p. 851. Emphasis in text.
40 Robinson 1966, p. 23.

underlying, deeper notion, value itself will remain with us as long as there is division of labour, as long as there are different activities to compare'.[41] Now, neither of these two authors seems to have paid enough attention to the passage immediately preceding the one cited here. In that passage, referring to a text of the economist Storch, Marx speaks of 'a *false abstraction*' which is made 'when one considers a nation whose mode of production is based on value, furthermore, organised capitalistically, as a collectivity which works simply for the needs of the nation'.[42] Here clearly, by collectivity Marx means the associated or socialist collectivity. For Marx value exists in the form of the commodity only when producers as private individuals produce use values independently of one another and exchange their products as commodities. Value is a specific social relation of which commodities are the material medium. Marx offers examples of collectivities where there is division of labour and shared activities among the members of the collectivity without a trace of value. In one of these examples, Marx refers to the patriarchal peasant family, labouring in common uniquely for their own needs of different types. Here the different labours which create useful articles are 'social functions', because they are the functions of the family, 'which has, in the same way as in commodity production, division of labour. The labour power of individuals operates here simply as a definite part of the total labour power of the peasant family and the measure of the expenditure of individual labour power by labour time takes directly the social character of their labour'.[43] Engels, following Marx faithfully,[44] neatly sums up the essential in his critique of Dühring. According to him, as soon as the society comes to possess the means of production and employs them in directly socialised production, labour becomes directly social. Even then society has to know how much time is necessary to produce an object of utility. It will set up the plan in conformity with the means of production to which especially the labour force belongs. 'Finally it is the useful effects of different useful objects, reciprocally balanced and in relation to the quantity of labour

41   Bródy 1970, p. 16.

42   Marx 1992, p. 871; 1984, p. 851. Emphasis in text.

43   Marx 1987a, p. 108; 1976a, p. 73; 1954, p. 82. About a decade earlier, Marx had already written, concerning the patriarchal family, that 'spinning and weaving were *social* labours within the limits of the family. The organisation of the family (*Familienzusammenhang*) with its natural division of labour stamped the product of labour with its specific social character'. See Marx, 1980a, pp. 112–13; 1970a, p. 33.

44   We recall here what Engels wrote concerning his *Anti-Dühring*: 'I have read out to him [Marx] the whole manuscript before it went to print'. See Engels 1962, p. 9.

necessary for their production, that will determine the plan. People will make everything without the intervention of the famous "value".[45]

On the question of socialism and directly social labour, there have been some significant works by the economists of Eastern Europe in light of the practical experience of what was widely supposed to be the 'socialist' countries. A very important contribution in this regard comes from an ex-Yugoslav economist – virtually ignored in the Western European economic literature – A.M. Vacic, in a paper in the late 1970s.[46] He points to the real operation of commodity production in all the existing socialist countries, thereby contradicting Marx's affirmation that there would be no commodity production in socialism. He observes that in Russia – the prototype of this system – the leaders started with the conviction that in conformity with Marx's ideas their socialist system must exclude commodity production. He notes, 'as long as the dominant opinion in Marxist economic theory was that the socialist economy involves the negation of commodity production, it was thought that labour under socialism was of a directly social character, following which the practice of the socialist countries started from the supposition that the labour of the socialist producer got its final social appreciation already in the course of production, in a natural, concrete form, and as such, constituted the basis for sharing in the total social product'.[47] In its most marked form, this conviction was translated during the period of the so-called 'war communism' into a system of distribution of personal income in kind, not money. The relations between units of production were determined in physical terms. Although such extreme forms were later abandoned, the principles remained in force for a long time. 'The fact that personal income is paid in money does not alter the situation since money is also treated as a means of the capitalist system utilised by socialist society to realize its own goals'.[48] This point of view was accepted in Marxist theory until after the Bolshevik victory, as late as 1952, when Stalin declared that the law of value asserted itself also in socialism. Following this proclamation, commodity production as an integral part of socialism was accepted by all the countries calling themselves socialist. Indeed, at the present stage of the development of the means of production, with the present material and social structure of production in these countries, the commodity form of production is found to be objectively necessary. Hence the commodity form of production as a normal phenomenon of socialism has gained universal acceptance in these countries.

---

45   Engels 1962, p. 288.

46   Vacic 1977, pp. 227–45.

47   Vacic 1977, p. 231.

48   Vacic 1977, p. 232.

The fact of the matter is that, following Marx – as we mentioned earlier – the commodity-producing nature of production and directly social labour mutually exclude each other. In these countries calling themselves socialist, labour, far from being directly social, is of an indirectly social nature in the sense that it gains its ultimate social recognition through the sale of produced goods taking the commodity form.[49] This idea of Vacic seems to have followed from the ideas expressed by some Russian economists earlier (and much less elaborately), who had recognised the non-directly social character of labour in their socialism – understood, following Lenin, as the first stage of communism – necessitating the calculation of labour expenses in the form of value. Thus M. Edelman – accepting Russian society as socialist – observed, while discussing the problem of balance of interbranch expenses of labour, that the cost of socially necessary labour 'cannot be measured directly in labour time given the specific character of the social production at the first stage of the communist society'.[50] The eminent dissident economist V.P. Shkredov – whose basic works remain untranslated in any principal Western European language as far as we know – in his turn held that while in each unit of production the division of labour as well as the products appear as the result of a 'directly social (*neposredstvenno obshchestovenni*) labour relation, the compatible directly social character of labour is not yet, over wide spheres, a technical necessity'.[51]

Labour Time and Non-labour Time

The least discussed subject in the debates on the question of socialist accounting is the question of the relation between labour time and non-labour time, with its huge implication for the freedom of the labouring individual in socialism – a question to which Marx attached the utmost importance. In a number of texts Marx raises this vital issue. In the chapter on 'Machinery and Modern Industry' in his master work, Marx refers to Aristotle's observation that if every tool, when summoned, could perform its appropriate function of its own accord, if the weaver's shuttle could weave of itself, then there would be no need of slaves for the lord. Similarly, Marx mentions, in the same text, the position of a Greek poet Antipatros, who welcomed the water-wheel for grinding grain as the giver of freedom to the female slaves.[52] In one of the 1861–3

49   Vacic 1977, p. 233.
50   Edelman 1964, p. 15.
51   Shkredov 1967, p. 56.
52   Marx 1987a, pp. 396–7; 1976a, pp. 290–1; 1954, pp. 384–5.

manuscripts Marx cites an anonymous English pamphlet of the early 1820s, which claims that 'wealth is disposable time and nothing more', and elaborates on the theme. Referring to this author, Marx stresses that if the productive forces bring about a situation in society where society produces in six hours the necessary abundance that it produces in twelve hours currently, everybody will have six hours of disposable time, that is, real wealth, making available time for enjoyment, free activity and development. 'Time is the space (*Raum*) for the development of faculties'.[53] 'The whole human development, in so far as it goes beyond the development immediately necessary for humanity's natural existence, consists simply in the employment of this free time and presupposes it'.[54] With the development of science and technology leading to increasing productivity of labour, labour time decreases. This means that the greatest possible abundance of material wealth is produced in the shortest possible labour time. 'The saving of labour time is equal to the increase in free time, that is, time for the full development of the individual. The free time – which is both leisure time and time for higher activity – has naturally transformed its possessor into a different subject, and as a different subject s/he enters into the immediate process of production; this saving is identical with the development of the productive power'.[55] Indeed, the 'whole economy is reduced to the economy of time'.[56] The productivity of a machine is measured by the human labour power it replaces. Less labour must be expended in producing the machinery than is displaced by the employment of that machinery. Under capitalism the purpose of introducing machines is to increase the production and realisation of surplus value. The capitalist, instead of paying for the labour, only pays the value of the labour power employed. 'The limit to his use of the machine is fixed by the difference between the value of the machine and the value of the labour

---

53   Marx 1962a, p. 254; 1971a, p. 256. In his discourse to the workers a few years later, Marx stressed in English that 'Time is the room of human development'. See Marx 1988a, p. 424; Marx and Engels 1970b, p. 219. In an earlier composition (1845), Marx had posed the question – in the context of the dependence of the cost of production of objects on labour time – 'has the society time for human development?'. See Marx 1972, p. 52; 1975, p. 49. One of the authors who seems to have inspired Marx to think along these lines was W. Schulz, whom Marx cites at length in his Parisian Manuscripts of 1844. There Marx cites this author: 'In order to be able to develop mentally in all freedom a people must not remain a slave of its physical needs. Before everything they must have time to create intellectually (*geistig*) and enjoy intellectually'. See Marx 1973a, p. 478; 1975, p. 290.

54   Marx 1976b, p. 168; 188b, p. 191.

55   Marx 1953, p. 599; 1993, p. 711.

56   Marx 1953, p. 89; 1993, pp. 172–3.

power replaced by it. Hence in a communist society there would be a very different scope for the employment of machinery than there can be in a bourgeois society'.[57]

Under capitalism, to the extent machinery develops along with the accumulation of science and the productive powers of society, it is no longer in labour but in capital that the whole social activity is manifested. In machinery knowledge is something alien and external to the labourer. While living labour is subordinated to the dead labour which acts in total independence, to the extent that the labouring individual's labour is not required for capital's needs, it becomes superfluous. It is important to underline that to the extent that labour, that is, the quantity of labour, is posited as the unique element determining production, direct labour as the principle of creating use values vanishes or at least is reduced to a subordinate role, quantitatively and qualitatively, in relation to the technological application of the natural sciences and the general productive power brought about by the social organisation of production as a whole. 'In this way capital works for its own dissolution. Capital right now unconsciously reduces human labour to its minimum. This will be of great advantage for the emancipated labour, and this is the condition of its emancipation'.[58] It is in this revolutionary sense, it seems to us, that Marx, referring to the social revolutions of 1848, told the British workers a couple of years earlier (1856) – in a 'little speech in English', as he informed Engels – that 'steam, electricity, and the self-acting mule were revolutionists of a rather more dangerous character than the citizens Barbès, Raspail and Blanqui'.[59] Indeed, to the extent that big industry develops, the creation of real wealth depends less on labour time and the quantity of labour employed in production than on the power of the agents put into movement during labour time, whose powerful efficiency has little relation to the direct labour time which production costs; it depends rather on the state of science and technological progress. Real wealth is manifested rather in the immense disproportion between the labour time employed and its product. 'The theft of the labour time of others on which to-day's wealth depends appears as a miserable foundation compared to the new development created by big industry itself. As soon as labour in its immediate form ceases to be the great source of wealth, labour time would cease to be the measure of labour, just as exchange value would cease to be the measure of use value, and

57   Marx 1987a, pp. 380, 382; 1976a, pp. 279, 280, 635; 1954, pp. 369, 370, 371.
58   Marx 1953, p. 589; 1993, p. 701.
59   Marx 1980b, pp. 655–6. These three were great revolutionaries of the epoch.

thereby production based on exchange value collapses, and the immediate process of material production casts off its form of misery and contradictions'.[60]

Socialist Accounting Framework

The social framework for accounting in socialism has to correspond to socialism's emancipatory character. In this regard there is still much to learn from what the Parisian communards of 1871 sketched as their future socio-political framework. Indeed, Marx was full of praise for this initiative of the communards, as can be seen in his 1871 *Civil War in France*. This Parisian project for the future was something *new* to him. Hints for this change can be read in the 1872 'Preface' to the German edition of the 1848 *Manifesto*. The revolutionary measures proposed at the end of the second section of the *Manifesto*, 'would, in many respects, be differently worded to-day' we read, becoming 'antiquated' due, most importantly, to the experience of the Paris Commune.[61] Thus, what appears as the principal task of the working class after it becomes the ruling class and has won the battle of democracy – namely, wresting all capital from the bourgeoisie 'to centralize all instruments of production in the hands of the State'[62] – goes directly against the experience of the Commune, which had destroyed the state machine in its first steps. The official programme of the Commune, announced on 19–20 April 1871, gives the outline of the project. It speaks of the 'absolute autonomy of the commune extended to all the localities of France, guaranteeing individual liberty, liberty of conscience, liberty of work'. The programme continues, 'the political unity such as has been imposed by the Empire and monarchy and parliamentarism is no more than a despotic and ignorant *centralisation*. The political unity which Paris wants is the *voluntary association* of all the local initiatives towards a common goal: well-being, freedom and security for all'.[63] Prosper-Olivier Lissagaray, the great chronicler-militant of the Parisian Revolution (and fighter on the barricade), as well as a merciless critic of the Commune's insufficiencies – and held in high esteem by Marx – while discussing the programme, wrote that 'the communal Revolu-

---

60   Marx 1953, p. 593; 1993, p. 705.
61   Marx and Engels 1970b, p. 32. This concerned basically the question of state. In the same
      sense, Engels, in his letter to Bebel many years later (18–28 March 1875), wrote, 'The whole
      talk about the state should be dropped, especially, since the Paris Commune, which was
      no longer a state in the proper sense of the term'. See Marx and Engels 1970b, p. 335.
62   Marx and Engels 1970b, p. 52.
63   In Schulkind 1974, pp. 150–1. Emphasis added.

tion, started by the people's initiative, and made under the slogan of Universal
Republic, [will] define the future Commune sufficiently expansively so as to
enable the citizens easily to combine their social action, the Commune of fifteen or twenty thousand souls, the Commune-canton, to express clearly their
rights and those of the collectivity'.[64] Marx, in his 'Address of the General Council of the International' (1871), elaborated on this position of the communards.
Once the Commune was established in Paris, eliminating its centralised government, in the provinces too the centralised government had to give way to
the 'self-government of the producers', the communes. The Commune was to
be the political form of even the smallest country hamlet formed by universal suffrage and revocable at short terms. The rural commune of every district
was to administer their common affairs by the assembly of delegates in the
central town, and these district assemblies were again to send deputies to the
National Delegation, each delegate to be at any time revocable and bound by
the imperative mandate of the particular constituents.[65] We thus see here the
portrait of a completely decentralised (non-state) administration.[66] In contrast with his analysis of the political project of the Commune, Marx does not,
generally, discuss anything concerning the economy, the organisation of the
units of production. However, Marx does emphasise that the 'Commune was
to serve as a lever for uprooting the economical foundation upon which rests
the existence of classes. With labour emancipated, every man becomes a working man, and productive labour ceases to be a class attribute'.[67] Further – and
this is vital to note – Marx stresses a very essential point directly concerning
the organisation of production in the *future* society. It is 'co-operative production superseding capitalist production'.[68] 'If co-operative production is not to

64   Lissagaray 2000, p. 214.
65   Marx, in Marx and Engels 1971, pp. 71, 72, 73.
66   It is important to emphasise that in the different versions of the *Civil War in France*,
     whenever he speaks of the governance on both sides of the war, Marx contrasts the 'state'
     of the Versailles forces with the 'government' or 'administration' of the communards. In
     his eyes – contrary to a later interpretation – the Commune was not a new kind of state
     after the elimination of the old state. The Commune was no state at all.
67   Marx, in Marx and Engels 1971, p. 75.
68   Marx, referring to Owen's Rochdale cooperatives, cites a British newspaper, the *Spectator*:
     'they showed that associations of workmen could manage shops, mills, and all forms of
     industry with success, and they immediately improved the condition of the men; but they
     did not leave a clear place for masters'. Marx comments '*Quelle horreur*'! Marx 1987a, p. 328;
     1976a, p. 623; 1954, p. 313. The newspaper's own term 'master', appearing in the first edition
     of *Capital*, was replaced by the word 'capitalist' in the second German edition, as well as

remain a sham and a snare, if it is to supersede the capitalist system, if *united co-operative societies are to regulate national production upon a common plan*, thus taking it under their own control, and putting an end to the constant anarchy and periodical convulsions, which are the fatality of capitalist production – what would it be but Communism, "possible" Communism?'[69] At the same time we should not forget that Marx never considered the 1871 Commune as a *socialist* society. As Marx observed, concerning the measures undertaken by the Communards, 'there is nothing socialist in them except their tendency'.[70] The Commune could serve only as a 'lever for uprooting' capitalist production, as mentioned above. So, naturally, Marx could not discuss the question of the organisation of the economy of the Commune in terms of a *socialist* society. But a broad outline of things to come could be seen depicted here. It should be stressed that for Marx 'cooperative society' and 'cooperative mode of produc-tion' 'are identical with "socialism" or communism'.[71] Speaking of cooperatives in the sense of Marx, let us add that there is no question of a separate set of consumers' cooperatives analogous to the producers' cooperatives in the new society, inasmuch as here, unlike what takes place in capitalism, articles are produced directly for consumption – productive as well as individual – without any sale or purchase to separate the producers from the consumers. In cap-italism – in the absence of collective production – an individual consuming particular products considers her/himself as a simple consumer without any direct involvement in the social production process. Hence the consumer/pro-ducer distinction is a projection into socialism of a character of the bourgeois world, where the individual capitalists consider people outside of their own labourers as simple consumers of their products. In a socialist society, let us add, all able-bodied individuals excepting the aged, the children and the dis-abled, are supposed to be producers.

On Planning and the Unit of Calculation

The habitual discussion of the possibility (or otherwise) and method(s) of rational economic calculation in socialism has been carried on in terms of the

---

in the French version and the English translation of the fourth edition of the book, though in the third edition the original term was retained.

69 Marx, in Marx and Engels 1871, pp. 75–6; emphasis added.

70 Marx, in Marx and Engels 1971, p. 165. In this regard see also Marx's important letter to the Dutch socialist F. Domela-Neuwenhuis (22 February 1881), in Schulkind 1974, p. 244.

71 See Marx, in Marx and Engels 1970b, p. 319; in Most 1989, p. 783.

opposites 'plan' vs 'market', where plan stands for socialism and market for capitalism. For socialists, planning is supposed to eliminate what Marx often calls
the 'anarchy of the market' reigning under capital, leading to economic fluctuations and crises. But what kind of planning for socialism is in question?
For a large number of people, both Right and Left, largely under the impact
of the experience of planning in post-1917 Russia, the type of planning considered in this connection has been central planning, on the basis of mainly
state ownership of the means of production, which has been taken as the hall-
mark of socialism. An outstanding example of this way of thinking we find in
the well-known Marxian economist Maurice Dobb. First, as regards socialist
production, for Dobb the 'specifically social character' of a socialist economy
derives from the 'transformation of the property basis', that is, 'expropriation
of the propertied class and socialisation of land and capital', where 'socialisation' means 'transference of land and capital into the collective ownership of
the workers' *State*'.[72] Regarding planning, he first cites, approvingly,[73] the economist Lionel Robbins – 'planning involves central control; and central control
excludes the right of individual disposal' – and then adds that here the 'essential contrast is between an economy where the multifarious decisions which
rule production are taken each in ignorance of all the rest and an economy
where such decisions are co-ordinated and unified'.[74] Years later, while survey-
ing the debate on economic calculation in a socialist economy, Dobb, referring
to 'economic development', underlines the importance of 'centrally planned
development as an organic whole', and observes 'major decisions controlling
economic development, and hence human welfare, must be taken as policy
decisions by some organ of the central government'.[75] Let us note *en passant*
that for anyone with some knowledge of the post-1917 development in Russia,
it should be clear that Dobb is completely 'buying' the official position of the
régime by standing Marx on his head when he affirms that the social character of the régime is derived from the change in the régime's property relations
(in the means of production). In other words, it is the juridical relation which
determines the real relation of production. Secondly – and this has immediate relevance for the discussion here – this view of planning, centralised at
the highest level, is the very opposite of the type projected by the 1871 communards for the *free society* of the future and summarised by Marx (as given
above) as *decentralised planning by the associated producers*. Let us add that

---

72   Dobb 1940, pp. 77, 270–1. Emphasis added.
73   Dobb 1940, p. 271.
74   Dobb 1940, p. 271.
75   Dobb 1965, pp. 76, 86.

another eminent Marxian economist, Paul Sweezy, also seems to have been arguing basically in the same way. He stressed that 'centralised planning' was an 'essential feature of any socialist society'.[76] Again, while, referring to the 'productive activity brought under conscious control replacing law of value by the planning principle', he very approvingly mentions Preobrazhensky's assertion that in Russia the 'centralised planned economy' has been established.[77] This indeed has been the common run of thought on socialist planning for the last several decades. For the purposes of this chapter, we will not proceed further with Dobb. He appears also in another chapter of the book treating 'market socialism'.

Let us now turn to the problem of the unit of calculation to be used for the allocation of resources and finished goods in the Association. Here allocation of the products of labour through exchange taking value form, that is, mediated by money, is excluded by definition. As Marx stresses in a well-known and much cited passage of his 1875 *Gothacritique*, 'Within the cooperative society based on common ownership in the means of production, the producers do not exchange their products; just as little does the labour employed on the products appear here *as the value* of these products'.[78] Note that Marx is referring here to the very beginning of the new society, right *after* the end of the 'revolutionary transformation period'.

As mentioned earlier, in the absence of money as the unit of calculation, there are only two ways of distributing the products of labour in society – either through labour time as the unit of measure or in-kind. Regarding the first alternative, the labour time serving as the unit of calculation in socialism has to be not only necessary labour time, but also directly socially necessary labour time, as was emphasised earlier. Here the 'community is posited before production',[79] 'individual labour is directly a component part of social labour'.[80] And of course the labour in question is total labour, both living and materialised labour. In a passage of Marx's 1857–8 manuscripts, we read of both types of measure of a product – natural measure and measure by labour time. 'In so far as the product has a measure, the measure can only be the natural measure of the object itself: volume, weight, length, measure of space, measure of utility etc. But as the effect, or as the existence of the force at rest (*als ruhndes*

76   Sweezy 1949, p. 24.

77   Sweezy 1970, pp. 53–4.

78   Marx, in Marx and Engels 1970b, p. 319. Emphasis in original.

79   Marx 1980a, p. 113; 1970a, p. 34.

80   Marx, in Marx and Engels 1970b, p. 319.

Dasein der Kraft) which has created it, it can only be measured by the force that has created this force itself; the measure of labour is time. Simply because the products *are* labour, they can be measured by labour time'.[81]

When people speak of labour time being the unit of calculation in socialism – both for and against – they very rarely, if at all, clarify what type of labour they are talking about. Generally the labour time for them is the labour time which Marx applies for his value theory, a couple of examples of which were given above. With such a unit of calculation one can never arrive at the correct measure since the labour time in relation to the value analysis is only indirectly social labour. The relevant labour time for the free Association of individuals is rather directly socially necessary labour time. As Vladimir Shkredov, following Marx, has put the matter succinctly, '(here) all members of society are directly (*neposredstvenno*) united with the means of production even *before* the start of the production process'.[82] Shkredov is speaking here of collective production. With such production, the labour of the individual is posited right at the beginning of the production process as social labour, and registered as such in bookkeeping. An example of the failure to specify the type of labour time involved, arriving at a doubtful solution, is seen in a 1930 brochure by the 'council communists' from Holland: *Basic Principles of Communist Production and Distribution*. After posing the question to what extent it is possible to calculate the number of labour hours that have gone into each industrial establishment, the brochure says that it is the 'modern cost accounting' – the 'thoroughgoing rationalisation developed under capitalism' – that offers the definite answer. This involves each separate productive process and each separate subsidiary labour function. 'At present they are all related to a common denominator – money. But nothing stands in the way of changing into another unit of calculation'. It is 'perfectly possible to impress upon each product the number of hours its production has cost'.[83] It must be stressed that in the method of cost accounting in the text cited here – which is the context of capitalist production – the labour in the cost calculation has to be only commodity producing labour, that is, labour which has to prove its social necessity only indirectly, only in the market. This character of labour will not change simply by adopting a new unit of calculation instead of money, and cannot serve as the unit of calculation of cost in the 'co-operative society' after capital. Unfortunately this libertarian brochure seems to be repackaging 'labour money', whose self-

---

81   Marx 1953, p. 507; 1993, p. 613. Emphasis in original.
82   Shkredov 1988, p. 30. Emphasis added.
83   *Kollektivarbeit* 1930, pp. 37–8.

contradictory character Marx had clearly exposed in his 1857–8 manuscripts and in his 1859 *Contribution to the Critique of Political Economy*.

Calculation by labour time in the sense of directly social labour time as the unit of measure, where this labour time is considered as necessary – directly determined by the criterion of satisfaction of social needs – should not be too difficult in a régime of collective production, given the pre-conditions of social accounting discussed earlier, that is, universal statistics of needs and resources corresponding to those needs, as well as a fully decentralised, *stateless* 'association of co-operatives' (in Marx's sense), built on a fully democratic basis with election and recall of delegates with strict mandates from the members of their own units of production, which Marx underlined in his discussion of the project for the future drafted by the Communards of Paris. Now, strictly speaking, the labour under consideration here is the total labour – both living labour and materialised labour. At the *start* of the new society – that is, *after* the end of the 'revolutionary transformation period', to which corresponds a political 'transition period'[84] – calculating *living* labour time in the units of production may not be too difficult with appropriate bookkeeping, However, it would be practically impossible to get the exact estimate of the labour time going into the material means of production – that is, materialised labour – inasmuch as most of these means of production would have been manufactured under the *ancien régime*, where the labour going into the means of production was indirectly social labour whose necessity was measured only in terms of its recognition in the market.

Only infrequently does Marx explicitly mention labour time as the *unit of calculation* in the 'cooperative society', while broaching the problem of distribution of the means of production and living labour in the new society. We should always remember that, for Marx, society's totality of means of production and living labour is equivalent to society's total labour time. Thus in his 1857–8 manuscripts he writes, concerning the new society: 'Society must distribute its time appropriately with a view to realizing production in conformity with its needs. The economy of time as well as the planned (*planmässige*) distribution of labour time in the different branches of production remains therefore the first economic law in the collective production'.[85] Again, in *Capital* Volume I, while discussing the distribution of the total product of the 'Union of free individuals', Marx opines that after setting aside one part of this product to serve the means of production, the other part meant for con-

---

84   See Marx, in Marx and Engels 1970, p. 327.
85   Marx 1953, p. 599; 1993, p. 711.

sumption has to be distributed among the individuals. 'Only for a parallel with commodity production' one could suppose that the share of each producer (in the means of subsistence) is determined by her/his labour time. Thus 'labour time would play a double role: its socially planned distribution regulates the right proportion of various functions of labour in relation to different needs. Simultaneously labour time serves as the measure of the individual share of the producers in the common labour and therewith the consuming part of the individuals in the common product'.[86] Shortly afterwards, in the second manuscript for the second volume of *Capital*, Marx wrote that 'on the basis of socialised production society distributes labour power and means of production to the different branches of production (*Geschäftszweige*). The producers receive paper vouchers on the basis of which they can draw from the consumer stocks the quantity corresponding to their labour time. These vouchers are no money (*kein Geld*). They do not circulate'.[87] Finally in the *Gothacritique*, where, given the particular question he has to deal with, that is, a criticism of the Lassallean approach to distribution, Marx focuses on personal distribution of the total consumption in the 'cooperative society'. To introduce this object of focus, he at first gives a brief sketch of the allocation of society's total product in view of satisfying society's different needs. In drawing the sketch of allocation, he does not explicitly use labour time as the *unit of calculation*, even though, naturally, the products are considered as 'products of labour'. He speaks only in

---

86   Marx 1987a, p. 109; 1976a, p. 75; 1954, p. 83. In the French version neither the term 'means of subsistence' nor the term 'planned' appears.

87   Marx 2008, p. 347; 1956a, p. 362. In his edition Engels altered somewhat the text. This labour voucher is neither money nor the ill-famed 'labour-money'. A critical discussant of Marx puts the matter fairly well: 'Each voucher ends its life once it has been exchanged for goods. This is not the same as a present day check, which transfers ownership of a deposited sum; although one physical check serves for a single transaction and then ends its life, an asset has been transferred to the payee, who can then transfer it to others'. See Steele 1992, p. 32. However, Steele, like most readers of Marx, fails to take into account the basic reason for the singularity of vouchers. In the text of the *Gothacritique* Marx, while discussing the exchange of equivalents governing the exchange of labour between society and individual in the lower phase of the socialist society, stresses the fundamental difference between this exchange and the one under commodity economy: 'the exchange of equivalents in commodity exchange only exists *on the average* and not in the individual case' (Marx and Engels 1970, p. 320. Emphasis in original). Marx underlines in several places – to some of which we have referred earlier – that in collective production each individual's contribution as a distinct share of the collectivity is known before production begins. That is why the voucher in question is singular, it does not circulate. It is neither money nor 'labour money'.

terms of products as use values. One could read this as distribution in kind, without mediation by money. After having excluded exchange value, broaching personal distribution (after the necessary deductions have been made for the common needs of society at large), Marx opines, for the initial phase of the new society, that 'the individual producer receives back from society – after the necessary deductions – exactly what s/he gives to it. What s/he has given to it is [her or] his individual quantum of labour ... S/he receives a certificate from society that s/he has furnished such and such amount of labour (after deducting her/his labour for the common funds), and with this certificate s/he draws from the social stock of means of consumption as much as costs the same amount of labour'.[88] As can be seen, it is only for personal distribution of consumption goods that labour time is used as the unit of calculation. The same idea we found earlier in his manuscript for the second volume of *Capital*, where Marx also uses labour time as measure explicitly for personal consumption, but simply speaks of distribution of 'labour power and means of production' – that is, in kind – 'to the different branches of production'.[89] In fact in some relevant passages of the same book, Marx does not even mention labour time as the unit of calculation. Here is one:

> If we imagine society to be not capitalist, but communist, there would be, to start with, no money capital or disguises of transaction accompanying it. The thing is reduced simply to this, that society has to calculate beforehand how much labour, means of production, means of subsistence society can employ without causing harm to the branches of production like building of railways which for a long time can deliver neither means of production, nor means of subsistence nor any kind of useful effect, but (on the contrary) will withdraw labour, means of production, means of subsistence from the aggregate product.[90]

Here, Marx is simply speaking of the need of calculation without any mention of labour time as the unit.[91] In another place Marx is discussing the movement

88   Marx, in Marx and Engels 1970b, p. 319.
89   Marx 2008, p. 347; 1956a, p. 362.
90   Marx 2008, pp. 306–7; 1956a, pp. 318–19.
91   Let us underline a very important point in connection with the text cited here. Here we see a contrast in the method of calculation in socialism (communism) as opposed to capitalism, 'calculation beforehand', and what appears a little later in the same text (not given here), calculation *post festum* in capitalism, that is, involving directly social labour time

of constant capital between different units of production within the department of means of production in the reproduction process of capital. Here the theme is re-entry of constant capital value in part in its own sphere of production, like corn in corn production, coal in coal production, iron in iron production. However, since the part products composing constant capital do not enter directly their specific spheres of production, they simply change their place. 'They enter in their *natural form* in another sphere of Department I while the product of other spheres of Department I replaces them in *natural form*'. The products, insofar as they do not directly serve as means of production in their own branches of production, move from their own sphere of production to another sphere, and reciprocally. 'If production were social (*gesellschaftlich*) and not capitalist, the products of Department I would clearly continue to be redistributed, one part remaining directly in the sphere of production from which it originated as a product, the other part moving to the other places of production giving rise to a to-and-fro movement between the places of production in the Department I'.[92] Here, again, there is no mention of labour time as the unit of calculation in the allocation process of the means of production between different branches of production.

In connection with the discussion of labour time as the unit of calculation in socialism, a brief mention must be made of an important 1959 monograph by a distinguished Russian Marxist mathematician-economist, V.V. Novozhilov. On the question of labour time as unit of calculation he is one of the very few who, directly following Marx, connects the increase of non-labour time, and hence free time for the labouring individual, to an increase in productivity via application of machinery. This emancipatory aspect of the question is largely absent in the 'Western' discussion of the subject. We should add that following the usual practice of the post-1917 régime in Russia, and contrary to Marx, Novozhilov, too, distinguishes socialism from communism, considering it as the preparation for and the first phase of communism (while considering Russia to be a socialist society). His object of research has been how to optimise the use of society's resources, including living labour, in the really existing 'socialism', but also in the 'communism' yet to come, given that investment needs have to reckon with the limited character of available resources. He poses this as a problem of measurement of cost in terms of what the mathematicians call the problem of 'extremum', that is (relative) maximum or minimum, subject

---

in socialism (precisely because of the collective character of production) and indirectly social labour time in capitalism. See Marx 2008, pp. 307; 1956a, pp. 318–19.

92   Marx 2008, p. 381; 1956a, pp. 428–9. Emphasis added.

to constraints, and solves the problem by what in mathematics is named the method of the 'Lagrange multiplier'. We can skip the purely mathematical part and give the gist of his general argument. According to him, though the general principles of measuring costs are the same in socialism and communism, the forms of calculation are different in the two systems. In socialism it is calculation in terms of value, in communism, which has no value relation, it is in terms of labour time. The latter is relevant for our discussion. For communism, according to our author, the most general problem of extremum is governed by the law of economy of labour. That is why the maximisation of the rate of growth of productivity of labour is the most general problem of extremum of economic development. He holds that the maximisation of the growth of productivity of labour in communism constitutes at the same time the process of the maximum increase of time freed from material production. He explicitly cites Marx's statement from the manuscript of *Capital* Volume III: 'the reign of liberty lies beyond the realm of material production'. More concretely, one has to find the minimum of labour costs in final production, which is linked with the maximisation of the growth of labour productivity. Hence, for the society as a whole, the magnitude to minimise is the quantity of living labour. Now, for the society as a whole, the past or materialised labour is a constant which cannot be modified, whereas the living labour is a variable magnitude. Hence for society as a whole the minimum of the totality of costs in both past and present labour for production is determined by the minimum of living labour (past labour being a constant). Of course the treatment of past labour as zero does not mean that the products of this past labour are free of cost, not having involved any labour cost. This implies only that the products of past labour enter the expenses not as cost incurred in the past, but only insofar as their utilisation economises the living labour of society.[93]

One important point regarding labour time as the accounting measure should be noted. The tendency of capital is to increase the productivity of labour and thereby decrease the necessary labour time to the maximum. This results in an ever-diminishing role for living labour in the creation of use values. The same process also creates plenty of use values, sufficient to satisfy more than the basic human needs even now. Even more than 150 years ago, Marx and Engels, while referring to the immense productive forces unleashed by capitalism, underlined that 'the conditions of bourgeois society are too narrow to

---

93   Novozhilov 1967, pp. 175–7. Here the author is following the method Marx had adopted – that is, assumed constant capital as equal to zero – when analysing the rate of surplus value. See Marx 1987a, pp. 222–5; 1976a, pp. 160–3; 1954, pp. 205–7.

comprise the wealth created by them'.[94] For example, in a calculation presented by A. Maddison concerning labour productivity for twelve West European countries (weighted average), GDP per hour worked (international $ per hour) increased from 1.38 to 28.53 between 1870 and 1998.[95] By the time humanity creates the new society it is almost certain that a situation will arrive where labour time even as an accounting measure for individual consumption – as Marx envisages in terms of labour vouchers corresponding to the individual's labour contribution for the early phase of socialism – will have become superfluous, and people can obtain directly in kind whatever suffices to satisfy their needs. It is interesting to note that personal distribution according to needs in communism appears in Marx and Engels in one of their incomplete and rather unsystematised texts in a manuscript for the *German Ideology*: 'the differences of *heads* and intellectual capacities (of individuals) do not at all determine the differences in stomach and physical *needs*; consequently, the false phrase – because it is founded on the existing conditions – to each according to one's capacities, in so far as it takes enjoyment in a narrow sense, must be changed into *to each according to one's needs*; in other words, the *differences* in activities do not justify any inequality or privilege in the possession of enjoyment'.[96]

For socialist accounting the alternative to calculation by labour time is calculation in kind. Otto Neurath – referred to earlier – is arguably the most important socialist advocating calculation in kind. In this system every individual's 'quality of life' – defined as encompassing both the happiness and unhappiness of the individual – is determined in a direct way without any mediation by money. 'Growing crops will be decided in light of people's nutritional needs in much the same way as building schools is decided in light of people's educational needs. This is the economy in kind (*Naturalwirtschaft*), no longer sums of money but things themselves are taken as the basis for decisions'.[97] The logic of such an approach already appears in Marx's discussion in several texts. It should be stressed that though the production and reproduction of capital is Marx's focus of attention, the material content, independently of social forms, could equally apply to any society including socialist society. 'Whatever be the social form of the process of production, it must have to be continuous, that is, periodically repeat the same process. The conditions of production are also the conditions of reproduction'.[98] Earlier in this chapter we referred to a text from

---

94   Marx and Engels 1970b, p. 41.
95   Maddison 2006, p. 351.
96   Marx and Engels 1962c, p. 528. Emphasis in original.
97   Neurath 2004, p. 383.
98   Marx 1987a, p. 523; 1976a, p. 402; 1954, p. 531.

the manuscript for *Capital* Volume II discussing what could be called input-output in the process of production. This approach is also seen in an earlier manuscript in connection with Marx's analysis of Ricardo's theory of accumulation:

> A large part of what appears in one sphere as constant capital is at the same time, the product in another, a parallel sphere of production. The commodities emerge from one sphere as product, enter another as commodities forming constant capital. The commodity produced in one sphere of production passes on into another sphere of production to be consumed there as constant capital. [There can be also] a part of constant capital which is itself industrially consumed in the production of constant capital. This part is replaced *in natura* either directly from the product of this sphere itself or through the exchange of a portion of the produce of the different spheres of production which produce constant capital.[99]

Note the in-kind method in the cited passage. Neurath very clearly shows that cost and benefit in the sense of capitalism do not have any sense in socialism based on this natural system. In contrast with capitalism's money calculation – telling us nothing about the real wealth of a people – a socialist economy is concerned with usefulness, with people's needs with regard to food, clothing, housing, health, education, entertainment.[100] To this end society seeks to employ raw materials, extant machines, labour power, etc., in the best possible way, giving due consideration to environment and non-wasteful exploitation of resources. All this is best done by in-kind calculation, in terms of use values.[101] To get a full picture of the movements of productive resources and final products in terms of use values in the society as a whole, Leontief's input-output analysis is of great help. In this analysis, inter-industry transactions that go into the production of the output of an economic system are arrayed in the form of a matrix, with the outputs of each industrial sector displayed along its row and the inputs it draws from other industries in its column. The ratio of each input to the output of the sector – called its input-output coefficient –

---

99   Marx 1959, pp. 468–69; 1968, pp. 471–2.
100   Already in his 1847 *Anti-Proudhon*, Marx, referring to the 'coming society without classes', wrote that the 'determinant of production would not be the *minimum* of (labour) time, but the production time employed for different objects would be determined by their social utility'. See Marx 1965, p. 37. Emphasis in text.
101   Neurath 2004, p. 468.

reflects the technological requirement for that input, which 'although it is usually expressed in monetary value, is *best visualised in the physical units appropriate to it, whether tons, bushels, barrels, kilowatts or (hu)man hours'*.[102] Such coefficients could be derived from the records of actual transactions or from engineering data. The double-entry bookkeeping of the input-output table thus reveals the fabric of the whole economy, woven together by the flow of use values which ultimately links each branch and industry to all others.[103] Input-output coefficients could also be read as an efficiency index. It is the great merit of Oskar Lange to have shown, referring to Marx's two sector reproduction schemes, that the Leontief input-output system is an extension of the division of the Marxian schemes into n branches.[104] In a socialist society, given its social framework as a decentralised 'association of cooperative' units of production – in Marx's sense – effecting the allocation of means of production, that is, materialised labour, and living labour to different branches of production, as well as distribution of personal consumption in kind, seems to be simpler than in terms of labour time as an accounting unit. However, an estimate of society's total labour time in production dictated by the law of 'economy of time' as society progresses is of prime importance in view of its emancipatory implications. As discussed above, less labour time in material production means more free time for the individual's enjoyment and all-round development. Here the accounting could be done only in terms of labour time. Let us recall that Marx and Engels already wrote in 1845 that the question is 'will or will not the society have time to develop humanly? That depends on the labour time'.[105]

Finally, the accounting social framework studied here looks rather stationary, apparently not taking into account changes in people's needs through time, and technological changes. However, temporal changes can be, without much difficulty, taken into account. Given the thoroughly democratic process of decision-making embodied in the 'association of cooperatives', assessing people's needs through periodic surveys at short intervals should be increasingly easy, given the federated, decentralised social structure and rapid changes in communication technology. Collection of data on material production and people's needs and processing them through the input-output method at short intervals should prove much less difficult than in the early years of Leontief's undertaking.

102   Leontief 1982, p. 203. Emphasis added.
103   Leontief 1986, p. 5.
104   Lange 1969, p. 47. A more elaborate discussion can be found in Lange's 1959 text.
105   Marx and Engels 1972, p. 52; 1975, p. 49.

Anarchist Communism

By and large communism – at least in Europe – had not been traditionally associated with anarchism. This association was started by some anarchists in the late 1870s, sometime after the 1871 Paris Commune. It was 'Collectivism', not communism, with which Bakunin – arguably the best-known anarchist in Europe – had qualified his anarchism. By Collectivism Bakunin meant that the institution of the state must be abolished, that there would not be any individual private property in the means of production, and that all means of production would come under common ownership of the association of producers. Bakunin even showed a totally negative attitude to communism. Thus at the 1868 Bern Congress of the 'League of Peace and Liberty' he declared,

> I detest communism because it is the negation of liberty. I am not a communist because communism concentrates and causes all the forces of society to be absorbed by the state. It necessarily ends in the centralisation of property in the hands of the state, while I desire the abolition of the state, which has until now enslaved, oppressed, exploited and depraved the humans, while I desire the abolition of the state – the radical extirpation of the principle of authority and the tutelage of the state. I desire the organisation of society and of collective property from below upwards by means of free association and not from above downwards. In this sense I am a collectivist and not a communist.[1]

In this chapter we treat anarchist communism in the writings of two of its foremost representatives: Peter Kropotkin and Carlo Cafiero.

Peter Kropotkin

Peter Kropotkin was a scientist, a geographer by training, before he became an anarchist. He tried to create a scientific foundation for anarchism in light of the broad, discernible tendencies in nature and society. The genesis of his anarchism he describes in his 1899 *Memoirs*:

---

1 Cited in Plekhanov 1895. Plekhanov was one of the founders of Russia's Social Democratic Party.

Having been brought up in a serf owner's family I entered active life with a great deal of confidence in the necessity of commanding, ordering, punishing. But when at an early age I had to manage serious enterprises and to deal with men and when each mistake would lead at once to heavy consequences, I began to appreciate the difference between acting on the principle of command and discipline, and acting on the principle of common understanding. The former works admirably in a military parade, but it is nothing where real life is concerned, and the aim can be achieved only through the serious effort of many converging wills ... I was prepared to become an anarchist.[2]

Kropotkin's Anarchist Communism

According to Kropotkin, anarchism is a principle or theory of life under which society is conceived 'without government', in which individuals do not have to submit themselves to an authority in order to have a harmonious existence. This is ensured by 'free agreements between different groups freely constituted for the sake of production and consumption, as also for the satisfaction of the infinite variety of needs and aspirations of a civilised being; in a society developed on these lines, voluntary associations would take all the fields of human activity so as to substitute themselves for the state in all its functions'.[3] Such a society cannot come about unless the human mind frees itself from ideas inculcated by 'minorities of priests, military chiefs and judges, all striving to establish their domination, and of scientists paid to perpetuate it'[4] – a society where there is no longer room for those dominating minorities.

The state is only one of the forms of social life which, however, has not existed for all eternity. In his work *The State: Its Historic Role* (1897), Kropotkin observes that the Roman Empire was a state, but that the Greek cities and the medieval city republics were not. The state, and particularly the centralised state, re-emerged in Europe rather recently – around the sixteenth century –

---

2 Kropotkin 1989, pp. 201–2.

3 Kropotkin 1910. At a philosophical-scientific level, Kropotkin viewed anarchism, in his 1901 work *Modern Science and Anarchism*, as a 'world-concept based on mechanical explanation of all phenomena, embracing the whole of nature – that is, including in it the life of human societies. Its method of investigation is that of exact natural sciences, and if it pretends to be scientific every conclusion must be verified by the method by which every scientific conclusion must be verified. Its aim is to construct a synthetic philosophy comprehending in one generalisation all the phenomena of nature – and therefore also all the phenomena of societies' (cited in Marshall 2008, p. 318).

4 Kropotkin, in Graham 2005, p. 141.

and it practically destroyed the free towns and their federations.[5] Fully recognising as a fact the equal rights of every member of the society to the wealth accumulated in the past, anarchism refuses to accept a division between the exploited and the exploiters, dominated and the dominators, governed and the governors. 'It seeks the most complete development of individuality combined with the highest development of voluntary association in all its aspects, in all possible degrees, ever changing, ever modified associations which carry in themselves the elements of their durability and constantly assume new forms which answer best to the multiple aspirations of all'.[6]

In his 1902 work *Mutual Aid*, Kropotkin stressed further the character of human society before the rise of the (centralised) state. As if to refute what was later called 'social Darwinism' – that is, the justification of human inequalities on the basis of the survival of the fittest – Kropotkin, basing himself on extant critical-historical studies of Europe, including Russia, held that mutual aid among fellow humans had been the rule till very recent times, and had been the foundation of social life. With a remote human origin, this tendency continued to exist and developed further from the tribes through progressively larger agglomerations. A new form of mutual aid appeared in the Middle Ages: a federation of communities covered by a network of fraternities and guilds across the land. Then, towards the end of the fifteenth century, they fell a prey to the growing military state. 'Only wholesale massacres by the thousand could put a

---

5   See Kropotkin 1897, 1898. We should point out that in his visceral animosity for anarchism, the eminent Marx scholar Hal Draper has distorted Kropotkin's account of the rise of the modern state. Bracketing Kropotkin with Bakunin, he calls him 'naïve' and derisively writes about Kropotkin's account of the evolution of the state: after quoting Kropotkin to the effect that the 'state, as far as Europe is concerned, is of recent origin, it barely goes back to the sixteenth century', Draper scornfully writes that the state 'apparently did not exist in feudalism! That is, Kropotkin saw the medieval state as non-despotic, *hence not a state*' (Draper 1990, pp. 124–5; his emphasis). First of all, Draper chooses not to mention that, according to Kropotkin, the Roman Empire was already a state which was destroyed by the 'barbarians'. The modern *centralised State* starts much later in the sixteenth century. Thus Kropotkin wrote: 'In Europe the centralized state dates from the sixteenth century after the medieval communes were defeated' (1898). It is also remarkable that our Marx scholar did not see that Marx's position on the rise of the modern centralised state, presented in his discourse on the Paris Commune (1871), is not much different from Kropotkin's. Thus in both the final version and in the second draft of the discourse, Marx says that the 'centralised state power dates from the days of the absolute monarchy serving the nascent middle class society' (Marx 1971, pp. 68, 218). This of course means that under feudalism there was no centralised state in Europe, which is exactly what Kropotkin had written.

6   Kropotkin, in Graham 2005, p. 142.

stop to this widely spread popular movement, and it was by the sword, the fire and the rack that the young states secured their first and decisive victory over the masses of the people. When the medieval cities were subdued in the sixteenth century by the growing military states, all institutions which had kept the artisans, the masters, and the merchants together in the guilds and the cities were violently destroyed'.[7]

In his 1901 article 'Communism and Anarchy' Kropotkin speaks of two kinds of communism – authoritarian and anarchist. But he does not sufficiently clarify what he means by 'communism'. He only cites some historical examples of communitarian life, for example, in Europe's middle ages. Kropotkin's criterion of desirability of communism is how far the individual is free under communism. 'Of all the institutions and forms of organisation that have been tried till now, communism is the one that guarantees the greatest amount of individual liberty – provided that the idea that begets the Community be Liberty, Anarchy'.[8] Kropotkin adds that 'communism, being an economic organisation, does not in any way prejudice the amount of liberty guaranteed to the individual, the initiator, the rebel against crystallising customs'.[9] It may be authoritarian or it may be libertarian, opines Kropotkin. Then he adds, 'the only durable form of communism is the one in which, following the close contact between fellow humans that it brings, every effort would be made to extend the liberty of the individual in all directions. With Anarchy as an aim and as a means, Communism becomes possible, without it Communism necessarily becomes slavery and cannot exist'.[10]

In his 1910 *Encyclopaedia Britannica* contribution, Kropotkin considers anarchists (also) as 'socialists of whom they constitute the left wing'. Further, he calls his own anarchism 'anarchist communism'.[11] It was Kropotkin's aim to prove that communism had more chances of being established than collectivism,[12] especially in the communes taking the lead, and that 'free or anarchist

---

7   Kropotkin 1902.

8   Kropotkin 1901.

9   Kropotkin 1901. Kropotkin seems to be unaware that long before him Marx and Engels, with a very different notion of communism, had stressed in their 1845 *German Ideology* that the organisation of communism was essentially economic. We discuss this whole point extensively in another chapter of this book.

10   Kropotkin 1901.

11   Kropotkin 1910.

12   Kropotkin uses the term 'collectivism' differently from Bakunin, whose usage we have mentioned earlier, and refers to a state socialism that is attributed to Marx. 'Anarchist communism differed from collectivism only on one point, the way in which the product

communism is the only form of communism that has any chance of being accepted in civilised societies; communism and anarchy are, therefore, two terms of evolution which complete each other, the one rendering the other possible and acceptable'.[13] In fact, in his 1906 work *The Conquest of Bread*, Kropotkin wrote: 'Anarchy leads to Communism, and Communism to Anarchy, both alike being expressions of the predominant tendency in modern societies, the pursuit of equality'.[14] Mooting the question of distribution, the share of each person in the wealth, Kropotkin observes that it is impossible to estimate the share of a person in the riches which *all* contribute to amass.[15] From this general synthetic point of view Kropotkin observes,

> We cannot hold with the collectivists that payment proportional to the hours of labour rendered by each would be an ideal arrangement, even a step in the right direction. The collectivist ideal appears to be untenable in a society which considers the instruments of labour as a common inheritance. A new form of property requires a new form of remuneration. A new method of production cannot exist side by side with the old form of consumption, any more than it can adapt to the old forms of political organisation.[16]

Continuing further with the economic conceptions of the anarchists, Kropotkin holds that the prevailing system of private ownership of land and the capitalist system of production for profit represent a monopoly which goes against the principles of justice and the dictates of utility. They are the main obstacles which prevent the success of modern technology from being brought into the service of all, so as to produce general well-being. 'The anarchists consider the wage system and capitalist production together as an obstacle to progress, but

---

of labour should be shared. In place of the mutualist and collectivist idea of remuneration according to hours of labour, the anarchist communists proclaimed the slogan: from each according to his [her] means, to each according to his [her] needs'. George Woodcock 1967, p. 114.

13   Kropotkin 1910.
14   Kropotkin 1906.
15   It is interesting to note that years before Kropotkin, and in direct opposition to Bakunin, Marx had held that in a communitarian society communal production is presupposed as the basis of production. The labour of the individual is posited as social labour from the beginning. Here, unlike what happens in commodity production, no ex post recognition of the individual's contribution is necessary. See Marx 1953, p. 88; 1993, p. 172.
16   Kropotkin 1906.

they also point out that the state was and continues to be the chief instrument for permitting the few to monopolise the land and the capitalists to appropriate for themselves a disproportionate share of the yearly accumulated surplus of production. Consequently, while combating the present monopolisation of land, and capitalism all together, the anarchists combat with the same energy the state, the main support of the system'.[17] As opposed to the collectivists, Kropotkin stresses that to hand over to the state all the main sources of life – the land, the mines, the railways, and so on – as also the management of all the main branches of industry, in addition to all the functions accumulated in the hands of the state, would mean to create a new instrument of tyranny. State capitalism would only increase the powers of bureaucracy and capitalism. True progress lies in decentralisation, both functional and territorial, in the development of the spirit of local and personal initiative, and of free federation in lieu of the present hierarchy from centre to the periphery.

Speaking of the process of social transformation, Kropotkin observes that, like all evolution in nature, the slow evolution of society is followed from time to time by periods of accelerated evolution which are called revolutions. 'Periods of rapid change will follow the periods of slow evolution, and these periods must be taken advantage of, not for increasing the powers of the State, but for reducing them in every township or commune of the local groups of producers and consumers, as also the regional, and eventually the international federations of these groups'.[18] Kropotkin explains that by 'Revolution' one should understand that it is not a simple change of governments. It is the taking possession by the people of all social wealth, it is the abolition of all forces which have so long hindered the progress of humanity. However, it is not by any government decree that this revolution – which is basically an immense economic transformation – can be accomplished. In order that the taking possession of society's wealth should become an accomplished fact, it is necessary that the people shake off slavery, to which they have been too much accustomed, that they act on their own will and march forward without waiting for any order from any one. In his 1892 work on *Revolutionary Government*, Kropotkin wrote that 'The economic change which will result from the Social Revolution will be so immense, so profound, it must so change all relations based on property and exchange, that it is impossible for any individual to elaborate the different social forms which will spring up in the society of the future. This elaboration of new social forms can only be made by the collective work of the masses;

---

17   Kropotkin 1910.
18   Kropotkin 1910.

any authority external to it will only be an obstacle, only a trammel on the organic labour which must be accomplished'.[19] In the same work, he emphasised that 'It is time to give up the illusion of a *Revolutionary* Government. It is time to admit this political axiom that a *government cannot be revolutionary*'.[20]

In his work *Fields, Factories and Workshops* (1912), Kropotkin takes up the issue of the increasing power of the human over the productive forces of nature. He asks – given the system of division of functions and production for profit – whether the means now in use for satisfying human needs lead to real economy in the expenditure of human forces. Then he mentions several fields of productive activity to illustrate the possibility of achieving economy in the expenditure of human forces. Thus, in agriculture, given well thought out and socially carried out permanent improvements of the soil, the duration of work to grow bread for a family of five would be less than a fortnight every year, while the work will be not only far less hard than that of a slave in earlier times, but, in fact, will be really agreeable, like work in the open air after a day's work in a factory. Kropotkin envisages a great variety of workshops and factories which are needed to satisfy infinite diversity of tastes among civilised humans, 'factories in which human life is more of account than machinery and the making of extra profit, in which men, women and children will be attracted by the desire of finding an activity suited to their taste, and where, aided by the motor and the machines, they will choose the branch of activity which best suits their inclination'.[21]

Finally we touch on Kropotkin's idea of what he considers to be agreeable work for individuals, or, in other words, what work becomes possible after society is liberated from the reign of capital. For example, a factory could be made as healthy and pleasant as a scientific laboratory. There can be no doubt that work will become a pleasure and a relaxation in a society of equals in which 'hands' will not be compelled to sell themselves and to work under any condition. Slaves can submit to them, but free humans will create new conditions, and their work will be pleasant and infinitely more productive. He stresses: 'A society, regenerated by the Revolution, will make domestic slavery disappear – this last form of slavery, the most tenacious, because it is also the most ancient. Servant or wife, man always reckons on woman to do the house work; but the woman too at last claims her share in the emancipation of human-

---

19   Kropotkin 1892.
20   Kropotkin 1892. Emphasis in text.
21   Kropotkin 1912.

ity, she no longer wants to be the beast of burden of the house'.[22] He refers to machines of all kinds which will be introduced into households to enable men and women to work without muscular effort. 'To emancipate woman is to free her from the brutalising toil of kitchen and washhouse. Let us fully understand that a Revolution intoxicated with the beautiful words, liberty, equality, solidarity would not be a Revolution if it maintains slavery at home; half humanity subjected to slavery of hearth would still have to rebel against the other half'.[23]

Carlo Cafiero[24]

By anarchist communism Cafiero means the revolutionary abolition of the state and wage system, voluntary association and distribution according to needs. In the existing society, anarchy starts with *attack* against every authority, every power, every state, whereas in the future society anarchy will be *defence*, which means preventing the re-establishment of any authority, any power, any state. The future society will be characterised by 'complete liberty of the individual who, freely driven by his [her] needs, tastes and sympathies, will unite with other individuals in an association; free development of the association, which is federated with others in the commune; free development of the communes which are federated in the region; the regions in the nations; the nations in humanity'.[25] Communism is the second term – the first being the term anarchy – of the anarchist revolutionary ideal. Communism today is the taking possession of all wealth existing in the world in the name of all humanity. In the future society communism will signify the enjoyment of all wealth by all individuals following the principle *'From each according to one's faculty, to each according to one's needs*, that is to say, from each to each according to one's will'.[26]

---

22   Kropotkin 1906.

23   Kropotkin 1906.

24   The whole section which follows is based on the author's fundamental work on anarchy and communism, delivered as a speech at the Jura Federation of Anarchists in 1880. We should mention here that this same Cafiero had prepared a small popularised compendium of Marx's *Capital* Volume 1 and had sent it to Marx. Marx in his reply (in French), dated 29 July 1879, praised the work, calling it much superior to similar attempts by some others at popularising his work. The anarchist writers seem to avoid any mention of this Marx-Cafiero connection.

25   Cafiero, in Graham 2005, p. 109.

26   Cafiero, in Graham 2005, p. 109. Emphasis in text.

Cafiero stresses that the act of possessing and enjoying society's wealth cannot be mediated by any representative, any government, any state. It must be the act of the people itself directly. And, since the common wealth is spread over the whole globe, since all of it belongs to humanity as a whole, those who find this wealth within their own reach and are in a position to use it, will use it in common. 'If an inhabitant of Peking came into this country, s/he will have the same right as the others; s/he would enjoy, in common with the others, all the wealth of the country in the same way that s/he had done in Peking'.[27]

Broaching the question of distribution in the new communist society – whether individuals will have the right to receive products at will without doing more work – Cafiero answers very positively: the principle 'from each according to one's faculty, to each according to one's needs' is possible because the future communist society will create useful products with such an abundance that there will be no need to limit consumption nor to ask individuals to do more work than they would be able or willing to perform. Cafiero offers three reasons for this possibility: (1) harmony of co-operation in various branches of activity replacing competitive struggles; (2) introduction of machines of different kinds on an immense scale; (3) considerable economy in the power of labour, instruments of labour and raw materials, arising from the suppression of dangerous or useless materials. As regards the first, 'this individualist principle of capitalist production, each for him [her] self and against all, and all against each, will be replaced in the future society by the true principle of sociability: each for all and all for each. What an enormous change will be obtained in the results of production, when each man (woman), far from having to struggle against all others, will be helped by them, s/he will have them not as enemies but as co-operators'.[28]

As to the machines, however great their power looks at present, it is only minimal compared to what it will be in the future society. One has only to take account of the number of machines remaining idle because of their inability to earn a profit for the capitalist owner. The workers themselves oppose the machines, since they drive the workers out of the factory, to starve them, to crush them. Yet one could imagine what a great interest the workers of the future will have in increasing the number of machines when workers will not be at the service of the machines, but, on the contrary, the machines will be at the service of the workers! Speaking of the possibility of great economies in the

---

27   Cafiero, in Graham 2005, p. 110. We have taken the liberty of changing the overtly sexist language of the text.
28   Cafiero, in Graham 2005, p. 111.

process of production as regards human labour, machines and materials, resulting from their proper use, Cafiero underlines 'how many workers, how many instruments, how many materials of labour are used to-day for the armies of land and sea to build ships, fortresses, canons, and all the arsenals of offensive and defensive weapons. And when all this strength, all these materials, all these instruments are used in industry for the production of articles which be themselves used for production, what a prodigious increase of production we shall see emerge'.[29] With such abundance in communism, each person will be able to receive from the common wealth whatever is required to satisfy their needs. At the same time, with the hugely diminished labour time due to technological development, work will cease to be a burden on the worker and will be turned into an agreeable endeavour.

Now after putting the instruments of labour and raw materials in common, if society retained the individual distribution of the products of labour, society would be forced to retain money, sharing a greater or lesser accumulation of wealth according to the greater or lesser merit of individuals. Equality would then have disappeared. In the future society, in the beginning, since the products would not be abundant enough, rationing has to be introduced, but in order that the society remains communist, the sharing of products must have to be carried out not according to merit (as it is done under capitalism), but still according to need. Cafiero gives the example of a large family where, though the individuals contribute unequally to the common fund according to their earning capacity, each one gets their share according to need, though the helpings are reduced. 'It cannot be otherwise in the great humanitarian family of the future'.[30]

Anarchism and Marx: The Relation

The conflict in the workers' First International – the International Workingmen's Association (1864–72) – between the majority represented by Marx and those members who were on his side, on the one hand, and Bakunin and his followers on the other, has very much coloured the representation of Marx's relation to anarchism.[31] In the following we will abstract from the *events* con-

---

29   Cafiero, in Graham 2005, p. 112.
30   See Cafiero, in Graham 2005, pp. 113–14.
31   Let us just note that Marx's charge against Bakunin in the context of the International had nothing to do with anarchism, but was solely about Bakunin's attempt to turn the International into something totally opposed to its basic aim and principles – to turn the body

nected with this conflict and stay almost exclusively within the realm of idea(s). In this question the focus is – given the anarchists' absolute opposition to the state – mainly on the relation of the state to socialism as Marx saw it. The first thing that comes to mind in this connection is that the position ascribed to Marx on this issue, that the state is an integral part of socialism, is ascribed, however paradoxically, by *both* of the two opposing political sides – anarchists and a large section of Marx's own followers, particularly the partisans of what, after 1917, passes for socialist régimes. This ascribed position, completely alien to Marx, enabled the anarchists in general to make an impermissible amalgam of Marx's position and the position of the 'Marxists' (Marxians), obfuscating Marx's own position on both state and socialism.[32] However, though the question of the state in relation to the society after capital has been the primary focus in the controversy, a few Marxians have also critically discussed some other aspects of anarchism from the point of view of what they consider to be Marx's own perspective. Given the somewhat extended analysis of the topic of the state in relation to socialism in another chapter in this book, we try here to deal with that part of the supposedly 'Marxian' critique which touches on the non-state aspects of the discussion. One of the few Marxians who have criticised the anarchists on both points – state as well as non-state – is Nikolai Bukharin. This mainly concerns the economic organisation of the society succeeding capital.

Let us first summarise Bukharin's arguments on this question. On the one hand, he holds that, for the communists, it is centralised production under large trusts, while, on the other, for the anarchists it is small, decentralised production. Further, the communists believe not only that the society of the future must free itself of the exploitation of human by human, but also that

into a headquarters of world revolution by conspiratorial means. This is confirmed by a great historian of anarchism who is also its sympathiser, Peter Marshall, in a book praised by Noam Chomsky. Marshall writes, 'It is difficult to refute the main thrust of the "Marxist camp". Bakunin undoubtedly tried to establish a secret, centralised, and hierarchical organisation with the intention of directing the International'.

32   Maximilien Rubel, arguably the most informed Marx scholar after Riazanov, has observed that 'Marxism as the ideology of the master class has succeeded in emptying the concepts of socialism and communism, as Marx and his forerunners understood them, of their original meaning and has replaced it with a picture of a reality which is its complete negation' (Rubel 2005). Again, the same writer stresses the peculiar fact that 'the triumph of "Marxism" as a state doctrine and party ideology preceded by several decades the publication of the writings where Marx set out most clearly and completely the scientific basis of his social theory' (Rubel 2005). This 'anachronism', added Rubel, 'has an analogy uniquely in the genesis of great religions where faith precedes canonisation' (Rubel 1994, p. xi).

it will have to ensure for the human the greatest possible independence from nature that surrounds her/him, that it will reduce to a minimum the time spent on socially necessary labour, developing to a maximum the forces of production, and likewise the productivity itself of social labour. Communists consider that the ideal solution to this is centralised production, methodically organised in large units. The anarchists, on the other hand, prefer a totally different type of relations of production. Their ideal consists of tiny communes which by their very structure are disqualified from managing any large enterprises, but reach 'agreements' with one another and link up through a network of free contracts. From an economic point of view that sort of production is closer to the medieval communes than to the mode of production destined to supplant the capitalist system. This system is not only a retrograde step, it is also utterly utopian. Any new order is possible and useful only insofar as it leads to the further development of the productive forces of the order which is destined to disappear. Naturally any further development is conceivable as a continuation of the tendency of the productive forces of centralisation. Seeing that capitalist centralisation is a method of oppression, the anarchists protest, in their simplicity, against all centralisation of production; their infantile naiveté confuses the essence of the thing with its social, historical forms. Then Bukharin concludes: 'So the distinction between communists and anarchists with respect to the bourgeois society lies not in that we favour the state and they are against the state, but rather in that we favour production being centralised in large units, fitted to the maximum development of productive forces, while anarchists favour small, decentralised production which cannot raise, but only lower the level of these productive forces'.[33]

This account of the anarchist position by Bukharin has to be taken with a table spoon of salt. It is an oversimplified representation, and to a large extent, a misrepresentation of the anarchist, particularly of the 'anarchist communist', position on the question of the economic organisation of the society after capital.

Remarkably, Bukharin does not give any specific reference to any particular text by the anarchists in his critique of their position. As can be seen in our discussion given above on the positions of the two anarchist communists – Kropotkin and Cafiero – with reference to their texts, Bukharin's description of the alleged defects of the anarchist position on the organisation of production in the society after capital is highly inaccurate. Kropotkin, we know, stresses the necessity of a countless variety of factories in order to satisfy an infinite

---

33   Bukharin 1918.

diversity of tastes. They are also needed to increase the power of humans over the productive forces of nature, enabling real economy in the expenditure of human labour power. Marx had already stressed the importance of machinery for gaining the 'economy of time'. Similarly, Kropotkin emphasises the necessity of 'modern technology' for producing general wellbeing. Naturally the scale of production would correspond to the technology applied.

In the same way we saw earlier that another anarchist communist, Cafiero, had spoken of the introduction of machines of different kinds 'on an immense scale'. As to the machines, their power under capitalism looks minimal compared to what it will be in the future society, where workers will not be at the service of the machines, but the machines will be at the service of the workers. For those familiar with Marx's texts this immediately brings to mind Marx's own position. Technology will 'hugely diminish' the amount of working time.

Finally, the federative communal structure of the organisation in society championed by the anarchist communists is only a version of what the 1871 communards had planned for France. It also touched precisely the organisation of industry. Engels, in his introduction to Marx's *Civil War in France*, wrote that the 'organisation of large scale industry was not only to be based on the association of the workers in each factory, but also to combine all these associations in one great union; which, in short, as Marx quite rightly says, must have led in the end to communism'.[34] The irony is that very interestingly Engels observed on the same page of his work that this scheme was the work of Proudhon (the anarchist), while adding that the end of the process, that is, communism, was the 'direct opposite of the Proudhon doctrine'.[35]

Going beyond these specific charges against the anarchists, Bukharin also undertakes a wholesale damnation and dismissal of anarchism without, again, referring to any particular text in the relevant literature. Bukharin, in the text under consideration here, opines that it follows from the anarchist theory that the 'consistent anarchist must be averse to soviet power and fight against it', that 'anarchists cannot have any special affection for the soviets', and that 'at best they merely exploit them and are ever ready to dismantle them'.[36] It is indeed ironical that the very year that Bukharin denounced the anarchists as the enemies of the soviets also saw the end of the *soviets as independent organs of power* of the labouring people of Russia. Bukharin himself, as a leading mem-

---

34   Marx and Engels 1971b, p. 31.
35   Marx and Engels 1971b, p. 31.
36   Bukharin 1918.

ber of the conquering group, and not the anarchists, was a party to this liquidation of the soviets.[37]

'Anarchy', continued Bukharin, 'is the ideology not of the proletariat, but
of declassed groups lacking a connection with all productive labour, ideology
of the lumpenproletariat, ruined bourgeoisie, decadent intellectuals, peasants
cast out by their families and impoverished, an amalgam of people incapable
of creating anything new'.[38] Not a word on how he arrived at this conclusion,
on what evidence. Now, if we follow the logic of facts, and not the argument of
abuse and vituperation soaked in ideology, and read the work of the eminent
American historian of anarchism, Paul Avrich, particularly his work on the role
of the Russian anarchists in the 1917 Revolution in Russia, we get a very different picture of the anarchists.[39] Far from being a bunch of idlers, delinquents
and lumpenproletarians, incapable of creating anything new, the anarchists
showed themselves to be the most energetic participants in the Revolution at
the side of the Bolsheviks. The anarchists were greatly impressed by Lenin's
ultra-radical statements of April 1917. Avrich writes that 'Lenin's appeal for a
"break-up and a revolution a thousand times more powerful than that of February" had a distinctively Bakuninist ring', and then Avrich quotes a 'prominent
anarchist' that 'there existed a perfect parallelism between the two groups'.[40]
There were at least four anarchist members of 'the Bolshevik-dominated Military Committee which organised the seizure of power on 25 October 1917'. With
the overthrow of the Provisional Government, 'the marriage of convenience
between the Bolsheviks and the anarchists had accomplished its purpose'.[41]

However, by the spring of 1918 the majority of anarchists had become sufficiently disillusioned with Lenin to seek a complete break, while the Bolsheviks,
for their part, had begun to contemplate the suppression of their former allies,
who had outlived their usefulness and whose incessant criticisms were a nuis-
ance the new régime no longer had to tolerate. An open break occurred in April
1918, when the Cheka launched a campaign to remove those anarchist cells,
considered particularly dangerous, from Moscow and Petrograd. The anarchists cried out in protest that the Bolsheviks had betrayed the masses and the
Revolution. We should remember that Bukharin's vituperative attack on the
anarchists occurred during just this period.

---

37 In the footnote accompanying Bukharin's text we read: 'The Italian editors note that the
    author was referring to what happened in Russia'.
38 Bukharin 1918.
39 We here draw on Avrich 1967, pp. 341–50.
40 Avrich 1967, p. 344.
41 Avrich 1967, p. 345.

But if the Golden Age was slipping from their grasp, the anarchists refused to despair; they tenaciously clung to the belief that ultimately their vision of stateless utopia would triumph. They proclaimed 'the Revolution is dead! Long live the Revolution'.[42]

Let us, for a change, take the anti-anarchist attack of a Marxist of a more recent vintage, the eminent scholar Hal Draper. Obsessed with Bakunin, out to demolish the 'Marx-Anarchist Myth', he presents anarchism almost as a generalisation of Bakuninism, ignoring the different tendencies within the movement. He refers to Marx's designation of the 1871 Commune as a 'workers' government ... a representative government based on universal suffrage', and then adds that 'both these institutions' were 'an anathema to *any anarchist* who knew what he was talking about'.[43]

Here is a counter-example. An eminent anarchist, a junior contemporary of Kropotkin, José Llunas Pujols, in his 1882 essay on 'What is anarchy', stressed that 'Administration is the only thing required and indispensable in any civilised society'.[44] Here obviously 'administration' signifies governance. He continued, 'since a collective as a whole cannot write a letter or do an infinity of tasks which only individuals can perform, it follows that *delegating* these tasks to the most qualified person *subject to a code of conduct prescribed in advance*, is not only not an abdication of freedom but rather an accomplishment of the most sacred duty of anarchy, which is the *organisation of administration*'.[45] Pujols stressed that 'All commissions or delegations appointed in an anarchist society should at all times be liable to *replacement and recall* through ongoing *balloting* of the Section or Sections by which they have been elected'.[46]

Just as many anarchists, affected by what happened in the International, have misrepresented Marx's (mainly political) ideas, the Marxians also – particularly those in the Bolshevik tradition – have misrepresented the ideas of the anarchists.

In fact, a closer reading of the literature on anarchism shows that the anarchists' stand that Marx was a statist draws mainly, not so much on what Marx himself wrote in his own texts, as on what the 'Marxists' said on this question claiming Marx's authority (not always strictly following his texts). Here an important role in this regard was also played by the political practice of the

42   Avrich 1967, p. 350.
43   Draper 1990, p. 172. Emphasis added.
44   Pujols, in Graham 2005, p. 126.
45   Pujols, in Graham 2005, p. 126. Emphasis in text.
46   Pujols, in Graham 2005, p. 126. Emphasis ours.

twentieth-century 'socialist' régimes. We take up this question of Marx's position on the state in some detail in another chapter.

It may not be totally out of place here if we present a couple of rather unusual statements from Bakunin in *praise* of Marx. The anarchist authors rarely mention these statements, and they seem to be mostly unknown to the Marxians, though these statements do not specifically refer to the question of state. The first statement was pronounced in Bakunin's address to the Berne Congress of the 'League of Peace and Liberty' (1869), where he compared Proudhon with Marx: 'Proudhon, in spite of all his efforts to get a firm foothold on the ground of reality, remained an idealist and metaphysician; his starting point is the abstract side of law from which he arrives at economic facts, while Marx, on the contrary, has enunciated and proved the truth, demonstrated by the whole of ancient and modern history of the human societies, of peoples and of states, that economic facts preceded the facts of political and civil law. This discovery and demonstration of this truth is one of the greatest merits of Mr. Marx'.[47]

The second statement appeared in a pamphlet that he composed during 1869–71 in which he called *Das Kapital* a 'magnificent work'. In continuation, he wrote,

> Nothing that I know of contains an analysis so profound, so luminous, so scientific, so decisive, so merciless an exposé of the formation of bourgeois capital and the systematic and cruel exploitation capital continues exercising over the work of the proletariat. The only defect of this work, based on a profound study of economic works, without admitting any logic other than the logic of facts – the only defect is that it has been written in part and in part only in a style excessively metaphysical and abstract which makes it difficult to explain, and nearly unapproachable for the majority of workers, and it is principally the workers who must read it nevertheless. The bourgeois will not read it ... This work is nothing other than a sentence of death, scientifically motivated and irrevocably pronounced, not against the bourgeoisie as individuals, but against their class.[48]

Let us conclude here by referring to some interesting remarks by Roberto Michels, the Italianised German sociologist, on what he thought was a conflu-

---

47   Cited in Plekhanov 1895.

48   Bakunin 1971.

ence of the two systems – Bakunin's and Marx's – here put in a nutshell by a
contemporary author:

> Marxism and Bakuninism functioned as two intimately related systems of
> radical thought. Both began as an obliterating indictment of capitalism.
> Both then sought the same socialist ends, though by different means ...
> One should not skip over the differences. But the conventional wisdom
> about Bakuninism and Marxism skipped over the similarities. Marxism
> entered the mentality of Italian socialists through Bakunin. In Michel's
> telling of the history of Italian socialism, Bakunin appears as a kind of
> John the Baptist, preparing the way for the gospel of Marxism. 'One can
> say that the Italian workers, saturated with Bakunin's ideas, were then psy-
> chologically prepared to receive the ideas of Marx'.[49]

---

49   Drake 2003.

CHAPTER 7

Concerning Guild Socialism

Introduction

Guild Socialism is a form of socialism which is almost entirely British and developed in the twentieth century over a relatively short period. This socialism is still a noteworthy episode in the history of the European working-class movement for its distinctly libertarian tendency at a time when the dominant Marxian socialism of the Second International, with its increasing compromise with the existing social order, was on its way to decay as an independent movement of the working class.

Guild Socialism advocated workers' self-government in industry through the national worker-controlled guilds. The guild theory, originated by Arthur Penty in his work *Restoration of Guilds* (1906), stressed the spirit of the medieval trust guilds.[1] The name 'Guild' is taken from the Middle Ages, during which the fundamental form of industrial organisation in Europe was the 'Gild' or 'Guild', an association of independent producers or merchants for the regulation of production or sale. Indeed, it was the common form of popular association in the mediaeval town. The element of identity between the mediaeval Guild and the National Guilds proposed by Guild Socialism in the twentieth century is, however, far more of spirit than of organisation.[2] Secondly, by 'guild' its partisans mean something based on trade unionism, but essentially different from the existing trade unionism in two particulars: (1) even if a trade union is what is called an industrial union including the entire body of workers, it is an incomplete body, because it excludes the technical workers attached to the industry, in other words, it does not include all of the persons engaged in that industry who are essential to its efficient functioning. One of the ways in which a guild would be different from a trade union is that it would include the whole of the workers by hand as well as experts – brain workers and manual workers of every kind – all the workers who are essential to the carrying on of that industry with efficiency as a public service. In their attitude to the trade union movement, the guild socialists 'have that object in mind: trying to create that sort of organisation that would be capable not merely of overthrowing capitalism –

---

1 See the article 'Guild Socialism' in *Columbia Electronic Encyclopaedia* (2012).
2 See Cole 1921, p. 46.

which is a comparatively easy job – but replacing capitalism – which is a very much harder job'.[3] (2) The second point of difference of the guild from the trade union, the guild partisans hold, is that the guild would be mainly concerned not with looking after the interest of its members in an economical sense but with the efficient functioning of industry. 'The main job of the guild would be not protection, not collective bargaining; it would be turning out the goods, seeing that the industry is efficiently conducted, actually *running and administering the industry*'.[4]

After Penty's work, mentioned earlier, later elaborations by three authors, A.R. Orage, S.G. Hobson and, above all, G.D.H. Cole, led to the incorporation of aspects of the Marxian critique of capitalism and of syndicalism. In what follows we draw on Hobson and Cole, though more on Cole than on Hobson, since it was Cole who covered the widest ground.

As a student of this system sums it up, 'Guild theory made three essential claims: it was to provide a critique of the existing system of industrial capitalism, to outline the basic requirements of an alternative social system, and to suggest the best method of transition from one system to the other'.[5]

Generally speaking, Guild Socialism accepts Marx's economic critique of capital(ism) as a system of 'wage slavery', though it does not always make clear the distinction between labour and labour power. Thus its theorists hold that by the system of wage slavery, *individuals* are turned into commodities subject to purchase and sale in the market. On the other hand, Guild Socialism distinguishes itself from most other left-wing movements by emphasising the *alienation* caused by wage slavery. Capitalism not only reproduces economic inequalities, but also vast inequalities of status, elevating a small group of individuals, while subjecting the mass of humanity to the indignity of being owned and controlled in the work process.

---

3 Cole 1968, p. 8.
4 Cole 1968, p. 9. Emphasis added.
5 Wright 1974, p. 169. He is however outright wrong to say on the same page that the Guild Socialists, while accepting the basic Marxian categories, went beyond Marx by asserting 'the human consequences of economic exploitation which we now describe in terms of "alienation"'. This shows only the author's profound innocence of Marx's own texts from his youth to the ultimate writings dwelling on this central theme, though not always using the same vocabulary.

Guild Socialism as Democracy

The starting point of Guild Socialism is that it is a form of socialism, not an alternative to socialism, a new interpretation of socialism, an attempt to make it a more complete and more balanced doctrine, more expressive of democracy, a doctrine that will make democracy more effective economically as well as politically. 'The desire of the guild socialists is not to found a new school, or a new organisation, but to convert the socialist movement to its point of view'.[6] Society is to be regarded as a complex of associations held together by the wills of their members, whose wellbeing is its purpose. Guild Socialists assume further that it is not enough that the forms of government should have the passive or implied consent of the governed, but that society will be in health only if it is in the full sense democratic and self-governing. The most vital assumption of all is that it regards this democratic principle as applying not only or mainly to some special sphere of social action known as 'politics', but to any and every form of social action and, in particular, to industrial and economic fully as much as to political affairs. 'Only a community which is self-governing in this complete sense over the length and breadth of its activities can hope to call out what is best in its members or to give them that maximum opportunity for personal and social self-expression which is requisite to real freedom'.[7]

Consequently, the 'workers as the dispossessed class' both economically and politically have to 'employ their industrial organisation as almost the sole means at their disposal for making their will felt'.[8]

The conception of democracy advanced by the Guild Socialists is very different from that which is commonly used. The Guild Socialist conception of democracy is that it is wrong to speak of one person representing another person or a number of persons, because by 'her/his very nature a human is such a being that s/he cannot be represented. This is of course not a denial of forms of representative government properly understood; it is merely to say that unless representative government conforms to certain canons, it will be misrepresentative government'.[9] The canon to which a representative must conform if it is to be really representative demands that the representative represent not another person but some group of *purposes* which people have in common. In other words, 'all true representation is not representation of persons, but only

6   Cole 1968, p. 4.
7   Cole 1921, p. 13.
8   Cole 1921, p. 17. This looks almost like a paraphrase of the Marx of the First International.
9   Cole 1968, p. 6.

representation of common purposes, that is, any real representation is necessarily *functional representation*.[10] The Guild Socialists hold that if we want a
democratic society we can only get it by making society democratic in all its
parts in relation to all the various functions which have to be performed in
that society. Thus, we must treat the problem of industry as one problem and
see that it gets organised on democratic lines by itself. Similarly, we must take
the problem of politics and see that it gets organised on democratic lines by
itself. The same is the case with all other spheres of society. Given that they
are dealing with an advanced industrial society, the guild socialists pay particular attention to the industrial sphere. Because 'unless you get the industrial
organisation straightened out you do not stand a chance of straightening out
anything else. Therefore that on which attention has first to be concentrated
is straightening out as far as may be the industrial system, bringing it into harmony with democratic principles, and then going on to introduce sanity into
the other parts of society as well'.[11]

Distribution and Allocation in Guild Socialism

Guild Socialists hold that it is futile to expect true democracy to exist in any
society which recognises vast inequalities of wealth, status and power among
its members. Most obvious of all is that, 'if in the sphere of industry one person
is a master and the other is a *wage-slave*, one enjoys riches and gives commands
and the other has only an insecure subsistence and obeys orders, no amount of
electoral machinery on a basis of "one person one vote" will make the two really
equal socially as well as politically; if we want democracy we must *abolish class
distinctions*'.[12]

Guild Socialists hold that equality of income cannot be made a condition of
the establishment of the guild system. The conditions – both moral and psy-
chological – required for making such equality realisable could develop only

---

10   Cole 1968, p. 6. Emphasis added.
11   Cole 1968, p. 7. Anthony Wright very pertinently comments: 'The main concern (of the
      guild socialists) was with industry, not simply because it is where, in a modern society,
      material production takes place, but also because here, under modern capitalism, there is
      a perversion of its social function through its production for profit, whereas its true func-
      tion, under democratic conditions, consisted in production for use, for human needs'. See
      Wright 1974, p. 173.
12   Cole 1921, p. 15. Emphasis added. We have taken the liberty of substituting 'person' for 'man'
      in the quotation, for obvious reasons.

in a free society, and even there only by a gradual process. It can only develop out of the actual experience of free and democratic industrial and social conditions. 'When it does come, it will come not in the absurd guise of the "equality of remuneration", but by the destruction of the whole idea of remuneration for work done, and the apprehension of the economic problem as that of dividing the national income, without regard to any particular work or service, among the members of the community. Until the consciousness arises that will make this possible, some inequalities of remuneration are likely to persist'.[13]

The guild partisans stress that the status and economic position of a guild worker are very different from those of a wage-worker. Unemployment as it exists in capitalism will have disappeared. Secondly, every guild person will be assured of her/his full income from the guild. Thus the person 'will have gained one thing which the wage worker most manifestly lacks in capitalism, economic security, and have gained it not by submitting to slavery (the slave has security of a sort), but as concomitant of industrial freedom'.[14]

The factory, the mine, the shipyard, and other places of work will be to a great extent internally self-governing, and will be the basis of the wider local or national government of the guild. The essential basis of the guild being associative service, the spirit of association must be given free play in the sphere in which it is best able to find expression. A factory under a guild is free to experiment in new methods, to develop new styles and products, and to adapt itself to the peculiarities of a local or individual market. The large guild organisations would consider the production of various factories so as to make supply coincide with demand. They would act largely as the suppliers of raw materials and as marketers of such finished products as were not disposed of directly from the factory.

The financial system, particularly industrial banking, obviously becomes an integral part of the guild organisation, and the banking system would be under the control of the guilds which it would have to finance.

Cole emphasises that though production is carried on with a view to satisfying the ultimate users of the product, a large part of production is really of an intermediate character, that is, it does not directly go to the ultimate consumers, but to other industries which employ it for further production. Thus a large part of the total exchange would take place directly between the industrial units themselves.[15]

---

13   Cole 1921, pp. 72–3.
14   Cole 1921, p. 74.
15   See Cole 1921, p. 69.

The guild socialists stress the importance of accumulation, that is, the provision for making new means of production, which can come only from the surplus produced by industry. In fact, an important reason for the guild socialists to want 'national ownership' – equated to 'public ownership' – of industry is that a surplus generated in a particular industry really belongs to the community as a whole and not to that particular industry alone. Cole affirms, 'We want public ownership of industry for this reason, that if any industry produces a surplus, we want that surplus to pass not into the pocket of the industry in question, but into the national exchequer, to become a part of the revenue of the whole country'.[16] In order to contribute to the creation of fresh means of production, guild socialism has to divide the total national product into two parts, such that one part provides for the immediate needs of the population while the other goes to replenish the industrial capital, in order to satisfy the needs of future production. '[S]aving will become an affair of the community, just as under collectivist socialism'.[17] As regards the financing of public services, the easiest basis for taxation, taxation at source of various industries, will be imposed on different guilds.

As regards prices, they are not determined by the free play of demand and supply, but regulated ultimately by the Commune bearing what Cole calls the 'just price', that is, 'a price satisfactory to the social sense of the community, which would be the normal method of determining prices in a guild society'.[18] The consideration of the question of prices leads on to a bigger problem – that of capital. The question is, how would industry and services be financed in a guild society? This question, already broached in Cole's first book – mentioned above – is further developed in his second book. We are told that it will not be by the existing methods, ranging from real savings out of income to capitalist credit by financial interests. Now, 'all additions to real capital take the form of a part of the productive power of labour ... using materials not for manufacture of ultimate products or rendering of ultimate services, but to the manufacture of products and the rendering of services incidental to such manufacture for purposes of further production'.[19]

It is essential for a community to preserve a balance between production for direct use and production for use in further production. 'The allocation, therefore, of the communal productive resources is a matter of the Commune as a

16   Cole 1968, p. 13.
17   Cole 1968, p. 15.
18   Cole 1921, p. 142.
19   Cole 1921, p. 148.

whole. Whether this is expressed in terms of money or not does not matter; it is essentially an allocation of material and labour, and ultimately of human productive power'.[20]

As regards the method of effecting the allocation in the right way, each guild has to prepare a budget showing its estimate of requirements of goods and services for immediate use and for extensions and improvements. Quite in harmony with the guild society's democratic character, the preparation of the budget undergoes inter-guild consultations leading to possible modifications in the original estimates, subject finally to the examination by the Commune statisticians. 'The various budgets will thereby be brought into harmony with the estimated national production, and the complete budget will come up before the Commune as a whole for satisfaction. Thus the allocation of the communal labour power and the provision of capital will become *directly regulated by the Commune*, and will not be left, as they are now, to the blind play of economic forces or the machinations of financiers'.[21]

This will amount to an ordered balance of saving and spending, and will mean an allocation of various resources – material and human – corresponding to the social needs in the Commune, and will be done by the method of self-government, where each service and interest will have a full opportunity of putting its point of view and with full representation in the communal decision.

Finally, the issue of credit would be controlled by the Commune – whether the guilds have their own banks or not – just as the Commune would control the currency.

Consumers and Producers

Concerning the commonly asked question, won't the guilds work for their own benefit, instead of working for the community as a whole – and, more particularly, won't they seek their own interest instead of seeking the interest of the *consumers*? – there are important differences between Cole and Hobson, centring on the conception of 'consumption' and its status in the economy. For Cole, to safeguard the interest of the consumer whose interest is not the same as that of the producer, it is necessary that the ownership of industry lies in the hands of the public and not with the guild whose basic function

---

20   Cole 1921, pp. 144–5.

21   Cole 1921, pp. 145–6.

is to administer industry on a democratic foundation. According to Cole, the guild socialists agree with the 'collectivists' in demanding *national ownership* of industry, that the industry should be taken over and owned by the public. For Cole, as opposed to the collectivists, this does not, however, mean that the public also has got to undertake the *administration* of industry, that is, industry need not be administered by government bureaucrats. 'The right way to administer an industry is to hand it over to be worked by the people who know the best possible way of working it efficiently. This involves both the technicians and the manual workers'.[22]

Hobson has a very different view of production and consumption. We give here a gist of his relevant ideas. The term 'producer' means one who produces. But, opines Hobson, 'the men and women who produce are no longer the producers; they sell only their labour (power); the product of their labour belongs to the entrepreneur who arrogates to himself the word "producer" '.[23] The wage earner not only forfeits her/his claim to the product by selling his/her labour as a commodity, s/he is helpless when her/his financial master usurps her/his title also. If the possessing and wage-earning classes are active and passive citizens, they can also be distinguished by the economic control of consumption, which belongs entirely to the active citizen. The transition from passive to active citizenship involving the abolition of the wage system has 'as its corollary the control of production by the producer instead of the consumer who can only be the capitalist. Production and consumption are not two separate and unrelated processes but the complementary stages of one and the same economic transaction, and it is the capitalist who controls the transaction as a whole, directing its main current to his own interest and amenity'.[24]

Transformation of the Existing Society

The Guild Socialists underline that the Russian Revolution – independently of the policies of the Bolsheviks – produced a powerful effect on the minds of the workers. A situation has been created in which distribution of social status and authority has lost all correspondence with the real balance of forces. 'The inevitable outcome is *revolutionary change* with or without violence. The object of the guild socialists is to inform this coming revolution with a constructive

---

22 Cole 1968, p. 12. The term 'collectivist' in that epoch signified state socialist, and public ownership meant basically state ownership.

23 Hobson 1920, p. 34.

24 Hobson 1920, p. 30.

spirit'.[25] As Hobson very pertinently observes, stressing the dual role of capitalism – negative and positive – 'Capitalism bore in its train unspeakable horrors,
but it was a dominant factor in a period of great and continuous achievement.
Its mission is now exhausted, its work completed; we are now moving into a
new era of industrial democracy, in which function supplants exploitation and
partnership ends servitude'. He then adds, 'economic and social developments
do not spring out of the blue, they are the offspring of preceding conditions,
the harvest of yesterday's seeds'.[26] This revolution is a transformation of the
existing relation(s) of production under capital, that is, mainly, wage slavery.

'The essence of the Guild idea is the abolition of the wage-system, it is to
smash the wage system, with the consequent elimination of the master class'.[27]
The essential thing, the supreme task, is wage abolition, the restoration of the
product to the producer. This automatically involves the end of capitalism,
though the Guild Socialists seem not to be always very explicit about this direct
connection. It is interesting to note that Hobson coins a new term for the wage
system – 'wagery' – denigrating, it seems, the system even further. He writes,
'Wagery is wagery, whether under State Socialism or private capitalism. Temporarily, at least, wage-conditions may be ameliorated by State Socialism – an
improvement in degree and not in principle. But there is this deadly objection:
State Socialism involves the secured continuance of rent and interest, and so
the more firmly and legally rivets the chain that binds labour to its commodity valuation'.[28] Hobson says, again, more pithily, 'We seek not a "permanent
improvement" in relation between employers and workers, but the abolition
of the wages system and of a master class'.[29]

A social revolution is conceived as a transformation of the social and economic system as well as of political institutions. To a great extent it will be not
the challengers but the defenders of the capitalist system who will have the
choice of weapons. According to the Guild Socialists, besides a plan for assumption of power, there is also a need for a plan of action for the oppressed class to
pursue, both in the course of and after the assumption of power, based directly
upon the workers' own organisation and assigning to them the leading role in
the process of transformation. The Guild Socialists distinguish themselves from
those socialists, 'whether they call themselves Marxian or not', who hold that
socialism would come about through the assumption by people or the workers

---

25   Cole 1921, p. 24. Emphasis added.

26   Hobson 1920, p. 38.

27   Hobson 1920, pp. vi, xii.

28   Hobson 1920, p. 18.

29   Hobson 1920, p. 80.

of the state-machine, that is, parliamentary and political power, and by the use of this power for the expropriation of the rich, the socialisation of the means of production and the re-organisation of industry under state ownership and under the full control of a parliament dominated by socialists. However, the Guild Socialists opine that the 'omnicompetent State, this *"great Leviathan"*, is utterly unsuitable to any really democratic community and *must be destroyed*. It will have no place for the survival of the factotum State of to-day'.[30]

Now the question arises: after the destruction of the 'omnicompetent State', what will happen to the state's function of *coordinating* the activities of the various functional bodies in society? The guild partisans emphasise that functional democracy as conceived by them must have a coordinating agency which, however, must neither be historically continuous with the present political machinery of society nor simply reproduce its structure, particularly its rootedness in direct non-functional election. Thus the Guild Socialists 'assume' that 'not only will the present political machine lose its economic and civic functions to new bodies, but that the task of coordinating these functions will also pass out of its hands. It will thus, at the least, *"wither away"*, will disappear altogether'.[31]

Hence a new form of coordinating body has to be sought which will not be inconsistent with the functional democracy on which the whole system will be based. This coordination must not be coercive and must have to be accomplished by 'the willing, collective action of the various bodies requiring coordination'. It will be the communal organisation of the Guild Socialist society. 'This communal body of the coming society is named simply the Commune'.[32]

Ambiguities and Contradictions

The idea of economic democracy dominates Guild Socialism. As we have seen, it considers private ownership of the means of production, the commodity character of labour power, and the wage system as the basic evils of the capitalist system, with the consequent tasks of socialism as the transformation of the relation of labour, socialising the means of production, and revolutionising the society. Compared with the Second International socialism of the day, Guild

---

30   Cole 1921, p. 32. Emphasis added.

31   Cole 1921, p. 123. Emphasis added. This is the famous expression from Engels concerning the post-capitalist society, which we discuss in another chapter of the present book.

32   Cole 1921, p. 125. The allusion to the 1871 Paris Commune, though not explicitly mentioned, is clear.

Socialism was certainly a great libertarian tendency. However, how to achieve these lofty aims is not very clear in the Guild Socialist literature. First of all, it is not always clear if the Guild Socialists are speaking of guilds functioning like the co-operatives under *capitalism*, or of guilds in the transition period to the non-capitalist society, or of guilds in the *society after capital*. Then there are problems which one detects in the discussion on the solutions offered by the Guild Socialists.

Let us take the question of the state as envisaged by Guild Socialists. We saw earlier that both Cole and Hobson have a pronounced anti-state position. They want the disappearance of the *'Leviathan'* with the advent of the new society, the Commune. The state will simply 'wither away'. On the other hand, the Guild Socialists 'stand with the *collectivists* in the demand for national ownership of industry; the industries ought to be taken over and owned by *the public*',[33] even when the public does not administer the industry. Cole, but not Hobson, justifies this public or state ownership as a way to protect the interests of the consumers as opposed to those of the producers, as we saw above. Again, 'public ownership' of industry is wanted for the interest of (capital) accumulation: so that a surplus produced in an industry can pass not into the coffers of the industry, but into the 'national exchequer, to become a part of the revenue of the whole country'. The smooth functioning of the process of accumulation is facilitated by the instruments of bank and credit where, again, the state plays a crucial role. So, while the state is banished through the front door of the Commune, it sneaks into the Commune by the back door.

Secondly, the principal aim of Guild Socialism is to eliminate the capitalist system and to replace it with communitarian socialism based on the self-governing guilds, which also means – the Guild Socialists insist – the abolition of 'wagery', of 'wage-slavery'. They indeed equate the two, that is, self-government and the elimination of the wage system, as we have seen. However, this elimination of capitalism along with wage slavery does not seem to entail the elimination of markets, or, in other words, the exchange of products in *commodity* form. Aspects of this characteristic we have already briefly described earlier in our discussion on accumulation, without, however, subjecting this to a critique. Let us now look at this position a little more closely. The 'coordination of production of different units of production', each self-governed, would – we read – have to function such that 'supply coincides with demand, that is, they would act largely as suppliers of raw materials and as *marketers* of such fin-

---

33   Cole 1968, p. 12. Emphasis added in order to stress that these 'collectivists' are the state
      socialists, that 'public' ownership is just another name for basically state ownership.

ished products as were not disposed of directly from the factory'.[34] The instruments for facilitating this production for *market*, namely, the financial system and industrial banking, are also the same as they are in capitalism. The only difference seems to be that now the functioning of these instruments would be under the control of the guilds. 'The financial system, and especially the industrial banking must obviously be under the control of the guilds which it has to finance'.[35] It is evident that this control does not eliminate the commodity character of the product.

It should be clear that we are dealing here not with 'simple commodity' production, but with commodity production which is the result of a production process that is capitalist, whoever owns the capital, an individual owner or a collective owner like the state. In other words, this kind of production indicates the existence and expansion of exchange value, and this is the very essence of the capitalist mode of production. Even when the prices of commodities are regulated communally and not by the blind play of economic forces – as Cole affirms[36] – the commodity as such continues to operate. To assert the need for commodity production for society and at the same time to deny the existence of capital and wage slavery in society is clearly contradictory.

In a critical assessment of Guild Socialism, Otto Rühle, a well-known 'council communist', while noting some of what he considers as the progressive aspects of this socialism – as compared with capitalism – observes, nevertheless, some important shortcomings.[37] In Guild Socialism, observes Rühle, state and guild are kept in a position of 'balance of power'. If the state is more powerful it will result in 'collectivism', if the guilds are more powerful it will mean 'syndicalism'. 'It seems guild socialism seeks the half way between the economic order of the state and that of the trade unions; it wants a synthesis of the centrally administered economy and federated economy. This looks like a mechanical construction'.[38] The advantage of the balance between centralism and federalism is bought at the expense of the disadvantage that the whole progress consists in introducing the predominance of group individualism in place of the predominance of singular individualism. This is certainly a considerable step beyond present-day capitalism. But it remains still just the smallest part of the big step that has to be taken towards socialism. 'It represents a half meas-

---

34   Cole 1921, p. 60. Emphasis added.
35   Cole 1921, p. 67.
36   See Cole 1968, p. 13; and 1921, p. 145.
37   See Rühle 1971, pp. 85 ff.
38   Rühle 1971, p. 87.

ure, an interim solution, a middle station; the economic-technical effect gained thereby stands in no relation to the magnitude of the problematic which it wants to overcome'.[39]

The original position of at least one of the chief spokespersons of guild socialism – Cole – soon began to be modified in favour of practicality, the rationale of which is enunciated by Cole thus: 'Sitting in our chairs we cannot lay down with scientific precision the strategy and tactics of the guild socialists, or any great social transformation. All we can do is to see what is the utmost, under the actual conditions, that any given method of action seems capable of achieving, and to make up our minds not to use an extreme method if a less extreme method promises to fulfil the same purpose'.[40] In a 1946 article, Anton Pannekoek cited the following lines of the 'English socialist G.D.H. Cole': 'It would be necessary under socialism, as much as under large scale capitalism, to entrust the actual management of industrial enterprise to salaried experts, chosen for their specialised knowledge and ability in particular branches of work ... there is no reason to suppose that the socialisation of any industry would mean a great change in its managerial personnel'.[41] Then Pannekoek observes, 'thus the workers will have new masters instead of the old ones; good, humane masters instead of the bad, rapacious masters of today, appointed by the socialist government or at best chosen by themselves, and once chosen, they must be obeyed. Workers are not masters over their shops, they are not masters of the means of production'.[42]

Finally, totally abandoning his earlier position on workers' self-government in the units of production and opposition to wage slavery as well as his position on the incompatibility of socialism with the state, Cole unambiguously considered Russia of the 1930s to be the 'one Socialist country' where the 'Soviet leaders are endeavouring to follow out the doctrine of income distribution of Marx'.[43]

---

39   Rühle 1971, p. 88.
40   Cole 1921, p. 178.
41   Pannekoek 1946, p. 270.
42   Pannekoek 1946, p. 271.
43   Cole 1937, pp. 81, 249.

CHAPTER 8

On Market Socialism

Market Socialism (MS for short) as a conceptual category signifies an economic system where (at least) the principal means of production are owned either by the state or by some form of collectivity – like for example self-managed workers' cooperatives – and where the allocation of goods and resources for productive and individual (personal) consumption follows the market rule by operating basically through the price-wage system. As a theoretical category MS arose in the inter-war period but had a new lease of life after the Second World War. This was accentuated within a section of Left academics after the collapse of the Party-State régimes in Russia and Eastern Europe and the apparent victory of 'neo-liberalism' across the globe. Considered as a viable alternative to capitalism, MS would combine – so it was thought – economic efficiency with democracy and equity while avoiding an authoritarian command economy with administrative allocation of goods and resources. For the purpose of this chapter we will be exclusively concerned here with MS as a theoretical category and leave aside the various practical measures of market socialism that were adopted in Eastern Europe and Russia, and later in China and Vietnam, in view of what was perceived as the economic inefficiency of the administrative command economy.[1]

MS arose in the inter-war period in the early twentieth century as a reaction to the denial by the anti-socialists of the possibility of rational economic calculation – uniquely based on the price system that was indissolubly associated with private ownership of the means of production – in socialism. The (market) socialists accepted that there could be no rational economic calculation in a society in the absence of the price system. However, they rejected the argument that a price system associated with rational economic calculation was impossible without private ownership in the means of production.

---

1   The eminent Hungarian economist Kornai distinguished between two types of market socialism, 'one is market socialism to replace capitalism, and the other market socialism as a system to replace old style, Stalinist, pre-reform socialism'. See Kornai in Bardhan and Roemer (eds.) 1993, p. 42. As mentioned above, the present chapter is about what Kornai considered as the first type of MS.

Origin of Market Socialism

Before treating MS as such (the subject of the chapter) let us give a short account of the circumstances in which it arose. The debate on MS arose in connection with the broader discussion on the possibility of rational economic calculation in a socialist régime. A pioneer of this discussion was Vilfredo Pareto, the famous Italian economist of the Lausanne school, who in 1897 discussed how the 'minister of production' of the new society should employ society's material and human resources through the determination of 'coefficients of fabrication' – helped by all the necessary statistical data – in such a way that the citizens' welfare would be maximised. Pareto then opined that the minister 'would arrive precisely at the same coefficients as those which will be determined by free competition ... the values of the fabrication coefficients will be identical in the two cases', which he thought 'extremely remarkable'.[2] In the same work Pareto distinguished between the two systems thus: 'Free competition employs the entrepreneurs acting automatically, the socialist régime makes the functionaries act following the rules imposed by the public authority'.[3] In his next work (1909) on the subject, written about ten years later, Pareto first distinguished between what he called 'three types of transaction': type I corresponds to a situation where the individual cannot change the data of the transaction, the situation of free competition; type II to a situation where the individual can modify the condition of transaction, the situation of monopoly; type III – a special case of type II – is the situation which prevails when one wants to organise 'the totality of the economic phenomena'. The third type corresponds to 'the collectivist organisation of society'.[4] For such a society Pareto poses the problem of prices,

> The problem which the socialist state will pose to itself is: what price should be fixed so that my administered subjects will enjoy the maximum welfare compatible with the conditions in which they find themselves. Even if the socialist state suppresses all the opportunities of exchange, prevents all purchase and sale, prices will not disappear for all that. They

---

2 Pareto 1964, pp. 91–2. The great economist Joseph Schumpeter mentions F. von Wieser 1889 together with Pareto among 'upward of a dozen economists' who 'had hinted at the solution before Barone' (see below) and emphasised that both Wieser and Pareto 'perceived the fact that the fundamental logic of economic behaviour is the same in both commercial and socialist societies'. See Schumpeter 1950, p. 175.

3 Pareto 1964, p. 370.

4 Pareto 1966, p. 167.

will remain at least as an accounting artifice for the distribution of commodities and their transformations. The employment of prices is the simplest means and the easiest [way] for resolving the equations of equilibrium. If one persists in not using them one will end up by making use of them under another name, there will then be a simple change of language but not of the things.[5]

A few years later (1908) in an article in *Giornale degli Economisti*, Enrico Barone, following the basic ideas of Pareto, to which he added his own, and, like Pareto, apparently without any value judgment on the 'collectivist' régime, discussed what he called the 'Ministry of Production in the Collectivist State' had to do 'in order to maximize the advantages from its operation'.[6] He used a general equilibrium framework to present mathematically the conditions for maximising the advantages. By means of a set of simultaneous equations showing the technical possibilities of production, cost and consumer demand, Barone demonstrated a formal similarity between a competitive economy and a collectivist economy. According to Barone, if one abstracts from the economic variability of technical coefficients, 'it is not impossible to solve on paper the equations of equilibrium'. But it is inconceivable that the economic determination of the technical coefficients can be made *a priori* in a way that satisfies the condition of minimum cost of production, which is an essential condition for obtaining the maximum. 'This economic variability of technical coefficients is certainly neglected by the collectivists'. The determination of the most advantageous technical coefficients 'could only be done *experimentally*'.[7] That is, it would not be possible for the Ministry to have the necessary information *a priori*. On the basis of his findings, Barone called 'fantastic' those doctrines which 'imagine that production in the collectivist régime would be ordered in a manner substantially different from that of "anarchic" (that is, competitive) production'.[8] Barone concluded like Pareto earlier: 'all the economic categories must reappear, though maybe with other names – prices, salaries, interest, rent, profit, saving etc.; [similarly] the two conditions which characterise free competition reappear, and the maximum is more readily obtained the more perfectly they are realised. We are referring to conditions of minimum cost of production and the equalisation of price to cost of production'.[9]

---

5 Pareto 1966, pp. 210–11.

6 In Hayek 1935, p. 246.

7 Barone, in Hayek 1935, pp. 287–8. Emphasised in text.

8 Barone, in Hayek 1935, p. 289.

9 In Hayek 1935, p. 289. About this work of Enrico Barone, Schumpeter noted, 'the economist

The modern debate really started at the beginning of the twentieth century with a 1902 article by the Dutch economist N.G. Pierson, published in the
Dutch periodical *De Economist*, in which he discussed the 'Problem of Value
in a Socialist Community', dealing with what the author considered to be the
impracticability of socialism. It was a response to a talk by Karl Kautsky in Delft
from the same year. This article is the first important contribution to the modern discussion of the economic aspect of socialism.[10]

Almost two decades later the discussion was taken up in a rather aggressive
fashion by Ludwig von Mises[11] as a reaction to Otto Neurath's presentation of a
socialist economy based on economic calculation in kind.[12] Almost at the same
time (1922), the great sociologist Max Weber, independently of Mises, reacted
to Neurath in basically the same way.[13] However, as Hayek stresses, 'The distinction of having first formulated the central problem of socialist economics
in such a form as to make it impossible that it should ever again disappear from
discussion belongs to Ludwig von Mises'.[14] Another work, this time by a Russian
economist, B. Brutzkus, demonstrating the impracticability of a socialist economy with no prices, also appeared almost simultaneously.[15] Referring to the
works of these scholars on the impracticability of a socialist economy, a modern scholar, R.M. Steele, quite pertinently observes

> The chief causes of the coincidence are clear: the growth of a powerful
> socialist movement in many countries, the accession to power of social-
> ist parties in Russia, Hungary, Germany and Austria, during 1917–19, the
> attempt to introduce a communist economic order in Russia, which had

---

who settled the question (of economic rationality in socialism) in a manner that left little
to do except elaboration and clearing up of points of secondary importance, was Enrico
Barone'. See Schumpeter 1950, p. 173.

10   Hayek 1935, p. 27.

11   Mises 1920.

12   See in this regard the account, given years later, in Hayek 1977. In the present book
Neurath's scheme of economic calculation *in natura* is discussed at some length – see
Chapter Five.

13   See Weber 1922.

14   Hayek 1935, pp. 32–3. The relevant main works by Mises are two. The first is an article titled
'Economic Calculation in the Socialist Commonwealth' ('Wirtschaftsrechnung in sozial-
istischen Gemeinwesen'), 1920, translated into English in Hayek 1935, pp. 87–130, and the
second is a book titled *Socialism (Die Gemeinwirtschaft)*, first edition 1922, second edition
1932, translated into English as *Socialism* by J. Kahane, with additions for the English edition by the author, 1936.

15   See Boris Brutzkus 1921.

to be openly abandoned in 1921, and the socialisation debate in Germany and Austria, along with the manifest disorientation of the German Social Democrats and their accelerated retreat from the Marxian notions of socialist revolution.[16]

On the question of economic calculation in socialism, Mises maintained that 'Every step that takes us away from private ownership of the means of production and from the use of money also takes us away from rational economics ... Where there is no free market, there is no pricing mechanism, where there is no pricing mechanism there is no economic calculation'.[17] He added that 'exchange relations in production goods can only be established on the basis of private property in the means of production'.[18] In his first work referred to above, Mises underlined what he meant by 'Socialism'. For him, under socialism all means of production are the property of the community. In the second place, the distribution of consumption goods 'must be independent of production and of its economic conditions'. The material of exchange will always be consumption goods only. 'Production goods in a socialist commonwealth are always communal'.[19] Given the existence of exchange of consumption goods, the 'socialist state will also afford room for the universal medium of exchange, that is, money. However, money could never fill in the socialist state the role it plays in a competitive society in determining the value of production goods. Calculation in terms of money will here be impossible'.[20] Turning to the possibility of calculation in kind (as Neurath had proposed), Mises observed, 'it is an illusion to imagine that in a socialist state calculation *in natura* can take the place of monetary calculation. Calculation in kind in an economy without exchange can embrace consumption goods only; it completely fails when it comes to deal with goods of higher order. And as soon as one gives up the conception of a freely established monetary price for goods of a higher

---

16   Steele 1992, p. 84.

17   Mises, in Hayek 1935, pp. 104, 111.

18   Mises 1936, p. 132.

19   Mises, in Hayek 1935, p. 91.

20   Mises, in Hayek 1935, p. 92. In all fairness it should be pointed out that Mises does not fail to recognise the limits of money's role: 'Monetary calculation has its limits' (in Hayek 1935, p. 98). 'If a man were to calculate the profitability of erecting a waterworks, he would not be able to include in the calculation the beauty of the waterfall which this scheme might impair. Such consideration might well prove one of the factors in deciding whether or not the building is to go up at all' (in Hayek 1935, p. 99).

order, rational production becomes completely impossible'.[21] Mises added, 'In the socialist commonwealth every economic change becomes an undertaking whose success can be neither appraised in advance nor retrospectively determined later. There is only groping in the dark. Socialism is the abolition of rational economy'.[22] In his second work – the book mentioned above – Mises held, referring to the earlier works of Pareto and Barone, that 'they did not penetrate to the core of the problem [of calculation] under socialism'.[23] In this work, while speaking of socialism, Mises treated the terms 'community', 'organised society' and 'state' as equivalent if not identical. Thus he wrote that 'It is the aim of socialism to transfer means of production from private ownership to the ownership of the organised society, to the state. The socialistic state owns all material means of production and directs it'.[24] After equating the 'material means of production' with capital, Mises observed that 'if we adhere to this terminology, we must also admit that the socialist community must also work with capital and therefore produce capitalistically'.[25] There was an energetic response to Mises's anti-socialist argument in the relevant German literature. The thrust of the early German reaction to Mises was aimed at eliminating 'bourgeois economics' and replacing it with some kind of non-monetary exchange, undertaking labour as the measuring means, and public distribution of consumer goods to the individuals. It should be stressed that these socialist opponents of Mises, for the most part, all accepted his notion of *socialism* as referred to above. We propose to discuss this rather neglected aspect later.

Following Mises's 1920 article and the first edition of his book (1922), Georg Halm devoted a whole brochure (1929), mainly with reference to the relevant German discussion, to the question as to what extent economic calculation was possible in socialism.[26] He first distinguishes communism from socialism. In communism a central authority disposes over all the means of production including labour, determines the direction of production and regulates consumption. 'The freedom of consumers' choice, as is known in the capitalist economy, cannot be combined with communist method of production'.[27] As 'an example of the communist economy', he takes 'Soviet Russia under the Five

21   Mises, in Hayek 1935, p. 105.

22   Mises, in Hayek 1935, p. 110.

23   Mises 1936, p. 135.

24   Mises 1936, p. 56.

25   Mises 1936, p. 142.

26   Translated from the German as 'Further Considerations on the Possibility of Adequate Calculation in a Socialist Community', in Hayek 1935.

27   Halm, in Hayek 1935, p. 133.

year Plan'.[28] In contrast, he holds, 'the protagonists of socialism reject communism. They wish to retain freedom of consumption and a certain degree of freedom of occupation, but to do this without falling into the mistakes of the capitalistic system'.[29] Then he adds, 'the socialist society must be thought of as a mixture of capitalistic and communistic elements. Like capitalism it permits freedom of choice in consumption and occupation; like communism, socialism envisages the nationalisation of capital goods and land, the elimination of unearned incomes and the central control of economic life by the State'.[30]

Halm underlines the *rapprochement* of socialism to capitalism: 'since there is to be free choice of occupation and a free market for determining wages in the socialist economy, the relationships that have been described as existing under capitalism can also be assumed to exist under socialism'.[31] Similarly, the socialist economy does not renounce capital goods in production. Thus 'everybody agrees that the socialist economy must in *this* sense be capitalistic also'.[32] However, Halms points to a problem here related to economic calculation in socialism. This arises from the necessity of the existence of the payment of interest in the price of the product over and above its labour cost in order to employ the scarce means of production so that they are distributed among all the wants in an economic manner. 'Now, it is unfortunate that this allowance for interest, the need for which is urgently dictated by economic considerations, cannot be adopted in the socialistic economy; perhaps this is the most serious objection that can be maintained against socialism. Thus, in whatever direction the problem of economic calculation in the socialistic economy is investigated, insoluble difficulties are revealed, all ascribable to the nationalisation of the material means of production which are no longer subject to free pricing process'.[33]

Much more interesting and serious discussion on the position of the neo-Austrian economists regarding the problem of rational economic calculation in socialism started with the entry of the English speaking neo-classical economists in the field in the late twenties and early thirties of the last century. H.D. Dickinson was one of the first to propose a solution for a socialist economy.[34] In his model there would be a free market for consumer goods for indi-

---

28   Halm, in Hayek 1935, p. 135.
29   Halm, in Hayek 1935, p. 136.
30   Halm, in Hayek 1935, p. 137.
31   Halm, in Hayek 1935, p. 153.
32   Halm, in Hayek 1935, p. 155. Emphasis in text.
33   Halm, in Hayek 1935, p. 168.
34   Dickinson 1933, pp. 237–51.

viduals, but the means of production and natural resources would be owned by the state. It was a mathematical model of the socialist economy with the central authorities estimating statistical demand curves and production functions towards solution of equilibrium prices through successive approximation. (A few years later Dickinson abandoned this approach).[35] Only after Hayek published his ideas on socialist calculation in 1935 did Oskar Lange, following the earlier lead of Fred Taylor, respond to Hayek with his now celebrated model of MS essentially based on the model of neo-classical general equilibrium.[36] Before coming to Lange, let us say a few words on the pioneering work of the unduly neglected economist Fred Taylor in the market socialist debate.[37] Lange's own work in this field was stimulated by Taylor's paper. Before Hayek and Robbins had made their attack, 'It is the first contribution which really goes beyond what is contained in Barone's paper'.[38] As noted above, Barone demonstrated the possibility of rational allocation of resources in socialism by the method of trial and error. He, however, did not clearly indicate how this method would be applied. This work was done by Taylor. The substance of Lange's later work on MS (1936, 1937) is already presented in Taylor's 'Address'. In this work Taylor did not name any names. There is no reference to any economist who had discussed the economic calculation problem in socialism before him, no reference either to Barone or to Mises. Hayek's contribution would appear only later.

Taylor first clarifies what he means by 'socialist state'. By this phrase he means a state in which the control of the whole apparatus of production and the guidance of all productive operations are to be in the hands of the state. 'As such a sole producer the state maintains exchange relations with its citizens, buying their productive services with money and selling to them the commodities which it produces'.[39] In view of setting up a correct socialist plan, the central economic problem is to fix the selling price of a particular com-

---

35   Dickinson 1939.

36   Lange and Taylor 1938. Mark Blaug, the noted historian of economic thought, writes, referring to Lange's work, that 'its significance was that it was the last time that general equilibrium theory figured in a public debate in more or less the same sense that it had figured in Walras's own time' (Blaug 1996, p. 357).

37   This refers to Taylor's presidential address to the American Economic Association in 1928, 'Guidance of Production in a Socialist State'. The reader will find an excellent account of the two works by Taylor and Lange in Benjamin Lippincott's Introduction to his edited book on Taylor's and Lange's works on market socialism, published in 1938.

38   Lange, in Lange and Taylor 1938, p. 65.

39   Taylor, in Lange and Taylor 1938, p. 43.

modity. The economic authorities would set that price at a point which fully covered the cost of the commodity in question. Here the problem is to determine the 'effective importance' of the 'primary factors' in the production process. By 'primary factors' Taylor means 'those economic factors of production behind which the economist does not attempt to go', such as land itself, the original raw materials like metallic ores, and different kinds of labour services, and by 'effective importance' Taylor means 'the degree of importance which is a resultant of the whole situation, the degree of importance which should be taken into account in deciding how to act'.[40] The effective importance of each primary factor is derived from and determined by the numerous commodities which emerge from the complex of the productive processes. Because the effective importance of the commodities is expressed in terms of money value, the importance of the several factors would be so expressed. As already mentioned, the price of the particular commodity would have to be set at the point where it covers the full cost of producing the commodity. 'The particular method of procedure which would seem most suitable for dealing with the problem in the case of a socialist state is a form of the so-called method of trial and error, that is the method which consists in trying out a series of hypothetical solutions till one is found which proves correct'.[41] To start with, a provisional monetary valuation would be assigned to each factor. The managers of socialist productive operations would then carry on their functions as if the valuations were absolutely correct. Then if the authorities had assigned a valuation to any factor which was too high or too low, this would show itself at the end of the production period, requiring necessary correction. If too high a valuation had been assigned causing the authorities to be too severely economical in the employment of that factor, a physical surplus in the stock of the factor would show itself at the end of the production process. In the opposite case of assignment of too low a valuation to the factor, the authorities concerned would be too spendthrift in the use of the factor, resulting in a deficit in the stock of the factor. 'The authorities would have no difficulty repeating this process until neither a surplus nor a deficit appeared, when they would rightly conclude that the valuation which was then attached to any particular factor correctly expressed the effective importance of that factor'.[42] Only after Hayek published his ideas on socialist calculation in 1935 did Oskar Lange, following the earlier lead of Fred Taylor, respond to Hayek with his now celebrated

---

40   Taylor, in Lange and Taylor 1938, p. 45.

41   Taylor, in Lange and Taylor 1938, p. 51.

42   Taylor, in Lange and Taylor 1938, p. 54.

model of MS (Lange and Taylor 1938), essentially based on the model of neo-classical general equilibrium.[43] Before Hayek had published his own criticism of the possibility of rational economic calculation in socialism, most of the discussion on the subject was carried out by the adherents of socialism, almost all of them in English. The most distinguished exception was Lionel Robbins. He wrote that

> On paper we can conceive this problem to be solved by a series of mathematical calculations. But in practice this solution is quite unworkable. It would necessitate the drawing up of millions of equations on the basis of millions of statistical data based on many more millions of individual computations. By the time the equations were solved, the information on which they were based would have become obsolete and they would need to be calculated anew. The suggestion that a practical solution of the problem of planning is possible on the basis of the Paretian equations simply indicates that those who put it forward have not grasped what these equations mean.[44]

In his 1935 edited volume, Hayek included two papers of his own. The first paper recorded in outline the development of the controversy beginning with the Dutch economist Pierson and covering the German and Austrian discussions including Von Mises. The second summed up the basic points of the controversy and included his own critique of market socialists via his extension and defence of Mises. Concerning the mathematical solutions, particularly that of Barone, Hayek admitted that there was no logical inconsistency/contradiction in the solutions proposed. However, he stressed that what was practically relevant here was not the 'formal structure' of this system, but the 'nature and amount of concrete information required if a numerical solution is to be attempted and the magnitude of the task which this numerical solution must involve in any modern community and ... how far one would have to go to make the result at least comparable with that which the competitive system provides'.[45]

---

43 Hayek published his own contribution as a sequel to the earlier work of Mises, mentioned above. This came out in a collection of articles by different economists on socialist calculation, which he edited and published in 1935. See Hayek 1935.

44 Robbins 1934, p. 151.

45 Hayek 1935, p. 208.

Let us return to Lange's work.[46] In the discussion on market socialism which follows, the bulk will concern Lange's own contribution – the prototype, the 'mother', of the other models of market socialism which have followed Lange's – and the criticisms of the Lange model. We will only briefly go over a few later models which seem important to us.

The Competitive Solution

In his model Lange takes up Mises's contention that a socialist economy cannot solve the problem of rational allocation of its resources. The purpose of his work, states Lange, is to 'elucidate the way in which the allocation of resources is carried out by trial and error on a competitive market, and to find out whether a similar trial and error procedure is not possible in a socialist economy'.[47] He starts by making clear the institutional setting of the socialist economy under consideration. There is the public ownership of the means of production. There is a genuine market for consumer goods and for the services of labour. But there is no market for capital goods and productive services outside of labour. The prices of capital goods and resources outside of labour are 'prices in the generalised sense, i.e. mere indices of alternatives available, fixed for accounting purposes'.[48] The prices, whether market or accounting, are determined by the condition that the quantity of each commodity demanded is equal to the quantity supplied.

'The incomes of consumers are composed of two parts: one part being the receipts for the labour services performed, and the other being a social dividend constituting the individual's share in the income derived from the capital and natural resources owned by society'.[49] The decisions of managers are no longer determined by the aim of maximising profit. Instead, certain rules are imposed on them by the Central Planning Board (CPB) with the aim of satisfying consumers' preferences. These rules determine both the combination

---

46   Lange's work on socialism first appeared in the *Review of Economic Studies*, No. 1, 1936 and
       No. 2, 1937. A second version was published as a book together with the article by Taylor, as
       mentioned above in 1938. This book version benefitted from A.P. Lerner's important criti-
       cism of the original version, appearing in the same journal in 1936. This is why the Lange
       model is often called the Lange-Lerner model. We should note that Lange never used the
       expression 'market socialism'.
47   Lange, in Lange and Taylor 1938, p. 65.
48   Lange, in Lange and Taylor 1938, p. 73.
49   Lange, in Lange and Taylor 1938, p. 74.

of factors and the scale of output. One rule must impose the choice of combination of factors which minimises the average cost of production. 'This rule leads to the factors being combined in such proportions that the marginal productivity of that amount of each factor which is worth a unit of money is the same for all factors. The second rule determines the scale of output by stating that output has to be fixed so that marginal cost is equal to the price of the product'.[50] The same objective price structure that prevails in the (capitalist) competitive market, Lange observes, can be obtained in a socialist economy if the parametric function of prices is retained. That is, the task of the CPB is to 'impose on the managers of enterprises the parametric function of prices as an *accounting rule* where, for the purpose of accounting, prices must be treated as constant, as they are treated by entrepreneurs on a competitive market'.[51]

Here the CPB performs the functions of the market. Besides establishing the rules for combining factors of production and choosing the scale of output of a plant, for determining the output of an industry, for the allocation of resources, it fixes the prices so as to balance the quantity supplied and demanded of each commodity. It follows that 'a substitution of planning for the functions of the market is quite possible and workable'.[52]

Coming to income distribution, citizens' income is divided into two parts as already mentioned: one part consists of receipts for labour services performed and the other part consists of the 'social dividend' constituting the individual's share in the income derived from capital and other non-labour resources publicly owned, due consideration being given to the needs of capital accumulation. The social dividend is to be distributed in such a way as not to interfere with the optimum allocation of labour services between industries and occupations. 'The social dividend paid to an individual must be entirely independent of his choice of profession'.[53]

As regards the accumulation of capital, its role cannot be determined by the market, capital being under public ownership, but has to be fixed arbitrarily by the CPB, which sets the appropriate rate of interest for this purpose. The rate of interest is determined by the condition that the demand for capital is equal to the amount available. This is for the 'short period' when the supply of capital is given. As for the 'long period' when capital could be increased by accumula-

---

50 Lange, in Lange and Taylor 1938, p. 76.

51 Lange, in Lange and Taylor 1938, p. 81. Emphasis in text.

52 Lange, in Lange and Taylor 1938, p. 83.

53 Lange, in Lange and Taylor 1938, p. 84.

tion, the function of saving for this purpose is not left to the preference of the individual, but the rate of accumulation can be determined by the CPB arbitrarily. 'This simply means that the decision regarding rate of accumulation reflects how the CPB, and not the consumers, evaluate the optimum time shape of the income stream'.[54]

After describing the theoretical determination of economic equilibrium in a socialist society, Lange goes on to demonstrate how the equilibrium is determined by a 'trial and error' method as in a competitive market. Here Lange clearly follows Taylor, whose discussion of this method we have noted above. This method is based on the 'parametric function of prices'. The CPB, acting as the Walrasian auctioneer, starts with a given set of prices chosen at random. If, as a consequence, the quantity demanded of a commodity is not equal to the quantity supplied, the price of the commodity has to be changed: raised if demand exceeds supply, lowered if supply exceeds demand. Thus the CPB fixes a new set of prices, resulting in a new set of quantities demanded and supplied. Through repetition of this process of trial and error equilibrium prices are finally reached, demand and supply are in balance, and the market is cleared. Lange adds that 'actually it is the *historically given* prices which will serve as the basis for the process of trial and error'.[55] As Lange stresses, there is no reason why a trial and error procedure, similar to that in a competitive market, could not work in a socialist economy to determine the accounting prices of capital goods and of the productive resources in public ownership. 'Indeed, it seems that this trial and error procedure would, or at least could, work *much better* in a socialist economy than it does in a competitive market since the CPB has a much wider knowledge of what is going on in the whole economic system than any private entrepreneur can ever have'.[56] Lange mentions two features which distinguish a socialist economy from a private enterprise economy. First, the distribution of incomes: 'only a socialist economy can distribute incomes so as to attain maximum social welfare'.[57] The second distinguishing feature is 'the *comprehensiveness* of the items entering into the price system'.[58] In other words, 'a socialist economy will be able to put *all* the alternatives into its accounting by evaluating all the services rendered by production and taking into cost accounts *all* the alternatives sacrificed ... and by doing so it would

---

54   Lange, in Lange and Taylor 1938, p. 85.
55   Lange, in Lange and Taylor 1938, pp. 72–3. Emphasis in text.
56   Lange, in Lange and Taylor 1938, p. 89. Emphasis in text.
57   Lange, in Lange and Taylor 1938, p. 99.
58   Lange, in Lange and Taylor 1938, p. 103.

avoid much of the social waste connected with private enterprise, such as fluctuations in business cycles and serious environmental problems'.[59]

Thus to determine the equilibrium prices the 'CPB does not need to solve
hundreds of thousands – as Professor Hayek expects – or millions – as Professor
Robbins thinks – of equations'.[60] Referring to the position of Hayek-Robbins –
admitting the *theoretical* possibility but *practical* impossibility of the Pareto-
Barone solution – Lange now asserted that 'Thus Professor Hayek and Professor
Robbins have given up the essential position of Professor Mises, and *retreated to
a second line of defence*'.[61] About three decades later Lange repeated the same
argument to refute the Hayek-Robbins position. Referring to their argument
that the Pareto-Barone solution was impossible in practice, Lange observed,
'Were I to rewrite my essay to-day my task would be much simpler. My answer
to Hayek and Robbins would be: so what's the trouble? Let us put the simultaneous equations on an electronic computer and we shall obtain the solution in
less than a second'.[62]

Criticisms

According to the so-called 'standard version' of the debate, Lange had successfully refuted the Mises-Hayek argument. The 'standard version' accepted
Lange's interpretation of Mises's objection to socialism on the basis of *practical* impossibility of rational economic calculation, the Pareto-Barone solution
being dismissed on the ground that 'it did not penetrate to the core of the
problem'.[63] 'Among the academics it quickly became accepted as the definitive
answer to the Austrian critique of socialism'.[64] Schumpeter vindicated the 'pure
logic of socialist economy', saying that 'the only authority standing for denial
of the economic rationality of the socialist system was Mises'.[65] Summing up
the debate in 1948 Bergson – referring to the question of the (im)practicality
of calculation – observed that if this was the only problem 'there hardly can

---

59   Lange, in Lange and Taylor 1938, pp. 104–5. Emphasis in text.
60   Lange, in Lange and Taylor 1938, p. 88.
61   Lange 1938, p. 63. Emphasis added.
62   Lange, in Kowalik 1993, p. 361. In this connection, Lange added on the same page that the
      'market process with the cumbersome trial and error appears old-fashioned'. Indeed, it
      may be regarded as a 'computing device of the pre-electronic age'.
63   Mises 1936, p. 135.
64   Howard and King 1992, p. 369.
65   Schumpeter 1950, p. 172.

be any room for debate: of course socialism can work'.[66] In the same vein Paul Sweezy opined that 'as far as the economics profession is concerned, Lange's paper may be regarded as having finally removed any doubts about the capacity of socialism to utilize resources rationally'.[67]

This accepted view changed during the late 1970s. Then the modern Austrian school returned to the debate with a new interpretation which challenged the 'standard version'.[68] This led to a total re-examination of the debate. The neo-Austrians focused on what they thought was the misreading of the Mises-Hayek position by their opponents; the original Austrian arguments, the neo-Austrians underlined, were much more sophisticated than their opponents had thought.

The distinguished historian of economic theory Mark Blaug has very aptly remarked, that 'The socialist calculation debate was a catalyst in stimulating F. Hayek to go beyond Mises in reformulating the notion of economic coordination as an informational problem, competition essentially acting as a discovery process'.[69] The neo-Austrians (after Hayek) particularly focused on market uncertainty, rivalry, discovery, and entrepreneurship. Underlining the principal points in the Austrian position, one of its partisans observed that in the course of the debate with the neo-classicals, 'the Austrians developed their specific conceptions of dynamics, knowledge and rivalry and employed them to argue the necessity of such institutions as dispersed private property rights, the entrepreneur, "speculation", capital markets and the stock exchange. It was only later that mainstream economics, seeking to overcome the limitations of neoclassical statics, developed its own theories of uncertainty and risk, contingent contracts, informationally decentralised models and incentive systems'.[70] Right at the start we should note the crucial difference between the Austrians and the neo-classicals on the nature of knowledge. While the neo-classicals assume all relevant data as 'given', according to the Austrians individuals base their decisions not on given data but on *subjective knowledge*, which instead of being given has to be continuously *discovered* in the entrepreneurial, competitive market process. 'The sort of knowledge with which I have been concerned',

---

66   Bergson 1948, p. 447.

67   Sweezy 1949, p. 232.

68   See in particular Lavoie 1985; Murrell 1983; Keizer 1989.

69   Blaug 1996, p. 557. He added, 'Competition is an active process of discovery, of knowledge formation, of creative destruction. This is the Austrian view of competition'. See Blaug 1996, p. 594.

70   Keizer 1989, p. 80.

wrote Hayek, 'is knowledge of the kind which by its nature cannot enter statistics and therefore cannot be conveyed to any central authority in statistical form. The statistics which such a central authority would have to use would have to be arrived at precisely by abstracting from minor differences between things, by lumping together, as resources of one kind, items which differ as regards location, quality and other particulars in a way which may be very significant for the specific decision'.[71]

Though Bergson thought, in line with the dominant academic thinking of the period, that Lange's neo-classical model was viable, the criticisms of the Austrians notwithstanding – as we saw above – he was more sympathetic to the Austrians on the question of the acquisition of knowledge by individuals. Thus, quite in the spirit of Hayek, Bergson, referring to Lange's CPB as a 'Board of Supermen', wrote, 'Let us imagine a Board of Supermen, with unlimited logical faculties, with a complete scale of values for different consumers' goods and present and future consumption, and detailed knowledge of production techniques. Even such a Board would be unable to evaluate rationally the means of production'.[72]

Mises had already stressed the dynamism of the real-life process against the stationary character of neo-classical equilibrium economics: 'The problem of economic calculation is of economic dynamics, it is no problem of economic statics'.[73]

The shortcomings of Lange's neo-classical model arise from the lack of dynamism intrinsic to the neo-classical conceptual framework, as Mises had stressed. The model's validity is based on static equilibrium in which initial market conditions remain unchanged while the CPB continues its trial and error exercise. All CPB calculations are based on present conditions only. They do not solve the dynamic problem raised by Mises. The CPB will find it difficult to respond quickly to continually occurring changes in demand and supply. So

---

71   Hayek 1945, p. 524. See also Hayek 1937, pp. 33–54. Referring to a later work by Hayek – *The Sensory Order* (1952) – a sympathiser of the Austrian school has very pertinently remarked that 'By analogy with Gödel's famous theorem (which says that it is impossible to prove the consistency of a formal system within the system itself) Hayek argued that for all rational processes there must be some rules which cannot be stated. One cannot even be conscious of them. We know more than we can speak of. Not all knowledge is objectifiable'. See Shand 1984, p. 8.

72   Bergson 1948, p. 446.

73   Mises 1936, p. 139. And he added that the economic problem was of 'dissolving, extending, transforming, and limiting existing undertakings, and establishing new undertakings'. Mises 1936, p. 215.

CPB prices will be in perpetual disequilibrium, leading to persistent imbalances between demand and supply and to resource misallocation.[74]

The model suffers from the lack of a satisfactory incentive system to motivate the managers. It excludes the possibility of self-interested behaviour on their part and with that the existence of a principal-agent problem between the Board and the managers, including asymmetric information between the two, requiring monitoring of the agent. The managers are supposed to act as passive price-takers. There is also a possibility, in the case of very large units of production, of the industrial managers being in the position of monopolists and using their power to engage in monopoly pricing.[75] On a different, but not unrelated, plane, the eminent Hungarian economist J. Kornai wrote about the Board that 'The people at the Central Planning Board are reincarnations of Plato's philosophers, embodiments of unity, unselfishness, and wisdom; they are satisfied with nothing else but strictly enforcing the "Rule", adjusting prices to excess demand. Such an unworldly bureaucracy never existed in the past and will never exist in the future'.[76] To Kornai's acute observation it appeared that 'the Lange of the [nineteen] thirties, although a convinced socialist, lived in the sterile world of Walrasian pure theory and did not consider the socio-political underpinning of his basic assumptions'.[77]

There were also criticisms of this model from the Left. We will say a few words on the criticisms of two well-known socialists, both economists within the broad Marxian framework – Maurice Dobb and Paul Sweezy.

As regards Dobb, he stressed the difference between socialism's centrally planned economy and capitalism's anarchy of the market. He stated – clearly aiming at the competitive-solution model of the anti-Mises socialists – that most of the critics of Mises 'have argued that a socialist economy can escape the irrationality which is predicted of it if and only if it closely imitates the mechanism of the competitive market'.[78] He faulted the 'socialist critics of Mises' for 'overlooking the full significance of the difference between socialism and capitalism' in the sense that they 'failed to appreciate the crucial significance of a planned economy', which consists in the 'unification of all the major decisions

---

74   See the lucid discussion in Bergson 1967, p. 662. Years later, while asserting the ability of electronic computers to solve the calculation problem, Lange recognised that the market 'treats the accounting problem only in static terms' and that 'long term investments have to be taken out of the market mechanism' (Lange, in Kowalik 1993, p. 363).

75   Bergson 1948, p. 435.

76   Kornai 1986, p. 1726.

77   Kornai 1986, p. 1727.

78   Dobb 1940, p. 273.

which rule investment and production, by contrast with their atomistic diffusion'.[79] This critique did not prevent him from being in agreement with these socialists on the question of a free consumer market along with the market for labour (power) in socialism.[80]

Referring to the position of the neo-classical socialists in their debate with Mises, Dobb pointed to their focus on 'equilibrium', avoiding 'dynamic problems', and thus excluding the 'most important considerations affecting economic development', whereas 'certain kinds of development may only come upon the agenda if development is centrally planned as an organic whole'.[81] Dobb added that 'the quintessential function of planning as an economic mechanism is that it is a means of substituting *ex-ante* coordination of the constituent elements in a scheme of development for the coordination *ex-post* which a decentralised pricing system provides'.[82] Further elaborating the point, Dobb stressed that 'the decisions which confront planners and policy makers under conditions of *economic change*, the key decisions affecting development, could not be left under socialism to the automatic adjudication of any market or pricing system'.[83]

In his turn Paul Sweezy was more sympathetic towards Lange's competitive model than Dobb. Sweezy very favourably refers to Schumpeter's view on Lange's model: 'Professor Schumpeter probably expresses the opinion of the great majority of competent economists when he says not only that socialism passes the test of logical "definiteness and consistency" but also that it is "eminently operational"'.[84] Sweezy then adds, 'there are of course still many who believe that socialism is impossible for economic reasons, but with their chief intellectual arsenal out of production it seems reasonable to suppose that they will gradually run out of ammunition and either give up the fight or resort to other weapons'.[85]

However, Sweezy still has critical remarks to make on the Lange exercise. For Sweezy the most striking feature of Lange's model is that the function of the CPB is virtually confined to providing a substitute for the market as the coordinator of the activities of the various plants and industries. 'The truth is that Lange's Board is not a *planning* agency at all but rather a *price-fixing*

---

79   Dobb 1940, p. 273.

80   See Dobb 1940, pp. 300.

81   Dobb 1965, p. 76.

82   Dobb 1965, p. 76.

83   Dobb 1965, p. 86. Emphasis added.

84   Sweezy 1949, p. 232. Cited from Schumpeter 1950, pp. 184, 185.

85   Sweezy 1949, pp. 232, 233.

agency; in his model production decisions are left to a myriad of essentially independent units, just as they are under capitalism'. Sweezy concludes that 'we may then regard it as established by both theoretical reasoning and practical experience that a socialist economy will be centrally planned in a sense very different from that in which Lange's model may be said to be centrally planned; in any actual socialist society it must be expected that the function of the Central Planning Board will be to lay down concrete directives which will be binding on the managers of socialised industries and plants'.[86]

Feasible Socialism

After Lange's model the most important model of MS is that of Alec Nove (1983, 1991). Nove calls it 'feasible socialism'. Here we give a short outline of this interesting model, drawing basically on his first book. There was no important change in the second version.[87]

The 'political assumption' of this model is multiparty democracy with periodic elections to a parliament. Nove stresses the importance of the 'need to avoid the feeling of alienation' of the working people while taking full account of consumer preferences and user needs in determining what to produce. To this effect there would be a preference for the small-scale as a means of maximising participation and a sense of belonging. Outside centralised or monopolised sectors, and a limited area of private enterprise, management should be responsible to the workers. Also the preferences of the working people – called 'producers' preferences' – should play a major role in determining how goods should be produced, bearing in mind 'the need for economy of resources and the technology available'.[88]

There would be state enterprises – centrally controlled and administered – called 'centralised state corporations'; state (socially) owned enterprises with full autonomy and a management responsible to the workforce, called 'socialised enterprises'; 'cooperative enterprises'; and small-scale private enterprises, subject to 'clearly defined limits'.[89] The first group includes banks and credit institutions. Clearly there would have to be devised criteria of efficiency, taking into account social and economic externalities. There would be tripart-

---

86   Sweezy 1949, pp. 233, 238. Emphasis in text.

87   In the second edition Nove introduced in the model a market for capital, absent in the first edition, without substantially changing the original model. See Nove 1991.

88   Nove 1983, p. 199. Emphasis in original.

89   Nove 1983, p. 200. Emphasis in original.

ite supervision with management responsible to the state, the users and the workforce.[90] There would have to be central management of current microeconomic affairs for the sectors where informational, technological and organisational economies of scale, and the presence of major externalities, render this indispensable.[91]

The big state-owned units constitute the 'commanding heights' of large-scale industry and public utilities, plus finance.[92] As regards the role of competition, 'it is inconceivable to imagine choice without competition among suppliers of goods and services'.[93] The large majority of goods and services should, whenever possible, be determined by negotiations between the parties concerned. 'This implies competition, a pre-condition for choice'.[94]

Socialised and cooperative enterprises would have managers appointed by an elected committee to be responsible to this committee, or if possible, to a plenary meeting of the workforce.[95] The Centre would have a number of vital functions. First, major investments would be its responsibility. There would have to be 'conscious planning' by an authority, 'responsible to an elected assembly', of major investments of structural significance.[96] Secondly, the planners would endeavour to monitor decentralised investments directly or through the banking system. Thirdly, the Centre would play a major role in administering such central production activities as electricity, oil and railways. In those sectors where externalities are likely to be significant, central intervention is essential; it can take the form of regulations – such as measures to protect the environment from pollution, or subsidies in such areas as public transport and research. 'As an unlimited market mechanism would in due course destroy itself, and create intolerable social inequalities, the state would have vital functions in determining income policies, levying taxes, intervening to restrain monopoly power, and generally setting ground rules of a competitive market. Some sectors such as education and health would be exempt from market-type criteria'.[97]

Finally, it is recognised that a degree of inequality in income distribution is needed to elicit the necessary effort by 'free human beings'. Indeed, 'a degree

90   Nove 1983, p. 201.
91   Nove 1993, p. 227.
92   Nove 1983, p. 202.
93   Nove 1983, p. 203.
94   Nove 1983, pp. 210, 227.
95   Nove 1983, p. 206.
96   Nove 1983, p. 227.
97   Nove 1983, p. 227.

of material inequality is a pre-condition for avoiding administrative direction of labour', but moral incentives would be encouraged and inequalities consciously limited.[98]

This model, which is within the general framework of neo-classical economics, has important shortcomings, and does not address the neo-Austrian criticisms of the neo-classical general equilibrium model(s). As has been justly pointed out, 'major, non-marginal change and investment, together with the regulation of enterprise behaviour, is assumed to be undertaken by the state, but there is no discussion of how this is to be done or of where the knowledge on the basis of which these decisions are to be made comes from. Thus, the principal-agent problem is not discussed and neither is the Austrian theoretical challenge'.[99] We propose to get back to Nove later.

Analytical Market Socialism

This American variety of MS is mainly the work of John Roemer, with some cooperation from Pranab Bardhan. Sharing some features of the Lange model, it goes beyond that model by taking account of the Austrian and (particularly) Hayekian criticisms of it that we discussed earlier in this chapter.

In this analytical model, market socialism is defined as 'any of a variety of economic arrangements in which most goods including labour are distributed through the price system, and the profits of firms, managed by workers or not, are distributed quite equally among the population'.[100] We are told that the 'central question' here is by 'what mechanism profits can be so distributed without unacceptable costs in efficiency'.[101]

Roemer focuses on three equalities which he believes to be what socialists want: (1) equality of opportunity for self-realisation and welfare; (2) equality of opportunities for political influence; (3) equality of social status. He stresses the equalisation of income without any unacceptable loss in efficiency – particularly in raising the income of the poor – as the most important single step towards improving the opportunities for self-realisation and welfare.[102] Criticising the earlier socialists for their 'fetish of public ownership', the model emphasises the importance of optimum choice of property relations in firms

---

98   Nove 1983, pp. 215, 227–8.
99   Adaman and Devine 1997, p. 65.
100 Roemer 1994, p. 456.
101 Roemer 1994, p. 456.
102 Roemer 1994, pp. 454, 455.

and land. This choice should fulfil two desiderata: distribution of income, and efficiency. Property relations should engender competition and innovation.

In their joint work Bardhan and Roemer call their MS 'competitive social-ism', in which there would be 'competitive politics and competitive allocation of most commodities and resources', but where in a major part of the economy there 'would not be a replacement of state or public ownership of the principal means of production with traditional private ownership'.[103] To the question of what should be planned, Roemer answers that the pattern and level of invest-ment in the economy should be planned. Investment planning is necessary because '(1) markets that are necessary for investment to be efficiently alloc-ated do not exist, and (2) there are positive externalities from investment so that even were such markets to exist, market-determined investment would be socially sub-optimal'.[104] What is not to be planned is clearly stated. This market socialist economy à la Lange would not plan the basket of consumer goods pro-duced, the allocation of consumer goods among consumers, or the allocation of labour.[105]

As regards income distribution, every adult citizen would receive from the state treasury an equal endowment of coupons that can be used only to pur-chase shares of mutual funds, and only coupons can be used to purchase such shares, not money. Only mutual funds can purchase shares of public firms, using coupons. A share of mutual fund entitles the owning citizen to a share of the mutual firm's revenues. Firm's investment funds come from two sources: bank loans and the state treasury through coupon exchange. The intention of the coupon mechanism is to distribute the firm's profits among the adult cit-izens quite equally.

The firms in this 'coupon economy' would be organised around a fairly small number of main banks. A main bank would be mainly responsible for put-ting together loan consortia to finance the operations of the firms in its group; it would correlatively be responsible for monitoring these firms. The 'banks would not be owned by the government but by mutual funds, and, ultimately, citizens'.[106] Finally, Bardhan and Roemer intend to solve the principal-agent problem – while maintaining a roughly egalitarian distribution of total profits of the economy – by 'designing for the firms to rely on banks as their main monitors'. The 'proposed bank-centric financial system largely mitigates the

---

103   Bardhan and Roemer 1994, p. 137.
104   Roemer 1992, p. 267.
105   Roemer 1992, p. 268.
106   Roemer 1994, p. 470.

planner-manager principal-agent problem. And does so in a way potentially superior to that of the stock market-centric system'.[107]

Market Socialism Proper

This version of market socialism is due basically to the eminent economist from Poland, W. Brus. It arose from Brus's close observation of the economic reform process undertaken in post-Stalin Eastern Europe in an effort to get away from the earlier (administrative) 'command system'.[108] Brus's theoretical point of departure is the 1938 Lange model of MS. Particularly referring to the Hungarian 'new economic mechanism' (NEM for short), he compares it to the Lange model and finds that while NEM meets the Lange requirement for the 'trial and error' method for establishing the prices of producer goods, it departs from the Lange model as regards the investment sphere, particularly with respect to the rate of accumulation and allocation of the investment funds among sectors, areas and projects determined directly by the central planners, and by assigning a secondary place to the role of the rate of interest in equilibrating demand and supply of capital. Referring to the NEM model, Brus opines that 'The interaction between an effective central plan and a market mechanism which requires enterprises to adjust to general rules and conditions makes the model of *central planning with regulated market mechanism* an approximately adequate description of the concept of the new economic mechanism'.[109] The model, however, failed to live up to expectations, and the question arose as to whether the failure was due to the 'deficiencies of the blueprint itself', and not simply 'due to its deviation from the blueprint'.[110] In a work written jointly with L. Laski, Brus comes to the view that putting the controlled product market side by side with central planning is flawed. The authors stress the necessity of the presence of a capital market in a market socialist economy. The capital market in this context is defined as 'a mechanism of horizontal reallocation of savings through transactions between the savers and the investors in the productive assets'.[111] With the existence of a capital market, along with the product and labour markets, as opposed to the 'half-way house system' of the product market alone, market socialism becomes '*market socialism proper*'.

---

107 Bardhan and Roemer 1994, pp. 143–4,145.
108 Bruce 1987, p. 338.
109 Brus 1987, p. 341. Emphasis in text.
110 Brus 1987, p. 341.
111 Brus and Laski 1989, p. 106.

Hence, according to these authors, 'The main innovation of market socialism (proper), compared with the half-way houses, consists of the introduction of the capital market'.[112]

The feature which market socialism shares with capitalism – Brus and Laski opine – is the position of the enterprise. This latter has to be fully responsible for its activities in a competitive environment while aiming at 'profit maximisation, both short and long term'. The only but important difference is 'the exclusion of private ownership of the means of production'.[113] It is remarkable that these authors, unlike the general run of authors on MS, directly connect MS with Marx's analysis of commodity production.

Market socialism means a truly monetarised economy in which all goods are supplied as commodities. They are produced for sale, and only after they are transformed into money, that is, into generalised purchasing power, is the production process complete. The transformation of commodities into money – their realisation, in Marxian parlance – constitutes the critical phase in the reproduction process of the monetarised economy.[114]

Brus and Laski add that within the market system there is considerable room for state intervention 'following the Keynes-Kalecki approach to economic dynamics. Thus market socialism does not need to be equated with a *laissez-faire* market system'.[115]

Saying that the logic of the full-fledged market mechanism seems to indicate the 'non-state enterprise as the most natural constituent of the enterprise sector', they recognise consequently the abandonment of the 'dominance of public ownership, central planning and distribution according to work', whereby 'the distinction between capitalist and socialist systems, as hitherto perceived, becomes thoroughly blurred'.[116] However, they insist that their model of market socialism 'does not imply the abandonment of a number of basic socialist values – equality of opportunity, major concern for full employment, social care, and so on'.[117]

---

112   Brus and Laski 1989, p. 105. Emphasis in text. It is interesting to note that these authors
       consider the 1938 Lange model of MS to contain a capital market for the purpose of alloc-
       ation of investment between different sectors and projects operating through the price of
       capital – the rate of interest – towards equalising demand and supply of capital. See Brus
       and Laski 1989, p. 74.
113   Brus and Laski 1989, p. 110.
114   Brus and Laski 1989, p. 110.
115   Brus and Laski 1989, p. 117.
116   Brus and Laski 1989, pp. 150, 151.
117   Brus and Laski 1989, p. 151.

Market Socialism – 'Marxian'

Finally, there is a variant of market socialism explicitly evoking Marx as the reference point. We discuss here two important models of this genre. One by David Schweickart, the other by Michael Howard.

Schweickart explicitly claims himself to be an 'anti-Stalinist Marxist'. There are two books, in particular, written by him where he lays down his model.[118] In order to be brief, however, we leave aside the books, and instead, in what follows, we draw on his two important articles, which he published in two different places at two different dates, and which give the essentials of his model.

Schweickart starts by stating that market socialism is a feasible, desirable alternative to capitalism within a democratic framework. It is a 'democratic economy'. A modern economy, to be viable and desirable, must deal with three basic problems – alienation of labour, anarchy of production, and bureaucratic inefficiency. The solution to these problems requires the correct synthesis of three elements: democracy, planning and the market.[119] The remedy for alienation is workplace democracy. Enterprises should be controlled by those who work there. As regards planning, what has got to be planned is not the entire economy. On the contrary, under socialism, what requires planning is investment. As regards the market, under the assumption of at least moderate abundance in the economy, Schweickart emphasises, the market is the best instrument for processing and transmitting economic information and providing effective incentives for minimising production costs and for seeking out and satisfying consumer desires. Without denying the market's great 'imperfections as an instrument for growth and development', the author underlines that 'for the day-to-day adjustments of supply and demand that economic rationality requires, no better instrument is available'.[120]

Clarifying further, the author writes that 'a market socialist economy eliminates or greatly restricts private ownership of the means of production, substituting for private ownership some form of state or worker ownership. It retains the market as the mechanism for coordinating most of the economy. It may or may not replace wage labour'.[121] Schweickart poses the question: why not advocate and struggle for a 'non-market, democratic, *decentralised* economy'? He then replies that such an economy, at the present state of economic devel-

---

118   Schweickart 1993, 2002.
119   Schweickart 1992, p. 30.
120   Schweickart 1992, p. 32.
121   Schweickart, in Ollman (ed.) 1998, p. 10.

opment, is 'neither viable, *nor* desirable' given the complexities of the techno-
logies and given the range of goods that modern consumers demand. 'If, instead
of decentralised autarky, one wants decentralised, participatory bottom-up
planning that results in a unified plan for a large industrialised economy, it can't
be done'.[122]

Schweickart designates his model 'Economic Democracy', which puts worker self-management at the heart of the system. While this is the first 'defining
feature' of the model, the second feature distinguishing it from capitalism is
its mechanism for generating and dispensing funds for investment. Economic
Democracy relies on taxation. Each enterprise must pay a tax on the capital
assets under its control. This tax functions as an interest rate on capital. The
proceeds of the capital-assets tax constitute society's investment fund, all of
which are ploughed back into the economy.[123] The market does not dictate
investment flows. 'Under Economic Democracy investment funds are returned
to the communities on a per capita basis, as a *prima facie* entitlement. Thus capital flows to where the people are. People are not forced to follow the flow of
capital'.[124] Once in the community, the investment funds are then loaned to the
communal enterprises in view of setting up new concerns through a network
of public banks following two criteria: projected profitability and employment
creation.[125]

Finally, Schweickart sums up his model of 'Economic Democracy'. It is 'an
economic system with three basic structures, worker self-management of enterprises, social control of investment, and a market for goods and services'.[126]
He then poses the question, 'is this really socialism?', and goes on, 'There is, after
all, still competition, still inequality, still potential unemployment. [However,]
Socialism emerges from the womb of capitalism, and is marked by its origin,
it is not a perfect society; it is a non-capitalist economic order that preserves
the best that capitalism has attained, while overcoming its worst evils'.[127] As
examples of applied market socialism in the image of his model, allowing for
their imperfections, he cites today's China and the Mondragon co-operative
enterprise.[128] Elaborating further, Schweickart adds

---

122   Schweickart, in Ollman (ed.) 1998, p. 15. Emphasis in original.
123   Schweickart 1992, p. 35; in Ollman (ed.) 1998, p. 17.
124   Schweickart in Ollman (ed.)1998, p. 17.
125   Schweickart in Ollman (ed.)1998, pp. 17–8.
126   Schweickart, in Ollman (ed.) 1998, p. 18.
127   Schweickart, in Ollman (ed.) 1998, p. 20.
128   Schweickart, in Ollman (ed.) 1998, particularly pp. 9 and 21.

Granted, it is still a market economy, enterprises still sell their goods, and workers still receive incomes. There is still money, and even competition. The economy is stable and solid. It is not driven by capitalism's grow or die imperative ... Such a society deserves to be called the 'higher stage of communism'. The society has left the 'realm of necessity' and entered the 'realm of freedom'. We have here the rational core of Marx's dream.[129]

Howard's model of MS is largely the same as Schweickart's – worker-managed, socially (that is, state) owned enterprises coordinated by market mechanisms, with investment funds generated through a tax on capital assets. It differs from Schweickart's model on one important point. While defending Schweickart's economic democracy, Howard additionally draws on the work of Philippe Van Parijs, by allowing, in his model, an 'unconditional, highest suitable basic income' (BI) for all citizens.[130] At the same time, Howard presents his MS as a 'left-wing variant of John Rawls's conception of justice'.[131] And there is one further point of difference with Schweickart. While Schweickart mentions Mondragon cooperatives as an example on whose 'lessons he draws heavily',[132] he does not elaborate the point. In contrast Howard presents his market socialism as market socialism of the cooperative type, as exampled by the Mondragon cooperative(s). Howard stresses that his 'preferred model of market socialism combines the best features of the Yugoslav (cooperative) model and the Mondragon cooperative model: workplaces controlled by their workers, coordinated by means of a market, with details of ownership, investment, and income distribution worked out with a view to efficiency, justice, and the maximisation of democracy'.[133] He calls his model 'a kind of revision of traditional Marxism'.[134] Howard finds in Marx two 'contrasting models of post-capitalist classless society' – the one in the *Communist Manifesto* 'with commodity exchange', and the other in *Capital* and the *Critique of the Gotha Programme* 'without commodity exchanges, functioning under government planning'.[135]

Could we characterise the units of production in cooperative market socialism, as we find them in Schweickart and Howard, as socialist enterprises? Marx, indeed, evaluates workers' (producers' as opposed to consumers') cooperatives

129 Schweickart, in Ollman (ed.) 1998, p. 176.
130 Howard 2000, p. 26.
131 Howard 2000, p. 5.
132 Schweickart, in Ollman (ed.) 1998, p. 21.
133 Howard 2000, p. 225.
134 Howard 2000, p. 225.
135 Howard 2000, p. 76.

in capitalism quite positively. We see this clearly stated both in his 'Inaugural Address' (1864) and in the Resolution on Cooperatives (1866) – also composed by him – of the First Congress of the First International. The cooperatives have shown, Marx maintains, that 'production on a large scale, and in accordance with the behests of modern science, may be carried out without the exist- ence of a class of masters employing a class of hands; that to bear fruit, the means of labour need not be monopolised as a means of domination over and of extortion against the labouring man himself'.[136] And in the Resolution on cooperatives Marx holds that the movement is 'a transforming movement of the present day society, and that its great merit is to show in practice that the present system of subordination of labour to capital – despotic and impov- erishing – can be superseded by the republican system of association of free and equal producers'.[137] In no text does Marx qualify workers' co-operatives (of production) within *capitalism* as *socialist*. Indeed, '*within* the co-operatives the opposition between capital and labour is superseded'. However, this hap- pens 'only in the form' that the 'workers as association are their own capitalist, i.e., they use the means of production for the valorisation [*Verwertung*] of their own labour'.[138] The last phrase is crucial, inasmuch as any question of 'socialist enterprises' is excluded as long as the 'valorisation of labour' continues. Now, merely using the means of production for employing labour would signify no more than what Marx calls the simple labour process, valid for any mode of pro- duction. It is only when, in the process, labour is valorised that we are dealing with a different 'beast' – commodity production in general, that is, *capital*.

With the co-operatives remaining within the capitalist system, 'valorising labour', there can be no question of the socialist form, though there is now a 'breakthrough' within the old form. Marx justly calls them not the 'socialist' but the 'transitional forms [*Übergangsformen*] from the capitalist to the asso- ciated mode of production'.[139] In a remarkable paragraph of the *Civil War in France* on the workers' co-operatives, Marx speaks of the '*unified* co-operative societies' which are 'to *regulate* national production upon a *common plan*, thus taking it under their own control' as 'possible communism',[140] which clearly precludes commodity production (our emphasis). There is no question of val- orising labour in these cooperatives. On the other hand, in market socialism each cooperative is a commodity producer where the workers 'valorising their

---

136   Marx 1964a, p. 285.
137   Marx 1965a, p. 1469.
138   Marx 1992, p. 504; 1984, p. 440.
139   Marx 1992, p. 504; 1984, p. 440.
140   See Marx, in Marx and Engels 1971b, p. 76.

own labour' are 'their own capitalist'. They are necessarily subject to 'compelling competitive pressures', as Schweickart rightly observes.[141] Given the exigencies of the self-expansion of values – the very logic of commodity production being the dominant form of production – associated with the likelihood of a secular increase in income inequality within the co-operative *à la* Mondragon (of which more below), a workers' co-operative has every potential of splitting itself into functionaries of capital – without necessarily owning individually the means of production – and mere wage-labourers, thus 'degenerating into a bourgeois share company', as Marx would say.[142]

Market Socialism is Capitalism

Quite properly, the point of departure of MS is capitalism, to which is opposed socialism as a superior alternative. However, it is rare to see any explicit statement among its adherents about the meanings of capitalism and socialism as concepts. Oskar Lange is one of the few to conceptualise these two categories at the beginning of his model of socialism. It is interesting to note that this conceptualisation is not essentially different from the corresponding conceptualisation by the dominant 'Marxism' of the Second and the Third Internationals. This particular approach notably abstracts from the question of real (social) relations of production and focuses on form(s) of juridical ownership of the means of production and the form of circulation of products. Thus capitalism is conceived by Lange – in its 'Marxian sense', as he claims – as an economic system based on private enterprise with a competitive régime.[143] Correspondingly, by 'socialist economy' Lange means 'public ownership' of the means of production – necessarily associated with central planning – and calls this the

---

141   Schweickart, in Ollman (ed.) 1998, p. 18.

142   Marx 1965, p. 1469. Already, some of the disturbing trends in this direction can be detected in the much-touted Mondragon. Howard, whose account of Mondragon is more objective than Schweickart's, cites a report which, in Howard's words, 'shows, convincingly, that the majority of workers, particularly manual workers, do not feel that the firm is theirs or that they are a part of the firm'. 'Workers perceive', Howard continues, 'clear lines of division between those above and those below. Conflicts erupt over job classification, pay differentials and control of the work process ... Ironically workers in a private firm were found to have more effective leverage through their union over labor process issues, and cooperative managers can change working conditions in ways not tolerated in private firms'. Howard 2000, p. 128.

143   Lange, in Lange and Taylor 1938, pp. 104, 107.

'classical definition of socialism'.[144] Paradoxically but unsurprisingly, the position of Mises is basically the same.[145] Capitalism and socialism in almost all the MS models which followed Lange's are conceived essentially in the same way as in this prototypical model, which itself, it appears, was much influenced by the dominant 'Marxism' of the Second and the Third Internationals.

What is the relation of *this* 'capitalism' and 'socialism' to those in Marx's work(s)? This question is important because our present work is explicitly situated within Marx's universe of discourse, including the central categories as Marx had conceived them, and also because many of the models of MS take Marx as their reference point. If by the 'Marxian sense' of capitalism and 'classical definition of socialism' is meant capitalism and socialism developed by Marx in his *own texts*, then, in the light of these relevant texts, the claim of inheritance appears to have no basis. For Marx, *capital* is literally equated with the 'separation of the conditions of production from the labourer'.[146] Or, the 'absolute divorce of the objective wealth from the living labour power'.[147] Correspondingly, and logically, Marx conceives socialism (the *same* as communism) as a union of free individuals where, as opposed to capitalism's 'separation', there appears the unmediated union of producers with their conditions of production.[148] This necessarily implies *social appropriation* of the conditions of production where *society* itself – that is, the collective body of the associated producers (and not the *state*, which has disappeared) – is directly the subject.[149] It is clear that this has little to do with the famous 'public (state) ownership' of the means of production, so much touted by most of the adherents of MS and the partisans of the earlier 'communist' Party-State as the central characteristic of socialism.

Some academic adherents of MS with Marxian inclination have argued – just like the earlier Party-State proponents of 'commodity socialism' – that if commodity production could exist independently of, and long before, capitalism, it could also continue to exist under socialism, the market serving as a rational and efficient instrument for allocation of resources and products. Among the academic adherents of market socialism, Oskar Lange – the composer of the prototypical model of market socialism – was also the first to make this argument clearly and explicitly, in more than one place over a long

144   Lange and Taylor 1938, pp. 72, 73, 81.

145   Mises 1936, pp. 28, 128, 241. The same concept of socialism we find also in Halm. See above.

146   Marx 1962a, p. 419; 1971a, p. 422.

147   Marx 1982, p. 2238; 1994, p. 201.

148   Marx 1962a, p. 419; 1971a, p. 423; 1970b, p. 208.

149   Marx 1987a, p. 109; 1954, pp. 82–3; 1976a, pp. 73–4; 1970b, p. 319.

period. First, he did this by distinguishing between 'capitalism and simple commodity production' in a 1935 article in the *Review of Economic Studies* – that is, even before his 1938 book.[150] Then in his 1942 lecture at the 'Socialist Club' of the Chicago University Economics Department, he distinguished 'prices and money', that is, 'market' from 'capitalism', and asked the audience not to confuse one with the other.[151] Again in his 1957 Belgrade lecture he observed that 'commodity production is carried on already in pre-capitalist societies ... In a socialist economy the law of value continues to operate because production continues to be commodity production'.[152] Years later, the well-known economist from (ex-)Yugoslavia, Branko Horvat, made a similar argument. He wrote, 'Commodity production existed under slavery, serfdom, and capitalism ... Since there are so many types of commodity production, it should not be surprising if we find socialist commodity production as well'.[153]

Finally, we have the eminent Japanese economist of the Uno school, Makoto Ito. His argument is not as direct as those advanced by the two economists just mentioned – his argument in favour of market socialism is somewhat roundabout. He develops this argument by making circulation independent of the process of production, that is, *'pure forms of circulation* without referring to social relations that structure labour processes'.[154] What Ito is saying here explicitly, is really the very foundation of 'market socialism', which by definition abstracts from the process of production of products and thereby abstracts from the specific mode of production of the products being exchanged as commodities in the 'market'. It is also important to stress that while some models of market socialism contain workers' cooperatives as the mode of labour, the market socialist models for the most part explicitly have a 'labour market', that is, wage labour, besides a market for products including capital. As regards workers' cooperatives, let us note *en passant* that in Marx's long 'questionnaire' to the workers (1880) – to which reference is made at some length in this book in the chapter on 'socialist accounting' – there is a specific question: 'are there cooperatives in your profession? Do they employ workers from outside in the same way as the capitalists do?'[155]

---

150   In Kowalik 1993, pp. 10, 11.
151   In Kowalik 1993, pp. 305, 310. However, Lange should be praised for having taken this kind
       of initiative in the Economics department of a major US university – something uncommon in that period.
152   In Kowalik 1993, p. 336.
153   Horvat 1982, p. 501.
154   Ito 1996, p. 99. Emphasis in text.
155   Marx 1965c, p. 1536.

Now, it is true that commodity production predated capitalism by hundreds of years. However, in pre-capitalism the economy was only partially commodified, mainly involving the exchange of surplus over immediate consumption, and the basic aim of production was use value and not exchange value (including its self-expansion). Naturally, there could be no question of capitalism. 'Prices are old, so is exchange. But the determination of prices more and more by cost of production and the (increasing) inroads of exchange into all the relations of production are first fully developed and continue to develop more and more completely only in bourgeois society'.[156] Indeed, 'just as commodity production at a certain stage of its development necessarily becomes capitalist commodity production, in the same way the law of ownership of commodity production is necessarily transformed into the law of capitalist appropriation'.[157] This is the situation where the whole or at least the major part of the economy is from the start commodified – which is what MS supposes the economy to be. 'Purchase and sale seize not only the surplus of production but subsistence (or "substance") itself – the commodity becoming the *universal form of product*'.[158] Thus the market-socialist hypothesis would imply that it is the second commodity circuit – buying for selling (M – C – M') – which dominates the circulation process, leading necessarily to the continuous self-expansion of values, which is just another name for capital. Market socialism turns out to be a *capitalist* alternative to capitalism. Last but not least, it must be stressed (a point very often neglected by even those opposed to MS) that commodity production *as such* represents an 'inversion' (*Verkehrung*). Here the social relations of production exist 'outside of individuals as object' and their relations in the process of production of social life appear as 'the specific properties of a thing'.[159] Indeed, in the 'society of commodity producers', where the 'social mode of production is commodity production' – the very stuff of MS – the 'producers' own movement takes the form of movement of things and controls the producers instead of being controlled by them',[160] which obviously contradicts a '(Re)Union of free individuals',[161] that is, socialism.

---

156   Marx 1953, p. 74; 1993, p. 156.

157   Marx 1987a, p. 538; 1954, p. 551; 1976a, p. 417.

158   Marx 1976b, p. 286; 1988b, p. 330.; 1988a, p. 27; 1994, p. 356. Emphasis added.

159   Marx 1980a, p. 128; 1970a, p. 49.

160   Marx 1987a, pp. 106–7; 1954, pp. 80–1; 1976a, p. 71. Of course, a (whole) 'society of commodity producers' could only be a capitalist society, where all or most of the products of labour are commodities.

161   Marx 1987a, p. 109; 1954, p. 82; 1976a, p. 73.

To sum up, the problem of rationally allocating labour and non-labour resources in an economy is common to all human societies, at least as long as they remain relatively limited compared to human needs. However, it does not necessarily follow that this allocation could be effected rationally only through the exchange of resources taking the commodity (price) form. The partisans of market socialism, in common with their opponents, confuse the rational alloc-ation of resources as such with the rational allocation of resources through the price system. The point is that the allocation of resources through the value/commodity form of the products of human labour is only 'a particular social manner of counting labour employed in the production of an object', characterising just that society in which 'the process of production dominates individuals, the individual does not dominate the process of production'.[162] Only the 'routine (*Gewohnheit*) of daily life' makes us accept as 'trivial and self-evident that a social relation of production takes the form of an object'.[163]

---

162 Marx 1987a, p. 111; 1954, p. 85; 1976a, p. 75, We have translated the term 'Mensch' by indi-vidual, not 'man', as we read it in the English and the French versions.

163 Marx 1980a, p. 114; 1970a, p. 34.

The Problematic of a Non-capitalist Road to Socialism

Capital's Positive Contribution

Earlier we argued that it was capital which through its own contradictions would create the material and spiritual conditions for the rise of a society of free and associated individuals beyond capital – socialism. From the fact that socialism in Marx and Engels arises from the reality of the capitalist society, which is revolutionised into a new society, it follows that their starting assumption is historically severely limited to the capitalist epoch, which itself is considered as historically transitory. In particular, it is advanced capitalism in which the society has already freed itself from the millennial fetters of the individual's personal unfreedom under slavery and serfdom. At the same time, here, the capitalist mode of production and correspondingly capitalist relations of production have sufficiently advanced to a point where the immense majority of the population is in a situation where they are neither themselves part of the means of production (as were the slaves and serfs) nor in possession of any material means of production of their own. They, on the contrary, have only their own labour power – manual and mental – to sell 'freely' to the possessors of the means of production in exchange for a wage/salary (high or low) in order to live and reproduce their labour power. In fact, they are now the 'wage slaves' of capital. In its turn, this society over time reaches a stage where it itself can no longer continue to exist due to the incompatibility between its relations of production and forces of production, in the sense that the progress of the forces of production – of which the 'greatest productive force is the revolutionary class' (Marx) – shows how capital creates the subjective and objective conditions of its own negation and, simultaneously, the elements of the new society destined to supersede it – socialism. In the 'Critique', socialism (equivalently communism) signifies a 'society of free and associated producers' based on the 'associated mode of production (AMP)'. This 'union of free individuals', the crowning point of the producers' act of self-emancipation, where individuals are subject neither to personal dependence – as in pre-capitalism – nor to material dependence – as in capitalism – excludes, by definition, private property in the means of production, the commodity form of the product of labour, wage labour and state. Here the freely associated 'social individuals' are the masters of their own social movement, subjecting their social relations to their own control.[1]

The Controversy

In recent years it has been widely argued that Marx in his last years – particularly and notably in his writings on Russia[2] – did *fundamentally* change, if not contradict, his earlier central position that the elements of the new society are generated contradictorily within capital through a process of creating the conditions of its own disappearance. This line of thought was initiated and especially emphasised not so long ago by Teodor Shanin and Haruki Wada, and Shanin authored a book that has exercised a certain influence on scholars – Marxist or otherwise.[3]

Now, in these writings, Marx was reacting to a question posed to him by his Russian correspondents: could the already existing Russian rural communes be the basis for building socialism (communism) in Russia without going through the capitalist mode of production, or must Russia pass through a capitalist stage in order to arrive at the new society?

In his reply, Marx first observed that in *Capital* he had underlined that his analysis of the CMP – its genesis and development generating, in the process, the elements of its own negation – was confined strictly to 'Western Europe'.[4] He derisively rejected any claim to possess a 'master key of a general historical-philosophical theory fatally imposable' on all peoples irrespective of the specific historical circumstances in which they found themselves.[5] Thus the analysis in *Capital* could not offer either a positive or a negative answer to the question posed by the Russian correspondents. But, added Marx, from his independent studies on Russia he had concluded that the Russian rural commune could serve as the point of departure of 'social regeneration' in Russia. However, this transition will not be automatic. The communal ownership in land, the

---

1   Marx 1987a, p. 110; 1976a, p. 74; 1954, p. 84.

2   These are Marx's letter to Mikhailovsky 1877, his letter as well as several drafts of the letter to Vera Zasulich (1881) and his and Engels's joint preface to the Russian edition (1882) of the *Communist Manifesto*. The correspondence with the Russians Marx wrote in French.

3   Shanin 1983.

4   Marx is here referring to the chapter on the 'Secret of the Original Accumulation of Capital'. The reference to 'Western Europe' in this connection was added in the French version of the book, not reproduced in any of the German editions. See Marx 1976a, p. 519.

5   To Mikhailovsky, in Marx 1968, p. 1555.

point of departure of this 'regeneration', has already been affected by adverse forces – working inside and outside the commune – tending to undermine the system. On the one hand, parcellary cultivation of land and private appropriation of its fruits by its members, and, on the other hand, the state's fiscal exactions and the fraudulent exploitation by usury and merchant capital that had been taking place since 1861, when the Tsarist state adopted measures for the so-called 'emancipation of the peasants'. Hence, 'social regeneration' is possible provided that the negative factors are eliminated, most importantly by a 'Russian Revolution' by the peasant masses. In the process the commune could benefit from the scientific and technological acquisitions of the existing capitalism of the west.

According to Shanin, Marx's new familiarity with the Russian situation caused Marx to uphold the position that a peasant revolution in Russia, leading to its immediate socialist transformation, would serve as the prototype of immediate revolutionary transition to socialism from the peasant societies in the backward countries, just as England served as the prototype for the capitalist world.[6] Following Shanin, the Russian case added a fourth dimension to 'Marx's analytical thought', where to the 'triple origin suggested by Engels – German philosophy, French socialism and English political economy' – should be added 'a fourth, that of Russian revolutionary populism'.[7] If this is the reading of Marx's correspondence (on Russia) by a non-Marxist, a Marxist scholar from Mexico asserted that Marx, confronted with the Russian communes, underwent a 'change of direction' (*viraje*). Though this does not mean a 'fundamental change in Marx's theoretical position', it does signify the 'opening up of a broad road for the development of Marx's discourse on the different ways' (to socialism) – one for the central, more developed capitalism, the other for the less developed countries of the periphery.[8] A few years later Michael Löwy considered Marx's Russian correspondence as the 'antipode of the evolutionist and deterministic reasoning of the articles on India in 1853', where Marx had argued for the 'historically progressive mission' of the English bourgeoisie in that country.[9] Another Marxist, in her turn, read this correspondence as if it signified that the Russian case lent itself to a 'concept of revolution which changed everything, *including economic laws*', as if it was on a par with the Western European case, 'choosing a different path'.[10]

---

6   Shanin 1983, p. 18.

7   Shanin 1983, p. 20.

8   Dussel 1990, pp. 260–1.

9   Löwy 1996, p. 200.

10   Dunayevskaya 2002, p. 259. Emphasis in text. We should, however, take note of another

Let us now put Marx's discussion on Russia in its proper perspective, in order to see, on the basis of his relevant texts, what exactly Marx was saying in 1877 and 1881. At the outset it is necessary to refer to the emphasis Marx put on what he called the 'uniqueness' of the Russian case, which of course automatically excludes its generalisation into some kind of a 'law' applicable to the backward peasant societies, as, for example, the 'law of motion of capital' would apply to the capitalist societies in general. To Marx, the Russian 'agricultural communes' offered a *'unique* situation, without any precedent in history'.[11] First, contrary to India, the victim of a foreign conqueror who had violently destroyed its rural communes with 'common land ownership', Russia had no foreign conqueror, and it was the 'only European country' where 'till today' its communes 'have maintained themselves on a national scale'. Secondly, along with communal property of the soil, its historical environment, the contemporaneity of capitalist production in Western Europe offers it 'ready-made the material conditions of cooperative labour on a vast scale', which allows it to incorporate all the 'positive acquisitions of the capitalist system', the 'fruits with which capitalist production has enriched humanity' sparing it the necessity of passing through the capitalist régime.[12]

However, while considering the positive side, Marx emphasises, one has to reckon with the negative side contained in the 'dualism inherent in the Russian communal constitution', namely that, along with the communal ownership of land, there is also 'parcellary labour, the source of private appropriation', enabling the communes' members to 'accumulate moveable property, money and sometimes even slaves and serfs, uncontrolled by the commune' – which constituted the 'dissolvent of the original social and economic equality'.[13] Thus the 'dualism' of the communes offers an alternative: 'either its (private) ownership element will prevail (*l'emportera*) over its collective element or its collective element will prevail over the (private) ownership element'.[14] One should

---

statement by the author which largely attenuates this rather strong position: 'When Marx describes that the accumulation of capital is not the universal, he does not mean that it is not the universal in capitalism. He does mean that it is no universal for the *world*, and that the undeveloped, non-capitalist countries can experience other forms of development. But even then he qualifies it by saying that they must do it together what the advanced capitalist countries do' (Dunayevskaya 2002, p. 312; emphasis in original). We are grateful to Peter Hudis for referring us to this statement.

11   Marx 1968, p. 1566. Our emphasis.
12   Marx 1968, pp. 1561, 1565, 1566.
13   Marx 1968, p. 1564.
14   Marx 1968, p. 1565.

not forget that the 'agricultural commune' constituting the 'last phase of the primitive formation of society' is 'at the same time the phase of transition to the society based on private property including the series of societies founded on slavery and serfdom'.[15] 'Theoretically speaking', the Russian commune could conserve its soil by developing its base, the communal ownership of the land, and by eliminating the 'principle of private ownership which it also implies', and thereby 'become a direct point of departure of the economic system to which the modern society tends'.[16] However, coming down from the theory to reality, 'nobody can hide the fact that the Russian commune today is facing a conspiracy of powerful forces and interests'. Besides exercising 'incessant exploitation on the peasants, the State has facilitated the domination (within the commune) of a certain part of the capitalist system, stock market, bank, railway, commerce'.[17] Similarly, the commune is 'exploited fraudulently by the intruding capitalists, merchants, landed proprietors' as well as 'undermined by usury'. These different factors have 'unleashed inside the commune itself the conflict of interest already present and rapidly developed its germs of decomposition'.[18] This 'concourse of destructive influences, unless smashed by a powerful reaction will naturally end in the death of the rural commune'.[19] Hence Marx's emphasis on the need for a 'Russian Revolution'.[20] The fruit of this revolution, Marx thought, should be the 'substitution of the existing governmental institution, *Volost*', by an 'assembly of peasants, chosen by the communes themselves and serving their interests as the economic and administrative organ'.[21]

---

15   Marx 1968, pp. 1564–5.

16   Marx 1968, p. 1565.

17   Marx 1968, p. 1570. This 'dualism', manifesting the contradictory reality of the Russian countryside, Marx notes also in *Capital* Volume II, in one of its last manuscripts, written one year after his letter to Mikhailovsky. There he observed that 'landowners now operate with wage labourers instead of unfree serfs', but that, at the same time, these landowners 'lack sufficient purchasable labour power at their own chosen moments following the as yet incomplete separation of labourers from the means of production – thus having "free wage labourers" – due to common landownership of the village' (see Marx 2008, p. 695; 1956, p. 34).

18   Marx 1968, pp. 1570–1. This is confirmed by recent research. 'According to the commune's practice, tools and livestock were privately owned, and it was widely recognized that the more prosperous could manipulate the decision-making process of village assemblies so as to exclude the poor and even deprive them of land' (Kingston-Mann 1990, p. 31).

19   Marx 1968, pp. 1570, 1571, 1572.

20   Marx 1968, p. 1573.

21   Marx, in Riazanov 1971, p. 324. It is noteworthy that there is no mention of the state in

However, even if this 'revolution' is victorious and defeats the commune's transformation into capitalism, the building of communism in the peasant (and technologically backward) Russia would absolutely require the help of the advanced productive forces, the 'positive acquisition elaborated by the capitalist system'.[22] This material aid Russia could almost certainly not obtain from the capitalist regimes, but only from the victorious proletariat in Western Europe, which naturally would also serve as a bulwark against any attempted capitalist armed intervention in Russia from the outside. This seems to be the clear message that we get from the 'Preface' to the Russian edition of the *Manifesto*, the last to appear under the joint signatures of its authors. There it is observed that although the Russian commune had already been 'seriously undermined' (*stark untergrebene*), it could still directly go over to the 'communist form of collective ownership' provided that there is a 'revolution' in Russia which gives the signal for a 'proletarian revolution' in the West and that the one complements the other.[23]

Shanin imputes to Engels uniquely the position that the Russian revolution needed a proletarian revolution as a complement and asserts that 'Marx was moving away from such views'.[24] Wada, in his turn, in an otherwise well-researched paper, adds that the 'Preface' of 1882 'expresses the opinion of Engels, more directly than that of Marx'. Marx, being 'in low spirits [due to his wife's death,] asked Engels to make the draft and simply put his signature to it'.[25] As if Marx resigned himself to putting his name to whatever Engels wanted to draft. Unbelievable! Dussel, in his turn, though not going to Wada's extreme, writes that:

> [The 1882 Preface] is a text of compromise between Marx and Engels on the question of the Russian commune (that is, between Marx's 'Russian Revolution' and Engels's 'proletarian revolution') and the 'compromise' contained a contradiction indicative of the future.[26]

---

this transformation. In fact, the state's administrative organ has given way to a communitarian administrative organ freely chosen by the peasants. The influence on Marx of the libertarian experience of the 1871 Paris Commune is clear.

22 Marx 1968, p. 1566.
23 Marx and Engels 1882.
24 Shanin 1983, p. 22.
25 Wada, in Shanin 1983, p. 70. The antipode of Wada's position is offered by the editors of Dunayevskaya 2002, p. 316, who refer to Marx as the *sole* author of the 1882 'Preface' and nowhere mention Engels as its joint author.
26 Dussel 1990, p. 262.

Now, in his different drafts and the final version of his letter to Zasulich, as well as in his letter to Mikhailovsky, Marx does not explicitly refer to 'proletarian revolution' (by name) in the West as a complement to the Russian (peasant) revolution, so that 'proletarian revolution' in the 1882 'Preface' seems to come uniquely from Engels, who had, in a polemic in 1875, 'at Marx's demand and developing their common point of view',[27] *explicitly* spoken of the necessity of this complement for successfully transforming the existing commune system into a higher form.[28] However, a careful reading of Marx's drafts shows that the question of a 'proletarian revolution' in the West as an aid to the peasant revolution in Russia is very much present there, though the specific term is not. In the very first draft (Engels was not aware of these drafts, later discovered by David Riazanov), Marx considers as a 'very favourable circumstance' for the agricultural commune to go over to a higher form of society without passing through capitalism the fact that, after having survived a period when the capitalist system still appeared intact, bearing its technological fruits, the commune is now witness to this (capitalist) system

> struggling, on the one hand with its *labouring masses* and, on the other, with science and the productive forces which it has itself engendered, in a word, in a *fatal crisis* which will end in the *system's elimination* by a return of the present society to a higher form of the most 'archaïque' type of collective ownership and production.[29]

---

27   Rubel, in Marx 1968, p. 1552.

28   In this polemic, Engels, affirming the possibility of the existing commune system changing into a higher form, 'without passing through the intermediate stage of bourgeois parcellary property', emphasised that this possibility could not be realised without the help of a successful proletarian revolution in Western Europe, which (alone) could offer the Russian peasant in particular the materials which the peasant needs to 'carry through a revolution in his whole agricultural system' (Engels 1874). At the same time Engels underlined the importance of a revolution in Russia, 'Undoubtedly, Russia is on the eve of a revolution ... Here all the conditions of a revolution are united ... a revolution of the highest importance for Europe, since it will destroy with one stroke the reserve of the whole European reaction till now remaining intact' (Engels 1874).

     The similarity with what Marx wrote two years later is striking: 'Russia has been standing at the threshold of a revolution for a long time. All its elements are ready ... The revolution this time begins in the East where the bulwark of the reserve army of counter-revolution has as yet remained unhurt' (Marx to Sorge, 27 September 1877).

29   Marx 1968, p. 1570; our emphasis.

What else is he saying here but indicating – as if paraphrasing his famous, much misunderstood, 'Preface' of 1859 – a situation of acute contradiction between the relations of production and the material forces of production within western capitalism, ending in a 'fatal crisis' of the whole system and leading to its elimination and its substitution by a society of a higher type – obviously only possible through a revolution by its 'labouring masses', that is, the proletariat. If our textual reading of Marx is correct, Marx's position here is basically the same as that of the 'Preface' (1882) – only expressed in a different way – and certainly not very different from Engels's, which is easily verified when one reads Engels's two texts closely, those of 1874 and of 1894, the first published at Marx's demand and with his full accord (Rubel asserts this and even Wada concedes it)[30] and the second without its author being aware of Marx's drafts.[31]

A couple of points should be stressed here concerning Marx's depiction of the future society (after capital) as a return, in a higher form, of the most 'archaïque' type. This is in fact a paraphrase of a sentence from Morgan – whom Marx mentions as an 'American author' – where this author speaks of a 'new system' as 'a revival in a superior form of an archaïque type' towards which the modern society tends. Now, Shanin cites Marx's expression[32] and argues (without mentioning Marx's source) that this represents a kind of (new) enlightenment for Marx, confronted with the Russian commune. We would, however, submit that the *idea* underlying Marx's expression here does not really represent a new position for Marx. Rather he found in Morgan's statement a re-affirmation of his and Engels's (yes, Engels's, *pace* Shanin, Wada *e tutti quanti*) earlier position, held, it is true, in a more condensed *theoretical* manner without much empirical reference. Thus in his 1865 lecture (in English) to the workers, Marx speaks of three 'historical processes' of the relation between what he calls the 'Man of Labour and the Means of Labour' – first, their *'Original Union'*, then their *'Separation'* through the *'Decomposition of the Original Union'*, third, the 'restoration of the original union in a new historical form' through a 'fundamental revolution in the mode of production'.[33] Earlier we referred to a passage from Marx's 1861–3 manuscript where Marx, in the same way, speaks of the 'Original unity between the labourer and the conditions of production', as in family agriculture and 'natural communism', separation between them under capital and

---

30   In Shanin 1983, pp. 53–4.
31   Engels 1874 and 1894.
32   Shanin 1983, p. 17.
33   Marx 1988a, p. 412; emphasis in original.

the 'restoration of the original unity by means of a working class revolution' (along with the rest of society).[34] Engels, in his turn, in his preparatory notes towards *Anti-Dühring*, writes:

> All Indo-Germanic peoples started with common ownership. In course of social development, in almost all of these, this common ownership was eliminated, negated, thrust aside by these forms ... It is the task of the social revolution to negate this negation and to restore (*wieder herzustellen*) the common ownership to a higher stage of development.[35]

A few years later, Engels wrote an essay (1892) on the primitive form of collective land ownership in Germany and the subsequent development of private property. In that work Engels advised the German peasantry to revive in a new, higher form their old rural commune, which would enable the peasants to embark in a non-capitalist way towards the modern form of large-scale agricultural production. Engels starts by reminding the modern-day peasants of the 'old common property of all free men, the free common inheritance', and concludes by affirming that 'the restoration of a free peasant class has this value, that it has put the peasant in a position, with the aid of his natural comrade, the worker, to help himself, as soon as he understands *how*'.[36]

Another point in the draft has to be noted in this connection. In the draft we find an interesting representation of the most archaic type of community. This representation in a 'right form' broadly corresponds to Marx's configuration of the society envisaged as succeeding capitalism, present long before Marx had read Kovalevsky and Morgan. We mean the portrait of communism drawn in a few bold strokes, particularly in *Capital* (1867) and later in somewhat greater detail in the *Gothacritique* (1875). Here is the laconic sentence in the draft characterising the most archaic type (as opposed to its derivative, the 'agricultural commune'): 'in the more primitive communities (besides the common ownership of land) labour is done in common and the product, which is also common, is distributed (to the members) according to the needs of con-

---

34   See Marx 1962a, p. 419; 1971a, p. 423. Krader paraphrases this passage and connects this with Marx's draft of a letter to Zasulich, but specifically with reference to the 'Asiatic mode of production' (Krader 1973, p. 178), not as illustrating the *general position* of Marx regarding the configuration of the new society in relation to the 'archaïque', as we are trying to do here (by also referring to Marx's 1865 London lecture).

35   Engels 1877.

36   Engels 1892. Emphasis in original. See the interesting discussion in Walicki 1969, p. 193.

sumption after having put aside the part reserved for reproduction'.[37] Now, with this text in front of us when we read in *Capital* Volume I about the 'union of free individuals' labouring with the common means of production where the product of labour is a 'social product' of which one part is reserved in order to serve again as means of production while the rest is distributed among the members for consumption[38] – when we read this, does not this look like the primitive, archaic society appearing at a higher level in a new form, as Marx reaffirms in his 1881 draft citing Morgan?

Controversy Continued

Now the crucial question: does Marx's position on the Russian commune constitute a *fundamental* departure as regards his basic point of view on the question of the transition to a society of free and associated labour? We have already referred to the *singularity* and 'uniqueness' of the Russian case (underlined by Marx more than once), sufficient to exclude any *generalisation* of this case (as a prototype) to the pre-capitalist peasant society anywhere else in the world. In this sense this unique example naturally does not affect Marx's *general* position.[39] It is quite clear from Marx's correspondence that in its effort to go over to a higher type of society, assuming a successful 'Russian Revolution', the commune cannot, after all, avoid capitalism, developed elsewhere, which, through the proletarian revolution produced by capitalism itself by its own contradictions, and the advanced forces of production which it had created and which would be made available precisely by the victorious proletariat in the West, would be indispensable for the commune's survival as well as its extended reproduction. Thus the commune's transformation into a higher type of society would be impossible in the absence of capitalism elsewhere. All this of course assumes a successful 'Russian Revolution'. However, even *before* arriving at this point, the Russian commune already faces a sombre future, which Marx discerns in his dissection of the elements of its decomposition, contained

---

37 Marx 1968, p. 1563.

38 Marx 1987a, p. 109; 1976a, p. 74; 1954, p. 83.

39 Shanin's and Dussel's effort to extend the Russian case to the peasant world in general has no basis in Marx's texts. Nor is there much in Marx's texts to support Dunayevskaya's affirmation referred to earlier. For in order to generalise this case for peasant societies, one has to show the existence, at a considerable scale, of the communal ownership in them and the availability of capitalism's positive acquisitions. This would not be easy. Certainly it does not appear in Marx's extant texts.

integrally in its 'dualism', on the basis of the 'Russian reality', as we saw earlier.[40] Even before he had composed his drafts of the letter to Zasulich, Marx's letter to Mikhailovsky (1877) already indicated the possibility of the decomposition of the commune and clearly emphasised that the path of 1861 which the commune was already traversing, if continued, would exactly fall within the general case of *Capital*, which in fact turned out to be the case.[41]

The Russian case also, far from invalidating, rather confirms Marx's 1860s assertion – referred to above – that the two basic pre-conditions of building

40 The enthusiasts of the 'Russian road' leading directly to communism seem to have paid little attention precisely to the 'dialectic of negativity' in the commune's 'dualism', as Marx calls it. These readers mainly saw the positive side of 'dualism', not the elements of contradiction contained in it, which Marx repeatedly stresses. For a recent example see the otherwise important work Anderson 2010. The recent work of a Russian scholar seems, broadly, to confirm Marx's position. He writes: 'The reform of the 1860s intensified bourgeois tendencies of development. The village was not left untouched by this progress, it too experienced the strong growth of commodity-money relations and a degree of involvement of the peasantry in the countryside market ... Despite the phenomenal vitality of the commune, its days were numbered because it did not exist in a social, economic and cultural vacuum. Certain phenomena in the commune itself (such as "commodity-money relations", "growth of individualism struggling against collectivism" etc.) contributed to this development. As yet no more than tendencies, these phenomena nevertheless undermined the commune and threatened to destroy it' (Mironov, in B. Eklof and S. Frank 1990, pp. 28, 31, 32).

41 More than a decade later, in a letter to Danielson (1892), Engels recalled Marx's 1877 letter to Mikhailovsky. Engels observed: 'our author said that if the line entered upon in 1861 was persevered in, the peasants' *'obshchina'* must go to ruin. That seems to me to be in course of fulfilment just now ... I am afraid we shall have to treat "obshchina" as a dream of the past and reckon, in future, with a capitalist Russia. No doubt a great chance is thus being lost' (in Marx, Engels 1972c, p. 338; written in English). In his 'Afterword' (1894) Engels would cite this letter again to make the same point, while stressing the importance of a 'Russian Revolution' both for 'preserving what remains of the commune' and for 'giving the workers' movement in the West a new push and new, better conditions of struggle and thereby hastening the victory of the proletariat without which today's Russia can neither from capitalism nor from the commune come to a socialist transformation' (Engels 1894). In a well-researched work, a contemporary historian of Russia emphasises this tendency towards the decomposition of the commune arising from economic factors both internal and external. Among the first he mentions land shortage, rural overpopulation and underemployment of labour leading large numbers of peasants to seek wage employment elsewhere. The external factor was the increasing demand for wage labour arising from the growth of urban centres and the development of modern industry aided by the construction of a national network of railways after the 1850s (Moon 1999, pp. 287, 383–4).

the new, 'free association', namely, the development of labour as social labour and a high development of the productive powers of labour, could not be generated by the 'original unity' between labour and the conditions of production as manifested in the different forms of natural 'communism' (and the small family mode of production). In Russia not only were the productive powers of labour very backward but also the rural commune was 'struck by a weakness, hostile in every sense' – besides the parcellary mode of labour – namely, its existence as a 'localised microcosm', the isolation and the 'lack of contact of its life with the life of the other communes'. In this sense it was far from developing labour as social labour.[42]

Now this 'weakness' of the commune system – even with common ownership of land – constituted an obstacle to its transformation into a society of a new type that Marx had earlier sketched *theoretically* in the first edition of *Capital* (1867) (reiterating his 1860s position), which is to say, *before* his exposure to Chernyshevsky in 1870, which, according to Wada, was a 'turning point for Marx'.[43] Very interestingly, in the second edition of *Capital* (1872), as well as in its French version (1875), Marx retained the same passage word for word. Here is the passage:

> The ancient social organisms, of production (in the 'modes of production of ancient Asia, of antiquity' etc.) are extraordinarily much simpler and more transparent than the bourgeois [mode]. But they are based either on the immaturity of the individual human who has not yet severed his umbilical cord connecting him with others in a natural community (of a primitive tribe), or the direct relations of lordship and bondage. They are conditioned by a low level of development of the productive powers of labour and correspondingly the narrowness of the relations of human beings as between themselves and with nature in the process of production of material life.[44]

As we see, much of this central idea about the old communal system is carried over and gets confirmed in the concrete case of Russia, as seen in Marx's 1881 correspondence (after he has read Kovalevaky and Morgan).

---

42   Marx 1968, p. 1567.
43   In Shanin 1983, p. 45.
44   Marx 1987a, pp. 109–10; 1976a, p. 74; 1954, p. 83.

Further Considerations

It would of course be wrong to affirm that there was nothing new in Marx's thought in his reflections on the Russian communes. Marx and Engels were undoubtedly impressed by the vitality of these communes, where still about half of the land remained under communal ownership, something which existed nowhere else at that period.[45] This is seen in their continued interest in the question for at least two decades, beginning with the early 1870s. Common ownership of the means of production by the producers themselves, being the very basis of the new society, its existence in the Russian communal system – absent elsewhere – would indeed be, so thought Marx (and Engels), a very favourable factor enabling, to that extent, the Russian peasant to skip the stage of capitalist private ownership and start right away with this great asset, provided of course they eliminate beforehand the Tsarist régime, the system's principal enemy, and are helped by capitalism's positive achievements, necessarily mediated by the victorious proletariat in the West. However, the reason why we hold that this does not change *fundamentally* Marx's thought *in general*, is simply because it does not affect Marx's *general* position on the transition to a 'reunion of free individuals' at a higher level, whose indispensable (pre-)conditions are first, the existence of *social* labour (with socialisation of production) not at a local level but at the level of the whole society and, secondly, a high level of the productive powers of social labour contributing

---

45   Years later, Rosa Luxemburg, in her posthumously (and fragmentarily) published lectures on political economy in the party school (beginning 1907), gave figures on the gradual erosion of communal land ownership in European Russia for the period of 1890–1900. In our calculation from these figures it appears that communal land ownership came down from about 34 percent to 31 percent of the total land ownership in European Russia during this period: see Luxemburg 1972, p. 97. Luxemburg did not cite her source. However, the relevant Russian official data cited by a modern authority on Russian history do not show much difference from Luxemburg's data. They show the extent of the rural communal land in Russia's total land area at the end of the nineteenth century to be 34.3 percent (Grünwald 1975, p. 169). The data on the proportion of communal land in the total Russian land, for the subsequent period from around 1905 to 1917, are subject to controversy (more importantly their interpretation). See the critical survey by D. Atkinson 1973, pp. 773–89. It is interesting to note that Luxemburg's view about the Tsarist policy regarding the Russian communes was directly opposite to Marx's, based on the findings of his Russian sources. Comparing the destiny of the rural communes elsewhere (India et al) where these communes were destroyed through the 'collision with European capitalism', in Russia 'history has followed another course', she wrote, where the 'state did not seek to destroy violently the rural communes, but sought to save and preserve them by all means', p. 95.

not only to an abundance of material wealth in order to free 'social individuals' from the struggle for necessity, as mentioned earlier, but also contributing to the increasing availability of 'free time' beyond labour time, thus enabling the individuals to enjoy the wealth produced, as well as giving them time for 'free activity' undetermined by the 'compulsion of an external necessity'.[46] Ideally, capitalism need not be the system where these conditions are created, and it would certainly be better if it were not. Historically, however, as Marx never tires of repeating, it is only capital which, through its contradictions, has generated these conditions. The Russian communal system – abstracting from its factors of decomposition already operating – even as an exceptional case due solely to its communal land ownership, had to depend on capitalism's positive achievements, particularly the 'ready-made material conditions of cooperative labour',[47] that is, the conditions of socialising labour and production at the level of society. Finally, it is only the Western proletariat, itself a product of capital, which could, through its own revolution, stand as a bulwark against all intervention from outside in order to ensure a successful Russian Revolution against the Tsarist régime, the traditional preserve and 'head of European reaction', as the 1882 'Preface' observes.[48] In short, what was new in Marx's thinking, confronted with the Russian commune, was his theoretical non-exclusion of the possibility for a society to go over directly to socialism without passing through capitalism, though not without the help of capitalism prevailing elsewhere, which would both generate a proletarian revolution and make available to the society in question, precisely mediated by the victorious proletariat, the fruits of its advanced technology. At the same time Marx severely qualified this idea by emphasising the *uniqueness* of the Russian case and underlining the negative factors inherent in the commune's 'dualism', working steadily towards its decomposition with the possibility of transforming the situation into the general case as depicted in *Capital*. In the event, history, the 'best of all Marxists', as Hilferding used to say,[49] vindicated Marx's dire prognostic.

---

46 Marx 1962a, p. 255; 1971a, p. 256. The expressions 'free time' and 'free activity' are in English in the text.

47 Marx 1968, p. 1566.

48 Marx, Engels 1882. It is interesting to note that at the same period when Marx was composing his correspondence in question – in 1880 to be precise – he, in a different context, also maintained that the 'material and intellectual elements of the collective form of the means of production are constituted by the development of the capitalist class itself' (Marx 1881).

49 In Howe 1972, p. 517.

At this point let us dispose of a serious confusion resulting from an *ideological* reading of Marx's writings on Russia in 1881–2. A number of distinguished people have read Marx's idea of a 'Russian Revolution' in his correspondence and in the 'Preface' (1882) to the *Manifesto* as the prefiguration of the twentieth-century revolutions, particularly those led by the Marxists, beginning with the Bolshevik seizure of power. Thus, according to Shanin, Marx's new position was vindicated by a 'victorious revolution' led by the Marxists 'in the backward countries, some of which starting with Russia', and which, led by 'Lenin, Mao and Ho, proved socialist in leadership and results', whereas 'no socialist revolution came in the West'.[50] Similarly Dussel has written:

> Russia has certainly followed the road foreseen by Marx (*siguio el camino previsto por Marx*). Without passing through capitalism it has realised its revolution allowing the rural Russian commune to pass, in great measure, *directly* from the communal ownership to the social ownership ... since the revolution of 1917.[51]

Michael Löwy, in his turn, writes that

> It is often forgotten that, in their preface to the Russian translation of the *Manifesto*, Marx and Engels envisaged a hypothetical situation in which socialist revolution could begin in Russia and then spread to western Europe.[52]

Similarly, Raya Dunayevskaya interpreted the 1882 'Preface' as 'projecting the idea that Russia could be the first to have a proletarian revolution ahead of the West'.[53]

Now, if one reads Marx's writings under consideration *non-ideologically*, it is easy to see that the mentioned texts contain no reference to a 'proletarian' or 'socialist' revolution in Russia. In the relevant texts it is always a question of the 'Russian Revolution' *tout court*. It is a question of a revolution by Russian communal peasants against the principal enemy of the communal system – the Tsarist régime. Naturally, in the thinking of Marx (and Engels), following the materialist conception of history, there could be no question of a proletarian

---

50   Shanin 1983, pp. 25, 254.
51   Dussel 1990, p. 261; emphasis in text.
52   Löwy 1998, pp. 18–19.
53   Dunayevskaya 1991, p. 187.

revolution in the quasi-absence of a proletariat (unless Marx's Russian experience had made him abandon his materialism, for which there is no textual evidence). The idea of the possibility of a proletarian revolution occurring in a technologically backward society where the proletariat constitutes at most a very small part of society gained its *droit de cité* through a theory propagated around the time of the First World War, proclaiming the possibility of a proletarian revolution breaking out in the 'weakest link' in the world capitalist chain.[54]

Apart from the absence of any idea of such a revolution existing in Marx's texts, there is a more important point that should be stressed in this connection. There is in fact an unbridgeable gulf between the socialist revolution envisaged by Marx – a socialist revolution led by the producers themselves towards a society of freely associated labour, on the basis of what Marx calls producers' 'self-activity' (*Selbstbetätigung*) – and the revolutions of the twentieth century that took place under the leadership, not of the producers themselves, but of a tiny group of radicalised intelligentsia acting in their name – undoubtedly with mass *support* at the *initial* stage – beginning, particularly, with the Bolshevik seizure of power, which far from inaugurating the 'rule of the immense majority in the interest of the immense majority', as the *Communist Manifesto* famously stresses, from the start excluded the immediate producers from all real powers except in name. Even taking Marx's relevant correspondence one is struck by the emphasis he places in the text on the creative power of the immediate producers in the transformation of their society. Absolutely nowhere does Marx mention the need for a special apparatus to substitute for the spontaneous self-activity of the masses towards their own emancipation.[55] Thus, as we have already mentioned above, Marx stresses the need of 'substituting the governmental institution *volost* by an assembly of peasants elected by the communes themselves and serving as the economic and administrative organ of their interests'.[56] This is clearly in stark contrast with the systematic elimination of the producers' organs of self-rule almost from the start of the Bolshevik regime, and culminating in the bloody liquidation of Kronstadt's soviet democracy, 'bustling, self-governing, egalitarian and highly politicised, the like of which had not been seen in Europe since the Paris commune [of 1871]', in the words of perhaps the most authoritative academic his-

---

54   However, the principal proponent of this idea at the same time correctly acknowledged, contrary to many later Marxists and non-Marxists, that such a revolution had not been foreseen by Marx and Engels.

55   See the pertinent remarks by Rubel 1957, p. 434.

56   Marx 1968, p. 1567.

torian of the question.[57] What would, *a contrario*, have broadly corresponded
to Marx's idea of a 'Russian Revolution' was Russia's popular uprising of February 1917, initiated by the producers themselves without any party guidance,
as an immense revolutionary mass movement in an open-ended, plural revolutionary process, though without 'socialism' being proclaimed as the immediate
aim. The Bolshevik seizure of power, putting a brake on the process, destroyed
this revolutionary democracy.[58]

57   Getzler 1983, p. 246.
58   See in particular, on the whole question, Anweiler 1958; Daniels 1967; Ferro 1967; 1980.

Epilogue. Illusion of the Epoch: Twentieth-Century Socialism

In the period after 1917, in several countries, those who considered themselves as followers of Marx and Engels seized political power by overthrowing the existing régimes in the name of the working class and established their own régimes which they baptised 'socialist'. In each case, and without exception, this claimed 'socialism' followed Lenin's concept of socialism as the first phase of the society after the demise of capital (the second phase being, according to Lenin, 'communism'), in opposition to Marx's own, which we have discussed in some detail in the chapter on socialism in this book. So, before we conclude, it is only proper to examine to what extent these epigones of Marx (and Engels) could claim to have built societies that could be considered as an 'Association' (in Marx's emancipatory sense of socialism) marked, *grosso modo*, by the features ascribed by Marx to this early phase of the new society.

Preliminaries

Let us recall that in our chapter on socialism we have already, on the basis of Marx's (and Engels's) **own** texts, drawn a portrait of a socialist/communist society as an Association of free individuals based on the Associated Mode of Production – as opposed to the Capitalist Mode of Production – with corresponding social relations of production, a society founded on the *self-emancipation* of the producing classes. Let us add that this emancipatory character of the new society starts right from its first phase, where already there exist no classes following the disappearance of capital, and where the (new) society or Association is already in charge, the state having disappeared from the scene.[1] We conclude our book by analysing to what extent these 'Marxists' have built their claimed socialism, which conforms at least to what Marx conceived as the lower phase of socialism following the disappearance of the capitalist mode of production and the corresponding social relations of production. It goes

---

1 Marx, in his 1847 critique of Proudhon, wrote that 'the labouring classes in the course of its development will substitute the old civil society with an association which will exclude classes and their antagonism, and there will no longer be a political power properly speaking, since political power is precisely the official résumé of antagonism in the civil society'. See Marx 1965b, p. 136.

without saying that there could be and there are models of socialism which are not Marxian, as we have shown in this book. Some of these socialisms, too, could legitimately be conceived as libertarian. We submit that Marx himself is not indispensable for a revolution by the working people to inaugurate the new Association of free individuals after the demise of capital. It should be noted that the 1871 communal uprising of the workers in Paris owes nothing to Marx. Rather, as Engels in his 1891 Introduction to Marx's *Civil War in France* reported, it was basically the work of Proudhonists and Blanquists – the opponents of Marx – though they did the opposite of what their doctrines prescribed.[2] No wonder, since only a handful of individuals in the leadership – those coming from the International (themselves only a very small minority) – were familiar with Marx. Similarly, how many of the individuals involved in the immense spontaneous uprising of the Russian working people in early 1917 had even heard of Karl Marx? Almost surely none. Social revolutions would occur, Marx or no Marx. The essential point is that it is not so much about following exactly what Marx himself had written, but about revolutionising the present society, where things govern humans, into a society where humans govern things; where producers collectively dominate their own products instead of being dominated by the products; and determine their own destiny. This self-emancipated society of free humans is infinitely more humane than the existing one, and this fundamental emancipatory message, it so happens – and this is what needs to be stressed – was articulated more clearly by Marx than by anybody else. Rather than denouncing people dogmatically on the score of 'deviation from Marx', what is important is to see whether this central emancipatory message of Marx has been compromised or suppressed altogether by particular political groups in order to serve their selfish group interest.

At the same time, it cannot be sufficiently stressed that Marx is *indispensable* as a great educator for our understanding of the 'economic law of motion of the modern society' and its ensuing fatal contradictions.[3] And this is precisely the educative role that he and Engels, in their famous 1879 'Circular Letter' – cited earlier – wanted the intelligentsia who intended to participate in the workers' revolutionary process to take on: to bring education to the workers, but never be allowed by the workers to exercise any influence on the leadership of the movement. A great example is provided by the way the first International was founded in 1864. Marx had no role at all in the foundation of this great association of workers, contrary to a widespread view, even shared by such a great

---

2   See Engels, in Marx and Engels 1971, pp. 30–1.

3   Marx 1987a, p. 67; 1976a, p. 13; 1954, p. 20.

scholar as E.H. Carr.[4] It was entirely the English and the French workers who founded it, and Marx was simply a member of the audience at its first meeting in September 1864, sitting as a 'mute figure on the platform', in his own words (*als stumme Figur auf der Platform*).[5] Later he was accepted as a representative of the German workers and designated as a member of the subcommittee in charge of drafting its rules, and finally asked to draft those rules.[6]

However, it so happens that the established twentieth-century régimes, beginning with the Russian, baptised 'socialist', all trace their heritage to Marx. That is why our analysis turns on the fundamental characteristics of these régimes – where the Russian case, the *prototype*, will serve as the illustration – in order to see to what extent these characteristics could be seen to conform to those of the early phase of Marx's Association, as we have discussed them in our chapter on Socialism.

Nature of Twentieth-Century Socialism

Let us start at the beginning of the whole process – the seizure of political power claimed to be the act of the proletariat. Now, there is no evidence to prove the claim of the official spokespersons of the régimes that this power was proletarian, seized by the 'independent movement of the immense majority in the interest of the immense majority', as the 1848 *Manifesto* emphasised.[7] In fact the labouring people neither initiated nor led the so-called 'October Revolution'. In the same way, this 'immense majority' had no role in setting up single-party rule. The fate of millions of Russians was decided by a handful of radicalised intelligentsia leading the 'vanguard', far removed from the locus of

---

4   Carr 1964, p. 19.

5   See Abramsky 1964, pp. 73, 74, 76.

6   One should see the contrast in the way the Third International was founded, not by the workers but by their 'leaders', Lenin taking the initiative. It is quite proper that the body was called not the workers' international, but the 'communist' international. Quite in consonance with the (self-)emancipatory character of the workers' movement, at the very first congress of the first International (1866), a resolution was adopted by the congress to the effect that 'The work of the International Association is to generalise and unify the spontaneous movements of the working class, but not to prescribe or impose on them any doctrinaire system whatsoever' (see Marx 1965, p. 1469). The contrast with the tenor of the Third International is clear. To her great honour, Rosa Luxemburg, true to her democratic values, opposed this way of founding the International.

7   Marx and Engels 1970b, p. 45.

material production-exploitation and without any popular mandate, accountable to none and irrevocable by the labouring multitude.[8] This group seized power in the name of Russia's working class, it should be stressed, precisely by totally ignoring the soviets, the independent self-governing organs of this very working class. It should also be observed that by the very fact that the group which seized power were 'professional revolutionaries', as Lenin considered them to be, the group's members could not be day-to-day ordinary workers, who, consequently, could only play the role of *followers*, making the revolution automatically a minority affair. Paradoxically, Trotsky's own words on this revolution explain very clearly the nature of the October seizure of power. Thus in his *Diary in Exile* (1935) Trotsky wrote

> Had I not been present in 1917 in Petersburg, the October Revolution would still have taken place – on the condition that Lenin was present and in command. If neither Lenin nor I had been present in Petersburg, there would have been no October Revolution: the leadership of the Bolshevik Party would have prevented it from recurring ... If Lenin had not been in Petersburg, I doubt whether I could have managed to conquer the resistance of the Bolshevik leaders.[9]

One can safely say that the rest of twentieth-century socialisms followed broadly the same general pattern, *mutatis mutandis*. So, strictly speaking, in these régime changes, one minority replaced another minority. These were *minority revolutions*, remarkably confirming Engels's conclusion on the history of revolutions beginning with the great French Revolution in his Introduction to Marx's *Class Struggles in France*:

> If we disregard the concrete content of each case, the common form of all these revolutions was that they were minority revolutions. Even when the majority took part, it did so – whether wittingly or not – only in the service of a minority; but because of this, or even simply because of the

---

8   In the chapter on Socialism, we have cited the relevant part of the 'circular letter' (September 1879) that Marx and Engels addressed to their friends in order to stress that the intelligentsia has only an educational role to play in the workers' revolutionary movement, and that this group must not be allowed to exercise any influence on the party leadership.

9   Cited in Knei-Paz 1978, p. 230. The author – the latter – very aptly remarks on the same page that 'here the vanguard was reduced to its absolute extreme: not even the Party but one individual – Lenin'. We have seen earlier that Lenin accepts the dictatorship of a singular individual representing the dictatorship of a class.

passive, unresisting attitude of the majority, this minority acquired the appearance of being representative of the whole people.[10]

It is immediately clear that this method of seizing power by a minority – party power (and that, too, a single party) substituting for class power – or of installing a Party-State regime, is the exact opposite of the proletariat *as a class* becoming the ruling class and signifying the 'conquest of democracy', to use the words of the *Manifesto*, as the 'first step in the working-class revolution'.[11] Far from inaugurating the protracted struggle for an emancipated society through the revolutionary process of transformation, the minority seizure of power signals the advent of a new kind of enslavement of the people, enslavement by the Party-State. Let us add *en passant* that neither of these two *avatars* – neither Party nor State – finds a place in any discussion of the future society by Marx and Engels.

It must also be stressed that the proletarian way of seizing class power – the act of the immense majority in the interest of the immense majority – cannot simply mimic the way in which a minority seizes power from another minority in a class society, particularly in bourgeois society, simply because the proletarian seizure of power has an emancipatory goal, directly aimed at establishing a society without classes, a society of free individuals. This is the way that the most oppressed of the existing society, the working class – the proletarians – achieve their own emancipation by their own collective self-activity, paving the way to the emancipation of the whole of humanity. This self-emancipatory character of the whole process has to be shown by the very way the working-class movement is organised in its struggle to gain political power. It should, by the way, be noted that the *Manifesto* nowhere says that some party, and certainly no single party elite, formed outside the autonomous working-class movement, is to seize power on behalf of the working class. On the contrary, it is the class as such that seizes power from the bourgeoisie and becomes the ruling class. The specific form of such an organisation cannot be laid down a priori. However, in light of the experience of the last century, one could at least say what kind of form such an organisation should **not** acquire. We mean the specific party form which was devised uniquely as a machine for seizing power,

---

10 Engels, in Marx and Engels 1970b, p. 645. The 1848 *Manifesto* had already declared that 'all previous historical movements were movements of minorities in the interests of minorities. The proletarian movement is the independent movement of the immense majority in the interests of the immense majority' (in Marx and Engels 1970b, p. 45).

11 Marx and Engels 1970b, p. 52.

incapable of serving as an instrument for liberation.[12] There have, however, been examples of working people's attempts to build self-governing organisations independently of any party, and without any party hierarchy to lead them, as, for example, in Russia itself, first in 1905 and then between February and October 1917.

In the Russian case the workers', soldiers' and peasants' councils – the soviets – arose spontaneously as independent, thoroughly democratic, self-governing organs of the working people all over the country as a parallel power to the official governmental power of Russia in February 1917. As it happened, the forward movement of these spontaneously arising independent self-governing organs of the working people of Russia was not allowed to continue for a long time. As we mentioned earlier, the Bolsheviks effectively seized the political power *from* these soviets, not from the Provisional Government, and destroyed any possibility for this initial (bourgeois) democratic revolutionary movement to advance further. Oskar Anweiler traces the uneasy (if not hostile) relation between the Bolsheviks and the councils (soviets) from the very birth of the soviet movement, with the general strike of 1905 in Russia. The Bolshevik treatment of these self-administering organs was in sharp contrast with the treatment of these newly born soviets by the Mensheviks, on whom the historical memory of the 1789 French Revolution and the Paris Commune of 1871 exercised considerable influence. 'The Mensheviks saw the new soviets as workers' revolutionary organs of self-administration. They directly spoke of the formation of revolutionary communes in the interest of promoting the uprising and disorganising the government'.[13] Anweiler stresses that 'as opposed to the Menshevik idea of the revolution as a spontaneous process in the course of which one could not fix any action beforehand, Lenin claimed that an uprising could be fixed if those who fixed it had influence on the masses and knew to assess correctly the moment'. In fact the Menshevik campaign for revolutionary self-administering organs of the workers and peasants was considered by Lenin to be a 'childish idea'.[14] In his turn, the distinguished historian Israel Getzler has observed that 'Lenin saw the revolution as a planned seizure of central power synchronised with an armed uprising. Martov saw it as the progressive replace-

---

12   Victor Serge cites two remarkable predictions by the pre-Bolshevik Trotsky: (1) 'that which is anti-revolutionary in Bolshevism poses a menace to us only in the case of a revolutionary victory' (1908–9); and, (2) 'Bolshevism could be a good instrument for the conquest of power, but afterwards it will reveal its counter-revolutionary aspects'. See Serge 2001, pp. 978, 793.

13   Anweiler 1958, p. 85.

14   Anweiler 1958, p. 92.

ment of a disintegrating government apparatus by an ever-widening area of revolutionary self-government'.[15] By the beginning of summer 1918, the soviets, as independent self-governing organs of Russia's working people, going through an exponential decay, evaporated, giving rise to the absolute dictatorship of the Party-State. Oskar Anweiler has observed that

> the strength of the soviets lay in their close link with the masses of workers and soldiers whose mouthpiece they were ... They were sensitive barometers of the voice of the masses of the moment ... The radicalisation of the masses had to make itself felt through the radicalisation of the soviets. When a group whose objective is totally opposed to the democratic character of the soviets succeeds in obtaining their leadership with the help and in the name of the masses the consequence has to be the general downfall of the soviets. This was the case of the Bolshevik victory in the October revolution. The soviet movement which began as a democratic movement transformed itself into the springboard of the Bolshevik dictatorship.[16]

Marx wrote in his *Eighteenth Brumaire* that 'All revolutions perfected the state machine instead of smashing it. The parties that contended in turn for domination regarded the possession of this huge state edifice as the principal spoils of the victor'.[17] This description remarkably characterises the 'socialist' régimes of the twentieth century beginning with their Russian prototype. To the Bolsheviks, aware that they did not have the majority of the population on their side, the idea of the victory of the socialist revolution could be associated not with a majority, but only with a minority. This essentially minority, that is, undemocratic character of the notion of 'victory of the socialist revolution' in the minds of the Bolsheviks has been well brought out by the noted Russian historian Roy Medvedev, even though he was a sympathiser of that party:

> The political force on which the October Revolution was based was by no means the majority of the population. The Bolsheviks never concealed this fact, on the contrary they made it clear and justified it. Lenin frequently said that for the victory of the socialist revolution the Bolsheviks did not have to wait for an 'arithmetic majority'. Victory is possible with

---

15   Getzler 2003, p. 109.

16   Anweiler 1958, p. 139.

17   Marx, in Marx and Engels 1970b, p. 169.

the existing forces, and it would be criminal to let the opportunity slip by when a *reliable and energetic minority* was willing to follow the Bolsheviks.[18]

This is also seen in Lenin's insistence on the Bolsheviks alone taking power, not sharing it with other socialist parties who were at best considered as wavering, if not outright reactionaries. Lenin held, simply on the basis of the Bolsheviks gaining a majority in the Petrograd and Moscow soviets, that the majority of people were on their side. One of Germany's leading historians of Russia has underlined that 'Lenin's view of what a majority was had a quality of its own, for it had nothing to do with elections or votes ... it is obvious that Lenin's deductions – a majority in the soviets of both capitals equals a majority of the vanguard of the people equals a majority of the people equals victory in revolution – were not immediately intelligible to his comrades'.[19] A dissident Bolshevik, a metal worker, Shlyapnikov, protested against this one-party rule and the dangers associated with it:

We consider that it is necessary to build a socialist government with all the socialist parties in the soviets in order to consolidate the results of

---

18   Medvedev 1979, p. 145. Emphasis added. One wonders how this way of gaining power differs *in substance* from the way Bakunin conceived it. See in this regard Bakunin's 1865 work on 'The International Revolutionary Society or Fraternity' (in French), in Daniel Guérin 1970. By the way, the party itself, to which belonged the handful of individuals deciding the fate of Russia's 170 millions represented, on its side, an infinitely small minority of the total population. As Victor Serge has observed, 'At the moment when the revolution began, the membership of all the revolutionary parties was less than 1% of the population of which the Bolsheviks constituted a fraction' (Serge 2001, p. 866). The great Austrian scholar Joseph Schumpeter, himself a convinced socialist, wrote that 'Lenin had no illusion concerning the Russian situation. He saw that the tsarist regime could be successfully attacked only when temporarily weakened by military defeat and in the ensuing disorganisation a resolute and well-disciplined group by ruthless terror could overthrow whatever other regime might attempt to replace it ... What was needed was a body-guard of revolutionist janissaries, deaf to any argument but his own, free from all inhibitions, impervious to the voice of reason or humanity'. See Schumpeter 1950, p. 329.

19   Geyer 1968, p. 168. In fact an eminent US historian, Alexander Rabinowitch, in his blow by blow account of the 1917 October events, has shown that the delegates to the Second Soviet Congress, among whom the Bolsheviks dominated, when asked what kind of government they wanted, replied almost unanimously 'all power to the soviets' – an answer implying a coalition of all socialist parties – and that none mentioned a government composed uniquely of the Bolshevik Party. See Rabinowitch 2004, pp. 291–2.

the heroic struggle of the working class and the revolutionary army in October and November. Outside of it there is only one road: *maintaining a purely Bolshevik government by means of political terror.* We think that this will end up by eliminating the mass proletarian organisations from the direction of political life, establishment of an irresponsible régime and the ruin of the revolution.[20]

In contrast to Leninist practice, Rosa Luxemburg, speaking for the Spartacus League, declared that 'the Spartacus League is no party that wants to seize power on the back of the workers. It will only ever seize the power if it has a clear, unambiguous mandate from the vast majority of Germany's proletarian masses; it will never seize power by other means than a conscious approval of its perspectives, goals, and means of struggle'.[21]

Another notable example was the short-lived council movement in Hungary in 1956. Oskar Anweiler, the great historian of the soviet movement in Russia, observed that as in Russia in 1905 and 1917, in Hungary in October 1956, councils sprang up everywhere, independently of one another, of the most disparate kinds. 'The council movement seized with indescribable speed the whole land where the factory councils formed the backbone of the revolution'.[22] Together with the factory councils 'they were formed in all kinds of places, offices, universities, the army. In the countryside sprung up the peasants' councils'. As in Russia in 1905 and 1917 these were 'improvised organs of struggle which sprang up from the needs of the moment'.[23] However, the movement lasted a little more than a month. It met the same fate as Kronstadt in 1921. In early November, 1956, the Russian Party-State crushed the libertarian movement by means of massacre.

Somewhat different was the case of the Spanish Revolution of the 1930s which showed – as opposed to the Bolshevik revolution in almost all respects – that a self-governing mass of working people, free from any bureaucratic vice, and aimed at creating a society without rank and class antagonism, is capable of great deeds. This was strikingly illustrated by the working people of Spain for a relatively short period during their revolution of 1936–9. These working people defeated the Franco fascists over two-thirds of Spain within a month

---

20   Cited by Bukharin as an example of breach of party discipline. Bukharin 1988. p. 299. Emphasis in original.

21   In Kuhn 2012, p. 106. Rosa Luxemburg declared this one year after the Bolsheviks had practised exactly the opposite. Might it be that she had in mind the Bolshevik seizure of power?

22   Anweiler 1956, p. 394.

23   Anweiler 1956, p. 396.

of the start of the fascist uprising. These were 'people in arms', who for the first time saw themselves not as employees or serfs, but as human beings freed from the tyranny of the boss, and with all the means of production at their disposal. They had gained sufficient consciousness to understand that 'their ends were libertarian communism, their means direct action independent of all party politics'.[24] George Orwell, fighting with the anarchists and dissident communists, made the following observation on some aspects of the organisational situation of the fighter-workers:

> General and private, peasant and militiaman, still met as equals; everyone drew the same pay, wore the same clothes, ate the same food, and called everyone else 'thou' and 'comrade'; there was no boss class, no beggars, no prostitutes, no lawyers, no priests, no boot-licking, no cap-touching.[25]

In a word, within the ranks of the militants, there was, to borrow a phrase from Karl Korsch, 'discipline without yoke and order without domination'.[26]

Given the widespread attempts both by the bourgeois and the 'communist' propaganda to present the struggle of the Spanish people simply as a struggle for democracy against Franco, and to suppress the movement of Spain's working people for a far-reaching social revolution, we may be permitted to give a broad idea about the way the working people of Spain conducted their struggle both for their self-liberation and against the fascists, freely drawing on the account given by Gerald Brenan in his justly celebrated work on the civil war and revolution in Spain.[27]

After defeating the fascist insurrection in Madrid and Barcelona, the workers, now become the rulers of the land, organised themselves into workers'

---

24 Richards 1983, p. 45. Leon Trotsky, comparing the Russian and the Spanish Revolutions, wrote that 'The Spanish proletariat displayed fighting qualities of the highest order ... economically, politically, culturally. The Spanish workers from the very beginning of the Revolution showed themselves to be not inferior, but superior to the Russian proletariat at the beginning of the October Revolution in 1917'. Cited in Broué and Témime 1961, p. 131.

25 Orwell 1966, p. 66. In the same book he adds, on the Spanish militia, 'They, while they lasted, were a sort of microcosm of a classless society. In that community where no one was on the make, where there was a shortage of everything but no privilege and no boot-licking, one got perhaps a crude forecast of what the opening stages of Socialism might be like. And, after all, instead of disillusioning me it deeply attracted me. The effect was to make my desire to see Socialism established much more actual than it had been before' (p. 102).

26 Korsch 1969, p. 48.

27 Brenan 1969.

committees. The function of these was triple: through the armed militias they carried on the war against the enemy; by terror they destroyed or intimidated the enemy in their midst; and they took over the factories and estates abandoned by their owners and continued to work in them. Where the committees were anarchist, 'there was a definite policy of collectivisation which was intended to prepare the way for a thoroughgoing social revolution. Far from regarding the war as a mere war of defence against fascism, they saw in it the opportunity for which they had long been waiting to create a new type of society'.[28] Drawing on his close observation Brenan writes,

> When the military uprising took place in July 1936, every village in the anarchist districts of Spain threw off its municipality and began to govern itself through its syndicates. This syndicate was simply an assembly consisting of every able-bodied man and woman in the village who belonged to the working classes, whether s/he was a member of the CNT (National Confederation of Labour) or not. They met one evening a week and for several hours discussed village problems. Anyone who chose had the right to speak. The syndicate elected a committee which governed the village.[29]

Brenan also reports, by way of contrast, on the actions of the Communists in the Spanish civil war.

The Communists' appetite for power was insatiable, and they were completely unscrupulous. To them the war meant winning it for the Communist Party. Thus they kept the Aragon front without arms to spite the anarchists and prevented a very promising offensive in Extramadura from taking place because the credit for its success might have gone to Caballero (the left-wing socialist leader). They seemed to have no programme that could not be reversed should its reversal promise them any advantage. Their going back on many of their past tenets recalled the feats of those Jesuit missionaries of the seventeenth century who, the better to convert the Chinese, suppressed the story of the crucifixion. The Communists showed that the great release of feelings that accompanies revolution was distasteful to them. In the midst of a war of liberation, the Communists appeared in the guise of professionals and experts, while, not content with harmonising such impulses and directing them towards the end of military victory, they proceeded as far as they could to suppress them altogether. For their whole nature and history made them

---

28   Brenan 1969, pp. 318, 320.
29   Brenan 1969, p. 201.

distrust the local and spontaneous and put their faith in order, discipline and bureaucratic uniformity.[30]

Finally, of course, the revolution was defeated, the heroic working people had to succumb to the counter-revolutionary forces, the Republicans and 'Communists' and to betrayal by a part of the anarchist leadership. Thus, while the 'people in arms' had won the Revolution in 1936, the "People's Army" lost the war in 1939'.[31]

The customary way of seizing power by a minority – in the name of the working class – from another minority was questioned by Anton Pannekoek in a famous debate with Karl Kautsky in 1912, that is, five years before the Bolsheviks seized power, in the pages of the theoretical organ of the German Social Democratic Party, *Neue Zeit*. Pannekoek argued in conformity with the emancipatory goal of the workers' movement – a rather uncommon case within the tradition of Marx's disciples. He emphasised:

> The battle of the proletariat is not simply a battle against the bourgeoisie for the state power, but it is a battle against the state power. The problem of the social revolution can be put in a nutshell: it is to raise the power of the proletariat to a level superior to the level of the power of the state, and the content of this revolution is the destruction and dissolution (*Auflösung*) of the state's sources of power by the proletariat's sources of power. The end result of the proletarian struggle is the complete annihilation of the state organisation.[32]

The most important source of the proletariat's power, following Pannekoek, is its organisation. But this organisation must not be confused with the present-day 'working-class' organisations, which continue to be marked by the relations of the existing bourgeois order. On the contrary, 'the character of this organisation is something spiritual, the complete revolutionisation of the character of the proletariat'.[33] It leaves behind the individualist, centred on self-seeking interests, and attains to the solidarist behaviour which arises precisely from the

---

30   Brenan 1969, pp. 326, 327.

31   Richards 1983, p. 260.

32   Pannekoek 1912.

33   Pannekoek 1912. One important aspect of the workers' mindset, absent in Pannekoek's polemic, is their inherited millennial attitude of submission to authority. Joseph Schumpeter, a great economist from Austria, a socialist by conviction, and with first-hand knowledge of the German Social Democratic Party during the early years of the twentieth century, observed that at least for a period the 'workers who entered the organisation accepted the intellectuals' leadership with utmost docility and hardly even pretended to

habit of organised class action. In a word, a whole present-day mindset has to be transformed. After all, as we know, 'the ruling ideas of each epoch have ever been the ideas of the ruling class'.[34]

Let us now try to see what kind of socialism was established by the different régimes following the Russian prototype. In our analysis of post-1917 'socialism' we will be guided by Marx's materialist conception of history – inexactly called 'historical materialism' – as summarily presented in his 1859 Preface to the *Contribution to the Critique of Political Economy*, where the notion of social relations of production is discussed.[35] In other words, the basic question of our analysis is the relation between the immediate producers and the conditions of production.

Whatever be the social form of production, labourer and the means of production always remain its factors. But in their state of separation from each other, either of them can be such only as a possibility. In order to produce at all, they must unite. The specific way in which this is accomplished differentiates the different economic epochs of the social structure.[36]

It is remarkable that most of the discussions – favourable or otherwise – on the post-1917 socialist régimes concern only their *political* aspects, and are little focused on their socio-economic aspects. And the political aspects are mostly defined around the (solitary) Leaders of the régimes, like, for example, Lenin's or Stalin's Russia, Mao's or Deng's China, etc. For Russia, what Trotsky said in his Diary was a reality, that is, the October régime change was decided singularly by one individual who on his own thought that Russia was prepared for a socialist revolution – or was at least prepared to begin one – given that political power had been gained by the bourgeoisie, independently of any change in the social relations of production. And that singular individual succeeded in imposing his view first on a rather reluctant leadership of the party – ultimately by threatening to quit the leadership. Roy Medvedev, the distinguished Russian historian whom we mentioned earlier (whose father was liquidated by the Stalin régime), was, as we said, a sympathiser of the Bolsheviks, particularly of Lenin, while on the whole remaining an impartial observer. He wrote

> The Bolshevik Party was Lenin's creation. He was irreplaceable as that party's leader. When sharp differences arose [about the seizure of power]

---

decide anything for themselves'. See Schumpeter, 1950, p. 328. Another aspect, not mentioned by Pannekoek, is the prevalence of quasi-universal patriarchy.

34   Marx and Engels 1970b, p. 51.
35   See Marx and Engels 1970b, p. 181.
36   Marx 2008, p. 672; 1956a, p. 36.

Lenin's threat to resign from the leadership was more effective than all other arguments.[37]

Let us now see what kind of socialism was established by the *nouveaux régimes*. In this respect, the Russian case being the prototype of all the socialisms of the last century, this will be the case that we analyse here. We already mentioned Lenin's *revision* of Marx's notion of socialism by considering it as the first phase of, *as well as* the transition to, communism. This Leninist position, as distinguished from the Marxian, apparently merely terminological and innocent-looking, had far-reaching consequences which were far from innocent and far from what Lenin himself presumably might have anticipated. It became a convenient instrument for legitimising and justifying every repressive act of the Party-State, beginning with 1917–18 onwards, in the name of socialism, which, it was held, was only a *transitional* phase to communism, thus shelving Marx's immense emancipatory project to a never-never land – 'full communism', as Lenin often calls it – and metamorphosing Marx's project for society after capital into an unalloyed utopia. This became the conventional wisdom for all the Party-State régimes and their partisans. A number of them started also with the seizure of political power *in the name* of the working class (proletariat).

In Russia, given the way political power was captured by a small minority from another minority, having little relation to what the 1848 *Manifesto* calls the 'autonomous movement of the immense majority in the interest of the immense majority',[38] the ultimate outcome of this 'revolution', it goes without saying, could in no sense be an Association of free individuals. As a matter of fact, Lenin's lofty pre-October promise to destroy the old state machine and replace it with a (Paris) Commune type of state-non-state, fell by the wayside, and instead of all officeholders being elected and subject to recall, there appeared, as in a class society, an increasingly bigger bureaucracy consisting of (single) party nominees, hierarchically organised from the top downwards, a formidable police apparatus with the dreaded secret police, and a professional army with ex-tsarist officers occupying higher positions in increasing number. And far from the Paris Commune's universal suffrage with election and recall of all officeholders, there would be, henceforward, no free election after the last abortive Constituent Assembly election. The increasing unpopularity of the régime found its climax in the 1921 mass massacre of Kronstadt sailors and toilers by the regime, after the sailors dared to proclaim a 'third revolution' for

---

37   Medvedev 1979, p. 14.
38   Marx and Engels 1970b, p. 45.

a social order under the watchword 'All power to Soviets and not to Parties'.[39] This massacre vividly reminds one of Goya's great 1814 painting 'The third of May'. Robert Daniels, the eminent American historian of Russia, writes that 'It was essential for the Communist Party to suppress the idea of Kronstadt as a movement which defended the principles of the October Revolution against the Communists'.[40] Daniels cites the *Izvestiya* of the Temporary Revolutionary Committee of the Kronstadt revolutionaries: 'The time has come to overthrow the commissarocracy ... Kronstadt has raised the banner of uprising for the Third Revolution of the toilers. We fight for the genuine power of the labourers, while the bloody Trotsky and the glutted Zinoviev and their band of adherents fight for the power of the party of the communist-ravishers'.[41] The behaviour of the régime confirmed what Marx had said in his second draft of his 1871 'Address' on the Commune, recalling the earlier revolutions: 'After each popular revolution ... the repressive character of the state was more fully developed and more mercilessly used, because the promises made, and seemingly assured by the Revolution, could only be broken by the employment of force'.[42]

Before we analyse the reality of this claimed socialism, let us have a brief look at the conceptual framework of this socialism which was entirely Lenin's creation, and which constituted the basis of all the Party-State régimes of the last century.

Lenin speaks of socialism basically in *juridical* terms, not in terms of a complex of *social relations of production*. For him socialism is 'social ownership' of the means of production, which he further specifies as 'ownership by

---

39   See the authoritative, thoroughly researched work by Israel Getzler 2001, p. 240. To the argument about Kronstadt's bustling workers' democracy, which we have cited above, Getzler added that 'Lenin's response [to Kronstadt] blocked what was still left of the revolution's open-mindedness, completed the formation of the highly centralised and bureaucratised single-party dictatorship, and put Russia firmly on the road to Stalinism'. See Getzler 2001, p. 258.

40   Daniels 1960, p. 144.

41   Daniels 1960, p. 144. We learn from the same author that 'many of the government troops, captured by the Kronstadters in the early days of the defence of the island fortress, on learning that the sailors and workers had overthrown the power of the commissarocracy, went over to the side of the rebels. Ordinary communists were indeed so unreliable in the face of the issues raised by the Kronstadt affair that the government did not depend on them either in the assault on Kronstadt itself or on keeping order in Petrograd. The main body of troops employed were Chekists and officer cadets from the Red Army training schools, and the final assault was led by the top officialdom of the Communist Party'. Daniels, 1969, p. 145.

42   Marx, in Marx and Engels 1971, p. 204.

the working-class state'.[43] Of course Marx also speaks of the ownership of the means of production in the new society as 'social', where *society* itself and not the state – absent from the new society – is the owner, but for Lenin it is the 'working-class *state*' which is the new owner (*sobstvennost' na sredstva proizvodstva v rukakh gosudarstva*).[44] Here Lenin has successfully stood Marx on his head. For Marx socialism – even in Lenin's *revised* sense of the first phase of communism – is already a *classless* society, a 'union of free individuals' coming into existence *after* the working class, along with the last form of state (the dictatorship of the proletariat), has vanished. The proletariat (wage labourers) have been transformed into simple producers as free individuals and it is their society (the collectivity of free individuals) – and not any state – which possesses the means of production. Lenin speaks not only of the working-class state but also of what he considers to be its equivalent, the 'socialist state'.[45] Needless to say, this last expression, an oxymoron, is nowhere to be found in Marx. Earlier we referred to Marx's texts, showing that there could be no state in socialism. The proletarian dictatorship, preceding the Association of free individuals, is the last form of state, and it goes out of existence in the Association that follows the end of the revolutionary transformation period. Lenin tries to smuggle 'the state' into Marx's text of the *Gothacritique* by brazenly *revising* it. This he does by connecting two independent ideas in two analytically separate places of the text on the *Gothacritique* – Marx's discussion of the continuation of 'bourgeois right' in the first phase of communism and Marx's speculation about the future of the 'present day functions of the state'. Lenin emphasises the need for the existence of the 'bourgeois state' to enforce 'bourgeois right' in the first phase of the new society. His logic is baffling. For Marx this first phase is inaugurated *after* the disappearance of proletarian rule – the last form of state. From Lenin's position it follows that in the absence of the bourgeoisie (by assumption), the producers themselves – no longer proletarians – would have to recreate, not even their old state, but the *bourgeois state*, to enforce bourgeois right. For Marx, from the start of the new society there are no classes and hence there is no state and no politics. Whatever bourgeois right remains in the area of distribution does not require a particular *political apparatus* to enforce it. It is now *society* itself which is in charge. One can read this textually in the *Gothacritique*. Similarly, for the first phase of communism (Lenin's socialism), as we have mentioned in our chapter on socialism, Lenin envisages

---

43   Lenin 1982b, pp. 300, 302, 669; 1975a, pp. 305, 306, 660; 1982c, pp. 711, 712; 1971, pp. 760, 761.

44   Lenin 1982c, pp. 711, 712; 1971, pp. 760, 761.

45   Lenin 1982c, p. 714; 1971, p. 763.

the economy as one 'state syndicate' or one 'single factory', where 'all citizens' are transformed into '*hired employees* of the state' (*sluzhashchikh po naymu*) with 'equality of labor, equality of wages (*zarabotnoyplatyi*)'.[46] For Marx what Lenin is saying boils down simply to the 'state itself as capitalist', 'in so far as it employs wage labour'.[47] So what Lenin presents to us as socialism is really *state capitalism* which with a 'single state syndicate' or a 'single factory', as Lenin puts it, will be – in Marx's terms, as we find in *Capital*'s French version – the 'total national capital constituting a single capital in the hands of a single capitalist'.[48]

Thus Lenin laid the foundation for a socialist society entirely on juridical grounds, on a specific form of ownership of the means of production, ownership of what he called the workers' state. This form of ownership posed as the negation of private individual ownership was supposed to have abolished private ownership of the means of production and thereby capitalism. The consideration of real relations of production and their transformation were not considered, or rather, were thought to change automatically with the change of the form of juridical ownership of the means of production. For Lenin private ownership (of means of production) signifies private ownership of 'separate individuals' (*otdelnyikh lits*).[49]

It was Stalin who, following Lenin's lead on the concept of socialism, gave it the finished form on which was founded the whole rationale of the post-1917 Party-States. Needless to add, Stalin totally subscribes to the Leninist identity of socialism with Marx's 'first phase of communism' and the Leninist idea of socialism as the transition to (full) communism. Stalin's inversion of Marx's materialist position goes even further than Lenin's. Whereas with Lenin socialism is conceived in terms of the ownership of means of production, that is, in juridical terms, independently of the real relations of production, Stalin specifically makes 'ownership of means of production the basis of production relations',[50] and state ownership of the means of production is, again, *à*

---

46   Lenin 1982g, pp. 306, 308; 1975a, pp. 310, 312. In his Parisian manuscripts of 1844 Marx characterises what he calls 'crude communism'. This considers 'community as simply a community of labour and equality of wages, which are paid out by the communal capital' (Marx 1975, pp. 346–7).

47   Marx 1881; 2008, p. 636; 1956, p. 100.

48   Marx 1976a, p. 448. This phrase does not appear in the (original) German edition or in its English version.

49   Lenin 1982g, p. 300; 1975a, p. 305. The term 'separate' does not appear in the Moscow English translation.

50   Stalin 1980, p. 505.

la Lenin, identified with socialist ownership.[51] Lenin's idea of citizens as hired wage labourers of the state in socialism is also taken over by Stalin. Stalin's 'improvement' on Lenin's position here lies in his statement that, given the absence of individual private property in the means of production in socialism, labour power has ceased to be a commodity and that there are no hired wage labourers here.[52] However, the labourers receive their remuneration 'in the form of the wage', reflecting a material incentive according to the quantity and quality of labour. But this 'wage under socialism' is fundamentally different from the wage under capitalism, because contrary to what happens in capitalism labour power is not a commodity in socialism.[53] In other words, the wage exists and labour exists but wage labour does not. It seems Lenin lacked this 'subtle' logic of his seminarist follower.

In our chapter on socialism we devoted a whole section to the property question in the Association, where we also discussed the meaning of private property in the means of production – both individual property and class property. As we have underlined, private property of the individual capitalist in the means of production changes its forms of appearance dictated by the needs of accumulation of capital till it becomes 'directly social capital' under 'associated capitalists'. Now, what remains invariant with respect to changes in the forms of appearance of property in the means of production under capital is the separation of the producers from the means of production, making them into wage labourers. This separation is the very meaning of capital. There is a one-to-one correspondence between the existence of wage labour and the existence of private property in the means of production. This separation at the same time signifies that the worker is deprived of all material means of production and thereby all means of life.[54] So the state ownership in the means of production does in no way remove the private character of this ownership as long the workers, supposed to constitute the great majority of society, remain separated from it, compelling them to continue to exist as wage workers.

The idea of socialism as the lower phase of and transition to communism based on public (mainly state) ownership of the means of production and wage labour and in the state form under a single party, founded by Lenin and perfected by Stalin (with the additional introduction of commodity production), this idea remained the central idea of socialism, accepted uncritically by the rulers

---

51   Stalin 1970, pp. 383, 386.

52   Stalin 1980, pp. 580–1.

53   Akademiya Nauk 1954, pp. 452, 453.

54   Marx cites from Shakespeare's *Merchant of Venice*: 'You take my life, when you take the means whereby I live'. See Marx 1987a, p. 466; 1976a, p. 655; 1954, p. 457.

of the whole system of Party-States across the globe and their international partisans. In this ironclad frame of socialism, the state substituted for society and the party substituted totally for the (working) class. It should be clear, following our earlier discussion above, that this socialism has nothing in common with Marx's socialism – not transitional to but equivalent to communism – conceived as a society of free and associated individuals with social ownership of the means of production and without the state, commodity production or wage labour.

The Party-State

At this point let us have a critical look at the two members of this pair, so inseparable in twentieth-century socialism – the Party-State – in order to understand better the reality of this socialism. It is remarkable that the *Communist Manifesto* does not assign any role to the communist party in the seizure of political power. It is the *proletariat as a class* which gains power and becomes the new rulers of society, thereby conquering democracy. Neither has the communist party any mentionable role in establishing the proletarian dictatorship which follows. It is remarkable that there is absolutely no text in Marx's published work where even the slightest mention of this figure makes its appearance in the framework of a discussion on socialism/communism. Years after the end of the Communist League, in a remarkable letter to his friend Freiligrath, Marx spoke of the Party not in the 'ephemeral sense of any particular political party, public or secret, but of Party, in the eminently historical sense, which is born spontaneously from the soil of modern [capitalist] society'.[55] In other words, political parties are born from the antagonism of classes, and will disappear with the class society itself.

As to the second member of the pair – the state – we propose to elaborate the theme at some length, considering Marx's lifelong interest in it, developed in the context of his preoccupation with the question of human freedom – consequent upon the self-emancipation of the labouring masses – and in view of the fact that the state has been an inseparable part of the post-1917 socialist régimes. But before we come to Marx's treatment of the state's role in socialism, let us not forget that it was Lenin who, to his great merit, restituted Marx's libertarian ideas on the state from the oblivion to which they were consigned by the Second International, and in particular by the German Social Demo-

---

55   Cited in Rubel 1957, p. 290.

cratic Party. In his polemic with the 'revisionists' published on 1 April 1917, he asserted that there would be no state in communism, and that 'we Marxists are opposed to every kind of state (*protivniki vsyakogo gosudarstva*)'.[56] However, Lenin's libertarian period was very short, and ended well before the Bolshevik victory in October.

As regards the existence of the state in socialism, Marx, beginning as early as the 1840s, considered this institution to be an apparatus of coercion and repression, which for this reason could not be a part of an Association of free individuals. Marx's theoretical quest for an emancipated human society started with his 1843–4 critique of Hegel's political philosophy. As he later noted in his 1859 Preface to the *Contribution to the Critique of Political Economy*, 'the first work which I undertook to clarify my doubts was a critical revision of the Hegelian philosophy of right'.[57]

Marx's initial target of attack arising from his critique of Hegel's political philosophy is bureaucracy, which arises from the separation of state and civil society. Bureaucracy, for Marx, is a particular self-contained society within the state, 'bureaucracy is the imaginary state within the real state; bureaucracy holds the state as its private property, bureaucracy is the state's consciousness, state's will, the power of the state as a corporation, therefore a particular, closed society within the state. Bureaucracy is a magic circle from which no one can escape'.[58] Since civil society is separated from the state, 'the citizen of the state is separated from the citizen as a member of the civil society; s/he must therefore divide up his [her] own essence'.[59]

Hegel's central idea, around which Hegel's construction of his political system is built, is that people and society are nothing by themselves; the State personified by the monarch is everything. Marx posits democracy against monarchy.

> In monarchy we have the people of the constitution, in democracy the constitution of the people. Democracy is the solution to the riddle of every constitution. Hegel proceeds from the state, and conceives of the state as objectified human, democracy proceeds from the human. The human does not exist for the sake of law which contrariwise exists for the human. It is the human existence. Such is the fundamental distinguishing character of democracy. [And then Marx adds very significantly:] In

---

56   Lenin 1982g, p. 42; 1975a, p. 60.
57   Marx 1980a, p. 100; 1970b, p. 20.
58   Marx 1975, pp. 107, 108.
59   Marx 1975, p. 143.

modern times the French have understood this to mean that *political State disappears* in a true democracy.[60]

In the same period, in a letter to Ruge (May 1843), Marx wrote that 'only with the reawakening of self-esteem and a sense of freedom which had vanished with the Greeks can society ever again become a community of humans that can fulfil their highest needs, a democratic state'.[61]

Also in the same period (1844) in Marx's polemic we read that 'the existence of the state is inseparable from the existence of slavery ... even the radical and revolutionary politicians look for the causes of evil not in the *nature* of the state but in a specific *form of the state* which they would replace with *another* form of the state'.[62]

In his critique of the state Marx advanced further in the *German Ideology*. In this work, Marx makes a clear distinction between the state and community and underlines the state's pretension of substituting for the community. As such, the state appears as an 'independent power in the face of the individuals, and for the subjugated class, a totally illusory community, and a new chain, whereas in the real community individuals acquire their liberty simultaneously in and through their association'.[63]

In the 1848 *Communist Manifesto*, Marx (and Engels) treats the state, 'the political centralisation', as an established fact of bourgeois society, a consequence of 'agglomerated population, centralised means of production and concentrated property in a few hands'.[64] In the same work we further read 'the executive of the modern state is but a committee for managing the common affairs of the whole bourgeoisie'.[65] The brochure also envisages that 'in the course of development, class distinctions will disappear, all production will be concentrated in the hands of the associated individuals, and public power will lose its political character'.[66]

---

60   Marx 1975, p. 88. Emphasis in original. The well-known Italian scholar Lucio Colletti, in his 'introduction' to Marx's early writings, comments on this point: 'what is really understood by democracy here is the same as, many years later, Marx was to rediscover in the actions of the Paris Commune of 1871'. In Marx 1975, p. 42.

61   Marx 1975, p. 201.

62   Marx 1975, pp. 411, 412. Emphasis in original. Note that within one year Marx's stand on the state changes – from his praise of the 'democratic state' (1843) to a wholesale denunciation of the state itself, considered as the cause of 'evil' (1844).

63   Marx and Engels 1845–6.

64   Marx and Engels 1970b, p. 39.

65   Marx and Engels 1970b, p. 37.

66   Marx and Engels 1970b, p. 53. Translation modified. The English translation in the Moscow

The next important work where Marx deals with the state and bureaucracy is his 1852 text *The Eighteenth Brumaire of Louis Bonaparte*, where Marx speaks of 'the executive power of enormous bureaucratic and military organisation with its ingenious state machinery embracing wide strata ... this appalling parasitic body enmeshing the whole body of French society like a net which chokes all pores, springing up in the days of the absolute monarchy'.[67] And he then adds, 'all revolutions perfected this machine instead of smashing it; the parties that contended for domination regarded the possession of this huge state edifice as the principal spoils of the victor'.[68]

Almost two decades later, Marx saw his anti-state position vindicated in practice, in the work of the 1871 Paris Commune, whose members were by no means Marx's followers, but, on the contrary, were the followers of his opponents, of Blanqui, the majority, and of Proudhon, the minority, as Engels reports in his introduction to Marx's *Civil War in France*, where he adds that 'both did the opposite of what their schools prescribed'.[69] In other words, one could say – however paradoxically – that they confirmed Marx, who was their opponent.

We saw earlier that the 1848 *Manifesto* broadly held, at least implicitly, that the proletariat could not gain power without, in the revolutionary process, destroying the state as a part of the 'superstructure' of the existing society. However, in the programme of the *immediate* tasks, following the political victory of the working class, the state occupies a dominant position. The programme lays down: 'the proletariat will use its political supremacy to wrest, by degrees, all capital from the bourgeoisie, to centralise all instruments of production in the hands of the state'.[70]

Nevertheless, in the 1872 Preface to the German edition of the *Manifesto*, the authors stressed the need for important changes in the programme, particularly as regards its second section, which lays down the immediate revolutionary measures after the political victory of the working class.

---

version is defective. Also to be noticed is the similarity of these ideas with those discussed in Marx's Proudhon critique one year earlier, which we cited at the start of this chapter. In the 1848 *Manifesto* there is another important point which should not be missed. The pamphlet asserts that 'the proletariat, the lowest stratum of to-day's society, cannot stir, cannot raise itself without the whole superstructure of strata of the official society being sprung into the air'. See Marx and Engels 1970b, p. 45. This obviously implies the destruction of the state, a part of the superstructure of the official society.

67   Marx, in Marx and Engels 1970b, p. 169.
68   Marx, in Marx and Engels 1970b, p. 169.
69   In Marx and Engels 1971b, pp. 30–1.
70   Marx and Engels 1970b, p. 52.

That passage would in many respects be very differently worded to-day. In view of the gigantic strides of modern industry in the last twenty-five years, and of the accompanying improved party organisation of the working class, in view of the practical experience gained first in the February Revolution, and then still more, in the Paris Commune, where the proletariat for the first time held political power for two whole months, this programme has in some details become antiquated. One thing specially was proved by the Commune, viz. that the working class cannot simply lay hold of the ready-made State machinery and wield it for its own purposes.[71]

Contemporary with this declaration, in an article in the *International Herald* of 15 June 1872 on 'Nationalisation of Land', Marx wrote that

National centralisation of the means of production will become the national basis of a society composed of associations of free and equal producers carrying on the social business on a common and rational plan ... There will be no longer any government or state power distinct from society itself. Such is the humanitarian goal to which the great economic movement of the 19th century is tending.[72]

Marx found that after the political victory, the Commune did not, contrary to what the 1848 *Manifesto* had laid down, concentrate the instruments of production and capital in the hands of the *state*. Instead, it 'transformed the means of production, land and capital ... into mere instruments of the free and associated labour'.[73] So, for the Communards, it is not the state but the 'society of free and associated labour' which is in charge. Let us add a word of caution here. It would be a mistake to see in Marx's discourse on the Commune only Marx pushing his own political agenda, as it were. More often than not he is faithfully reporting with great admiration the self-emancipatory measures that the Communards themselves were trying to implement, some of which Marx had even not foreseen – proving thereby the workers' own capacity of generating new ideas independently of any outside 'leaders'. Basically Marx interspersed the narrative with his own interpretations and comments on what he thought to be the far-reaching significance of these communal measures. For example,

71   Marx and Engels 1970b, pp. 31–2.
72   Marx 1973d, p. 290.
73   Marx, in Marx and Engels 1971b, p. 75.

It was essentially a working-class government, the produce of the struggle of the producing against the appropriating class, the political form at last discovered under which to work out the economical emancipation of Labour. The Commune was therefore to serve as a lever for uprooting the economical foundations upon which rests the existence of classes.[74]

Again, Marx here credits the Parisian workers themselves for 'discovering' this political form. Also, it is notable that in his Address on the Commune he always employs the term 'government' and never 'state' for its rule, and these are of course not equivalent terms.[75]

In the very first 'outline' of the discourse *The Civil War in France*, Marx called the Parisian movement a 'Revolution not against this or that ... form of state power. It was a Revolution against the *State* itself ... a resumption by the people of its own life'.[76] Hal Draper writes, 'For Marx the "abolition of the state" could come only at the *end* of a sufficient period of socialist reconstruction of society'.[77] So, this will mean the existing state will still continue for some time during the period of *socialist* reconstruction. Significantly Marx declares in the third section of his 'Address' on the Paris Commune that 'the working class

---

74   Marx, in Marx and Engels 1971b, p. 75.

75   By state Marx means basically a centralised military-bureaucratic state (machine) integral to a class society, whereas the term 'government' signifies administration, valid for any society.

76   Marx, in Marx and Engels 1971b, p. 152. Hal Draper, desperate to keep Marx free from contamination by anarchism, dismisses this expression of Marx's as 'ambiguous' and holds as proof the absence of such expressions in what he calls the 'anti-anarchist exposition' in the second 'outline', and its absence from the published version of the discourse (Draper 1990, pp. 172–3). Most unfortunately for him, in both these places Marx clearly expresses the opposite view, presenting what the Communards were doing as the destruction of the bureaucratic-military state machine (see Marx in Marx and Engels 1971b, pp. 73, 202, 206). Surprisingly, Draper never mentions Marx's continuing hostility to the state, beginning with his early works, some of which we mentioned above. Nor does he draw his definitive conclusion from a serious reading of the final text of the 'Address', where Marx clearly speaks of the Commune 'breaking the modern state power', as mentioned here.

77   Draper 1990, p. 174. Emphasis Draper's. He does not pay attention to the fact that for Marx and Engels there is no state in the absence of classes, and there is no question of socialist reconstruction till the classes exist. Only at the end of the revolutionary transformation period do classes still exist; classes then disappear, ushering in the first phase of the Association.

cannot simply lay hold of the ready-made state machinery, and wield it for its own purposes'.[78] Draper ignores this crucial pronouncement, nor does he mention anywhere, as far as we can see, the 1972 preface to the *Communist Manifesto* where one can clearly see Marx and Engels's new position contrasted with what appeared in the original version of the text. A wholly contrary view, in relation to Draper, we also find in Engels in his letter to Bebel (18–28 March 1875). He wrote, 'With the *introduction* of the socialist order of society, the state will dissolve of itself and disappear'.[79] And then he added, 'the whole talk about the state should be dropped, especially since the Commune, which was no longer a state in the proper sense'.[80] Recently, some scholars have found the 'smashing of the state and the withering away of the state' to be 'worn-out concepts'.[81] They observe, referring to Marx's critical comments on Bakunin, that (according to Marx), 'socialism involves doing away with the state only in the sense of being an agency of class domination and capitalist reproduction, not in the sense of developing institutions for democratic decision making, accountable representation and administration in a classless society'.[82] Now, if it is already a classless society, does this not mean automatically that there is no state either? So how can then a state still remain, even for democratic decision-making etc? On the other hand, why cannot society itself take charge of reforming the institution, why do we need the state for that purpose? For the rest, we have not found any textual evidence in Marx's Bakunin-critique, or indeed in any of his other works, of what these scholars ascribe to Marx.

Marx's anti-state position continues in his 1875 *Critique of the Gotha Programme*. In the envisioned post-capitalist communist/socialist or 'co-operative society', as Marx calls it, there is not a trace of the state. Only during the revolutionary transformation period, *preceding* the appearance of the 'co-operative society', does the proletarian political power take on the state form, but this state, bereft of the bureaucratic-military machine and requiring no special coercive apparatus, is no longer a state in its usual sense, as Engels stressed in his already-cited 1875 letter to Bebel. Indeed, the proletarian dictatorship representing the immense majority in the interest of the immense majority, is naturally the least repressive form of state. Besides portraying the possible

---

78   Marx, in Marx and Engels 1971b, p. 68.
79   Engels, in Marx and Engels 1971b, p. 335. Emphasis added.
80   Engels, in Marx and Engels 1970b, p. 335. Emphasis added.
81   Panitch and Gindin 2015, p. 19.
82   Panitch and Gindin 2015, p. 19.

form of the 'co-operative' society, Marx strongly attacks the ideas of the statist Ferdinand Lassalle, and denounces the 'servile belief in the state' of the Lassalleans.[83]

Finally, a couple of years before the end of his life, Marx was asked by the Russian 'populist' revolutionary Vera Zasulich (1881) whether in his view it would be possible for Russia, given the strength of its peasant communes, to accede to socialism without passing through capitalism. In his reply, while underlining the importance of the communes as a favourable factor in this regard, Marx stressed that 'to save the Russian communes there must have to be a Russian Revolution'.[84] Then, pointing to the isolated character of these communes in their reciprocal relations, generating thereby the possibility of the rise of a central despotism dominating them, Marx, in order to eliminate this obstacle, added that 'it would be necessary to substitute the *volost*, a governmental institution, by an assembly chosen by the communes themselves and serving as the economic and administrative organs of their interests'.[85] Thus, as we see it, Marx, in one of his last writings, wanted the working people to substitute the existing state administrative machinery with their own freely elected assembly, in the manner, one could say, of the 1871 Parisian communards, who Marx certainly had not forgotten.

The Fundamental Question

The Soviet Union was not considered socialist by its rulers till the late 1930s. Till then it was considered a proletarian dictatorship. The victory of socialism was formally proclaimed on the basis of the fulfilment of the second Five Year Plan (1933–7), with 98.7 percent of the means of production under state and cooperative-collective ownership. The party declared that 'in our country ... the first phase of communism, socialism, has been basically realised'.[86] The régimes which, following the post-1917 Russian regime, call themselves socialist, justify this appellation on the same basis, that is, the alleged absence of private ownership in the means of production as shown by the predominance of public ownership in the means of production. Private ownership here is taken in the Leninist sense of ownership by separate individuals, that is, in the

---

83   Marx, in Marx and Engels 1970b, p. 29.

84   Marx, in Riazanov 1971, p. 329.

85   Marx, in Riazanov 1971, p. 324. 'Volost' is a unit of local administration (a district). This question is elaborated in another chapter of this book.

86   *KPSS v resoliutsiakh* 1971, p. 335.

sense of bourgeois jurisprudence, originally taken over from the Roman law.[87] However, this leaves untouched private ownership in the form of *class* private ownership in the sense of Marx, as we have already discussed in the chapter on socialism. This class private ownership of the means of production is equivalent to the non-ownership of these means by the great majority of society, compelled to work as waged/salaried workers. In other words, these means of production are the property of the capitalist class. The question of the nature of *social relations of production* in these economies has rarely, if ever, been raised. So, what has been the character of the social relations of production in these régimes, principally in Russia – the prototype – and in particular the relation between the producers and the means of production? In other words, to paraphrase Marx's expression, cited above, in what manner were these two factors of production united in order for production to take place? This is equivalent to asking, following another of Marx's statements, what was the direct relationship of the owners of the means of production to the immediate producers?[88] From the point of view of the materialist conception of history a definitive answer to this question would show the real character of the régime. 'The specific way in which the combination of the two factors, labourers and the means of production, is accomplished (*bewerkstelligt*), distinguishes the different economic epochs of the social structure'.[89] This separation between the two factors is unique to commodity production as an 'historically determined social mode of production'.[90] In other words, to the capitalist mode of production, where the products of labour, including labour power, are all commodities. So the starting point is the separation of the workers from the means of production, and it is the capitalist whose task it is to unite the two factors with a view to production. This signifies the existence of wage labour, and, by the same token, the existence of class private ownership of the means of production, whether the owner is an individual capitalist or a capitalist collective. The same argument holds when the state itself owns legally the means of production and employs wage labour. Here capital directly assumes the form of social capital in oppos-

---

87   It should be noted that Lenin did not introduce this concept of private ownership in the juridical sense. Kautsky had already used private ownership in this sense in his work on the Erfurt Programme (1891), which Engels had criticised in his 'Critique of the Erfurt Programme' (1891), where he had distinguished between 'capitalist production' and 'capitalist private production' (in Engels 1891). Here obviously 'capitalist production' includes class private ownership.

88   Marx 1992, p. 732; 1984, p. 791.

89   Marx 2008, p. 672; 1956a, p. 36.

90   Marx 1987a, pp. 106–7; 1976a, p. 72; 1954, p. 80.

ition to private capital. 'This is the abolition/sublimation of capital as private ownership within the limits of the capitalist mode of production itself'.[91] Here the ownership of means of production as capital is completely separated from the process of production, it is also separated from *all labour* connected with the process of production, including the labour of the active capitalist, the non-owner of capital, such that 'only the functionary remains, the capitalist disappears as superfluous from the process of production'.[92] Marx adds that it is 'the functioning capitalist who *really* exploits labour'.[93]

All the post-1917 régimes calling themselves 'socialist' have been character-ised by the separation of workers from the conditions of production, resulting in the existence of the commodity mode of production (with wage labour) as the basis of production. In a word, their mode of production is capitalist. In one of his 1860s manuscripts, let us recall, Marx identified *Capital* with 'separation of the conditions of production from the worker'.[94]

Now, the countries – beginning with Russia – where the seizure of power took place in the name of the working class, were materially backward. Here, for a large measure, pre-capitalist and non-capitalist relations of production prevailed. So the task for the victors was first to remove those backward rela-tions before any significant progress could be made. A few months after seizing power, Lenin told the Party Congress that 'the most developed form of capital-ist relation embraced only the small top part (*nebol'shie verkhushki*) of industry and hardly touched agriculture'.[95] As he pointedly observed four years later, 'medievalism' had first to be removed, and he declared that 'our task was to consummate (*dovesti do contsa*) the bourgeois revolution'.[96] So the régimes in question could not have capitalist relations as the dominant relations right from the start. They had first to create conditions separating the great majority of working people from the means of production, thus completing the bour-geois revolution first. This does not mean that there was no capitalist produc-tion in Russia before October. Capitalist production existed – even at a higher level compared to the level in most of the rest of the Party-State régimes at their starting point – in the few urban centres where it was carried on in big industries. Nevertheless, most of the vast countryside remained under peasant

---

91   Marx 1992, p. 502; 1984, p. 438.
92   Marx 1992, p. 459; 1984, p. 388.
93   Marx 1992, p. 460; 1984, p. 389. Emphasis in original.
94   Marx 1962a, p. 419; 1971a, p. 422. Of course, 'conditions of production' include 'means of production'.
95   Lenin 1982d, p. 532; 1975c, p. 529.
96   Lenin 1982f, p. 648; 1971, p. 705.

production, requiring a process of 'original expropriation' or 'primitive accumulation', in Marx's vivid phrase. In the case of post-October Russia this was carried out in the case of agriculture, pursued by the country's rulers with astonishing rapidity. From a well-known economic historian of the USSR, we learn that the percentage of the peasant households collectivised rose from a mere 1.7 in 1928 to 93 in 1937.[97] 'The twin goals of collectivisation – to feed gratis the non-agricultural segments of the economy and at the same time provide a flow of labour for the public works of government – were largely achieved'.[98] Alongside this process, it should be noted, commodity production itself was growing uninterruptedly. During the so-called 'war economy' (1918–1920/21), in spite of all official attempts to supress commodity production, the latter continued to prevail. A noted economist-historian, Alec Nove, has written about 'the sleepless leather jacketed commissars working round the clock in vain to replace the free market'.[99] The eminent Yugoslav economist Alexander Vacic, to whom we have already referred in the chapter on socialist calculation, very pertinently observed, referring to 'several socialist countries' (including the USSR), that 'in spite of the organised economic, political, and sometimes even physical pressure, commodity production maintained itself, it spread, renewed itself and extended to many fields', and that those countries were 'now more of a commodity-producing nature than they had been before the revolution'.[100] And as we know, generalised commodity production, where labour power itself is a commodity, is capitalism.

So, given the type of social relations of production on which these régimes were based, they could only be capitalist régimes in essential reality, however different they could be, compared to the standard 'Western' capitalist regimes, in *phenomenal* reality. In a justly famous passage, Marx wrote:

> It is always in the direct relations between the owners of the conditions of production and the immediate producers that one must look for the innermost secret relation, the hidden basis of the whole social structure, as well as the political form of the relations of sovereignty and dependence, in short, the form of state of a given historical epoch. Under their different aspects these relations naturally correspond to a definite stage of the methods of labour and of social productivity. This

---

97   In Prokopovitch 1952, p. 163.
98   Gerschenkron 1966, p. 148.
99   Nove 1982, p. 74.
100   Vacic 1977, p. 233.

does not prevent the same economic basis – the same as regards the main conditions – due to innumerable different circumstances, natural environment, racial factors, historical influences acting from outside, etc., showing infinite variations and gradations in appearance, which can be grasped only through the analysis of empirically given circumstances.[101]

Anti-Stalinists in general, beginning with the followers of Trotsky, have held that before Stalin consolidated his power, there was a 'workers' state', which under Stalin was transformed into its opposite, a state capitalist society. One of the most illustrious and articulate representatives of this tendency has been the well-known Marxist humanist, Raya Dunayevskaya, who hardly bothered herself with the fundamental *materialist* question of what type of production relations prevailed in Russia beginning with October 1917, that is, *before* Stalin came to power.[102] Quite rightly concerned with the brutal régime of Lenin's nominated successor, Stalin, she focused her attention almost singularly on the nature of Stalin's state power, which is really a question about society's super-structure or edifice (*Überbau*), but left out the problem of material basis – its social mode of production, in other words, the social relations of production. This superstructural question has indeed been the dominant question within the Left when it comes to the analysis of the Party-State régimes, completely standing Marx on his head. This kind of analysis either leaves out the facts of history or cannot properly analyse these facts. And facts are stubborn things, as the saying goes. Thus, against all evidence, Dunayevskaya accepted uncritically the claim of the spokespersons of Russia's post-October régime that Russia's working class had taken possession of the state power, and that it had done so in consequence of the successful proletarian revolution, called by her 'the greatest of all proletarian revolutions'.[103] By contrast, the non-partisan histori-ans (who nevertheless maintain basically progressive views) who have studied

---

101   Marx 1992, p. 732; 1984, pp. 791–92.
102   Dunayevskaya contends that, as opposed to what happened under Stalin, under Lenin 'production relations were different. In Lenin's time, before the worker entered the factory, he had his production conference, where he could decide the plan' (Dunayevskaya 1992, p. 28). Now, if this type of production relation was prevailing, but if the worker remained a wage labourer, then we cannot say that the production relation was different. Signific-antly, Dunayevskaya never mentions Lenin's 1918 work *The Immediate Tasks of the Soviet Government*, which we have already analysed as regards the coercive character of labour in the factories.
103   Dunayevskaya 1991, p. 108. Trotsky had made the fantastic claim that the 'proletariat as a whole seized the power'. See Trotsky 1987, p. 185.

the relevant events *à fond*, give us a very different picture.[104] It is the (single) Party, acting without popular mandate, substituting itself for and presenting itself in the name of the working class, which snatched and confiscated power from the soviets under the slogan 'all power to the soviets'. And the soviets as the self-governing organs of the working people were made to evaporate within a few months of 'victory'. As regards Russia's 'factory committees', which, in the words of a great authority, Paul Avrich, were the 'proletarian centres of the ele-mental revolutionary forces unleashed by the fall of the tsarist régime', these were brought under control by the Bolshevik régime by 'centralising the syndic-alist movement in the factories through the Bolshevik controlled trade unions'. 'By this process', adds Avrich, 'factory committees became "state institutions" as Lenin desired'.[105]

Dunayevskaya, a Hegel enthusiast, writes that Lenin's *Philosophical Note-books* laid the 'philosophical foundation for the Russian Revolution',[106] for which she has not given any evidence. Nor has she made clear what exactly this proposition means. As far as we know, Lenin never made this claim. If it means that the philosophy of this 'Russian Revolution' was based on Lenin's reading of Hegel's *Science of Logic*, then would it not be more proper to connect this foundation not with Hegel's *Science of Logic* but, rather, with *Hegel's Philo-sophy of Right*, whose crowning point is anti-democratic political absolutism, where people and society are nothing by themselves, but the state personified in the monarchy is everything? This latter question is very relevant in view of the reality of this much touted 'Russian Revolution', which had culminated in a society enslaved by the Party-State.

It is remarkable that the anti-Stalinists, beginning with the Trotskyists, have paid all their attention to the Stalin régime's super-repressive character, but almost never enough attention to the basic materialist point, namely, the régime's claim to socialism (beginning with 1936) based not on the social rela-tions of production but on the juridical relations of ownership of the means of production. Their denial of the régime's claim to socialism almost exclus-ively comes from its 'betrayal of the revolution', conceived in purely political terms, not in terms of the relations of production. We saw earlier that, following Lenin's pre-Marxian notion of private ownership of the means of production, and its negation through ownership belonging to the 'socialist state', Stalin had made the ownership relation the basis of production relations, thereby

---

104   See, among others, Anweiler 1958; Daniels 1967; Ferro 1976; Rabinowitch 2004.

105   Avrich 1963, p. 161.

106   Dunayevskaya 2002, p. 217.

'legislating away' (*wegdekretieren*), in Marx's words, capitalism.[107] Paradoxically, this analysis, based on the ownership criterion originating in Lenin, is also shared by the anti-Stalinists. It should also be noted that, besides the ownership criterion, Lenin also initiated the idea of the superstructural criterion as a determinant of social revolution, when on the basis of a change in government, independently of any change in the production relations, he claimed that the bourgeois revolution had been completed in Russia.[108] It should be stressed that in general people concerned with the characterisation of the régimes in question (either for or against) hardly refer to the *production relations* as the focal point for their analysis. It is always the political superstructure which dominates their thinking, where, at best, the juridical question of ownership is referred to. So any discussion of capital involves only capital as an investible thing, not as a relation of production. The eminent dissident Russian ('soviet') economist, V.P. Shkredov, has very justly summed the matter up, underlining that Marx's 'discovery of the difference as well as the connection' between capital as a social relation and capital as a (material) thing constitutes *a revolutionary upheaval* (*revolyutsionnogo perevorota*) in political economy.[109]

The fairly widespread notion that there had been a restoration of capitalism in Russia after Lenin is revealed as a fiction in the face of the continuing development of commodity production and wage labour in the country, as testified by Lenin's own pronouncements cited here. Again, in the Party Congress of 1919, Lenin told his assembled comrades, with particular stress, that 'In Russia the capitalist commodity economy is alive, operates, develops and generates the bourgeoisie as in every capitalist society'.[110] A latter-day critic of Russia's capitalist restoration has been the well-known scholar, I. Mészáros, an uncritical partisan of Lenin.[111] He has nailed Gorbachev and his followers for their sin of opening up and trying to free Russian society from the way it existed ever since the Bolshevik seizure of power from the soviets. We submit that the short Gorbachev period was the best in the history of Russian *capitalism*, when for the first time an attempt was made to introduce democratic reforms which might later have paved the way for the rebuilding of an independent working-class movement. It is no accident that the fall of Gorbachev was celebrated by

---

107   Marx 1987a, p. 67; 1976a, p. 13; 1954, p. 20.
108   See Lenin 1982b, pp. 19, 51; 1975d, pp. 37, 68.
109   Shkredov 1973, p. 165. Emphasis added.
110   Lenin 1982e, p. 120; 1971, p. 187.
111   Mészáros 2008, p. 32.

the Stalinists. Without offering any evidence on the basis of a change in the real relations of production, this eminent scholar came to the conclusion that capitalism had been 'restored' in Russia.

As a matter of fact, in Russia, as later in other lands ruled by a Party-State, the revolutions could only have a bourgeois character, given the objective and subjective conditions, too backward for inaugurating an 'Association of free individuals'. 'Humankind always sets itself only such tasks as it can solve, and the task itself arises only when the material conditions for its solution already exist, or are at least in the process of formation'.[112] Let us emphasise that Russia's February 1917 movement, content-wise a bourgeois democratic revolution in process, given its spontaneous mass character with its open-ended plurality, had, it appears, the potential of passing over, at a later date – given appropriate material conditions – into an authentic socialist revolution, if the labouring masses who participated had been allowed unfettered freedom – through their (own) self-governing organs – to continue their march forward. The Bolshevik seizure of power by a pre-emptive strike destroyed the democratic part of the revolution, and accelerated the bourgeois part.[113]

The immediate task for the victors in these countries was to build and perfect capitalist relations. The New Economic Policy (NEP) in Russia was precisely intended to play this role. This is very clear from Lenin's own pronouncements, some of which were cited above. A government decree of September 1921 described the wages system as 'a fundamental factor of industrial development, wages and employment being considered as a matter of relation between

---

112   Marx, in Marx and Engels 1970b, p. 182.

113   It is important to stress that the unique value of the soviets for Lenin was not their importance as working people's revolutionary independent self-governing organs, but as a mechanism for gaining the Bolsheviks' power, his championing of the slogan in public of 'all power to the soviets' notwithstanding. This is clearly seen in his confidential letters to his comrades on the eve of the seizure of power in the piece 'The Crisis has matured', end of September 1917. Some historians have noted this attitude in Lenin, faced with the rise of the soviets even in 1905. Here the much-maligned and neglected Julius Martov, the Menshevik Internationalist, in sharp contrast with Lenin, 'recognized at once the embodiment of the idea of revolutionary self-government', as Israel Getzler has written (Getzler 2003, p. 109). See also Marc Ferro 1967, p. 21. The outstanding German historian of the soviet movement, Oskar Anweiler, has observed that while the Mensheviks saw in the soviet movement the 'realisation of their idea of workers' revolutionary self-government', the Bolshevik revolutionary programme was based on the leading role of the party, and, in fact, Lenin characterised the Menshevik campaign of revolutionary self-government as 'a wholly infantile idea'. See Anweiler 1958, pp. 85, 92, 93.

the workers and the concerned enterprise'. In less than a year 'NEP had reproduced the characteristic essentials of a capitalist economy'.[114]

The fact that the seizure of political power in the countries of the nouveaux
régimes occurred in the name of the working people but without their active
involvement, either in the initiative or in the leadership of the people – who
at best accepted the régime somewhat passively, without any sustained, organised resistance – together with the fact that the ruling power was the power of
a single party, not only unprepared to share this power with any other socialist party, but even considering such other parties as enemies of the revolution and outlawing them, could only result in a minority government, which
remarkably confirmed what Engels had established in his 1895 Introduction to
Marx's *Class Struggles in France*, in the light of the earlier revolutions (which
we cited earlier). Thus a minority (of minorities) established its power, displa-
cing another (earlier) minority. Each of these minority governments, 'uniting
in its hand the power of political oppression and economic exploitation', in the
1891 words of Engels,[115] has exercised dictatorship over the majority, completely
reversing the process of the 'immense majority', constituted by the proletariat
as the ruling class, exercising its dictatorship over a small minority of expropriators, as the *Communist Manifesto* had envisaged, and not requiring a special
apparatus of coercion. No wonder that each of these régimes, by the sheer logic
of things, had to be *coercive* even if only to survive.[116] Indeed, we cited earlier
Shlyapnikov's prognosis that, given the way the government was formed under
Lenin, the rule could be exercised only by *terror*.[117] By the same logic there could
be no question of democracy – in its usual meaning of majority rule – under

---

114   Carr 1963, pp. 320, 321, 323.

115   Engels 1891.

116   Marx wrote in *New York Daily Tribune*, 28 January 1853, that 'Punishment is nothing but a
        means of society to defend itself against the infraction of its vital conditions. What kind
        of a miserable society is that which knows no better instrument for its own defence than
        the hangman!'

117   Lenin's comrade in the party leadership, L. Kamenev, also saw clearly, in Lenin's tactic of
        seizure of power, involving a merciless fight against the other socialist parties, the inevit-
        able drive towards the isolated rule of the Bolsheviks, which he and his associates thought
        would be dangerous. They wanted 'a mass party of the revolutionary proletariat' and not
        'a group of communist propagandists', who, in the event of seizure of power, 'could main-
        tain this power only with the help of *terror*' (Anweiler 1958, p. 195, emphasis added). In
        his turn Victor Serge, speaking of the Bolshevik regime, wrote that the Russian Marxists
        'formed at the school of despotism did not dare to show themselves as libertarians ... the
        fear of freedom, which is the fear of the masses, characterises the whole of the Russian
        Revolution' (Serge 2001, pp. 834–5).

these régimes. In fact, as shown above, Lenin, quite logically, openly expressed contempt for the 'notorious democracy' at the Ninth Congress of his party. Quite rightly so, inasmuch as democracy might have ended the régime's *raison d'être*.

So, then, to what extent have the régimes in question established socialism, even following Lenin's interpretation of Marxian socialism as the first phase of communism?[118] We have seen that the régimes in question, contrary to the Leninist position, have in fact been based on the commodity mode of production, that is, they have been *capitalist*, if we examine their social structures in terms of real *relations of production*, and not in terms of juridical forms of ownership. In other words, the key question is: how do the workers relate to the means of production?

Now, it is true that these régimes not only accepted Lenin's *idea* of socialism as the 'first phase of communism', but also the *content* of Lenin's socialism, in which the two central institutions are the state and wage labour, as we earlier emphasised in our analysis of his book *The State and Revolution*.

What about their claim to Marx's heritage? It is clear that these régimes illegitimately substituted Lenin for Marx in their construction of socialism. What is singularly absent in this 'Marxist-Leninist' tradition is Marx's immense emancipatory vision for the society after capital. It is interesting to note that the watchword is always 'proletarians of all lands unite' – this unity being understood as unity organised under the communist party. The slogan is almost never the 1864 clarion call of the first International: 'the emancipation of the working classes must be conquered by the working classes themselves'.

The idea of human emancipation based on the self-emancipation of the workers is an abiding message in Marx's writings almost from the beginning of his adult life. And this human emancipation boils down to the emancipation of the human individual. Already in the 1840s, Marx stressed that under capitalism individuals live only as contingent individuals, where all individuality is abstracted. Here individuals exist as individuals of a class. Under the commodity mode of production, in the conditions of a 'false community', individuals

---

118   Let us recall that the two-phase portrait of the Association appears basically in Marx's 1875 *Gothacritique*, with only a passing mention in his 1844 Parisian economic and philosophical manuscripts. Outside of the *Gothacritique*, whenever Marx discusses socialism/communism (including in the famous fourth section of the first chapter in *Capital* Volume I), it is always the first phase of the future society that Marx has in mind, without naming it as such. And in this first phase, reached after the revolutionary transformation period, there are no classes and hence no state, no commodity production, no wage labour.

are dominated by their own products. Contrariwise, the Association, the 'true community', creates the conditions of free development of individuals.

Marx had conceived human emancipation to be centred on the emancipation of the human individual from both subjective and objective constraints. We read in the *Communist Manifesto* that after the disappearance of the bourgeoisie, 'we shall have an association in which the free development of each is the condition of the free development of all'.[119] About two decades later in *Capital* Volume I, these words are repeated almost word by word: 'the real basis of a higher form of society, a society in which the full and free development of every individual forms the ruling principle'.[120] In the 'socialist' régimes of the twentieth century, it is precisely human individuals as persons who have been totally subjugated by the Party-State. It is an irony that while in April 1917, Lenin noted that the Russia of the time – that is, let us underline, under a 'bourgeois' government, on Lenin's own reckoning – was the 'freest country among the belligerent countries of the world',[121] precisely under the Bolsheviks it turned out to be one of the most viciously repressive countries of the world. This was a situation even worse than Pizzarro's dungeon in Beethoven's *Fidelio*, with no Leonara to rescue the prisoners.

---

119   Marx and Engels 1970b, p. 53.
120   Marx 1987a, p. 543; 1954, p. 555. This sentence is absent in the French version.
121   Lenin 1982b, p. 12; 1975d, p. 30.

References

Abramsky, C. 1964, 'Marx and the General Council of the International Workingmen's Association', *La Première Internationale: Colloques internationaux du CNRS*, Paris.

Akademya Nauk SSSR 1955, *Politicheskaya Economiya (Uchebnik)*, Moscow: Gosudartstvennoye Izdatel'stvo Politicheskoi Litratury.

Adaman, F. and P. Devine 1997, 'On the Economic Theory and Market Socialism', *New Left Review*, 221: 54–80.

Albert, Micheal 2003, *Parecon*, London: Verso.

Anderson, Kevin 2010, *Marx in the Margins*, Chicago: University of Chicago Press.

Anweiler, Oskar 1958, *Die Rätebewegung in Russland (1905–1921)*, Leiden: Brill.

Anweiler, Oskar 1958, 'Die Räte in der Ungarschen Revolution (1956)', *Osteuropa*, 8: 393–400.

Arendt, Hannah 1963, *On Revolution*, New York: Viking.

Arthur, Chris 1999, 'Marx, Orthodoxy, Labour, Money', *Beiträge zur Marx-Engels Forschung*, Neue Folge: 5–11.

Atkinson, Dorothy 1973, 'The Statistics on the Russian Land Commune 1905–1917', *Slavic Review*, 32, 4: 773–87.

Avrich, Paul 1963, 'Russian Factory Committees in 1917', *Jahrbücher für Geschichte Osteuropas: Neue Folge* Band 11, 2: 161–82.

Avrich, Paul 1967, 'The Anarchists in the Russian Revolution', *Russian Review*, 26, 4: 341–50.

Backhaus, Hans Georg 1997, *Dialektik der Wertform*, Freiburg: Ça ira Verlag.

Backhaus Hans Georg and Helmut Reichelt 1994, 'Der politisch-ideologische Grundcharacter der Marx-Engels Gesamtausgabe: eine Kritik der Editionsrechtilinien der IMES', in *MEGA Studien*: 101–18.

Bakunin, Mikhail 1971 [1869–71], *Recollections of Marx and Engels*, in Anarchy Archives.

Banyan, J. and H.H. Fisher 1934, *The Bolshevik Revolution: 1917–1918: Documents and Materials*, Stanford University Press.

Bahro, Rudolf 1978, *The Alternative in Eastern Europe*, London: NLB.

Bardhan, P. and J. Roemer 1994, 'Market Socialism: A Case for Rejuvenation', in *Foundations of Analytical Marxism*, edited by John Roemer, Vermont: Edward Elgar.

Barone, E. 1935 [1908], 'Ministry of Production in a Collectivist State', in *Collectivist Economic Planning*, edited by Friedrich Hayek, London: George Routledge.

Bebel, August 1879, *Woman and Socialism*, available at https://www.marxistsfr.org/archive/bebel/1879/woman-socialism/index.htm.

Bergson, A. 1948, 'Socialist Economics', in *A Survey of Contemporary Economics*, volume 1, edited by H. Ellis, Illinois: Homewood.

Bergson, A. 1967, 'Market Socialism Revisited', *Journal of Political Economy*, October: 657–73.

Bettelheim, Charles 1970, *Calcul économique et formes de propriété*, Paris: Maspêro.

Blackburn, Robin 1991, 'Fin de Siècle: Socialism after Crash', *New Left Review*, 185: 5–66.

Blaug, M. 1996, *Economic Theory in Retrospect*, Cambridge: Cambridge University Press.

Borkenau, Franz 1962, *World Communism*, Ann Arbor: University of Michigan Press.

Brenan, Gerald 1969, *The Spanish Labyrinth*, Cambridge: Cambridge University Press.

Bròdy, Andras 1970, *Proportions, Prices and Plannning*, Budapest: Akademiai Kiado.

Broué, Pierre and Émile Témime 1961, *La Révolution et la Guerre d'Espagne*, Paris: Minuit.

Bruce, W. 1987, 'Market Socialism', in *Palgrave: A Dictionary of Economics*, edited by J. Eatwell, M. Milgate, P. Newman, London: Macmillan.

Bruce, W. and J. Laski 1989, *From Marx to Market*, Oxford: Clarendon.

Brutzkus, B. 1935 [1921], *Economic Planning in Soviet Russia*, London: Routledge.

Bukharin, Nikolai 1918, 'Anarchy and Scientific Communism', available at http://www .marxistsfr.org/archive/bukharin/works/1918/ps.htm.

Bukharin, Nikolai 1970 [1920], *Ökonomik der Transformationsperiode*, Hamburg: Rowohlt.

Bukharin, Nikolai 1988, *Izbrannyie Proizvedeniya*, Moscow: Politizdat.

Bukharin, Nikolai 1989, *Problemy Teorii I Praktiki Sotsialisma*, Moscow: Izdatel'stvo Politichestkoi Literatoorii.

Bukharin Nikolai /Preobrazhenski Evgenii 1922 [1920], *The ABC of Communism*, available at https://www.marxists.org/archive/bukharin/works/1920/abc/.

Cafiero, Carlo 2005 [1880], 'Anarchy and Communism', in *Anarchism: A Documentary History of Libertarian Ideas*, edited by Robert Graham, Montreal: Black and Rose.

Carr, E.H. 1963, *The Bolshevik Revolution*, volume 2, London: Macmillan.

Carr, E.H. 1964, *The Bolshevik Revolution*, volume 1, London: Macmillan.

Chambre, H. 1974, *L'évolution du Marxisme Sovietique: théorie économique et droit*, Paris: Seuil.

Cleaver, Harry 2000, *Reading Capital Politically*, Edinburgh: A.K. Press.

Cole, G.D.S. 1921, *Guild Socialism Re-stated*, London: Leonard Parsons.

Cole, G.D.S. 1968 [1919], *Guild Socialism*, London: The Fabian Society.

Constantin de Grunwald 1975, *Société et civilisation russe au XIXe siècle*, Paris: Editions du Seuil.

Daniels, R.V. 1960, *The Conscience of the Revolution*, Cambridge: Harvard University Press.

Daniels, R.V. 1967, *The Red October*, New York: Charles Scribner.

Deutscher, Isaac 1960, *Russia in Transition*, New York: Grove Press.

Deutscher, Isaac 1963, *The Prophet Armed: Trotsky 1979–1921*, New York: Oxford University Press.

Devine, Pat 1988, *Democracy and Economic Planning*, Cambridge: Polity Press.

Dickinson, H. 1933, 'Price Formation in a Socialist Community', *Economic Journal*, June: 237–51.

Dickinson, H. 1939, *Economics of Socialism*, London: Oxford University Press.

Dobb, Maurice 1940, *Political Economy and Capitalism*, London: Routledge and Kegan Paul.

Dobb, Maurice 1965, *On Economic Theory and Socialism*, London: Routledge and Kegan Paul.

Dobb, Maurice 1966, *Soviet Economic Development since 1917*, New York: International Publishers.

Dobb, Maurice 1973, *Theories of Value and Distribution*, Cambridge: Cambridge University Press.

Dognin, P.D. 1977, *Les 'Sentiers escarpés' de Karl Marx*, Paris: CERF.

Draker, Richard 2003, 'Carlo Cafiero', in *Apostles and Agitators: Italy's Marxist Revolutionary Tradition*, Cambridge: Harvard University Press available at www.fdca.it/fdcaen/historical/biogs/cafiero/htm.

Draper, Hal 1986, *Karl Marx's Theory of Revolution*, volume 3, New York, Monthly Review Press

Draper, Hal 1990, *Karl Marx's Theory of Revolution*, volume 4, New York: Monthly Review Press.

Dunayevskaya, Raya 1944, 'Teaching of Economics in the USSR', *American Economic Review*, September: 501–29.

Dunayevskaya, Raya 1944, 'A New Revision of Marxian Economics', *American Economic Review*, September: 531–7.

Dunayevskaya, Raya 1991, *Rosa Luxemburg, Women's Liberation and Marx's philosophy of revolution*, Chicago: University of Illinois Press.

Dunayevskaya, Raya 2002, *The Power of Negativity*, Lanham, Maryland: Lexington Books.

Dussel, Enrique 1990, *El ultimo Marx* (1863–82), Mexico: Siglo veintiuno editors.

Edelman, M. 1964, 'La Balance interbranche des dépenses de travail et sa signfication économique en URSS', *Cahiers d'Etudes des Sociétés Industrielles et d'Automation*, Paris: CNRS: 15–36.

Engels, Friedrich 1973 [1868], 'Konspekt über "Das Kapital"', *Einführungen in 'Das Kapital' von Karl Marx*, Berlin: Dietz Verlag.

Engels, Friedrich 1976 [1845] 'Speeches in Elberfeld', 243–8, in MECW, vol. 4.

Engels, Friedrich 1877, *Anti-Dühring* available at https://www.marxists.org./archive/marx/works/1877/anti-dühring.

Engels, Friedrich 1874, 'Social Relations in Russia', available at: hiaw.org//defcon6/works/1874/refugee-literature/cho5.html

Engels, Friedrich 1894, 'Social Relations in Russia: Afterword', available at https:11marxists.anu.edu.au/archive/marx/works/1894/01/russia.htm.

Ferro, Marc 1967, *La Révolution de 1917*, volume 1, Paris: Aubier Montagne.

Ferro, Marc 1976, *La Révolution de 1917*, volume 2, Paris: Aubier Montagne.

Ferro, Marc 1980, *Des soviets au communisme bureaucratique*, Paris: Aubier Montaigne.

Foley, Duncan K. 1986, *Understanding Capital*, London: Harvard University Press.

Gerschenkron, Alexander 1966, *Economic Backwardness in Historical Perspective*, Cambridge: Harvard University Press.

Getzler, Israel 1983, *Kronstadt (1917–1921), The Fate of a Soviet Democracy*, Cambridge: Cambridge University Press.

Getzler, Israel 2003, *Martov: A Political Biography of a Russian Social Democrat*, Cambridge: Cambridge University Press.

Geyer, Dietrich 1968, 'The Bolshevik Insurrection in Petrograd', in *Revolutionary Russia*, edited by Richard Pipes, Cambridge: Harvard University Press.

Gramsci, Antonio 1996, *Il materialismo storico e la filosofia di Benedetto Croce*, Rome: Editori riuniti.

Halm, G. 1935 [1929], 'Further Considerations on the Possibility of Calculation in a Socialist Community', in *Collectivist Economic Planning*, edited by F.A. Hayek, London: George Routledge.

Harold, Isaacs 1910 [1938], *The Tragedy of the Chinese Revolution*, Chicago: Haymarket Books.

Hayek, F.A. 1935, *Collectivist Economic Planning*, London: George Routledge.

Hayek, F.A. 1937, 'Economics and Knowledge', *Economica*, 4: 33–54.

Hayek, F.A. 1945, 'The Use of Knowledge in Society', *American Economic Review*, September: 519–30.

Hecker, Rolf 2001, *In Memoriam Wolfgang Jahn*, Berlin: Argument Verlag.

Heinrich, Michael 1996–7, 'Engels's Edition of the Third Volume of "Capital" and Marx's Original Manuscript', *Science and Society*, 60, 4: 452–66.

Heinrich, Michael 2003, *Die Wissenschaft von Wert*, Münster: Westfälisches Dampfboot.

Heller, M. and A. Nekrich 1982, *L'utopie au Pouvoir: Histore de l'U.R.S.S. de 1917 à nos jours*, Paris: Calmann-Levy.

Hilferding, Rudolf 1968 [1909], *Das Finanzkapital*, Frankfurt am Main: Europäische Verlagsanstatalt.

Hilferding, R. 1972, 'State capitalism or Totalitarian-State Economy', in *A Handbook of Socialist Thought*, edited by I. Howe, London: Victor Gollancz.

Hobson, S.G. 1920, *National Guild and the State*, London: G. Bell and Sons.

Horvat, Branko 1982, *Political Economy of Socialism: A Marxist Social Theory*, New York: M.E. Sharpe.

Howard, M. 2000, *Self-Management and the Crisis in Socialism*, London: Rowman and Littlefield.

Howard, M. and J. King 1992, *A History of Marxian Economics*, volume 2, Princeton: Princeton University Press.

Ito, M. 1996, 'Money and Credit in Socialist Economics: A Reconsideration', *Capital and Class*, Autumn: 95–118.

Kautsky, Karl 1892, *The Erfurt Programme*, available at https://www.marxists.org/history/international/social-democracy/1891/erfurt-program.htm.

Kautsky, Karl 1902, *The Social Revolution*, volume 2, *On the Day after the Revolution*, available at https://www.marxists.org/archive/kautsky/1902/socrev/.

Kautsky, Karl 1924, *The Labour Revolution: The Economic Revolution*, available at https://www.marxists.org/archive/kautsky/1924/labour/index.htm.

Keizer, W. 1989, 'Recent Reinterpretations of the Socialist Calculation Debate', *Economic Studies*, 16, 1: 63–83.

Kingston-Mann, Esther 1990, 'Peasant Communes and Economic Innovation', in *Peasant Economy: Culture and Politics of European Russia (1800–1921)*, edited by Esther Kingston-Mann and Timothy Mixter, Princeton, NJ: Princeton University Press.

Knafo, Samuel 2012, 'Value-form Approach', *Elgar Companion to Marxist Economics*, Cheltenham: Edward Elgar.

Knei-Paz, Baruch 1978, *The Social and Political Thought of Leon Trotsky*, Oxford: Clarendon Press.

Kollektivarbeit 1930, *Grundprinzipien kommunistischer Produktion und Verteilung*, Berlin: Neue Arbeiter-Verlag.

Kornai, J. 1986, 'The Hungarian Reform Process: Visions, Hopes and Reality', *Journal of Economic Literature*, December: 1687–737.

Kornai, J. 1993, 'Market Socialism Revisited', in *Market Socialism: The Current Debate*, edited by P. Bardhan and J. Roemer, New York: New York University Press.

Kornai, J. 2009, 'Marx through the eyes of a European Intellectual', *Social Research*, Fall: 965–85.

Korsch, Karl 1969, *Schriften zur Sozialisierung*, Frankfurt am Main: Europäische Verlagsanstalt.

Korsch, Karl 1971 [1932], *Three Essays on Marxism*, London: Pluto Press.

Korsch, Karl 1972, *Karl Marx*, Vienna: Europa Verlag.

Kowalik, Tadeusz 1993, *Economic Theory and Market Socialism: Selected Essays of Oskar Lange*, Cheltenham: Edward Elgar.

Kozlov, G.A. (ed.) 1977, *Political Economy: Socialism*, Moscow: Progress.

KPSS v Rezoliutsiyakh i Resheniyakh S'ezdov Konferentsii I Plenumov 1971, Moscow: Izdatel'stvo politicheskoi literaturi.

Krader, Lawrence 1973, *The Asiatic Mode of Production*, Assen: Van Gorcum.

Krader, Lawrence 1974, *The Ethnographical Notebooks of Karl Marx*, Assen: Van Gorcum.

Kropotkin, Peter 1892, 'Revolutionary Government' available at http://dwardmac.pitzer.edu/Anarchist_Archives/kropotkin/revgov.html.

Kropotkin, Peter 2005 [1896], 'Anarchism', in *Anarchism: A Documentary History of Libertarian Ideas*, edited by Robert Graham, Montreal: Black Rose.

Kropotkin, Peter 1897, 'The State and its Historical Role', available at: https://www
.marxists.org/reference/archive/kropotkin-peter/1896/state/index.htm.

Kropotkin, Peter 1899, 'Memoirs of a Revolutionist', available at: https://libcom.org/
library/memoirs-revolutionist.

Kropotkin, Peter 1901, 'Communism and Anarchy', available at: https://www.marxists
.org/reference/archive/kropotkin-peter/1900s/01_07_x01.htm.

Kropotkin, Peter 2005 [1902], 'Mutual Aid', in *Anarchism: A Documentary History of
Libertarian Ideas*, edited by Robert Graham, Montreal: Black Rose.

Kropotkin, Peter 1906, 'Conquest of Bread', available at: https://theanarchistlibrary.org/
library/petr-kropotkin-the-conquest-of-bread.

Kropotkin, Peter 1910, 'Anarchism', in *Encyclopedia Britannica*.

Kropotkin, Peter 1912, 'Fields, Factories and Workshops' available at:
https://theanarchistlibrary.org/library/petr-kropotkin-fields-factories-and-
workshops-or-industry-combined-with-agriculture-and-brain-w.

Kropotkin, Peter 1920, 'The Wage System', available at: https://theanarchistlibrary.org/
library/petr-kropotkin-the-wage-system.

Kuhn, Gabriel (ed.) 2012, *All Power to the Councils: A Documentary History of the German
Revolution of 1918–1919*, Oakland: PM Press.

Kuruma, Samezō 2009, *Marx's Theory of the Genesis of Money*, Denver: Outskirts Press.

La Grassa Gianfranco 1975, *Valore e formazione sociale*, Editori Riuniti: Rome.

Lange, Oskar and Fred Taylor 1938, *On the Economic Theory of Socialism*, Minneapolis:
University of Minnesota Press.

Lange, Oskar 1993 [1935], 'Marxian Economics and Modern Economic Theory', in *Economic Theory and Market Socialism*, edited by Tedeusz Kowalik, Cheltenham: Edward Elger.

Lange, Oskar 1945, 'Marxian Economics in the Soviet Union', *American Economic Review*, March: 127–132.

Lange, Oskar 1959, *Introduction to Econometrics*, London: Pergamon.

Lange, Oskar 1969, *Theory of Production and Reproduction*, London: Pergamon.

Landauer, Carl 1959, *European Socialism*, volume 2: *A History of Ideas and Movements*
Berkley and Los Angeles: University of California Press.

Lapidus, I. and Ostrovitianov K. 1929, *Précis D'Economie Politique: L'économie politique
et la théorie de l'économie sovietique*, Paris: E.S.I. Press.

Lavoie, D. 1985, *Rivalry and Central Planning: The Socialist Calculation Debate Recon-
sidered*, Cambridge: Cambridge University Press.

Lenin, V.I. 1962a [1917], 'Marxizm O Gosudarstve', in *Polnoe Sobranie Sochinenii*, volume 33, Moscow: IPL.

Lenin, V.I. 1962b [1918], 'Pervonachalnyi variant stati ocherednye zadachi sovetskoi
vlasti', in *Polnoe Sobranie Sochinenii*, volume 36, Moscow: IPL.

Lenin, V.I., 1970 [1905], 'One Step Forward Two Steps Back', in *Selected Works*, volume 1,
Moscow: Progress.

Lenin, V.I. 1971a [1919], 'Economics and Politics in the Era of the Dictatorship of the Proletariat', in *Selected Works*, volume 3, Moscow: Progress.

Lenin, V.I. 1971b [1921], 'Tax in Kind', in *Selected Works*, volume 3, Moscow: Progress.

Lenin, V.I. 1975a [1917], 'The State and Revolution', in *Selected Works*, volume 2, Moscow: Progress.

Lenin, V.I. 1975b [1917], 'The Tasks of the Proletariat in Our Revolution', in *Selected Works*, volume 2, Moscow: Progress.

Lenin, V.I. 1975c [1918], 'Extraordinary Seventh Congress: The Political Report of the Central Committee', in *Selected Works*, volume 2, Moscow: Progress.

Lenin, V.I. 1975d [1918], 'Immediate Tasks of the Soviet Power', in *Selected Works*, volume 2, Moscow: Progress.

V.I. Lenin 1982a [1905], 'Shag Vpered, dva shaga nazad', in *Izbrannye Proizvedenyia*, volume 1, Moscow: Izdatel'stvo poliiticheskoi Literatury.

Lenin, V.I. 1982b [1917], 'O Zadachakh proletariata v dannoyi revolyutsi', in *Izbrannye Proizvedeniya*, volume 2, Moscow: Izdatel'stvo politicheskoi Literatury.

Lenin, V.I. 1982c [1918] 'Ocherednye zadachi sovietskoi vlasti', in *Izbrannye Proizvedeniya*, Moscow: IPL.

Lenin, V.I. 1982d [1918], 'Syed'moi extrennyi s'ezd R.K.P.(b): Politicheskoi otchet tsentral'nogo komiteta', in *Izbrannye Proizvedeniya*, volume 2, Moscow: IPL.

Lenin, V.I. 1982e [1919], 'Ekonomika I Politika v Epokhu Diktaturyi Proletariata', in *Izbrannye Proizvedeniya*, volume 3, Moscow: IPL.

Lenin, V.I. 1982f [1921], 'O prodovol'stvennom naloge', in *Izbrannye proizvedeniya*, volume 3, Moscow IPL.

Lenin, V.I. 1982g [1917], 'Gosudarstvo i Revolyutsia', in *Izbranie Proizvedenia*, volume 2, Moscow: Izdatelstvo Politichiskoi Literaturi.

Leontief, Wassily 1982, 'The Distribution of Work and Income', *Scientific American*, September 1982: 188–204.

Leontief, Wassily 1986, *Input-Output Economics*, New York: Oxford University Press.

Lippincot, B. 1938, 'Introduction', in Oskar Lange and Fred Taylor, *On the Economic Theory of Socialism*, Minneapolis: University of Minnesota.

Lissagaray, Prosper-Olivier 2000 [1876], *Histoire de la Commune de 1871*, Paris: La Découverte.

Löwy, Michael 1996, 'La dialectique du progress et l'enjeu actueldes mouvements sociaux', in *Congrès International: cent ans du marxisme*, Paris: PUF.

Löwy, Michael 1998, 'Globalisation and Iternationalism', *Monthly Review*, November, 16–27.

Lukács, Georg 1978, *The Ontology of Social Being: Marx*, London: Merlin Press.

Luxemburg, Rosa 1972 [1925], *Einführung in die Nationalökonomie*, Rohwolt Taschenbuch: Hamburg.

Luxemburg, Rosa 2004, 'From the Unfinished Manuscript "the Russian Revolution"', in

The Rosa Luxemburg Reader, edited by Peter Hudis and Kevin Anderson, New York: Monthly Review Press.

Maddison, Angus 2006, *The World Economy*, volume 1, Organisation for Economic Co-operation and Development (OECD).

Manevitch, V. 1972, 'Ob osveshchenii theorii tovarnogo proizvodstva pri sotsialisme v ekonmicheskoi literature 40–50-x godov', *ekonomicheskie nauki*, 9: 66–73.

Marx, Karl 1932 [1844], *Aus den Exzerptheften: Ökonomische Studien Marx-Engels Gesamtausgabe* (MEGA¹) I.3.

Marx, Karl 1953 [1857–8], *Grundrisse der Kritik der politischen Ökonomie*, Berlin: Dietz Verlag.

Marx, Karl 1954 [1890], *Capital*, Volume I, Moscow: Progress.

Marx, Karl 1956a [1885], *Capital*, Volume II, Moscow: Progress.

Marx, Karl 1956b (1861–3), *Theorien über den Mehrwert*, volume 1, Berlin: Dietz.

Marx, Karl 1959 [1861–3], *Theorien über den Mehrwert*, volume 2, Berlin: Dietz.

Marx, Karl 1960 [1875], *Nachwort zu 'Enthüllungen über den Kommunisten – Prozess zu Köln'*, in *Marx-Engels Werke* (MEW), volume 8, Berlin: Dietz.

Marx, Karl 1962a [1961–3], *Theorien über den Mehrwert*, volume 3, Berlin: Dietz.

Marx, Karl 1962b [1880], Randglossen zu Adoiph Wagners 'Lehrbuch der politischen Ökonomie', MEW volume 19, Berlin: Dietz. Available (English version) at: https://www.marxists.org./archive/marx/works/1881/01/wagner.htm.

Marx, Karl 1963 [1861–3], *Theories of Surplus Value*, volume 1, Moscow: Progress.

Marx, Karl 1964a [1864–8], 'Inaugural Address', in *General Council of the First International 1864–1868*, Moscow: Foreign Language Publishing House.

Marx, Karl 1964b [1894], *Das Kapital*, Volume III, Berlin: Dietz Verlag.

Marx, Karl 1965a [1866] 'Résolutions du Premier Congrés de L'A.I.T.', in *Oeuvres: Économie*, volume 1, Paris: Galimard.

Marx, Karl 1965b [1847], 'Misère de la Philosophie', in Karl Marx *Oeuvres: Économie*, volume I, Paris: Gallimard.

Marx, Karl 1968a [1861–3], *Theories of Surplus Value*, volume 2, Moscow: Progress.

Marx, Karl 1968b [1877,1881], 'Sur la commune rurale et les perspectives revolutionnaires en Russie', in *Oeuvres*, volume II, Paris: Gallimard.

Marx, Karl 1970a [1859], *A Contribution to the Critique of Political Economy*, New York: International Publishers.

Marx, Karl 1970b [1849], 'Wage Labour and Capital', in Karl Marx and Friedrich Engels, *Selected Works* (in one volume), Moscow: Progress.

Marx, Karl 1971a [1861–3], *Theories of Surplus Value*, volume 3, Moscow: Progress.

Marx, Karl 1971b [1871], 'The Civil War in France', in Marx and Engels, *On the Paris Commune*, Moscow: Progress.

Marx, Karl 1973a [1844], *Ökonomisch-philosophische Manuskripte* in MEW, *Ergänzungsband* I, Berlin: Dietz.

Marx, Karl 1973b [1849], *Lohnarbeit und Kapital*, MEW 6, Berlin: Dietz.

Marx, Karl 1973c [1847], 'Arbeitslohn', in MEW 6, Berlin: Dietz.

Marx, Karl 1973d [1872], '*The Nationalisation of the Land*', in Marx-Engels *Selected Works*, volume II, Moscow: Progress.

Marx, Karl [1874–5], *Conspectus of Bakunin's 'Stateism and Anarchy'* available at https://www.marxists.org/archive/marx/works/1874/04/bakunin-notes.htm.

Marx, Karl 1975 [1844], *Early Writings*, New York: Vintage.

Marx, Karl 1976a [1875], *Le Capital*, volume I, Paris: Editions Sociales.

Marx, Karl 1976b [1861–3], *Zur Kritik der politischen Ökonomie Manuskript*, in Marx Engels *Gesamtausgabe* (MEGA²), Section 2, Volume 3, Part 1, Berlin: Dietz.

Marx, Karl 1976c [1867], 'The Commodity', in A. Dragstedt, *Value: Studies by Karl Marx*, London: New Park.

Marx, Karl 1978 [1867], 'The Value Form', *Capital and Class*, 4: 130–50.

Marx, Karl 1980a [1858–61], *Ökonomische Manuskripte und Schriften*, MEGA², Section 2, Volume 2, Berlin: Dietz.

Marx, Karl 1980b [1856], 'Speech at the Anniversary of the *People's Paper*, April 19', in *Marx Engels Collected Works* (MECW), volume 14, New York: International Publishers.

Marx, Karl 1982a [1861–3], *Zur Kritik der politischen Ökonomie*, MEGA² II.3.6, Berlin: Dietz.

Marx, Karl 1982b, Oeuvres III, *Philosophie*, Paris: Gallimard.

Marx, Karl 1982c, Manuskript [1861–3], MEGA² volume 3, part 6, Berlin: Dietz Verlag.

Marx, Karl 1983a [1867], *Das Kapital: Kritik der Politischen Ökonomie*, Erster Band, Berlin: Dietz.

Marx, Karl 1983b [1858], *Letter to Engels* (April 2), MECW volume 40, New York: International Publishers.

Marx, Karl 1984 [1894], *Capital*, Volume III, Moscow: Progress.

Marx, Karl 1985 [1861,1862], *Letters* (to Engels, 9 December 1861); (to Kugelmann, 28 December 1862), MECW volume 41, New York: International Publishers.

Marx, Karl 1986 [1851], *Exzerpte und Notizen* März bis Juni 1851, in MEGA², Section 4, Volume 8, Berlin: Dietz.

Marx, Karl 1987a [1872], *Das Kapital* Volume I, in MEGA², Section 2, Volume 6, Berlin: Dietz.

Marx, Karl, 1987b [1858], 'Original Text of Second and Beginning of Third Chapter' of *Contribution to the Critique of Political Economy*, in MECW, volume 29, New York: International Publishers.

Marx, Karl 1987c [1867] *Letters* (to Engels, 16 June, 22 June, 24 August, 7 November); (to Kugelmann, 30 November), MECW 42, New York: International Publishers.

Marx, Karl 1988a [1863–7], *Ökonomische Manuskripte*, in MEGA², Section 2, Volume 4, Part 1, Berlin: Dietz.

Marx, Karl 1988b [1861–3], *Economic Manuscripts*, MECW 30, New York: International Publishers.

Marx, Karl 1988c [1868], *Letter to Kugelmann* (11 July), MECW 43, New York: International Publishers.

Marx, Karl 1989 [1880], 'Notes on Wagner's Textbook of Political Economy', in MECW, volume 24, New York: International Publishers.

Marx, Karl 1991 [1879], *Letter to Carlo Cafiero*, 29 July, MECW volume 45, New York: International Publishers.

Marx, Karl 1992 [1863–7], *Ökonomische Manuskripte* in MEGA², Section 2, Volume 4, Part 2, Berlin: Dietz.

Marx, Karl 1993 [1857–8], *Grundrisse: Foundations of the Critique of Political Economy*, London: Penguin.

Marx, Karl 1994 [1963–7], *Economic Manucripts* (1863–7), in MECW, Volume 34, New York: International Publishers.

Marx Karl 2008 [1868–81], *Manuskripte zum Zweiten Buch des 'Kapitals'*, Berlin: Akademie Verlag.

Marx, Karl and Friedrich Engels 1962 [1845–6], *Die Deutsche Ideologie*, MEW, volume 3, Berlin: Dietz. Also available at https://www.marxists.org/archive/marx/works/1845/german-ideology/.

Marx, Karl and Friedrich Engels 1968 [1845–6], *The German Ideology*, MECW, volume 5, New York: International Publishers.

Marx, Karl and Friedrich Engels 1970b, *Selected Works* (in one volume), Moscow: Progress.

Marx, Karl and Friedrich Engels 1972 [1845], *Die heilige Familie*, MEW volume 2, Berlin: Dietz. Also available in English at https://www.marxists.org/archive/marx/works/1845/holy-family.

Marx, Karl and Friedrich Engels 1975 [1845], *The Holy Family*, MECW volume 4, New York: International Publishers. Available at https://www.marxists.org/archive/marx/works/1845/holy-family/.

Marx, Karl and Friedrich Engels 1879, 'Circular Letter', available at https://www.marxists.org/archive/marx/.../1879letters/79-09-15.htm.

Medvedev, Roy 1979, *The October Revolution*, New York: Columbia University Press.

Meek, Roland 1956, *Studies in the Labour Theory of Value*, London: Lawrence and Wishart.

Meek, Ronald 1967, *Economics and Ideology and Other Essays*, London: Chapman and Hall.

Mészáros, István 2008, *The Challenge and Burden of Historical Time*, New York: Monthly Review Press

Mironov, Boris 1990, 'The Peasant Communes after the Reform of 1860s', in *The World of the Russian Peasant: Post Emancipation, Culture and Society*, edited by Eklof Ben and Frank Stephen, Boston: Unwin Hyman.

Mises, Ludwig Von 1935 [1920], 'Economic Calculation in the Socialist Commonwealth', in *Collectivist Economic Planning*, edited by F. Hayek, London: George Routledge.

Mises, Ludwig Von 1936 [1922], *Socialism*, New York: Macmillan.

Moon, David 1999, *The Russian Peasantry (1600–1930)*, Longman: London and New York.

Morishima, M., and G. Catephores 1975, 'Is there an "Historical Transformation Problem"', *Economic Journal*, June: 309–28.

Most, Johann 1989 [1876], *Kapital und Arbeit*, MEGA² Section 2, Volume 8, Berlin: Dietz.

Murrell, P. 1983, 'Did the Theory of Market Socialism Answer the Challenge of Ludwig von Mises? A Re-interpretation of the Socialist Controversy', *History of Political Economy*, 15.1, Spring: 92–105.

Neurath, Otto 2004, *Economic Writings: Selections 1904–1945*, Dordrecht: Kluwer Academic Publishers.

Nove, Alec 1983, *The Economics of Feasible Socialism*, London: Allen and Unwin.

Nove, Alec 1982, *An Economic History of the USSR*, Harmondsworth, Middlesex: Penguin.

Novozhilov, V.V. 1967, *Problemy izmereniia zatrat i rezultatov pri optimal'nom planirovanii* (Problems of measurement of cost and results in optimum planning), Moscow: Ekonomika.

Orwell, George 1966, *Homage to Catalonia*, New York: Penguin Books.

Panitch, Leo and Sam Gindin 2015, 'Marxist Theory and Strategy', *Historical Materialism*, 23, 2: 3–22.

Pannekoek, Anton 1912, 'Massenaktion und Revolution', *Neue Zeit*, XXX Jahrgang, 2 volumes, available at: https://www.marxists.org//deutsch/archiv/pannekoek/1912/xx/massenaktion.htm.

Pannekoek, Anton 1946, 'The Failure of the Working Class', in *Politics* (New York), III.8, September: 270–2.

Pannekoek, Anton [1948] 2003, *Workers' Councils*, London: AK Press.

Pareto, V. 1964 [1896–7], *Cours d'Économie Politique*, Geneva: Librairie Droz.

Pareto, V. 1966 [1909], *Manuel d'Économie Politique*, Geneva: Librairie Droz.

Plekhanov, Georgi Valentinovich 1895, *Anarchism and Socialism*, in https://www.marxists.org/archive/plekhanov/index.htm.

Preobrazhenski, E. 1926, *Novaya Ekonomika*, Moscow: Izdatelst'vo Kommunichestkoi Akademii.

Pujols, José Llunas 2005 [1882], 'What is Anarchy', in *Anarchism*, edited by Robert Graham, Montreal: Black Rose Books.

Rabinowitch, Alexander 2004, *The Bolsheviks Come to Power*, Chicago, IL: Haymarket Books.

Rabinowitch, Alexander 2007, *The Bolsheviks in Power*, Bloomington: Indiana University Press.

Rawls, John 1971, *A Theory of Justice*, Cambridge: Harvard University Press.

Reichelt, Helmut 1973, *Zur logischen Struktur des Kapitalbegriff bei Karl Marx*, Frankfurt am: Europaïsche Verlagsanstalt.

Riazanov, David (ed.) 1971 [1928], *Marx-Engels Archiv* I, Erlangen: Politladen.

Ricardo, David 1951 [1821,1817], *On the Principles of Political Economy and Taxation*, in *The Works and Correspondence of David Ricardo*, edited by Piero Sraffa, Cambridge: Cambridge University Press.

Robinson, Joan 1966, *An Essay on Marxian Economics*, London: Macmillan.

Robbins, Lionel 1934, *The Great Depression*, London: Macmillan.

Roemer, Jon 1992, 'Can there be Socialism after Communism?', *Politics and Society*, vol. 20, no. 3: 261–76.

Roemer, Jon 1994, 'A Future for Socialism', *Politics and Society*, 22, 4: 451–78.

Rubel, Maximilien 1957, *Karl Marx: Essai de Biographie Intellectuelle*, Paris: Marcel Rivière.

Rubel, Maximilien 2005 [1973], 'Marx, theoretician of Anarchism', in https://www.marxists.org/archive/rubel/1973/marx-anarchism.htm.

Rubel, Maxmilien 1965, in Marx *Oeuvres: Économie*, volume 1, Paris: Gallimard.

Rubin, I.I. 2012, 'Studien zur Geldtheorie von Marx', in *I.I. Rubin, Marxforscher-Ökonom-Verbannter*, Hamburg: Argument.

Rühle, Otto 1971, *Baupläne für eine neue Gesellschaft*, Hamburg: Rowohlt Taschenbuch.

Saad Filho 2002, *The Value of Marx*, London: Routledge.

Schulkind, Eugene 1974, *The Paris Commune: The View from the Left*, New York: Grove Press.

Schumpeter, J.A. 1950 [1942], *Capitalism, Socialism and Democracy*, New York: Harper and Row.

Schumpeter, J.A. 1994, *History of Economic Analysis*, New York: Oxford University Press.

Schweikart, David 1992, 'Socialism, Democracy, Market, Planning', *Review of Radical Political Economics*, Fall and Winter: 29–45.

Schweikart, David 1993, *Against Capitalism*, Cambridge: Cambridge University Press.

Schweikart, David 1998, 'Market Socialism: A Defence', in *Market Socialism: The Debate among Socialists*, edited by Bertel Ollman, New York: Routledge.

Schweikart, David 2002, *After Capitalism*, New York: Bowman and Littlefield.

Schwarz, Solomon 1987, 'Die Geldform in der 1. und 2. Auflage des "Kapital"', *Internationale Marx-Engels Forschung*, 1: 200–13.

Serge, Victor 2001, *Mémoires d'un Revolutionnaire 1908–1947*, Paris: Robert Laffont.

Shanin, Theodor (ed.) 1983, *The Late Marx and the Russian Road*, New York: Monthly Review Press.

Shkredov, V.P. 1973, *Metod issledovaniya sobstvennosti v 'Kapitale' Karla Marksa* (Method of Investigation into Property in Marx's *Capital*), Moscow: Izdatel'stvo Moskovskogo Universiteta.

Shkredov, V.P. 1987, 'Die Untersuchungsmethode der Entstehung und Entwicklungsgeschichte der kapitalistischen Produktionsweise im "Kapital"', *Marxistische Studien*, Jahrbuch der IMSE 12, 1: 232–7.

Shkredov, V.P. 1988, 'Sotsialism i sobstvennost' (Socialism and Property), *Kommunist*, 12: 28–37.

Shkredov, V.P. 1997, 'Über Engels' Historismus in seinem "Kapital"-Verständnis', *Beiträge zur Marx-Engels-Forschung*, Neue Folge: 114–30.

Shand, A.H. 1984, *The Capitalist Alternative: An Introduction to Neo-Austrian Economics*, New York: New York University Press.

Stalin, J.V., 1970, *Selected Writings*, Westport: Greenwood.

Stalin, J.V. 1972 [1952], *Economic Problems of Socialism in the USSR*, Peking: Foreign Languages Press.

Stalin, J.V. 1980, *Oeuvres choisies*, Tirana: Nëntori.

Steele, David Ramsay 1992, *From Marx to Mises*, LaSalle, IL: Open Court.

Suny, R.G. 1987, 'Revising the old story: 1917 revolution in light of new sources', in *The Workers' Revolution in Russia, 1917: the View from Below*, edited by Daniel Kaiser, Cambridge: Cambridge University Press.

Sweezy, Paul M. 1949, *Socialism*, New York: Mcgraw-Hill.

Sweezy, Paul M. 1970, *The Theory of Capitalist Development*, New York: Monthly Review Press.

Sweezy, Paul, M. 1980, *The Post-capitalist Society*, New York: Monthly Review Press.

Sweezy, Paul 1993, 'Socialism: Legacy and Renewal', *Monthly Review*, January.

Trotsky, Leon 1987, *The History of the Russian Revolution*, New York: Pathfinder Press.

Vacic', A.M. 1977, 'Distribution according to Work and Commodity Production', *Acta Oeconomica*, 18: 227–45.

Vernon, Richards 1983, *Lessons of the Spanish Revolution (1936–1939)*, London: Freedom Press.

Weber, Max 1978 [1922], *Economy and Society*, Berkeley: University of California Press.

Wolf, Dieter 2004, 'Fiction eines Wertbegriffs', Dieter Wolf/Heinz Paragenings, *Zur Konfusion des Wertbegriffs*, Hamburg: Argument Verlag.

Wright, Anthony 1974, 'Guild Socialism Revisited', *Journal of Contemporary History*, 9, 1: 165–80.

Index

Adorno, Theodor 80

agriculture 130–31, 138, 175, 277, 290

alienation 47, 57, 67, 75, 130, 145, 187, 217, 223

AMP (Associated Mode of Production) 20, 22, 29, 47, 50, 53–54, 59, 226, 232, 249

anarchism 169–72, 178–79, 181–83, 272, 286, 289–90, 295–96

Anti-Dühring 28, 107, 114, 150, 240, 287

Anweiler, Oskar 248, 254–55, 257, 279, 281–82, 285

Arendt, Hannah 45–46, 285

Arthur, Chris 105, 285

Asiatic mode of production 240, 289

Associated Mode of Production. *See* AMP

association of free individuals 1, 27, 29, 31, 33, 35, 37, 39, 41, 43, 45, 47, 49, 51, 53

Backhaus, Hans-Georg 80–83, 85–86, 88–89, 105–6, 109, 116, 285

Bahro, Rudolf 19, 285

Bailey, Samuel 88

Bakunin, Mikhail 33, 169, 171–73, 178–79, 183–85, 256, 273, 285, 293

banks 128, 133–34, 192, 196, 217, 220, 236

Banner of Marxism 132

Baran, Paul 136

Barone, Enrico 200–201, 204, 206, 208, 285

Bettelheim, Charles 136, 286

Blackburn, Robin 15, 21–24, 26, 286

Blanqui, Louis Auguste 33, 154, 270

Blaug, Mark 79, 206, 213, 286

Böhm-Bawerk, Eugen 105

Bolsheviks 6–13, 18, 25–26, 44, 120–21, 124, 137, 182, 193, 254–57, 260–61, 279, 282, 284, 295

Bonaparte, Louis 46, 270

bookkeeping 149, 160–61

Borkenau, Franz 6, 13, 286

bourgeoisie 5, 13, 19, 28–29, 36, 38, 44, 125, 155, 253, 260–61, 264, 269–70, 280, 284

Brutzkus, Boris 202, 286

Bukharin, Nikolai 6, 23, 42–43, 126–32, 180–82, 257, 286

bureaucracy 44, 146, 174, 262, 268, 270

Cafiero, Carlo 176–78, 180–81, 286

capital 1–4, 17, 27–29, 31–36, 48–51, 56–59, 63–64, 70–72, 79–81, 101–24, 154–56, 224–30, 232–33, 275–76, 292–93

accumulation of 59, 141, 210, 235, 266

Capitalist Mode of Production (CMP) 3, 5, 20, 22, 28–29, 36–37, 39, 50, 54, 59, 102–5, 107, 113, 232–33, 275–76

Carr, E.H. 6–7, 14, 251, 282, 286

Chinese Revolution 25, 288

classes 4–5, 7, 18–19, 21, 35–36, 46, 48–49, 86, 226, 249, 252–53, 267, 272, 275, 283

antagonism of 122, 267

CMP. *See* Capitalist Mode of Production

commodity exchange 77, 95, 122–23, 162, 225

commodity production 18–20, 63, 65–67, 73, 93, 97, 99–100, 102–4, 110–16, 118–19, 123–25, 134–38, 144–45, 147–51, 228–30

communism 27–29, 40–42, 50–51, 53–55, 59–60, 124–27, 163–66, 169, 172–73, 176, 178–79, 181, 204–5, 242–43, 265–66

Communist Manifesto 18, 21, 35, 38, 43, 46, 48–49, 225, 233, 247, 267, 269, 273, 282, 284

consumption 54–55, 72, 131, 134, 139, 141, 143, 157, 161, 163, 170, 173, 192–93, 204–5, 240–41

CPB (Central Planning Board) 209–12, 214–17

credit 24, 134, 136, 142, 192, 196, 259, 272, 288

crisis 32, 54, 74, 96–99, 158, 288

commercial 78, 96, 99

Deng's China 261

Deutscher, Isaac 9, 14–15, 23, 286

Devine, Pat 145, 219, 285–86

dictatorship 6–7, 9, 19, 41–42, 44, 46, 122, 125, 252, 264, 282, 290

Dobb, Maurice 10, 103, 158–59, 215–16, 287

Draper, Hal 39, 171, 183, 272–73, 287

Dussel, Enrique 234, 237, 246, 287

Dunayevskaya, Raya 132, 246, 278

economic calculation   21, 139, 158, 202–5, 214, 294

Engels, Friedrich   13–15, 27–31, 34–41, 43–46, 48–52, 55–58, 82–86, 100–116, 155–57, 237–40, 242, 244–47, 249–53, 269–75, 287

Ferguson, Adam   58
Frankfurt School   80, 105
free individuals   1, 27, 29, 31, 33, 35, 37, 39, 41, 43, 45, 47, 49, 249–50, 264

German Ideology, The   57, 84, 166, 172, 269, 294
Gindin, Sam   273
Gorbachev, Mikhail   21, 280
Gothacritique   3, 27–28, 44–45, 60, 120, 159, 162, 240, 264, 283
Gramsci, Antonio   36, 288
Grundrisse   81, 85, 87, 105–6, 292, 294
guilds   171–72, 186–87, 190–92, 195–97
guild socialism   22, 186–89, 191, 193

Hayek, Friedrich   201–8, 212–14, 288, 294
Hecker, Rolf   104–5, 110–11, 288
Hegel, G.W.F.   19, 30, 84–85, 88, 96, 116, 268
Heinrich, Michael   80, 107, 288
Hilferding, Rudolf   102, 121, 123–24, 245, 288
Hobson, J.A.   187, 192–94, 196, 288
Horvat, Branko   229, 288
Howard, Michael   212, 225, 227, 288
Hungary   202, 257

industry   31–32, 130, 154, 156, 167–68, 174, 178, 181, 186–87, 189–93, 195–96, 198, 210, 216, 276

Kautsky, Karl   35, 45, 118–21, 275, 289
Kornai, Janos   15–21, 26, 199, 215, 289
Korsch, Korsch   85, 121–22, 258, 289
Kronstadt   257, 263, 288
Kropotkin, Peter   170–76, 180–81, 183, 289–90
Kugelmann, Ludwig   46, 86–87, 139, 293
Kuruma, Samezō   80, 89

labour   47–48, 51–52, 54–55, 57–61, 63–65, 71–76, 91–95, 133–35, 139–41, 144–54, 159–63, 191–95, 226–27, 242–43, 276–78

Lange, Oskar   102, 115, 136–37, 149, 168, 206–16, 220, 227–29, 289–90
Lenin, Vladimir Ilyich   3–8, 10–15, 21, 23–25, 35–36, 41–44, 121–22, 125, 182, 251–52, 254–56, 261–68, 275–76, 278–84, 290–91
Leontief, Wassily   144, 168, 291
Löwy, Michael   234, 246, 291
Luxemburg, Rosa   25, 36, 102, 114, 244, 291

Mao   15, 246, 261
market socialism   22, 24, 100, 199–201, 203, 205–7, 209, 211, 213, 215, 219, 221–23, 225–31, 285–86, 289–90
Martov, Julius   7–8, 23, 25, 254, 281
Marx, Karl   1–5, 13–41, 43–53, 55–58, 60–71, 73–117, 136–42, 145–68, 178–79, 183–85, 225–47, 249–53, 261–78, 280–89
Medvedev, Roy   9, 11, 255, 262
Mészáros, Istvan   39, 280
Mises, Ludwig von   122–23, 202–4, 206, 208, 212–16, 228, 294–95
Mondragon   224–25, 227
money   67–73, 75–78, 82–83, 87–90, 94–99, 118–23, 125–26, 132–35, 143–47, 151, 159–60, 162–63, 166, 203, 222
   category of   83, 87
   determination of   90, 96

nature   50, 57–59, 63, 68, 75–76, 92–93, 128–29, 140–41, 169–70, 174–75, 180–81, 208, 213–14, 275, 278
NEP (New Economic Policy)   127–28, 132, 281–82
Neurath, Otto   119–20, 142, 144, 166–67, 202–3
New Economic Policy. See NEP
Nove, Alec   138, 217, 277

Pannekoek, Anton   143–44, 198, 260, 295
Pareto, Vilfredo   200–201, 204
peasants   10–11, 13, 112, 130–31, 236–38, 240, 242, 254, 257–58, 276
Plekhanov, Georgi   10, 169, 184, 295
private ownership   2, 16, 20, 48–50, 119, 124, 195, 199, 203–4, 222–23, 236, 244, 265, 274–76, 279
productive forces   16, 31, 33, 49, 54–55, 60–61, 73–74, 122, 129, 153, 180, 238

Rabinowitch, Alexander   9, 24, 256, 279
Rawls, John   146
Reichelt, Helmut   80–81, 83, 85–86, 88–89,
    105–6, 116
revolution   3–4, 6, 14–15, 30–31, 35–36, 38–
    43, 174–76, 182–83, 236–39, 245–47,
    252, 254–60, 262–63, 281–83, 285–
    87
revolutionary transformation period   39–41,
    46, 120–22, 159, 161, 264, 272–73, 283
Ricardo, David   14, 32, 74, 79, 85, 96, 111, 114–
    16, 149, 296
Robbins, Lionel   206, 208, 212, 296
Robinson, Joan   149, 296
Roemer, John   199, 219–21, 285, 289
Rubel, Maximilien   5, 36, 179, 238–39, 247,
    267
ruling class   21, 37–40, 43, 127, 155, 253, 261,
    282

Schumpeter, Joseph   8, 79, 200–202, 212, 216,
    256, 260
Schweickart, David   223–25, 227
Second World War   22, 199
Serge, Victor   254, 256, 282
Shanin, Teodor   233–34, 237, 239, 241, 243,
    246
Shkredov, V.P.   106–7, 117, 152, 160, 280
simple commodity production   53, 100–117,
    197, 229
slavery   7, 31, 35, 37, 41, 47, 57, 61, 112, 172, 174–
    76, 190, 229, 232, 236
    domestic   175
Smith, Adam   57–58, 76, 114–15
socialism   1–4, 13–15, 27–31, 37–41, 118–31,
    133–38, 151–52, 157–60, 194–99, 202–6,
    227–28, 248–52, 261–68, 285–91

non-capitalist road to   232–33, 235, 237,
    239, 241, 243, 245, 247
socialist accounting   119, 139, 141–45, 147, 149,
    151–53, 155, 157, 159, 161, 163, 165, 167, 229
Stalin, Josef   6, 15, 134–36, 151, 265–66, 278–79
state ownership   16, 22–23, 49, 158, 193, 195–
    96, 265–66
surplus value   54, 59, 67, 109–11, 127, 130, 153,
    165, 292
Sweezy, Paul   14–15, 39, 103, 114, 159, 213, 216–
    17
Spain   257–9

transition period   39–42, 45, 125–28, 132, 161,
    196
Trotsky, Leon   6, 9, 23–24, 26, 44, 252, 261,
    278, 286

use value   64–75, 90, 94–95, 97, 99, 109, 112,
    140–41, 144, 146, 149–50, 154, 163, 165,
    167–68

value form   51, 53–54, 63–64, 66, 79–81, 85,
    87–88, 92–94, 99, 130, 159
value theory   79, 82–83, 105, 136, 149, 160
    pre-monetary   83

Wada, Haruki   237, 239, 243
wage labour   14, 23, 102, 105, 120–21, 123, 127,
    223, 229, 232, 242, 265–67, 275–76, 280,
    283
Wagner, Adolph   84
Weber, Max   122–3, 202, 297
Wolf, Dieter   80, 83

Zasulich, Vera   233, 238, 240, 242
Zinoviev, Grigory   6

CPSIA information can be obtained
at www.ICGtesting.com
Printed in the USA
JSHW022355190919
1541JS00002B/3